MAKING JOURNALISTS

Diverse models, global issues

Edited by Hugo de Burgh

Foreword by James Curran

R Routledge
Taylor & Francis Group

LONDON AND NEW YORK

First published 2005
by Routledge
2 Park Square, Milton Park, Abingdon, Oxon OX14 4RN

Simultaneously published in the USA and Canada
by Routledge
270 Madison Ave., New York NY 10016

Routledge is an imprint of the Taylor & Francis Group

Typeset in Galliard by
Taylor & Francis Books
Printed and bound in Great Britain by
Antony Rowe Ltd, Chippenham, Wiltshire

British Library Cataloguing in Publication Data
A catalogue record for this book is available
from the British Library

Library of Congress Cataloging in Publication Data
Making journalists / edited by Hugo de Burgh.
p. cm.
Includes bibliographical references.
ISBN 0-415-31502-6 (alk. paper) -- ISBN 0-415-31501-8 (pbk. : alk. paper)
1. Journalism. I. Burgh, Hugo de, 1949-
PN4731.M285 2005
070.4--dc22
2004024809

ISBN 0–415–31502–6 (hardback)
ISBN 0–415–31501–8 (paperback)

MAKING JOURNALISTS

12/04

UNIVERSITY OF
WOLVERHAMPTON
ENTERPRISE LTD.

If jour
taught
 Ma
countr
the U
taught
societi
educat
tions
assum
 Wh
we are

Hugo
and Di

CONTENTS

CONTRIBUTORS

Rosental Calmon Alves holds the Knight Chair in International Journalism at Texas in Austin and directs the Knight Center for Journalism in the Americas. A professional journalist since 16, he spent most of his career in *Jornal do Brasil*, a Rio de Janeiro newspaper, serving as a foreign correspondent for more than a decade and eventually as director and managing editor.

James Curran is Professor of Communications at Goldsmiths College, University of London. He is the author of *Media and Power* (2002), co-author of *Power without Responsibility* (6th edition, 2003), and co-editor of *De-Westernizing Media Studies* (2000) and *Mass Media and Society* (4th edition, 2005) among other books.

Hugo de Burgh is Professor of Journalism at the University of Westminster. His publications include *Investigative Journalism* (2000), *The Chinese Journalist* (2003) and *Can Vote Won't Vote: Is the Media to Blame?* (editor, *Journal of Public Affairs* special issue, 2004). He is Director of the China Media Centre, London.

Theodore L. Glasser is Professor of Communication and Director of the Graduate Program at Stanford University, California. He has written (with James Etterna) *Custodians of Conscience: Investigative Journalism and Public Virtue* (1998), and he is editor of *The Idea of Public Journalism* (1999).

Chin-Chuan Lee is Professor of Journalism and Mass Communication at the University of Minnesota and Chair Professor of Communication at the City University of Hong Kong. Among his many publications, the most recent are *Chinese Media, Global Contexts* (editor, 2003), *Global Media Spectacle* (with Joseph Man Chan, Zhongdong Pan and Clement So, 2002), and *Money, Power and Media: Communication Patterns and Bureaucratic Control in Cultural China* (editor, 2000).

Brian McNair is Professor of Journalism and Communication at the University of Strathclyde. His publications include *Glasnost, Perestroika and the Soviet Media* (1991), *The Sociology of Journalism* (1998), *Journalism and Democracy*

(2000), *News and Journalism in the UK* (4th edition, 2003) and *Mediated Access* (with Matthew Hibberd and Philip Schlesinger, 2003).

Paulo Mancini is Professor of the Sociology of Communication and Academic Director of the School of Broadcast Journalism at the University of Perugia. His publications in English include *Politics, Media and Modern Democracy* (with David L. Swanson, 1996).

Lise Marken is a PhD student in the Department of Communication at Stanford University, California. Her interests include journalism, the role of mass media in democracy, and feminism.

Betty Medsger is founder of the Center for Integration and Improvement at San Francisco State University, where she was the head of the journalism programme for ten years. A former reporter for the *Washington Post*, she is adjunct faculty member at the Graduate School of Journalism at Columbia University. She conducted the 1996 comprehensive study of journalism education in the United States, *Winds of Change: Challenges Confronting Journalism Education*. As a consultant, she has worked with journalism educators in South Africa, China and Europe, as well as in the United States.

John V. Pavlik is Professor and Chair of the Department of Journalism and Media Studies at the School of Communication, Information and Library Studies, Rutgers, the State University of New Jersey. He is also Director of the Journalism Resources Institute. His books include *Journalism and New Media* (2001), and *Converging Media* (with Shawn McIntosh, 2004).

Angela Phillips is a journalist on the *Guardian* and Head of Practice at Goldsmiths College, Department of Media and Communications. She has published extensively on social issues and their representation by the media. Her current research is into the ability of ethnic-minority journalists to influence agendas and treatments in the media in which they work.

Marina Prentoulis is a research assistant and visiting lecturer in the Department of Sociology at City University, London. She is currently completing a PhD at the Department of Government, University of Essex, on the institutionalization of English radical journalism during the nineteenth century. Her research interests include the history and sociology of journalism, political communications and discourse analysis.

Helge Rønning is Professor in the Department of Media and Communications, University of Oslo. He has published widely on literary, social, political, media and cultural issues. He has conducted research in Nigeria, Zimbabwe and Mozambique. He has been very active in Norwegian public life, serving on public bodies including the Freedom of Expression Commission, and chairing the Norwegian Non-Fiction Writers Union and the board of *Kopinor*.

Naomi Sakr, a specialist on Arab media, teaches in the School of Media, Arts and Design at the University of Westminster. She is the author of *Satellite Realms: Transnational Television, Globalization and the Middle East* (2002) and the editor of *Women and Media in the Middle East* (2004). Her research interests are media policy and governance, and media development and human rights.

Michael Schudson has written extensively on the roles of the media in society and is a specialist in the sociology of culture. He is Professor of Communication and Adjunct Professor of Sociology at the University of California at San Diego. His books include a history of American public life, *The Good Citizen* (1998), and have covered topics such as the idea of Watergate, objectivity and the power of news.

Daya Kishan Thussu is Professor of Communications and the Global Media at the University of Westminster. A former Associate Editor of Gemini News Service, a London-based international news agency, he is the co-author (with Oliver Boyd-Barrett) of *Contra-Flow in Global News* (1992), editor of *Electronic Empires: Global Media and Local Resistance* (1998) and author of *International Communication: Continuity and Change* (2000).

Howard Tumber is Professor of Sociology and Dean of the School of Sciences at City University, London. His many publications include *Media at War: The Iraq Crisis* (co-author, 2004); *Political Scandals and Media Across Democracies*, a two-volume edition of *American Behavioral Scientist* (co-editor, 2004); *Media Power, Policies and Professionals* (editor, 2000); and *News: A Reader* (editor, 1999). He is the founder and co-editor of the journal *Journalism: Theory, Practice and Criticism*.

David H. Weaver is Roy W. Howard Professor in Journalism and Mass Communication Research at Indiana University-Bloomington. The most recent of his many books are *Mass Communication Research and Theory* (2003) and *The Global Journalist* (1998); among his recent journal articles have been those on media roles in the 2000 election, foreign correspondents in the US, and mass communication research trends from 1980 to 1999.

FOREWORD

James Curran

If you walk into a good academic bookshop in a major American city like New York or Philadelphia, you are likely to find several shelves of books devoted to journalism. No other country in the world has so many studies that scrutinise and appraise the performance of their news media. Alongside the inevitable dross, distinguished books on American journalism appear with remarkable frequency. They are mostly written with elegance, draw on extensive empirical evidence, and advance a central argument about the nature of American journalism, the influences shaping it, or its wider influence on politics and society (for example, in the past two years, Gans 2003; Schudson 2003; Hamilton 2004). In most cases, they are also critical in tone – indeed, sometimes elegiac or angry. These are not vainglorious exaltations of the virtues of American journalism.

American journalism research is based on enormous resources that are not matched elsewhere: a large number of well-endowed universities with big journalism schools, wonderful libraries and well over a hundred university presses. The use of large-scale surveys, and the routine references that are made to research assistants' help at the beginning of books, are further testaments to the material support available to American journalism research. This tradition is also rich because it has retained roots in different disciplines, and not become over-specialised. Indeed, fields like history, sociology and political studies regularly generate books that enhance our understanding of American media (e.g. Patterson 2003; Starr 2004), and keep alive their connection with journalism studies.

However, perhaps the most admirable aspect of American journalism research is that it matters. Its main inspiration is the tradition associated with the Hutchins Commission that seeks to reconcile the needs of the market and democracy by fostering a culture of public service within the journalism 'profession'. The American media, it is hoped, will serve the public because their staff are encouraged to owe allegiance first and foremost to the public interest. Out of this noble project has developed a dialogue between the media industries and journalism schools in which it is accepted that American universities have a legitimate role in supporting, monitoring and interpreting the ideals of journalism. American journalism schools play a prominent part in educating future journalists, recruit former distinguished journalists as professors, and generate research that is recognised to be relevant. This includes a strong historical strand that celebrates good journalism and excoriates the bad, in this way helping to transmit professional values from one generation to the next; a strong audit tradition that examines through careful case studies the performance of contemporary news media; and an interpretive strand that seeks to uncover the dynamics shaping American journalism. The latter often comes out of communication rather than journalism departments, and tends to get up the noses of journalists. In the 1970s, 1980s and early 1990s, it advanced a critique of the way in which 'objectivity journalism' lent itself unintentionally to elite manipulation and control (e.g. Tuchman 1978; Fishman 1980; Hallin 1989 and 1994). More recently its main theme has been that American journalism is being undermined by hypercommercialism (e.g. McChesney 1999 and 2004; Shanor 2003; Hamilton 2004). Both these critiques are advanced with such compelling evidence that they are impossible to ignore.

In other words, American journalism research is impressive in numerous ways. It is extensive, intelligent, relevant and influential. It is also amazingly parochial. Journalism research in the USA is almost exclusively *American* journalism research. The books on journalism in American bookshops are, apart from a tiny number, overwhelmingly about American journalism. It is assumed that everything that is worth saying about journalism – how it is practised, how it is shaped, how it influences society – can be confined more or less to one country: the United States. This self-absorption is perhaps to be expected from a country where less than 20 per cent of its citizens have a passport. It is also a product of what Niall Ferguson calls an 'empire in denial' (Ferguson 2004): a country that has yet to acknowledge to itself that it is an imperial power.

Yet, it is worth clinging to the possibility that there are valid ways of doing journalism that are not prescribed by the American model of fact-based, neutral professionalism. For this reason, it makes sense to examine the experience of other countries in case these have anything to offer as a way of improving journalism or extending its repertoire. There are in fact compelling reasons, as I have argued elsewhere, for thinking that democracy is best served by having different kinds of journalism, each of which contribute different things to the democratic process (Curran 2005).

It is also worth entertaining the fugitive possibility that the libertarian, market-based model of organising journalism in the United States is not the best way of doing things. There are a number of alternative approaches. These include public-service broadcasting (of which there are four main kinds); the social-market approach that sustains media competition and diversity through selective subsidies; and the participant model that supports media staff rights and influence. Again, it makes sense to look outside the United States to examine the efficacy of these alternatives.

Indeed, to engage with the variety of different kinds of journalism that exist in the world, it is necessary to develop conceptual frameworks that adequately describe and evaluate these experiences. This is not to suggest that we should abandon universalistic values (such as a commitment to freedom, equality and mutuality). But it is to suggest that an American-based model can get in the way of properly understanding different contexts. This applies not only to journalism scholars immured within one tradition, but also more bizarrely to journalists in different countries steeped in the ideology of American journalism. In Latin America, some journalists concealed from themselves that they were implicitly colluding with military regimes in the 1980s by priding themselves on being neutral professionals, as extolled in American journalism theory (Waisbord 2000). Similarly, Paolo Mancini (2000) found that numerous Italian journalists failed to acknowledge that they were political actors rather than neutral intermediaries because they viewed themselves in terms of the rhetoric of American professionalism.

If the hubris of American journalism scholarship takes the form of self-absorption and the involuntary export of its ideas, its counterpart in Western Europe is manifested in a different way. There is a strong theoretical tradition in European media and cultural research that advances confident generalisations on a wide variety of subjects – such as the nature of postmodernity, the emancipatory properties of the virtual world, the role of the media in society, the part played by sources in the 'making' of news. Yet, while these generalisations are usually presented as if they have a universal or near-universal application, they are often based on evidence and examples derived from a small number of unrepresentative countries in Western Europe and North America. This encourages the experience of most of the world to be both disregarded and misunderstood. It also gives rise to tendentious theorising that is seldom explicit about its geographical limitations.

These two forms of myopia – the inward orientation of American journalism research and the spurious universality of European media and cultural theory – are now prompting a growing reaction. An increasing number of studies argue that media theory needs to be recast on the basis of a wider sample of countries, or more simply that media studies should become less parochial. For example, John Downing (1996) and Colin Sparks (1998) challenged conventional media theorising on the basis of a comparative examination of countries in Eastern Europe. Daniel Hallin and Paolo Mancini (2004) took this one step further by identifying three competing media systems – the liberal model (North Atlantic countries), the democratic corporatist model (North/Central Europe) and the polarised pluralist model (Mediterranean countries) – arguing that all are the products of different structures of social and political power, and of different cultures. *De-Westernizing Media Studies*, a project supported by the Korean Research Council, sought to cast the net wider by evaluating media theory in relation to the experience of different media systems around the world. Its essays challenged doctrinal simplification, arguing among other things that market influences on the media could be positive in authoritarian, state-dominated societies, but debilitating in certain other contexts (Curran and Park 2000). More generally, the rapid growth of the literature on globalisation during the last decade can be viewed as a protest against academic parochialism. Globalisation was a process that was already well advanced by the end of the nineteenth century (Ferguson 2003, among others). The fact that globalisation should now be attracting so much attention is an indication of a new dissatisfaction with traditional, geographically bounded ways of looking at things. It also registers an increased awareness that the world is changing rapidly in response to the end of the Cold War (and its replacement by the 'war on terror'), the rise of the Asian economies and of new communications technologies; and that, as dramatised by climate change, the world is becoming more interdependent in ways that need to be understood.

This book is a welcome product of this sea-change. Its contents are surveyed in the editor's introduction, and so do not need to be reviewed in detail here. It is sufficient to say that *Making Journalists* extends our field of vision, and deepens our understanding of journalism, by not being confined to what used to be called 'the West'. David Weaver's key comparative surveys, summarised in this book, reveal the existence of some kind of shared intellectual heritage and common set of occupational beliefs among journalists around the world, while at the same time highlighting significant differences of interpretation and emphasis between them. Yet, the book's national case studies tend to emphasise rather more than this survey divergences of journalistic convention, ranging from the tradition of instruction in China (predating the Communist regime) to that of advocacy in Italy, from the dualism of journalistic traditions in Latin America to state conscription and resistance in Africa and the Middle East, through to the libertarian professional model in the United States (with, as Michael Schudson persuasively argues, distinctive American cultural accretions). From this conspectus, it is possible to obtain a better insight into the different definitions of journalism that are practised around the world, and a better understanding of the influences (by no means all cultural) that shape these.

One way in which society can intervene to influence the development of journalism is through education. A number of contributors to this book raise fundamental questions about what the role of journalists should be, and what part universities should play – if any – in their education. These questions are surprisingly rarely asked but need to be addressed if journalism educators are to succeed, even modestly, in their vocation of making the media better. This constitutes the second, subsidiary focus of this book.

In short, this volume breaks free from some of the customary limitations of journalism and media research. It charts new waters, and invites us to adjust our normal, geographically confined perspectives. It is to be welcomed as a new and important contribution to the globalisation of journalism studies.

References

Curran, J (2005) 'What democracy requires of the media' in G. Overholser and K. Jamieson (eds) *The Press*, New York: Oxford University Press.

Curran, J and Park, M.J (2000) *De-Westernizing Media Studies*, London: Routledge.

Downing, J (1996) *Internationalizing Media Theory*, London: Sage.

Ferguson, N (2003) *Empire*, London: Allen Lane.

—— (2004) *Colossus*, London: Allen Lane.

Fishman, M (1980) *Manufacturing the News*, Austin: University of Texas Press.

Gans, H (2003) *Democracy and the News*, New York: Oxford University Press.

Hallin, D (1989) *The 'Uncensored War'*, Berkeley and Los Angeles: University of California Press.

—— (1994) *We Keep America on Top of the World*, London: Routledge.

Hallin, D and Mancini, P (2004) *Comparing Media Systems*, New York: Cambridge University Press.

Hamilton, J (2004) *All the News That's Fit to Sell*, Princeton: Princeton University Press.

Mancini, P (2000) 'Political Complexity and Alternative Models of Journalism: The Italian Case', in J. Curran and M.Y Park (eds) *De-Westernizing Media Studies*, London: Routledge.

McChesney, R (1999) *Rich Media, Poor Democracy*, Urbana, Il: University of Illinois Press.

—— (2004) *The Problem of the Media*, New York: Monthly Review Press.

Patterson, T (2003) *The Vanishing Voter*, New York: Vintage.

Schudson, M (2003) *The Sociology of News*, New York: Norton.

Shanor, D (2003) *News From Abroad*, New York: Columbia University Press.

Sparks, C (1998) *Communism, Capitalism and the Mass Media*, London: Sage.

Starr, P (2004) *The Creation of the Media*, New York: Basic Books.

Tuchman, G (1978) *Making News*, New York: Free Press.

Waisbord, S (2000) 'Media in South America. Between the Rock of the State and the Hard Place of the Market', in J. Curran and M.Y Park (eds) *De-Westernizing Media Studies*, London: Routledge.

INTRODUCTION

Journalism and the new cultural paradigm

Hugo de Burgh

> The growth of scientific knowledge and technological expertise has not produced a convergence in values, or a universal civilisation. Instead, it interacts with the diverse cultures humans have always had and gives them new weapons with which to propagate their different values.
>
> (Gray 1998: xxii)

About this book

This book offers three opportunities. The first – *Journalism and journalists* – is to provide an update on the subject and its practitioners today. The second opportunity – *Journalism and location* – is that of obtaining an overview of journalism in different cultures, in this case the USA, India, the Arab world, China, Sub-Saharan Africa, Latin America and Europe. The perceptive reader will immediately bridle at the idea of a chapter on journalism in Europe without Poland[1] or one on Africa without the Maghreb, or of trying to do justice to a region as complicated as Latin America in single chapter, but we hope that the writings themselves will prove that the experiment has value. If nothing else, the combined message is that, despite similarities, there are great differences. The similarities are relatively easy to enumerate, but what is really interesting are the differences, however we account for them, and it is that theme which distinguishes this book.

The third opportunity – *Journalism and the future* – is to investigate something of the ways in which people come to be turned into journalists and the common problems for journalism formation thrown up by institutional and technological changes today, and to explore the possible future of journalism.

Nowhere are journalists more acknowledged in their roles and responsibilities than in the USA and from no country are the initiatives and issues affecting journalists appearing thicker and faster than the USA. It is therefore fitting that our concluding chapter, which looks at the journalists the world needs for the future and how it might get them, comes from there, and from Ted Glasser.

1

Why this book?

As Brian McNair suggests in Chapter 1, journalists are becoming more and more important in creating, rather than reflecting, the reality we live. Yet journalism is a neglected topic of analysis, and journalism education ever more so. Journalism Studies has only recently won acceptance in academic life, even though journalism itself has been a subject to be studied at US universities since the early 1900s and in Chinese universities since the 1920s.

This book, then, may serve as an introduction to Journalism Studies for those who will then go on to read the academic journals. It contributes to the body of work which shows that Journalism Studies is distinct from, though within, Media Studies. But it does more than that. It internationalises Journalism Studies, in the way that James Curran and Myung-yin Park's *De-Westernizing Media Studies* (2000) has done for the parent discipline. We believe that, with this work, we are exorcising homogenisation, by demonstrating that the old fallacy that all journalisms were at different stages on the route to an ideal model, probably Anglophone, is *passé*. In the past, some books were written about journalism as if there were only Anglophone journalism and undeveloped attempts at it. The fact that this book is being produced and refutes that view is the result of what I explain below as 'the new cultural paradigm'.

The book begins by asking the question:

What is journalism?

'Familiar notions of what it means to be a journalist, how best to practise journalism, and what different publics can reasonably expect of journalists in the name of democracy' have been undermined, as Brian McNair observes in his chapter. Although generally from an Anglophone, often from a British, perspective his examination has a bearing upon journalism everywhere.

Journalism has become the pre-eminent cultural form of our age, he argues, and although in existence for hundreds of years has only now expanded to involve a 'vast universe of information providers' and become in many ways 'the centre of public life'. In explaining these assertions, McNair clarifies for us just why we, as students and scholars of journalism, exist, and why our discipline matters.

The academic student of journalism needs to ask the kind of questions he raises, from 'who is the journalist?' to 'what cultural role does he or she perform?' Journalism has various functions and there are many expectations of it, some of which McNair illustrates with examples from another medium, the film. We now see journalism as one among several modes of telling tales, 'reported reality', and understand the difficulty of truth telling even as we uphold accuracy and impartiality.

The fact that authorities find it much more difficult to control information today means that journalists have new powers and responsibilities, ironically just when commercial pressures make it more difficult to be responsible. Other challenges to journalism include the erosion of temporal and spatial barriers in information provision; and the erosion of the distinctions between acting as a watchdog, punditry and entertainment functions of journalism – McNair sketches the development of these and other genres. He also shows different ways in which the increasing prevalence, popularisation and power of journalism can be interpreted. The journalist, advances McNair, thanks to technological enlargement of his or her scope, needs now to be thought of as 'information architect'.

Why do people become journalists? What kinds of people become journalists? What are their socio-economic and educational backgrounds, and their motivations? These are some of the questions which David Weaver (1998) addresses in his report of extensive international research. He shows us that there are similarities around the world; for example, journalists tend to be young and on their way to more lucrative jobs, and have rarely studied journalism at university but are usually graduates. Journalists are predominantly from the established and dominant cultural groups in their societies and may increasingly be conforming to emerging universal ethical and professional norms. However, there are marked differences between societies as to standards, roles, practices, career specifics and images of the audience. These differences may be more to do with political institutions than cultural predilections.

Weaver's well-established expertise in mapping the development of journalism around the world is of particular value in this book, rooting our local and often qualitative analyses in empirical studies, globally undertaken such as to provide cross-cultural comparability.

'Is journalism a profession?', 'should it be?' and 'could it be?' are questions that have exercised many for many years, which is why Howard Tumber and Marina Prentoulis' chapter is timely. Starting with early attempts to understand what professions are about, undertaken by the founding fathers of sociology, they go on to the specific case of journalism, and whether it can fit in to the models or whether it shares a development history with occupations generally accepted as professions. In doing so, they show just how journalism differs from those occupations against which it is compared, as well as demonstrating how journalism has nevertheless undergone a similar development process. They also clarify how journalism can be distinguished from other communication occupations, and the significance of the claim to objectivity. The functions of professional institutions and codes of practice are discussed, leading on to the place of education and training in their diffusion and of the relationship between education and training with professional status.

Tumber and Prentoulis move on in their final pages to look at the changing roles of journalists, who are becoming more engaged, increasingly interpretative and more multi-skilled and independent of the technical operatives on whom they were, until recently, dependent. There are grounds for believing that these developments are making it even more difficult to envisage journalists attaining formal professional status, even as they continue to take on professional characteristics.

After the essays on journalism in different societies, to be introduced below, the final section of the book touches on the formation of journalists.

Betty Medsger's chapter on journalism education deals exclusively with the USA, but there are good reasons for this. First, the earliest schools of journalism were established in that country, and have been the examples from which much of Asia and Latin America have learned. Many journalists throughout the world have therefore been powerfully influenced by the approach to journalism education that developed in the USA from the late nineteenth century, and it is valuable to have that history spelt out for us. Second, the matters that bedevil the discipline in the USA bedevil it elsewhere, and Medsger describes them well. The confusion of functions between communication studies, media studies and journalism education (not to mention journalism studies); the increasing academicisation of journalism education; the widening gulf between academic careers and practical teaching: all these are confusing the formation of journalists. If these are not issues in your country, they will be: in an up-to-date report from the front line, Medsger shows us Lee Bollinger's solution at Columbia University, which should give the rest of us pause for thought. Third, there is no satisfactory way to write a 'world' account of journalism education. As long ago as 1990 Hugh Stephenson and Pierre Mory provided us with an overview of it in Europe, but developments since then have been momentous and Eastern Europe was, and is, unmapped. There are studies of journalism education in China (Lu 2004) and the UK but that still leaves large areas of the world about which we hear only anecdotes as new faculties and schools of media and journalism are set up almost daily.

Medsger makes very clear the importance of the subject. As the factual media have grown in political power, in the Anglosphere at least, they have also been subjected to scrutiny and critique for the way they use that power, for their perceived partiality, for their failure to obey rules of evidence, for their sensationalism and their treatment of others. There is a growing belief among ordinary people – who are reported to despise journalists – and the opinion-forming classes that journalists are a danger to civilised society, rather than its custodians (Lloyd 2004). The critics always call for better-educated journalists. That is only part of the need, for journalists are subject to conditions not of their making or comprehending, from the political economy of the media to the power of political, commercial and ideological pressure. Nevertheless, as Medsger makes clear, an educated, informed, responsible and aware journalist is a journalist armed.

In an account rooted in her experience of practising journalism and of teaching it in London, Angela Phillips addresses an issue vital to journalism courses everywhere: who should call the shots? She points to the problems of journalism educators, answerable to both industry and universities, neither of whose high authorities have much understanding of their work, and all too often calumnied by journalists too.

Phillips shows how wrong headed is the failure of the profession to acknowledge the part played by education in the development of the very skills its members most value – analytical and critical ones. She argues the importance of educating aspirants to understand how knowledge is acquired and what conditions it, and that universities are the best places for doing that, and for the mixture of academic and practical learning which is better preparation for adaptability and professionalism than either traditional academic study or mere vocational training.

While journalists argue, employers are busy raising the entry barriers for journalists, even as they run down their own in-house training. Insisting that applicants have degrees, British employers now want to gain control of university courses by setting up 'Centres of (technical) Excellence' and enforcing accreditation. The trouble is that concentration of funds in a few industry-orientated centres, and obliging courses generally to conform to industry ideas of what is needed, will almost certainly squeeze out the very modules and attitudes that educate journalists in the wider responsibilities of their profession. The dilemma Phillips identifies goes to the heart of journalism education in all countries: are our students merely to hold down jobs as information processors or are they to hold authorities to account?

The world of journalism is being utterly transformed by new media, or digital information technology and their convergence in a networked environment, holds John Pavlik. His essay, coming from the USA as it does, contradicts some of the consequences of new technology discerned in, for example, India and China, but this may be because the starting points are different, and it may well be that his predictions do indeed hold good for us all.

Today, thanks to changes in technology and management practices, there are too many outlets and too few customers. The resulting intense competition combines with digitisation in its various manifestations (Pavlik identifies five distinct but converging areas) to cause less and less investment in research, analysis and evaluation. The implications for quality of journalism, for its integrity and its role in the public sphere, are great. Almost all the developments he discusses reduce the time spent upon actual journalism, and the emphasis is increasingly upon its packaging and distribution. Not that everything is negative: Pavlik reports a dramatic growth in ethnic media, which supports the underlying theme of this book. But the well-known fact that the dominant media of the twentieth century are suffering steady long-term decline will not be reversed by the new media – quite the opposite. Those who consider that journalism matters will have to take up the technological gauntlet and fight to ensure that it survives.

So much for the environment shared by journalists everywhere. What can we say about journalism in different societies?

Culture and journalism: what's in common, what's not

There are still people who do not watch television, usually because their communities are cut off from modern society but also, in some cases, out of conscious

5

rejection. When you show such people news programmes from Shanghai, Atlanta, Buenos Aires or Kiev, what strikes them is the similarity of format. When you visit newsrooms the world over it is notable how not only the technology but also the working practices appear universal. It is an understandable assumption that technology has globalised news production and homogenised it.

News suppliers are international, so that images bought from the same supplier may be deployed everywhere; begging, for a moment, the questions of how they are used and how received, we can acknowledge that images digested in common join global brands, transnational songs, series and formats to delocalise our world and subject our own communities to more and more ideas and pressures from far away.

And yet, as research such as that of Kevin Robins (2000) has shown, and as John Thompson (1995) has so convincingly argued, information technology can also have the opposite effect. Middle Eastern minorities in Britain are not dependent upon the media of the host country but can hook up to media produced in the country from which they originated, keeping the shared identity alive. Differences between them and the host society may even grow deeper if there does not exist that impetus for incorporation into a common identity for which the USA has been famous. Cultures which, a century ago, would have been assimilated may now survive, thanks to new media.

The facility with which ideas now travel does not necessarily mean that what Anglophones might think of as the appropriate interpretations win.[2] The Baghdad torture pictures will be understood differently in different countries. Chinese neo-conservatives have been stimulated by books from the West on such topics as cultural imperialism (Tomlinson 1999), the clash of civilisations (Huntingdon 1996) and the failure of the Enlightenment project (Gray 1995). It is a reasonable guess that the Western writers did not foresee that they would embolden Chinese conservatives who wanted to restore Confucianism. Al Quaeda marries modern attitudes and technological opportunities with medieval beliefs (Scruton 2003). In these examples, the globalisation of new ideas and capabilities has consequences unforeseen in their places of origin, including the strengthening of indigenous cultures.

The point here is that appearances are deceptive. Modes of organisation and formats may be universal, but content and application are not. As Shi Anbin (2004) tells us, the idea of professionalism is universal but it is interpreted differently – according to culture.

What's this to do with journalism?

The academy has been universalist too. Early textbooks on journalism suggested that the media went through various stages and ultimately ended up free, as in the USA and the UK. Left academics pointed out that there were many flaws in the Anglo-American models but in general omitted to consider circumstances other than the economic which made for differences between the media in the

Anglosphere and elsewhere. They subscribed, in other words, to the same general scheme without agreeing with the hierarchy.

Although there are references to English journalism in this book, there is no chapter identifying it, perhaps because it is so familiar to students of journalism as to be regarded as a kind of benchmark. What are the characteristics of English journalism? A particular myth of origins; easily distinguished subcultures (distinct elite and popular press); a particular public-service tradition; an ideology of detachment, individualism and empiricism. In other words, English journalism is exceptional in some of the ways that the anthropologists tell us (MacFarlane 1987, 1992) that English society is exceptional.[3] Just as certain factors in England's early history gave rise to certain types of social or political institution, so they spawned particular cultural phenomena, including, eventually, particular modes of journalism. For those who accept cultural differences as significant, if not determining, this is not surprising.[4]

We can speculate that the particular characteristics[5] of English society which made it so dynamic and entrepreneurial in another era have made it easier for free-market approaches to dissolve bonds of interpersonal solidarity today (Gray 1998: 74).[6] On the other hand Anglophone societies have held onto a reasonably open political culture; a public-service tradition; a thriving civil society of voluntary associations; relative mutual trust (what Sicilians, lamenting its absence in the Mediterranean, refer to as *bonu fidi*); belief in the common weal, particularly today the environment, and concern for strangers, those dying of plague in faraway places; charitable donations.[7]

If we accept the idea of distinct cultures having institutional and behavioural consequences, then we have some sort of explanation for the high value placed upon factuality, public service and independence in Anglophone journalism. If investigative journalism has a particular style and performs a particular role in any given society, then that is not by chance but because it comes out of a tradition shaped by factors which, for want of a better word, we call 'cultural'.

Culture is one of the influences upon journalism, along with political economy and technology. At different times these, and doubtless other contexts, have greater or lesser influence than each other, and upon each other, too. Thus, while we can explain some of the manifestations of journalism, such as tabloidisation (Sparks and Tulloch 2000), by references to changes in the political economy, and attribute the enhanced speed of newsgathering to technological change, neither are mutually exclusive. And what journalists put *into* the tabloids depends upon culture.

How can we describe the relationships between journalism and culture?

The influence of the media upon our thinking and our behaviour – upon our culture – is increasingly studied, with mixed success, but I want to step back and look at the other side as it were: the influences of the culture upon journalism.

In the newsroom, the typical way in which events are identified as news-worthy, the criteria applied to check ('proximity', 'immediacy', and so on), the ranking, the professional processes brought to bear upon them that they may be reconstituted as news – these are culturally determined. The cultures may be growing closer together ('immediacy' is by no means just an Anglophone crite-rion today) but there are discernible differences. In the Chinese case, how much these are due to political fiat and how much to cultural predisposition is a legiti-mate question. At one extreme of journalism – usually far from the newsroom – much journalism may be phatic communication. In the UK, you only have to look at one edition of the *Guardian* and compare it to the simultaneous *Daily Mail* to see that the transmission of information may be less the point than the affirmation of orthodoxy. Here again is a subject of study. What is it that jour-nalists in a particular culture like to reaffirm for, and share with, their customers? What categories of ideas are thought appropriate to news in this society? And how startling does a Venezuelan find English or Russian choices?

Examining *investigative journalism*[8] within the cultural context, and comparing it with that of other societies, leads us to the conclusion that inves-tigative journalists, while certainly pointing out transgressions of their culture's values, are also fulfilling the expectations of their cultures as are scholars or mothers, adolescents or judges (Xu 2000; de Burgh 2003). After all, our very questions are conditioned by our institutional and cultural lives, our answers are shaped both by the nature of the questions and by the repertoire of possible responses of which we are capable, and which are conditioned or delimited by our culture as well as by the surrounding institutions.

If there are different ways of running societies, worthy of respect even if not liking, then the different institutions of societies must have their differentness acknowledged, no matter that they are, confusingly, called by similar names. Relative to the Dutch parliament, the British parliament often seems powerless to influence the executive; the parliaments of Turkey and Italy have different relationships to their respective polities than does the US Congress to its. So, I suggest, is it with journalism. Journalism does different things in different socie-ties. Of course there are aspects in common, apart from the name, but these we all know about. It is the differences that are fascinating.

Paulo Mancini published an article in 2000 which drew our attention to just how different Italian journalism is, in its aims as in its functions, from Anglophone journalism. And yet, because of the prestige of Anglophone jour-nalism, Italian journalists have tended to deny that difference.

Mancini (2000) argues that, in Italy, the 'professional model of journalism based on neutrality, autonomy and detachment from power' is widely accorded respect on account of the need, still forcefully felt by journalists, to prove that they are repudiating the fascist legacy. And because of media imperialism. The need to reject any whiff that the media of other countries are superior obliges non-Anglophone media institutions to represent themselves as the same kind of institution, whereas the true fact may be that they are simply performing roles which are determined by and in their own cultures. In other words, journalists may characterise themselves using the discourses of Anglophone journalism studies, yet, in practice, are very distant from them. In Mediterranean and Hispanic countries, where tyro journalists assiduously study the Anglophone model, they nevertheless act in accordance with quite different sets of conventions. Psychologists call that 'cognitive dissonance'.

Mancini also observes that the press in Italy has always been 'more literary, comment and advocacy orientated', as does Chalaby (1996) of the French press. Journalism is expected to be a tool in struggles for commercial or political gain. He emphasises that news organisations are closely tied to organised interests and political parties, and many suggest that this is the case in the Hispanic media too (Quesada 1997), although Waisbord (2001) has re-examined this question and come up with a more nuanced understanding. Mancini argues that the objectives of the media channels are to 'transmit ideas, protect interests and organise people who already share the same point of view', accounting for this by saying that although in a two-party system such as those of the USA and the UK, objectivity may be possible:

> Objectivity is almost impossible within an intricate and fragmented panorama in which a greater number of political forces act and in which even the slightest shades of meaning in a story risk stepping on the positions of one of the forces in the political field.
>
> (2000: 273)

In this book, Mancini broadens out his discussion to consider Europe more generally. Thanks to him we can now lay to rest the infuriating assumption often made that European and Anglo-American journalism are the same. Mancini admits Anglophone journalism to be the only universal model, yet simultaneously shows us that there are marked differences between American and English journalism; some characteristics of English journalism bring it closer to the 'European model' that he adumbrates.

The journalism of the Anglophone countries has certain clear differences from that of the European continent. The most obvious one is the relationship with politics; another is the value put upon 'factuality'; a third is that European journalism is far more literary, with journalists being more part of the cultural elite than are their Anglophone counterparts. The practical results of these distinctions are considerable.

England is more akin to Europe in that its newspapers are highly partisan, while existing side by side with the BBC's public-service broadcasting. For the continental countries have generally sought to keep some broadcasting public and find, in the links between public broadcasting and the political systems, major matters of public debate and constant tension.

There are many differences even within continental Europe. In Scandinavia there exists a high degree of professionalism and common standards even where newspapers are politicised, and in Sweden newspapers are subsidised to ensure a plurality of views, whereas in the Mediterranean journalists take sides as members of the political, and literary, elites. A combination of the media's traditional dependency upon sponsors, of journalists being part of the cultural intelligentsia and of the French revolutionary tradition of polemical journalism has meant that that factuality and reportage associated with Anglophone journalism are less prevalent than are comment, interpretation and evaluation.

What Mancini does in his chapter is to demonstrate how different cultural traditions have resulted in journalisms that can be called 'European' and 'Anglophone'. He has also pointed out the ways in which English journalism belongs to both. Although any discussion of this kind, as he writes, 'tends to sacrifice the complexity of the phenomena observed', nevertheless 'constructing typologies always has a significant and important cognitive value'. He makes the familiar look different.

US journalism, avers Michael Schudson, 'emerges out of a unique history and it has been shaped by a relationship to distinctive political institutions and a unique political culture', a statement which encapsulates the core sentiment of this book, for it could of course be made about all the journalisms here described. And Schudson neatly summarises how US journalism, emerging from English traditions, changed in accordance with the geographical and political circumstances of the new republic and gradually took upon itself those characteristics which make it the distinctive institution we know today.

In particular, Schudson explains how it is that American journalists' 'passion should be dispassion', how the ideal and practices of impartiality came out of the nineteenth-century transformation of American culture to bring about 'ardent professionalisation' and how the wealth and profitability of the media helped sustain the new journalistic practices. Furthermore, he notes the degree to which journalism in the USA and journalism in Europe have grown apart.

Schudson's cultural interpretation of US journalism is by no means triumphalist. He considers that there is a downside to factors that have made his country's media so effective: 'limits on governmental constraints in the United States have made the American news media more vulnerable to censorship by private media companies themselves'. Countries can attain the same ends by different routes: 'very different positions elsewhere may serve democracy as well or better than the liberal-libertarian First Amendment tradition in the United States'.

In China in the 1920s and 1930s journalists trained in the USA worked to adapt the US model to home conditions. The attempt was abandoned after the victory of the Soviet-inspired Communist Party in 1949, and the media was stifled more or less until around 1992, since when they have undergone rapid changes in re-adapting to the market economy. China is the world's most populous country and Chinese-language media in the world probably rival English-language media in scope.

Chin-Chuan Lee (2001) provides us with a clear history and a number of key messages of modern relevance. He points out the similarities between Confucian and Maoist models of communication and the significant differences, including the latitude for moral choice allowed to individuals in the traditional Chinese order. He notes that the target of journalists, their audiences, have always been seen as subordinate, never as citizens in some equally shared public sphere. Confucianism saw them as objects of instruction or guidance; Maoism wanted them indoctrinated and mobilised while the present-day media, which Lee, with pleasing irony, terms 'The Communist–Capitalist Media', seek conformity and exploit them for profit.

A sense of public service imbued leading journalists during the development of the early modern press, with cynosure Liang Qichao envisioning them as a 'bridge' between rulers and ruled, but it was a sense deriving from the moral responsibility of members of the ruling class[9] rather than from any democratic sentiment. They prided themselves on being instructors and experts.

Mao wrecked this by making journalists mere mouthpieces of propaganda; they therefore fell short of reporting abuse, investigating atrocities or forestalling economic calamities. His romantic notions helped ensure that China failed to establish the legal and institutional mechanisms to resolve the contradiction between political centralisation and popular participation and, though there have been fluctuations in journalism's situation since the 1980s, the problem remains. It has, however, been further complicated by the marketisation of the media which not only has vastly expanded the scope of journalism and its involvement with economic development and political affairs, but also brought about unprecedented corruption.

Above all, Lee reminds us that journalists in China, regardless of which of the three models you turn to, have seen themselves as instruments of China's mission to wealth and power, to which any ethic or practice must be subjected.

The experience of India could not be more different, although in the early years after Independence journalists were strongly influenced by their recent past when they had been activists in the nationalist movement, as Daya Thussu reminds us. They saw their role as 'following a developmental agenda set by an activist state', yet, gradually, thanks to the government's relative tolerance of criticism, the press was able to develop a professional independence, with norms unsullied by political interference, and to become the kind of 'early warning system' for crises that was not possible for journalists in China.

India is the world's largest democracy yet until the early 1990s broadcasting was government controlled. Once there was competition from the many new channels that followed deregulation, so came cultural hybridity and new, competitive challenges for journalists. Thussu reports a study of Indian journalists suggesting that they have found more career opportunities, that they have retained a strong public-service orientation and that, although they fear foreign ownership of Indian media, they watch Western TV (and in particular BBC World).

Similar, though as yet less rich, opportunities are coming to journalists elsewhere. Arab journalists were, until recently, trapped in history: having been the cheerleaders of anti-imperialism and anti-Zionism in the 1950s, they were expected, by the harsh and narrow-minded political regimes under which they operated, to be advocates and mobilisers. That some journalists had the courage to step out of line is a tribute to their courage and foolhardiness.

Naomi Sakr outlines the development of the modern Arab media from the 1870s and then, while warning against over-simplification, shows how the arrival of satellite television in the 1990s began to change them. The competition of foreign coverage, upon which most media users relied to get credible reportage, impelled editors to try to make their vehicles interesting enough to maximise circulation but uncontentious enough to satisfy the politicians; more private vehicles developed and more diversity too, although it remained typical of editors to see their role as one of fighting for causes rather than simply informing.

In the 1980s, Saudi-financed *émigré* ventures, based usually in London, persuaded their sponsors that credible journalism requires sourcing own stories, reporting relatively freely and investigating. What the sponsors found impossible to accept was that conflicting views might be aired. It was the BBC's closure of its Arabic Service in 1998 and the subsequent establishment, in Doha, of Al-Jazeera TV, that were to infiltrate that concept into the Arab media. Al-Jazeera built upon some innovations that pre-dated it, yet innovated: Viewpoints previously unheard were reported and expressed (Al-Jazeera was widely criticised for interviewing Israeli spokesmen!); stories were covered that were never covered before (Sakr reminds us that the Massacre of Halabja was ignored by the Arab media in 1988); investigations took place; public participation was introduced. Old media have tried to adapt, while new ones are attempting to emulate; what Al-Jazeera reports is difficult to ignore, and how Al-Jazeera screens is on every competitor's agenda. Not only are there many more jobs for journalists, and training opportunities, but their roles and conditions are changing as they have earned new respect, improved their contracts and can move posts. Rarely in the history of media can the advent of one vehicle in an important culture area have had such impact so quickly upon the industry and the profession of journalism.

Is the Arab development an example of technological determination? Or cultural change? Their colleagues in Sub-Saharan Africa must look enviously at the progress being made in the Arab world.

There is little reference to Africa in mainstream media and journalism studies, so that Helge Rønning's chapter rights a wrong. He demonstrates that the urge to tell truth to power is as fierce in the continent where it is most dangerous, and he does so by giving impressive instances. He places the courage of the few within the contexts they suffer. Low wages, poor resources, inadequate training and low social standing are endemic. Broadcast journalists are commonly forced to be mouthpieces of the ruling clique, newspaper journalists have tiny readerships and even smaller internet audiences. In consequence of these factors, the media do not cover the lives and interests of the majority of the populations, the rural poor.

Journalists are dependent, whether upon the local political elites or international funders. Their backers usually have very different ideas from them as to what journalism is about and, at least in the case of the politicians, are willing to enforce their views with violence. Privatisation of the media at the behest of international development organs has not provided a solution but new versions of old problems. Advertising is still inadequate and fickle; corruption is routine; fear is everywhere. Nevertheless, as Rønning shows with examples from Zimbabwe, Zambia, Mozambique, Ivory Coast, Cameroon, Malawi, Senegal, Tanzania, South Africa and Kenya, many journalists do contrive to keep the opinion formers apprised of issues and protests, and to expose abuse and corruption. From being the mouthpieces of nationalism in the days of colonialism's retreat, then the cat's paws of politicians and their plans for development, journalists are, haltingly, managing to represent diverse voices and serve as the watchdogs of power. Rønning's chapter on Africa is magisterial in its sweep, managing both to explain the commonalties and to teach us the specifics.

This book reports changes in the activities and prospects of journalists in many countries, but perhaps the changes have nowhere been more remarkable or more pregnant with possibilities than Latin America, where, as Alves shows us, the media have played important roles in the transition of Latin American countries to democracy which has been such a notable feature of the past twenty years.

The alternative or vanguard press has usually led the way, demonstrating its value as critic and source of information, pushing more mainstream media institutions to risk turning from lapdogs into watchdogs. Journalists and proprietors have managed this by establishing unwritten rules of engagement with political power holders, sometimes allying with them, sometimes spearheading democratic movements against them. The press has become a very popular institution in many countries, generally surpassed in the polls only by the Catholic Church.

All sides have struggled to understand the roles and the potential of the media in democratic society. In countries where journalists are free from external political pressures for the first time, they have run into internal constraints, when media proprietors are still reluctant to exert independence after so many years of being muzzled. Journalists, on the other hand, are frequently unprepared to use the freedom and commit abuses in their eagerness to denounce malfeasance, sometimes without proper evidence or attention to ethical considerations.

Nevertheless, the dangers to journalists have been great, by no means always from authority but also from criminal interests. Some 200 have been murdered. Alves' chapter explores the complex transition from a lapdog press to a watchdog press, and provides inspiration as well as examples for study.

The new cultural paradigm

Once upon a time there was a belief, general to the educated in Europe and the USA, that humanity was moving towards, and should be helped by all right-thinking people towards, a universal civilisation. This was the natural end towards which human society was tending, thanks to the spread of knowledge, understanding and the liberating achievements of science and technology. Most recently, globalisation has been seen as accelerating this process.[10]

Various versions of this vision, and the belief that it is beholden upon us to push this process along, have been influential and often dominant from the early nineteenth century to now.[11] In the nineteenth century the imperialists excused their conquests of other peoples by claiming that they were importing progress; simultaneously the forgers of new nations made the same boast as they ground down the religious and ethnic minorities which did not fit. In the twentieth century there arose, essentially from the same philosophical foundations and claiming to be creating a universal civilisation as they extirpated people, the Russian Bolsheviks, German Nazis and Chinese Maoists, to name only the major players. Each of the countries that succumbed has had, painfully, to try to return to the position it was in before the utopian revolution. So the dream is over? Not yet. Although one version of this dream, what John Gray calls 'Plan and Slaughter', may never be revived, Enlightenment universalism has reappeared in an updated version of its nineteenth-century manifestation, as the Anglophone countries and their allies seek to impose their own way of doing things upon (so far one of the) Arab countries.[12] However the Iraq War appears not only to have incited terrorism, but also to have strengthened critics of activist 'enlightenment' missionary politicians of both left and right, and the universalist paradigm is giving ground to an antique sense of the way things ought to be, more familiar to Yuan Dynasty Chinese or Ottoman Turks than to the modern world.

The return of the repressed

Over the past decade, political and religious movements have emerged which reject the idea that we are all destined to be Anglophones, which is what globalisation has seemed to threaten for many. In Indonesia, Malaysia, Egypt, Algeria and Iran it is Muslim identity that is contested. But in different ways many different people are baulking at the homogenising vision, whether Hindus, Mexicans, or Sami, seeking ways to be modern which derive from their own. Chechens, Tibetans and Eastern Turks are fighting a different kind of cultural assault from that of their nineteenth-century forebears, and the fact that they do so reflects a modern phenomenon: the politics of identity.

Nationalists tend to 'essentialise' national or religious culture in ways that infuriate the historian. They may be doing so as much in reaction to perceptions of foreign domination as on account of their own, autonomous, yearning. Nevertheless it is surely undeniable that, even as they don *multiple* identities, many people are becoming more sensitive to their *local* identities.[13]

The world of scholarship has been going in the same direction. On the one hand, Stuart Hall, working with Gramsci's concept of hegemony, turns economic determinism on its head to argue that cultural production determines the social and economic climate (Procter 2004: 18), while on the other, market liberals undergo a comparable conversion in the very remarkable *Culture Matters: How Values Shape Human Progress* (Harrison and Huntingdon 2000). Departments of business studies publish treatises on the specifically Italian ways of doing commerce – connected to anthropology, artisanship and a very particular network culture – and establish degrees in Chinese management, both to prepare Anglophones and to codify the rules for Chinese practitioners themselves!

The recognition of culture as determinant of institutional and individual behaviour has an old history and, in Europe, can probably be attributed to the seventeenth-century Gianbattista Vico, appropriately a Neapolitan. He recognised 'the existence of a variety of autonomous cultures, entire ways of life, each with its own outlook and values flowing out of one another, which are not merely a succession of efforts, attended by varying success, to achieve the same universal goals' (Berlin 2000: 141). He went further, holding that

> there is a pervasive pattern which characterises all the activities of any given society: a common style reflected in the thought, the arts, the social institutions, the language, the ways of life and actions of a entire society ... [such that] works of art must be understood, interpreted, evaluated, not in terms of timeless principles and standards valid for all men everywhere, but by a correct grasp of the purpose and therefore the peculiar use of symbols, especially of language, which belong uniquely to their own time and place, their own stage of social growth.
>
> (ibid.: 9–11)

It sounds modern, especially given the lip service paid to multiculturalism in the Anglophone societies today – at least until the start of the 2003–4 Iraq War. It sounds modern because the Cultural Studies movement has alerted us to the varieties of cultures that may exist within any given national culture, and, hand in hand with Saussurian and structuralist insights, made us aware of the significance of manifestations of culture which we once innocently thought of as 'teapots', 'jeans' or 'antimacassars'. It is also unsatisfying, because it explains neither what culture is nor in what ways culture acts upon circumstances, any more than either the Birmingham School founded by Hall, or Bourdieu, have been able to do.

What is culture?

Culture is 'the social practices and beliefs of a given group of people who share them' (Jandt 1995: 157), a more generally acceptable definition than those advanced by Arnold, Leavis, then Hoggart and Williams, which tended to leave

Anglophones with an uncomfortable divide between high culture and low culture, and which also have failed to help us distinguish between popular culture and commercialised culture. Although contested by, *inter alia*, Hannerz (1992), this kind of definition is still useful.

We may wish to identify cultural differences as huge as in childrearing or as minor as in body language. As Raymond Williams wrote: 'many of our communication models become, in themselves, social institutions. Certain attitudes to others, certain forms of address, certain tones and styles become embodied in institutions which are then very powerful in social effect' (quoted in Carey 1989: 33). Although this reminds us just how many cultures there are for us to belong to, from professional cultures to class cultures to kinfolk cultures and minority subcultures of every kind, in which the differences from the norms of the culture of the geographical, or national society, can be quite great, ordinary people probably think simply of 'national culture' when they hear the term. In doing so they (and we) tend to essentialise, stereotype (over-simplify) or reduce the subject to the object of one's own cultural urges, producing orientalism or occidentalism. And still we are not really helped to grasp how Vico's 'pervasive pattern' or 'common style' have come about.

While common sense may satisfy us in our daily lives – we know the differences between an Italian and a Chinese, don't we? – academics need to delve further if they are to make a useful tool out of culture. One of the most interesting attempts to understand the underlying structures of culture has been made by Todd,[14] who argues that the culture, politics and economic development potential of societies are primarily determined by the prevailing family form (de Burgh 1999). Thus he can explain why certain areas of Italy have embraced socialist parties and certain areas reject them in favour of monarchism, why Meiji Japan developed so rapidly by contrast with other societies apparently faced with similar circumstances, and so on. Family form is the basic building block upon which we grow those attitudes and habits that result in culture, which then determine a society's choice of religion, polity and economy, and the society's mode of reacting to, or ability to adapt to, stimuli from outside (imperialism, technological change, media revelations). He would take any given social phenomenon and understand it in terms of the underlying realities of the society, and has done so impressively with French electoral politics (Todd 1988). Fei Xiaotong was thinking along the same lines when his career was cut short in the 1940s (see Fei 1992).

Culture Matters: How Values Shape Human Progress, referred to above, is, in particular, an attack upon modernisation theory and dependency theory. It is written by (mainly) economists and

> development practitioners ... focusing on the role of cultural values and attitudes as facilitators of, or obstacles to progress. They are the intellectual heirs of Alexis de Tocqueville, who concluded that what

made the American political system work was a culture congenial to democracy; Max Weber, who explained the rise of capitalism as essentially a cultural phenomenon rooted in religion; and Edward Banfield, who illuminated the cultural roots of poverty and authoritarianism in Southern Italy, a case with universal applications.

(Harrison and Huntingdon 2000: xxi)

None of its authors quoted Joseph Levenson,[15] but a crude application of his ideas on Confucianism in the spirit of Todd or Harrison would interpret the Chinese Communist Party as a reflection of the needs of Chinese culture rather than a function of the stage reached by the Chinese economy (Marxism–Leninism), the will of the masses (Maoism) or a product of Bolshevik entrepreneurialism (Western university departments of politics at various times).

In short, an idea repressed for many years has returned, that culture is fundamental and cannot be explained away by economics. It has returned at the very moment that we are all agog with globalisation.[16] We now need to find ways of applying our new understandings, but in the debate on structure and agency – the attempt to understand in what ways 'objective' supra-individual social reality and the subjective mental worlds of individuals are inextricably bound up together, how traditions, economic circumstances, new technology and domestic circumstances interact – there is no simple solution. Even more is this so now that we must consider the culture industries themselves as amounting to powerful actors. And journalism is part of those industries.

Conclusion

How journalism operates in a given society, no less than musical expression or eating habits, is the product of culture. And if we accept, following Carey (1989: 30), that communication is most revealingly examined as ritual rather than as transmission, then it is also in order to identify the ritual that we study journalism. We recognise journalism as profoundly influencing our thinking, and replacing or supplementing traditional sources of knowledge. Globalisation has meant a sharing of techniques, and formats and professional attitudes but also, paradoxically, globalisation has brought about an intensified awareness of the power of culture such that we cannot afford to ignore it.

Notes

1 Journalism in Eastern Europe is in such flux that it seemed wiser to exclude a subject which needs a volume all to itself.
2 The economic success of the Anglosphere, the spread of English as the world language and the universalist pretensions that are powerful in their culture seem to make Anglophones particularly clumsy in their dealings with others. Many

people in the world today live two lives – they pretend to be what Anglophones think they are, while preserving their own identities in regions which Anglophones, so often monolingual, cannot penetrate. The tragic events in Iraq this year seem to me to be as much about Anglophone cultural incompetence as about oil, or Israel, or geopolitics or whatever. The same mindset makes it difficult for Anglophones to accept that countries which do not value what they value can nevertheless achieve modernity, even, perhaps, be more successful, not only materially but in the sense of having greater social cohesion and opportunities for individual happiness. Anglophone prejudice in this regard is tribalism disguised as universalism.

3 The detached way in which Anglophones have historically treated their offspring, their ideas about inheritance and gender have been very distinct for as long as we have any knowledge, according to MacFarlane (1987).

4 The Anglo-Saxon society which provides the common roots of today's Anglophone countries has been distinct from that of its continental European neighbours ever since the earliest times that it has been possible to study. The very different relations between and within families (Todd 1987), and much earlier commercialisation of the land-ownership system (MacFarlane 1992), are among the basic characteristics which have developed into those typical characteristics of Anglophone culture: empiricism, individualism and distance. These characteristics enabled Anglophone societies to take advantage of economic and technological developments and create the institutions appropriate to them, from the sixteenth century onwards.

5 There is a risk that by 'characteristics' I am thought to mean old chestnuts beloved of books attempting to explain the English, such as 'tolerance' or 'reticence', whereas we should judge cultural differences more by institutions. Early traditions in child-rearing, family formation, inheritance and so on are the kind of institutions which have themselves led to others, from the joint-stock company to common law.

6 England has a culture of hire and fire, Japan does not. England has an excluded indigenous underclass, Mediterranean Europe hardly. That there are dysfunctional aspects to these characteristics is not in doubt today: Anglophone societies lead the world in broken families, restless mobility, workaholism, the gulf between rich and poor, incarceration rates, suicide.

7 It is not a coincidence that Amnesty International, Save the Children, Friends of the Earth and thousands of comparable initiatives were initiated in Anglophone Societies. But the point being made here is that the distinctiveness of Anglophone society accounts for many things both good and bad.

8 For the UK, see de Burgh (2000); for the USA, see Ettema and Glasser (1988); for China, see de Burgh (2003); for Germany, see Wallraff (1978); for Spain, see Quesada (1997).

9 By which I mean, of course, Confucian literati.

10 For a critique of this view, see Sparks (1998).

11 Although temporarily eclipsed during periods of pessimism after the First World War and in the 1950s, as the full horror of the Nazi and Communist experiments in social transformation became apparent at the moment that nuclear war seemed nigh.

12 I want to quickly affirm here my own admiration for many aspects of US society and for its enormous contribution to human happiness, progress and security. The error being made by leading US policy-makers and opinion formers is to assume that, simply because the USA has been so successful and has attracted so many immigrants by its opportunities and ideals, the rest of the world, 'Old Europe' or Arabia, China or Mexico, want only to be like it.

13 Local is not meant geographically. As John Thompson has so well described, identities once thought of as geographically fixed have become 'delocalised' (1995: Ch. 6).

14 Starting from his work as an anthropologist, demographer and student of electoral sociology, Todd has gone on to theorise a correlation between family form and ideological systems. In *The Explanation of Ideology* (1989) he argued that ideologies correspond to sets of attitudes determined by family form, which has predisposed adherents of those ideologies to particular kinds of doctrines; indeed ideologies spread only so far as the geographical diffusion of the family forms with which they have affinity, because, far from being determinants of behaviour, they are reflections of it. In *The Causes of Progress* (1987) he found that family form rather than economics accounts for the rate of industrial development of a given society, and in particular that societies in which women have higher status have greater potential for socio-economic development. The failure of the academy to explain why particular religious or political ideas and institutions take root where they do is a reason for us to pay attention to Todd, who offers insights to development economists, public-policy specialists and students of history and culture alike.

15 Levenson argues that communism suited Chinese intellectuals because it enabled them to feel superior to the hated West and more advanced. They could 'reject Confucianism from a superior position, while rejecting capitalism too' (Levenson 1958: 134). I would add that another appeal of communism was surely that it offered that great unity which the messy compromises of Anglophone democracy did not. While not assuming that Levenson would agree with that, I will quote from him to back up my point:

> To suggest, therefore, that Chinese communism has a role to play as a device for an intelligentsia in its efforts to escape an intellectual dilemma is not to deny but to confirm the fact that Chinese communism has come to the fore because of awesome social pressures. Alienation from Chinese tradition is inseparable from restlessness in Chinese society; and a revolutionary effort to cure the malaise which alienation engenders is the inescapable counterpart, in intellectual history, of the effort, by revolution, to pass through social restlessness to a social equilibrium.

(1958: 145)

16 For the best demolition of the idea that there is a global public sphere, see Sparks (1998).

References

Berlin, Isaiah [1976] (2000) *Three Critics of the Enlightenment: Vico, Hamann and Herder*, Princeton, NJ: Princeton University Press.

Carey, James W. (1989) *Communication as Culture: Essays on Media and Society*, London: Routledge.

Chalaby, JK (1996) 'Journalism as an Anglo American Invention: A Comparison of the Development of French and Anglo-American journalism 1830s–1920s', *European Journal of Communication* 11(3): 303–326.

Curran, James and Park Myung-jin (2000) *De-Westernizing Media Studies*, London: Routledge.

de Burgh, Hugo (1999) 'Todd, Emmanuel', in Ellis Cashmore and Chris Rojek (eds) *Dictionary of Cultural Theorists*, London: Arnold.

—— (ed.) (2000) *Investigative Journalism: Context and Practice*, London: Routledge.

—— (2003) 'Kings without Crowns? The Re-emergence of Investigative Journalism in China', *Media Culture & Society* 25(6) November: 801–820.

Ettema, J. and Glasser, T. (1988) 'Narrative Form and Moral Force', *Journal of Communication* Summer: 8–26.

Fei Xiaotong [1947] (1992) *From the Soil: The Foundations of Chinese Society,* trans. G. Hamilton and Wang Zheng, Berkeley, CA: University of California Press.

Gray, John (1995) *Enlightenment's Wake,* London: Routledge.

—— (1998) *False Dawn: The Delusions of Global Capitalism,* London: Granta.

Hannerz, Ulf (1992) *Cultural Complexity: Studies in the Social Organisation of Meaning,* New York: Columbia University Press.

Harrison, Lawrence E. and Huntingdon, Samuel P. (2000) *Culture Matters: How Values Shape Human Progress,* New York: Basic Books.

Huntingdon, Samuel P. (1996) *The Clash of Civilisations and the Remaking of World Order,* New York: Simon and Schuster.

Jandt, F.E. (1997) *Intercultural Communication,* Thousand Oaks, CA: Sage.

Lee, Chin-Chuan (2001) 'Beyond Orientalist Discourses: Media and Democracy in Asia', *Javnost: The Public* 8(2): 7–20.

Levenson, Joseph R. (1958) *Confucian China and its Modern Fate,* vol. 2, London: Routledge.

Lloyd, John (2004) 'What the media are doing to our politics', London: Constable.

Lu Ye (2004) Working paper prepared for Bellagio Conference, 17–21 May

MacFarlane, Alan (1987) *Marriage and Love in England: Modes of Reproduction 1300–1840,* Oxford: Blackwell.

—— (1992) 'On Individualism', *Proceedings of the British Academy* 82: 171–199.

Mancini, Paulo (2000) 'Political Complexity and Alternative Models of Journalism: The Italian Case', in J. Curran and M.Y Park (eds) *De-Westernizing Media Studies,* London: Routledge.

Procter, James (2004) *Stuart Hall,* London: Routledge.

Quesada, M. (1997) *Periodismo de investigacin o el derecho a denunciar,* Barcelona: CIMS.

Robins, Kevin (2000) 'Beyond Imagined Community? Transnational Media and Turkish Migrants in Europe', Inaugural Lecture, University of London, 31 October.

Scruton, Roger (2003) *The West and the Rest: Globalisation and the Terrorist Threat,* London: Continuum.

Shi, Anbin (2004) 'Transnational Media Corporation and National Media System: China after Entry into the WTO', working paper prepared for Bellagio Conference, 17–21 May.

Sparks, Colin (1998) 'Is There a Global Public Sphere?', in Thussu, D (ed.) *Electronic Empires: Global Media and Local Resistance,* London: Arnold.

Sparks, Colin and Tulloch, John (2000) *Tabloid Tales: Global Debates over Media Standards,* New York: Rowman & Littlefield.

Stephenson, Hugh and Mory, Pierre (1990) *La Formation Au Journalisme en Europe,* Bruxelles: AEFJ.

Thompson, John (1995) *The Media and Modernity,* Cambridge: Polity.

Todd, Emmanuel (1987) *The Causes of Progress: Culture, Authority and Change,* Oxford: Blackwell.

—— (1988) *La Nouvelle France,* Paris: Hachette.

—— (1989) *The Explanation of Ideology,* Oxford : Blackwell.

Tomlinson, John (1999) *Globalization and Culture,* Cambridge: Polity.

Waisbord, Silvio (2001) *Watchdog Journalism in South America,* New York: Columbia University Press.

Wallraff, G. (1978) *The Undesirable Journalist*, London: Pluto.

Weaver, David (ed.) (1998) *The Global Journalist*, Cresskill, NJ: Hampton Press.

Xu, Hua (2000) 'Morality Discourse in the Market Place', in Hugo de Burgh (guest ed.) 'Of the Party and in the Market: the Social Functions of Chinese Journalism Today', special edition of *Journalism Studies* 1(4) November: 637–648.

Part I

JOURNALISM AND JOURNALISTS

1

WHAT IS JOURNALISM?

Brian McNair

What is journalism and why should we care?

To answer the second question first: a reasonable claim can be made for journalism as the pre-eminent cultural form of our era, occupying more resources in its production and distribution, and routinely consumed by more people in most countries than any of the many other ways in which we experience the world through mass media. We love our movies and our music, of course; are addicted to our TV soaps and our game shows, perhaps; have reverence and respect for our literature and visual art. But journalism *matters* more than them all, if only because it is the end product of a major industry employing hundreds of thousands of people, and daily supplying hundreds of millions – billions, across the globe – with information about every conceivable aspect of the world around them. Journalism, in all its varieties, is the constant background and accompaniment to everyday life.

And in this, straightforwardly industrial sense, journalism matters more with each passing year. Journalism has existed as a recognised mode of communication – 'the staple of news', as Ben Jonson referred to it in 1624 – for more than four centuries, but since the early 1980s its production has expanded as print and broadcast outlets have been joined by teletext services, then, with the arrival of cable and satellite technologies, by 24-hour real-time news channels on TV and radio, and in recent years by a proliferation of mobile-telephone and online news sites. The journalistic sector of the media economy is a vast universe of information providers, a public sphere of practically (from the individual's perspective, at least) infinite size and depth. The established brand leaders in journalism – the BBC, the *Wall Street Journal*, the *Financial Times*, the American TV networks, Reuters – have been joined in an ever more crowded multi-platform marketplace by new players like CNN, Sky News and Fox; by gossipy, often scurrilous yet enormously impactful online news sites such as the *Drudge Report*; by Arab language real-time broadcasters like Al Jazeera; and now, in what some have termed the blogging 'revolution', the thousands of journalistically inclined web logs jostling for attention in the networked, digitised media environment of the twenty-first century. The consumers of journalism have been moved from a position, not that far distant in the past, of relative information scarcity to one of surplus and excess. If it is true, as some argue, that in the early twenty-first century we inhabit a culture of information overload, a communicative Tower of Babel, then journalism is that culture's currency.

More than all this, journalism matters because it has a uniquely *privileged* cultural status, placing it (and journalists) at the centre of public life and political debate ever since journalists first began to irritate kings, queens and popes in early modern Europe. In recent times, journalism has been the trigger for the Monica Lewinsky scandal which nearly brought down US President Bill Clinton, the sleaze scandals which did much to put an end to eighteen years of Conservative government in the UK, and the continuing demystification (some would say undermining) of the British monarchy in the tabloid press and elsewhere. As this chapter was being written, public debate in the United Kingdom was dominated by a bitter dispute between the Labour government and the BBC.[1] That controversy, and the suicide of a senior official to which it led, forced the setting up of an independent judicial inquiry before which even the prime minister himself was required to appear. As for the BBC, its reporters, editors and managers were subjected to an unprecedented examination of their journalistic methods and principles, from which they did not emerge unsullied. The intense political and public interest in the Hutton inquiry[2] illustrates that journalism is not just the most important cultural form of the twenty-first century, if measured by the billions of pounds, dollars and euros spent globally on its production and consumption; it is also the most influential and contentious, with the capacity to shape the agenda of public debate, destabilise governments and cause immense misery to individuals in all walks of life.

Journalism's perceived importance (*perceived* because it is not always clear what its actual consequences on specific events and processes are) means that competing interest groups constantly struggle to define what, from their perspective, it *should* be, as well as what goes into it and what it says. Political actors in today's democratic societies inhabit a world where public opinion is crucially important. Journalism is the fuel, the raw material of public opinion, and a key tool in its management by elected politicians, lobbyists, pressure-group activists and even terrorists like Al Quaeda and ETA, for whom journalism provides the essential 'oxygen of publicity' which enables their causes to be noticed and (they hope) addressed. The communication techniques, tactics and strategies popularly referred to as 'spin' or *public relations* have evolved to their current state as a means of managing (or attempting to manage) journalistic coverage of events.

Journalism in transition

We should care about what journalism is, not least, because its practitioners are currently going through a period of rapid and unsettling change, driven principally by developments in communication technology, the fuller implications of which are described in John Pavlik's chapter later in this volume. These have opened up new possibilities for newsgathering and reporting. Satellite and cable, digitalisation and the internet, CCTV and lightweight recording equipment – all have problematised long-standing notions of what journalism is, and what it is not. They have transformed the processes of news production and distribution in ways which challenge the journalist's traditional relationship to his or her material, and his or her cultural role. They have transformed the economics of journalism, and challenged normative definitions of what the journalistic agenda should be. They have expanded the parameters of journalistic form and encouraged the emergence of hybrids. Journalism has become part of a wider culture of *factuality*, by which I mean our societies' growing fascination with the real and the actual (as opposed to the imagined and the fictional). The emerging culture of factuality is seen in the explosion of reality TV, makeover shows and other media forms in which traditional boundaries between news and commentary, education and entertainment, objectivity and subjectivity, detachment and commitment, reportage and reconstruction are eroding.

These processes have been welcomed by some, condemned by others. They have made life easier for journalists in some respects, and in others more difficult. They make it timely for a consideration of what are journalism's core values, its definitive characteristics, its unique selling propositions.

It is not just a question of what journalism is, though, but of what we think it should be, and the tensions between the two. It is a question of what journalism is becoming, when the technological, political and economic environments within which it is practised are, as they are now, in flux. And because, for all the technological wizardry now available to the industry, journalism is ultimately the product of human beings, one should also ask – who is the journalist, and what cultural role is he or she expected to perform in the twenty-first century?

This chapter proposes some answers to these questions, with occasional assistance from another branch of the culture industries. Since its origins, mainstream cinema has been fascinated with journalism and journalists, from whose working lives have been drawn a memorable set of heroes and villains. Journalists have been portrayed by the greatest stars of their era, including Clark Gable, Cary Grant, Rosalind Russell, James Stewart, Burt Lancaster, Kirk and Michael Douglas, Richard Gere, Geena Davis, Kate Winslet, Kevin Spacey, Jim Carrey and Angelina Jolie. The involvement of these stars in films centred on news media says something about the romantic allure of the journalist in our societies (something of a paradox, given the public hostility often recorded towards the profession in opinion polls). Journalists, no matter what the polls say, are glamorous and sexy in a way that accountants and bank managers are not, a fact reflected not least in the rise of journalism studies as a degree subject in higher education. But journalists are also mistrusted, despised, feared, in some cases loathed, and movies about the profession play on these ambivalences for dramatic effect.

Apart from their sheer entertainment value, therefore, these films also present a useful source for students of journalism interested in the social role of the profession. An entire book could easily be written about what the cinema tells us of the changing role of journalism in the twentieth century, and the pressures the journalist has been under from competing demands and interests. I will select here for the purposes of illustration just a few films in which journalists feature as central characters. They help us to understand, through the eyes of cinematic artists, not necessarily what journalism is but what we collectively, as a society, would like it to be, and how those expectations have changed.

What journalism is – an overview

Since the 'invention' of journalism sometime in the sixteenth century (Raymond, 1996) it has been required to be at least three things, often at the same time:

1 A supplier of the information required for individuals and groups to monitor their social environments; what Denis McQuail (1987) has characterised as a medium of *surveillance*.
2 A resource for, support to and often participant in public life and political debate – in liberal-democratic societies particularly, the discursive foundation of what Habermas (1989) famously called the *public sphere*.
3 A medium of education, enlightenment and entertainment – what might be grouped together as its *recreational* or *cultural* functions.

These three functions often overlap, of course, and reconciling them within texts which are at the same time (for example) politically useful and entertaining has generated professional tensions. These have structured public and political debate around the performance of journalists for as long as news media have existed. In seeking to define what journalism is, we must also consider the competing positions adopted in those debates.

Journalism as information – some distinguishing features

Journalism was born as a commodity for sale in the cultural marketplace. If not the first cultural form to exploit the technologies of text and image reproduction which drove the Enlightenment in early modern Europe (Elizabeth Eisenstein (1983) notes that religious, scientific and pornographic texts also benefited from the printing revolution), then journalism was certainly in the vanguard. Early printed pamphlets, corantos and newsheets were produced for profit. Even before print, when news was dispatched through the medium of handwritten letters as *correspondence*, journalists were suppliers of a commodity with, to use Marxian terminology, both use value (information about the world was needed for the pursuit of government and business, trade and war – journalism was *useful*) and exchange value (the price this information could command in a marketplace, when packaged and offered for sale as news). From the beginning the correspondence supplied by journalists depended on the existence of a market of paying customers who could read, or who had access to those who could read on their behalf.

For a variety of reasons, not all journalistic media have adhered to this straightforwardly commercial model, being financed, like the BBC, through taxation or other means of public support. The newspaper of the Communist Party of Great Britain, the *Morning Star*, was supported throughout most of its history by donations from Communist Party members and supporters, as well as subsidies from the Soviet Union. Throughout the communist world, until its collapse in the late 1980s, the party maintained journalistic media from state funds, seeing words as being, to paraphrase Lenin, 'much more dangerous than bullets' and thus, in the interests of political self-preservation, part of the cultural apparatus of the totalitarian state. They remain so in the decaying outposts of Marxism–Leninism, such as Cuba and North Korea. In China, where capitalism has been introduced in all but name, the Communist Party retains its monopoly on the control of journalistic media.

Local and even national newspapers in some European countries enjoy state subsidies designed to ensure healthy and diverse media in remote or under-populated areas which might be unable to support them by sales revenue alone. These deviations from the commercial model have been exceptions to the rule, however. Journalism is principally about packaging information for sale directly to an audience willing to pay for it through a cover charge, or indirectly by selling access to that audience on to other businesses, who will pay for advertisements placed alongside journalistic material. Often, especially in print (although the UK and other countries have seen an explosion of 'metro' free newspapers in recent years, distributed free to commuters on their way to and from work), the two means of revenue generation are combined. A commercial company such as Independent Television News (ITN), whose bulletins are received by its UK audience on ITV and Channel 4 free of charge, depends on the size and quality of its audience to generate advertising income. Even the BBC, free of the direct commercial pressures felt by ITN and Sky News in Britain, must pay attention to its audience share if it is to maintain political and public support for its licence fee funding. Journalism here, as elsewhere, is a business, manufacturing and selling a product. As such, and like other businesses, journalism has always been required to meet the expectations of its audiences, as well as seeking to create new markets.

So what, as consumers, do we expect from journalistic commodities? What are we buying when we pay for a newspaper, or subscribe to a news service on cable or satellite, teletext, e-mail or mobile phone?

First and foremost, we are paying for *useful information* – for knowledge which has been extracted, processed and refined from the raw material of the world's happenings, and within which some order has been imposed on the chaos of events. We can experience directly only what happens in our immediate

29

physical environments. What happens at a distance may well impact on us, however, and we need (or think we need) to know about it. Journalism meets that need, at a price which reflects the costs of the inputs which have gone into its production. In agreeing to pay that price we are purchasing what we believe to be a reliable account of the real beyond our immediate experience, mediated through the professional skills of the journalist and the resources of the journalistic organisation. Journalism can be defined, in this sense, as *mediated reality*.

Novelists address the real, of course, as do painters, poets and scientists (natural and social) when they use their artistic or scholarly tools to investigate and then communicate something about the meaning of life and the workings of the world to their audiences. The journalist, like the novelist and the historian in their different ways, tells stories, but the former's stories are presented to potential audiences as *factual*, rather than fictional, artistic, or scientific.

Journalistic stories tell us about things *that actually happened*, as opposed to things imagined by the novelist or the playwright, or interpretatively reconstructed from forensic analysis of relics and documents by the archaeologist or the historian. Journalism presents snapshots of the real, narratives of contemporary events rather than those of the past (although historical context is crucial to much journalism, and the uncovering of hitherto unknown historical facts can become news if it can be contextualised in terms of the present).

To have value as information, journalism has to be accepted as *true*, or at least an acceptable approximation of the truth. To this extent it is trusted, and acquires its privileged status over prose fiction and other discursive modes which, though they may address the real in terms which are profound and deeply affecting, cannot claim to be true in quite the same way. This despite the qualification that the reality which journalism aspires to represent is, by necessity, mediated through various processes and technologies. This mediation distinguishes the journalistic representation of reality from the reality itself, and obliges the student of journalism to consider the choices made and decisions taken in the production process. To assist here we can distinguish between three categories of the real:

- what *actually* happened (and what, by implication, would have happened anyway, in the absence of an observer to record it – the asteroid or comet which devastated much of Siberia in 1908 *did* crash to earth, despite the fact that no reporter witnessed it);
- what is *perceived* to have happened by those present at an event (who may or may not include journalists); and
- what is *reported* as having happened, or journalism.

There is no necessary correlation between these three dimensions of the real, and irrespective of the claims for objectivity made for it (see below), journalism is not and never could be reality in the first, absolute sense. It can be, at best, only a *version* of reality, constructed according to rules, codes and conventions which we associate with journalistic discourse.

At the most basic level of 'constructedness', news is a sampled version of reality. Journalists learn *news values* which, when applied to the unceasing flow of events, allow sifting and sorting to take place, bestowing newsworthiness on some and not others. News values are cultural, and reflect subjective assumptions about what is important to the members of a society at any given time. Commercial news media have values which reflect the need to sell journalism in a marketplace (prioritising conflict and drama, for example), whereas the state-controlled media of the USSR operated news values designed to produce an ideologically functional journalism (the meeting of production targets was 'news', for example, as was any evidence, no matter how slight, of popular dissatisfaction with capitalism in Western countries).

Once bits of reality have been awarded news value and given a place on the journalistic agenda, narratives are constructed around choices about such matters as camera angle, verbal language, framing and contextualisation of events, editing of material and use of sources. Special effects will be deployed, such as graphics and computerised image manipulation. Some broadcast news bulletins even accompany their stories with soundtrack music. All these narrative devices represent subjective choices made by human beings (prescribed by technology, ethical codes, market conditions, and so on) as they strive to manufacture *stories*. That said, journalistic stories must still be accepted as both *true*, and *new*, providing us with information which in some respect or other we have not had access to before, and which can be relied upon to be accurate in what it tells us of the real events and processes it addresses.

Journalistic information is further distinguished in that it always concerns the human, or the *social*, as opposed to the natural scientific discourses of, say, physics, biology and meteorology. Discoveries in science may be both true and new, but become *news* only when they are perceived to have some impact on the social reality of human beings. The discovery of a black hole far off in the cosmos will have little value to the mainstream news media. A black hole found sitting on the edge of our solar system would probably make headlines, as in September 2003 did the asteroid found to be hurtling in the general direction of earth (estimated time of arrival, 11 March 2014). It is not the lump of rock silently orbiting the solar system which is news, but its potential impact on human societies. Weather data become news, and the subject of journalism when, as in the baking European summer of 2003, temperatures are so extreme and unusual that people die in large numbers, or are burnt out of their homes in forest fires.

Objectivity and its discontents

To be useful in the information marketplace, as already noted, journalism (or those who make it) must persuade us of its accuracy and reliability, or more precisely, its *objectivity* – those qualities of detachment and independence in newsgathering and reportage which have been at the core of journalism's unique selling proposition since the mid-nineteenth century. With the rise of mass literacy and consumer affluence, the market for news expanded in the nineteenth century, along with the number of organisations producing it for profit, and objectivity developed as a professional ethic of journalism – what Gaye Tuchman famously termed a 'strategic ritual' (1972, p. 661). Some scholars have argued that journalists embraced objectivity precisely to allow their products to be marketed as reliable and accurate in a market of many providers (Schudson, 1978; Schiller, 1981). Inspired by the successful application of positivist epistemology in natural science, objectivity allowed media organisations to brand their output with a universally accepted standard of excellence which could be bought into by all, regardless of their ideological and political biases.

The sophisticated news consumers of the twenty-first century are aware that journalism is not the absolute truth, and that the claim of journalistic objectivity refers to an aspiration, a never-quite-achievable searching after the closest possible approximation to the truth of what really happened. Journalism, like other discourses of knowledge, has left behind the age of epistemological innocence and entered its postmodern phase, characterised by a loss of faith in the possibility of disinterested truth, and a growing recognition that even for journalism – the medium of record and honest reportage – a certain degree of relativism and subjectivity is inevitable. For Ben Bradlee, 'our goal in journalism is still truth, absolute truth. But truth today is harder and harder to define. Today's truth is all too often tomorrow's half-truth, or even falsity.'[3] For Alan Rusbridger, editor of the *Guardian*, 'the newspaper that drops on your doorstep is a partial, hasty, incomplete, inevitably somewhat flawed and inaccurate rendering of some of the things we have heard about in the past twenty-four hours'.[4]

If the fundamental impossibility of absolute truth in journalism is now widely accepted, some dispute that even the next best thing, the aspiration to objectivity, is seriously held by all media organisations. Although no organisation, not even the public-service BBC, has been immune to accusations of bias or deliberate distortion of the truth (as in the Labour government's attack on BBC reporter Andrew Gilligan for his coverage of its dossier on weapons of mass destruction[5]), the main source of tension around this issue has been the perceived negative effect of commercial pressures and the fact, as already noted, that journalism must succeed as a commodity in a marketplace.

Several Hollywood movies have explored this tension, dramatising the manner in which 'truth', and the journalist's duty to report it, can be sacrificed to venality. Often, these movies suggest, reality itself is distorted to make it more sellable. In *His Girl Friday* (Howard Hawks, 1938) Cary Grant's unscrupulous editor and Rosalind Russell's principled reporter come to epitomise the clash between the former's desire to dress up or enhance events to make them more sensationalistic, and the latter's professional ambition to 'tell it like it is'. At the serious core of the film's romantic comedy is a sophisticated exploration of how easily objective truth may be transformed into something rather less noble.

Billy Wilder's *Ace in the Hole* (1951) takes an even more cynical view, with Kirk Douglas as a ruthless print journalist in desperate need of a story, who stumbles upon a minor accident in the desert and proceeds to turn it into sensational and lucrative drama, even at the cost of lives (including, in the end, his own). Wilder's film depicts how news media feed off what he suggests is the public's unhealthy desire for spectacle and drama (the film was called *The Big Carnival* in the USA, referring to how the tragedy of a man stuck down a hole in the desert becomes a tourist attraction for the thousands of voyeurs who flock to the scene). A real-life tragedy is made worse by the commercial imperatives of the media, and transformed into entertainment.

The same strand of cinematic cynicism resurfaced four decades later in Costa-Gavras' *Mad City* (1998), starring Dustin Hoffman as a TV news reporter who stumbles across a hostage-taking incident in a public library (John Travolta plays the hostage taker). Here, too, the demands of his employers for a 'good' story, and his own professional ambitions, transform an unfortunate misunderstanding into a real tragedy in which people are killed.

In Stephen Frears' *The Accidental Hero* (1996) Hoffman plays not the journalist, but the victim of this tendency for commercially competitive media to distort reality in pursuit of sales and professional success. In this case Geena Davies is the journalist who witnesses petty thief Hoffman's act of genuine heroism which saves the survivors of an air crash. The film shows how Hoffman's reluctant act of selflessness is mythologised, dramatised, reconstructed and transformed into sentimental pathos by Davies' news organisation, as she becomes more uneasy. In a key speech, delivered at an awards ceremony where she is being honoured (and just before the plane crash where she encounters Hoffman's accidental hero), Davies' character highlights the tension at the core of the film when she attacks her profession's tendency to manufacture 'reality' and destroy lives:

This is an onion [holds up an onion, and begins peeling it]. It's a metaphor for a news story. Only a few hours ago I was sitting on a ledge, sixteen stories above the street, interviewing a man who subsequently jumped to his death. $40 million in the bank, happily married, good health, great story.

But there's gotta be more. I mean, we're pros, right? Extramarital hanky panky, maybe? [continues peeling] Another great story. Maybe the guy's been accused of child molesting? Terrific story. What? Turns out the accusations were false? Wonderful, more story. Maybe the alleged mistress was lying, setting the guy up, huh? Sensational story. So we keep going, keep digging, expose the guy's family, his whole life. Why? Because we're pros. Because we're looking for the truth. What if it turns out, for all our digging, for all our painstaking investigation, what if it turns out there wasn't any truth? Just stories. One story after another, layer after layer, until there's nothing left, and if it's like that, do we have any obligation to stop at any point? Or do we just keep going, digging, digging, peeling, peeling, until we've destroyed what we were investigating in the first place?

The competitive need for a story, any story, creates 'the news', which exists independently of the real core of events.

Objectivity is also perceived to be threatened by the interests of those who own and control journalistic media. If news is a business, it is owned by businessmen (and they are generally men) with political preferences and ideological biases. The views of the world's leading media baron, Rupert Murdoch, are well known and have often been detected in the editorial standpoints of his many newspapers and broadcast media. During the US and British invasion of Iraq in early 2003, Murdoch's Fox News channel in the USA was deemed by most observers to have adopted a more patriotic stance in its coverage of the conflict than, say, the big US networks or the BBC. On the other hand, the journalistic output of Sky News in Britain has maintained a reputation for balance, principally because Murdoch and his managers have understood that the broadcast news market in the UK would not allow the flag-waving Murdoch can get away with in America, where the terrorist attacks in New York of September 11, 2001, had an understandably more direct, emotional impact (Zelizer and Allan, 2002). In Britain, even after those attacks and the onset of the war on terrorism, succeeding in the information marketplace means competing with the BBC and ITN, both renowned across the world for the high standards of objectivity (or impartiality, as UK broadcasting regulations demand of the public-service broadcasters) which they apply to their output.

The commodity status of journalism, then, need not produce declining standards, if high standards of objectivity are the market standard. On the contrary, as the information marketplace has become more competitive in recent years, the commercial value of reliably accurate information increases, not decreases, and old-fashioned objectivity remains a key marketing tool for global news brands like the BBC and CNN.

That the aspiration to seek out and report the truth remains important to journalism, for commercial reasons as much as any other, was illustrated by the plagiarism scandal which overwhelmed the reputation of the *New York Times* in June 2003. In that case the exposure (by other news organisations and weblogs) of a number of deceptions committed by star reporter Jayson Blair undermined the newspaper's reputation for objectivity, and forced the resignation of its senior editors. By the scandal's end the trustworthiness of that paper's reportage had been seriously tarnished. Although such scandals are nothing new to journalism, and certainly not unique to the *New York Times*, the Blair case illustrates the enduring commercial importance of public trust in the integrity of the journalistic commodity. While newspapers and periodicals such as the *National Enquirer*, *The Onion* or *Private Eye* can succeed by delivering something other than objective journalism, usually in the name of political satire or entertainment, the core business of the journalism industry remains the production of accurate, up-to-date information on events deemed important by its various audiences. Putting these elements together, one can define journalism in terms I have used in earlier work, but which remain useful in distinguishing it from other forms of discourse about the real. Journalism is:

> Any *authored* text, in written, audio or visual form which *claims* to be (i.e. is presented to its audience as) a *truthful* statement about, or record of, some *hitherto unknown* (new) feature of the *actual, social* world.
>
> (McNair, 1998, p. 4)

Journalism as political action

There are of course many ways of telling the truth, and any authored account of reality, even one which claims to be objective, inevitably bears the imprint of its author's subjectivities and biases, whether these are conscious and acknowledged in the text as part of the narrative, or unconscious and thus not explicit. Journalism is selective, as we have seen, simply because any account of reality has to sample from the chaos of events, and focus on some aspects rather than others. In doing so, journalism highlights and draws attention to some events, processes and accounts while ignoring or downplaying others. This, of course, is fertile ground for contestation and dispute, and for this reason journalism has always been about more than the simple provision of information. It has always been ideological, and deeply *political*.

Although it acquired its essential use value as *correspondence*, or what we would today think of as *straight reportage*, intended for those with a need to monitor and survey the world around them, it was inevitable that the information contained within journalism would have political and ideological resonance. News of an obscure religious movement for reformation in one part of Europe could have serious consequences for the established Catholic Church in Rome. News of a military defeat in a far distant part of the empire could have implications for the popularity of ruling elites at home (and still can). If journalism found its market as useful information, much of that information was politically charged, and thus subject from the outset to state control and censorship.

This is not the place to detail the various and often brutal means by which the religious authorities and absolute monarchs of Europe sought to prevent inconvenient or potentially destabilising information from emerging as news. Suffice to say that all such regimes did so, as do their contemporary equivalents. In these countries – the Arab states of the Middle East; China and other nominally Marxist regimes – as in medieval and early modern Europe, journalistic information is subject to rigorous political control, and journalists must subordinate themselves to the demands of the ruling elite.

This control is becoming steadily more difficult to sustain in the digitised environment of online journalism and real-time news (see below), and, as the rise of Al Jazeera shows, is gradually giving way to the more unruly, independently minded journalism which first emerged in early modern Europe as the transition from feudalism to capitalism gathered pace. At that time, journalism acquired the function of servicing those struggling for freedom from the European aristocracies. Journalists were sucked into political events, with some aligning themselves to liberal reformers, others to their conservative opponents. As the bourgeois revolutions and religious struggles intensified, journalism became what Joad Raymond calls 'a bitter and aggressive instrument of literary and political faction' (1996, p. 13), enthusiastically taking sides in the English Civil War, the French Revolution, the American War of Independence and the other key battles which shaped modernity. Journalism, rooted as it was in the reporting of events, became at the same time a rhetorical tool in the process of persuasion about the *meaning* of events, as absolute monarchies were replaced with democracies in the advanced capitalist world.

In the course of that lengthy historical process, the evolution of journalism was inseparable from the intellectual revolution which produced such concepts as individual freedom and private rights. The struggle for democratic reform throughout Europe and then in America became a struggle for freedom of thought, and for institutions which could facilitate the pursuit and exercise of that freedom in the public domain. John Milton's *Areopagitica*, Tom Paine's *Rights of Man* and other key works established the idea of the journalist as a voice independent of the state (if not necessarily of particular parties), licensed to scrutinise and criticise the powerful, and to advocate political standpoints. To the function of information provision was added the role of *watchdog*, of 'Fourth Estate' as Edmund Burke termed it, alert to the potential abuse of power by king, prime minister or president.

And in the chaos of events, now accessible to public scrutiny through the mass medium of printing, journalists were also called upon to act as analysts, interpreters and sense-makers. The journalist became a *commentator*, as well as a correspondent. By the mid-1600s, notes Raymond, 'the detailed reporting of news was concomitant with strong interpretation and passionate persuasion' (1996, p. 168). The most successful of these passionate, persuasive journalists became participants in, as well as reporters of, events in the political sphere. In modern times we refer to this dimension of the journalistic function as *punditry*. Now as then, the journalist-pundit is a political actor in his or her own right, a figure of some authority, often in competition with career politicians (indeed, journalists sometimes become politicians in their own right. In Britain this has been the path trod by Alistair Campbell, who became a key political figure in the Labour government elected in 1997, or by columnist Boris Johnson, who became a Conservative Member of Parliament in 2001.)

One of the greatest films about journalism ever made explores the notion that some journalists can become too powerful, to the point of megalomania. In Alexander Mackendrick's *The Sweet Smell of Success* (1957) Burt Lancaster is cast as columnist J.J. Hunsecker, a ruthless and manipulative figure modelled on Walter Winchell. Hunsecker, like Winchell, trades in gossip and scandal, but is taken seriously by politicians, and has policemen in his pocket. He is a king-maker, and a destroyer of careers. As his lackey, press agent Tony Curtis, describes him, 'he's told presidents what to do and where to go'. The story of Hunsecker dramatises what had, by the 1950s, become a recurring criticism of the excessive political power of some journalists – no longer watchdogs over the powerful, but bullies of the powerless, just as prone to corruption as any elected senator or member of a legislature. Except, of course, that journalists are not elected. In the half century since the fictional J.J. Hunsecker stalked the nightclubs of New York, anxiety about the excessive power of journalistic pundits – the king-makers – has continued to surface in debates about journalism. This has often taken the form of criticism of the alleged blurring of news and commentary in much journalism. As the star columnist and special correspondent (in broadcasting) has risen in importance, the traditional separation between reportage and interpretation has been eroded. A 'commentary explosion' has been detected by some critics, to the detriment of the core information function of journalism.

The columnist as commodity

As its interpretative dimension evolved, journalism was increasingly sold on the quality of those interpretations, and the pleasure to be derived from their consumption. Journalists became valued not just as reporters, but as rhetoricians and prose stylists. Journalism of this type became something akin to an art form, their leading practitioners treated as celebrities, able to command high fees. And to this day, a significant part of what we buy when we pay for a newspaper or a magazine is the aesthetic abilities of a particular journalist whom we admire – the iconoclastic political satire of the late Hunter S. Thompson (dramatised in Terry Gilliam's 1999 film of Thompson's *Fear and Loathing in Las Vegas*), the 'new journalism' of Tom Wolfe, the political insights of Thomas Friedman, the calculated offensiveness of Julie Burchill, the combination of neo-conservatism and progressive sexual politics seen in the work of Andrew Sullivan, and their equivalents in broadcasting – Louis Theroux's weird weekends spent with American survivalists or LA porn producers, Michael Moore's angry assaults on US corporations and militarists. Some of these celebrity journalists specialise in politics, others cast their net more widely. All have value in the journalistic marketplace not necessarily because of the correctness of their opinions, but for the manner of their expression. They are paid large sums to sell newspapers and increase broadcast-news ratings in the same way that music by Madonna or movies by Spielberg shift CDs and sell cinema tickets.

Journalism as entertainment

This brings us to journalism's recreational and cultural functions, which I listed above as those of education, enlightenment and entertainment. Clearly, part of what makes the journalism of a columnist such as Julie Burchill a valuable commodity is its capacity to entertain. Even those who find her views objectionable may enjoy being enraged by them. Left-wingers may enjoy the forthright 'neo-con' opinions of Andrew Sullivan. Conservatives may hate everything Michael Moore says, but love the way he says it. We love some columnists, and love to hate others. Either way, there is pleasure involved.

Journalism can entertain even when it aspires merely to inform. Reviews and journalistic essays, sports journalism, journalism about lifestyle, travel and the doings of celebrities – all present useful information, but all are consumed for pleasure rather than necessity. They may educate, in so far as they teach us things about art, culture, science, and so on. They may enlighten in the old-fashioned sense of teaching us to appreciate and enjoy the products of culture. But above all, they entertain. They are, in short, *infotainment.*

Entertainment has been a function of journalism since the early news-sheets printed graphic accounts of public executions, royal scandals and witch burnings, and has steadily increased in importance over time. As the literate population of capitalist societies expanded, and as these populations acquired greater wealth and leisure time, the demand for recreational news media expanded with them, and journalism's capacity to entertain has become integral to its commercial success. The rise of the star columnist and the interview form in the late nineteenth century, the growth of the weekend newspaper supplement in the late twentieth, the intense journalistic interest in lifestyle and leisure, all reflect the increased dedication to entertainment and recreation of all news media, whether broadsheet, mid-market or tabloid.

Dumbing down and other anxieties

Some see this as a negative trend, to be resisted at every opportunity. From their perspective, the rise in the quantity of journalism which can reasonably be described as infotainment is a further consequence of commercialisation, part of an alleged 'dumbing down' of news media. Douglas Kellner typifies this cultural pessimism when he writes that 'the commercial media have sacrificed the imperatives of journalism and news in the public interest for focus on spectacle and entertainment'. In a recent book he identifies US news coverage of the O.J. Simpson trial as 'an important episode in the transformation of news into infotainment and the decline of journalism in a media culture' (2003, p. 96). The irreconcilability of quality news with entertainment is here taken for granted.

Cultural pessimism about the deterioration of news is not new, however. As John Carey's study *The Intellectuals and the Masses* shows (1992), the fear of dumbing down is as old as popular journalism itself, reflecting the ongoing efforts of intellectual elites to control what the masses consume at the cultural level. Early tabloids such as *Tit Bits* in the UK were denounced in very similar terms to those which greet popular newspapers in the current era, and for the same reasons – inappropriate content would, it was feared, rouse the masses to inappropriate behaviours and attitudes, undermine popular respect for authority, and challenge the elite monopoly on aesthetic judgment. An alternative view sees these trends as part of a long process of democratisation of Western culture, which has been accompanied and facilitated by a huge expansion in the quantity and quality of information to people of all classes and tastes. Rather than dumbing down, this perspective argues that journalism, and its audience, is steadily 'braining up' (McNair, 2000).

Journalism in a changing environment

These are subjective matters, however, and the student must assess the meaning of the trends for him or herself. The only certain thing is that journalism, like all cultural forms, has been changing and evolving since its emergence, paralleling changes in the environment within which it is practised. And as I have noted, many current anxieties about dumbing down, commercialisation and the like can be found in discussions of journalistic evolution going back centuries. In recent times, however, journalists have been passing through particularly eventful times for their profession.

Technological change, and the journalist as information architect

Most obviously, journalists are currently living through the dramatic expansion and acceleration of information flows, and the globalisation of the public sphere. More and faster media have shrunk the world, while connecting it in new and more intimate ways (Gleick, 1999). The launch of Ted Turner's Cable Network News (CNN) in 1980, and the subsequent growth of 24-hour, 'rolling' or real-time news have changed the definition of at least one kind of news from *that which has happened* to *that which is happening*. Journalism on rolling news channels is not a medium of record, but a flow medium, constantly updated and never 'definitive'. Journalism on CNN, BBC News 24 or Sky News comprises rolling commentaries on events which, because they are happening right now, are hazy and unresolved, slow moving and confused. Events progress in real time, glacially, and yet we have instantaneous, ubiquitous access to that progress.

The sociological consequences of this new mode of perceiving distant reality for audiences are as yet unclear. For journalists themselves, the advent of real-time news, and its increasing cultural centrality following September 11 and the wars in Afghanistan and Iraq, mean that there is less time for investigation and analysis of complex stories, and more airtime to fill with speculation and opinion. Satellite phones and other mobile newsgathering technologies have allowed correspondents on the scene to be constantly present on air, but often with nothing of substance to say. On the other hand, as the real-time coverage of September 11 demonstrated with horrific clarity, there is now virtually nothing which is not instantly accessible to a global public via the medium of live TV news. Temporal and spatial boundaries have been substantially eroded.

Journalism has been further transformed by the internet, possibly the most important leap in communications technology since the invention of print more than half a millennium ago. Since the early 1990s, established print and broadcast news media have gone online to service a community of net users estimated at 550 million by 2002. New journalistic organisations like Slate and the Drudge Report have emerged, as has a growing community of 'bloggers' – individuals who maintain their own news sites with material of variable quality, from the diary entries of enthusiastic hobbyists to the professionally managed sites of columnists like Andrew Sullivan. During the 2003 attack on Iraq one resident of Baghdad fed the world with exclusive insider information via his weblog. As the Iraqi regime on the one hand, and the US–British military on the other, fought a propaganda war for global opinion, this source supplied an alternative perspective on events.

The internet has allowed for a proliferation and diversification of journalistic voices, and added to the communication chaos unleashed by the rise of real-time news. Information flows with ever greater speed and volume, while making it more difficult for any individual to keep up with. If this is cultural democratisation, it is also information overload, and for that reason recent technological innovations have not meant, thus far at least, the 'death' of traditional print and broadcast news media. In an information environment of real-time news flowing instantaneously around the globe, further complicated by a global net of online providers, the old-fashioned newspaper or TV bulletin, produced to a more leisurely and considered schedule, with more time for reflection and analysis, becomes more, not less important. The sense-making, interpretative functions of journalism are enhanced, not made redundant in the era of real-time and online news.

The journalist, meanwhile, must learn to perform his or her craft across print, online and broadcast platforms, becoming an *information architect* who builds news around whatever technological means are available, and be adaptable to all. TV reporters produce packages for radio. Prime-time bulletins lend to, and borrow from, rolling news. Online sites make newspapers printed in Scotland, or TV and radio broadcasts made in London and Dallas, available to the world.

Infotainment, postmodernisation and the hybridisation of journalism

Technology is also driving the growth of what was earlier described as infotainment, and in particular the rise of new media genres which combine journalistic techniques and narratives of real life with elements of drama and game show-style competition. These journalistic hybrids include makeover shows like *Changing Rooms* in the UK, interactive reality TV formats like *Pop Idol, Big Brother* and *Survivor*; sensationalistic documentaries on such topics as *Neighbours From Hell, Holidays From Hell, Facelifts From Hell* and *Drivers From Hell*, often based on CCTV footage; and docu-soaps (as the term suggests, a combination of documentary and soap-opera techniques).

These journalistic hybrids are produced for entertainment, and while this has always been a legitimate function of journalism, the overt incorporation of techniques previously associated with game shows, soap operas and TV drama has blurred traditional boundaries between journalism and not-journalism.

Journalism after September 11, 2001 – the changing political environment

At the same time as new technologies have been transforming the work of the journalist, the changing political environment has challenged the traditional role of the journalist as objective reporter of events. In the latter years of the Cold War, when US foreign policy was supporting the death squads of Central and South America, Oliver Stone made *Salvador*, which dramatised the experiences of a real-life reporter in the aforementioned country. James Woods, playing a Hunter Thompson-like adventurer, has to come to terms with the US-sanctioned atrocities he witnesses. His commitment to journalistic objectivity is challenged by the sight of peasants slaughtered, dissidents tortured and nuns raped in the name of anti-communism.

In Michael Winterbottom's *Welcome to Sarajevo*, like *Salvador*, based on real events, the ideological confusion and amoral inhumanity engendered by the end of the Cold War and its replacement by genocidal ethnic strife lead a journalist to question his role as detached witness to events, and to become instead a participant, who rescues an orphan child and takes her home to England.

After September 11, 2001, a much more fundamental challenge to the notion of objectivity was mounted, throughout the Western world, but in the United States in particular. In their introduction to *Journalism After September 11* Zelizer and Allan note that 'shaken to their foundations [by the events of September 11, 2001] have been familiar notions of what it means to be a journalist, how best to practice journalism, and what different publics can reasonably expect of journalists in the name of democracy' (2002, p. 16). The book contains essays by several journalists asking if objectivity could be an adequate response to events involving the deaths of thousands a few hundred yards from one's own office in New York; if patriotism and pro-American bias were now part of the journalist's duty. Organisations such as Fox News and Clear have been accused of abandoning any pretence to objectivity in their coverage of the post-September 11 wars in Afghanistan and Iraq, substituting it with cheerleading in support of 'the war on terror'. In Britain, on the other hand, despite the Blair government's enthusiastic participation in that war, the

41

need for journalistic objectivity, political independence and emotional detachment has been defended by the BBC and ITN, not without criticism from the government at times. That debate will continue.

Meantime, the post-9/11 world is a more dangerous one for journalists, especially those like Daniel Pearl who saw it as his role to be there, at the heart of the conflict, and paid for it with his life. More journalists were killed in the attack on Afghanistan which followed September 11 than American or British soldiers. As of August 2003 eighteen journalists had been killed reporting the Coalition invasion of Iraq. Across the world from Zimbabwe to Russia to South America, wherever there is political conflict and struggle, journalists are in the firing line.

Summary

I began by defining journalism as *mediated reality* to highlight the fact that, although presented by its authors as more or less true, new, and so on, journalism is always a manufactured account of the real, not the real itself, which emerges to find acceptance in the information marketplace only after a number of production processes have been gone through. I have also characterised journalism as a cultural commodity, an art form, an entertainment medium and a mode of political action. It can be more than one of those things at the same time.

In the end, the question 'what is journalism?' can have only one answer. Journalism is many things, and often different things to different people. For some it is a set of technical skills – a craft, to be learned and practised according to traditions handed down over the centuries. For others it is a noble profession, with a special responsibility to defend democratic processes, and an associated set of core ethical values. For others still, journalism is a creative medium, an art form even, as dependent upon fertile imagination and aesthetic sensibilities as a technical knowledge of shorthand or interviewing techniques. Fortunately, journalism is big enough to contain all of those, and the diverse ambitions of those thousands of students now preparing for journalistic careers. They, and their audiences, will define in the end what journalism is going to be in the twenty-first century.

Notes

1 The Hutton inquiry into the suicide of Dr David Kelly began in August 2003, and concerned the circumstances behind the BBC's reporting of claims that the Blair government had 'sexed up' (i.e. enhanced in order to sensationalise the implications of) key information on Iraqi weapons of mass-destruction capability.
2 For the text of the Hutton report and other inquiry documents, see http://www.the-hutton-inquiry.org.uk/
3 Quoted in A. Rusbridger, 'Taming the beast', *Guardian*, 18 February 2002.
4 Ibid.
5 For the detail of these accusations, see the Hutton report: http://www.the-hutton-inquiry.org.uk/

References

Carey, J., *The Intellectuals and the Masses*, London: Penguin, 1992.

Eisenstein, E., *The Printing Revolution in Early Modern Europe*, Cambridge: Cambridge University Press, 1983.

Gleick, J., *Faster: The Acceleration of Just About Everything*, London: Abacus, 1999.

Habermas, J., *The Structural Transformation of the Public Sphere*, Cambridge: Polity, 1989.

Kellner, D., *9/11 and Terror War: The Dangers of the Bush Legacy*, Lanham, MD: Rowman and Littlefield, 2003.

McNair, B., *The Sociology of Journalism*, London: Arnold, 1998.

—— *Journalism and Democracy*, London: Routledge, 2000.

McQuail, D., *Mass Communication Theory*, 2nd edition, London: Sage, 1997.

Raymond, J., *The Invention of the Newspaper*, Oxford: Clarendon Press, 1996.

Schiller, D., *Objectivity and the News*, Philadelphia, PA: University of Pennsylvania Press, 1981.

Schudson, M., *Discovering News*, New York: Basic Books, 1978.

Tuchman, G., 'Objectivity as strategic ritual: an examination of newsmen's notions of objectivity', *American Journal of Sociology*, 1972, vol. 77, no. 4, pp. 660–70.

Zelizer, B. and Allan, S. (eds), *Journalism after September 11*, London: Routledge, 2002.

2

WHO ARE JOURNALISTS?

David H. Weaver

The question of who journalists are has never been definitively answered, in part because journalists themselves often don't want to be licensed, certified or classified by any official authority or by anyone outside journalism, and in part because there is no specific body of knowledge that journalists must master to practice their craft.

In the United States, the occupation of journalist has been vaguely defined from the early days of the republic. During the 1700s to the mid-1800s, journalism was basically an apprenticeship system where aspiring novices such as Benjamin Franklin learned the trade in print shops, and where the role of journalist was fulfilled largely by the town printer and correspondent.

By the middle of the nineteenth century, as society became more complex and many of its journalistic operations resembled corporate enterprises, the term journalist came to describe reporters, writers, correspondents, columnists, newsmen (and a few newswomen), and editors who worked mainly for newspapers and magazines. In the twentieth century, the word was broadened to include radio and television news announcers, reporters, editors, and some online writers and editors.

This chapter tries to sketch a rough portrait of journalists in various countries by drawing on the most comprehensive surveys of these news people carried out in the United States and 20 other countries and territories. It compares their demographic characteristics, their educational backgrounds, their views about which roles they find most important, their ethical values, which aspects of their work they see as most important, and their images of their readers, viewers, and listeners.

Comparing journalists across national boundaries is difficult. There are many characteristics, attitudes and behaviors that depend on the specific setting. Yet there are also similarities that cut across the boundaries of geography, culture, language, society, religion, race, and ethnicity.

This chapter points out similarities and differences in the basic characteristics and professional values of journalists from 21 countries and territories. (For more details, see Weaver, 1998.) These include Algeria, Australia, Brazil, Britain, Canada, Chile, China, Ecuador, Finland, France, Germany, Hong

Kong, Hungary, Korea, Mexico, New Zealand, the Pacific Islands, Poland, Spain, Taiwan, and the United States. The surveys were conducted between 1988 and 1996, mostly by letter and telephone, and include interviews with more than 20,000 journalists in total.

The point of trying to draw comparisons between journalists in these different areas of the world is the hope of identifying some similarities and differences that may give us a more accurate picture of where journalists come from and whether they are becoming more professional as we leave the twentieth century behind and begin a new millennium. The major assumption is that journalists' backgrounds and ideas influence what is reported (and how it is covered) in the various news media around the world, and that this news coverage matters in terms of world public opinion and policies.

Backgrounds and demographic profiles

Why journalism?

One of the most fundamental questions about the backgrounds of journalists is why they chose journalism in the first place. Our 1992 and 2002 national surveys of U.S. journalists asked them to tell us, in looking back, why they became journalists. In 1992, the most common answer centered on a love for writing, followed by the enjoyment of gathering news and reporting it. A close third reason was the desire to "make a difference" and to right wrongs by bringing injustices to public attention (Weaver and Wilhoit, 1996, pp. 51–56). Other answers mentioned the intrinsically interesting work of journalists and an interest in current events, and still others mentioned their experiences on college newspapers and other media, as well as the influence of teachers of journalism in high school and college.

The initial analysis of our 2002 survey data suggests that a love for writing is still the most common answer, followed by an enjoyment of reporting, a desire to be involved in current events and history, an interest in politics, and the enjoyment of telling a story (Weaver *et al.*, 2003). These findings are similar to those of Henningham and Delano (1998), who found that being good at writing was the main reason for both British and Australian journalists to enter the field, followed by the perceived excitement and interest of the occupation, and an interest in current events. Wilke (1998) also found the journalists in Chile and Mexico were most likely to be attracted to journalism because of the possibilities for writing and the non-routine nature of the work, as well as the chance to uncover various abuses.

Socio-economic backgrounds

Another fundamental question about the backgrounds of journalists has to do with their socio-economic backgrounds. One recurrent criticism of journalists is that they no longer come from working-class backgrounds, but rather from professional or upper socio-economic families, and are therefore less able to empathize with the concerns of working-class people.

In the 1992 U.S. presidential campaign, then Vice-President Dan Quayle referred to journalists as the "cultural elite" (Weaver and Wilhoit, 1992, p. 63), prompting a local newspaper columnist in Bloomington, Indiana, to write that he called home to say, "Hey Ma, didja hear that the vice-president says I'm elite. *Culturally* elite?" He concluded, "And we always thought we were lower middle class." With a bachelor's degree from a public university and a $31,000 average salary in 1992, it was a bit hard to imagine how the average U.S. journalist could be a member of the cultural elite who, in the vice-president's words, reside in "the newsrooms, sitcom studios and faculty lounges across America" (Weaver and Wilhoit, 1992, p. 63).

Although entertaining, this anecdote does not provide systematic evidence that bears directly on the question of U.S. journalists' socio-economic backgrounds. Unfortunately, we do not have such evidence because we have not asked about the educational levels, occupations, and incomes of journalists' parents in our 1982, 1992 and 2002 surveys—nor have many other studies of journalists for that matter.[1] Johnstone *et al.* (1976) found in their 1971 national survey of U.S. journalists that nearly half of their fathers (49 percent) were employed in professional or managerial occupations, and 62 percent were in the white-collar sector of the labor force. In our studies since then (Weaver and Wilhoit, 1986, 1996; Weaver *et al.*, 2003) we have found that U.S. journalists are much more likely to have earned a college degree than the population at large and to come from the dominant ethnic and racial groups in society, but we have no evidence about the occupations, educations or incomes of their parents.

Profiles

In our 1992 national study of U.S. journalists, we found that the statistical "profile" of the typical U.S. journalist in 1992 was much like that of 1982–83: a white Protestant male with a four-year bachelor's degree, married, and in his 30s (Weaver and Wilhoit, 1996). But there were some changes from the early 1980s—an increase of four years in median age to 36, more minorities, and more journalists earning college degrees, but no increase in those majoring in journalism in college (about 40 percent).

In 2002, this profile had changed only slightly to include mostly white married males in their very early 40s with four-year college degrees (Weaver *et al.*, 2003). The median age had increased from 36 to 41, the proportion of minorities had increased slightly to nearly 10 percent, and the percentage earning college degrees had also increased to nearly 90. This demographic profile of U.S. journalists is similar in some ways to the profiles of journalists in other areas of the world, but there are some notable differences as well.

Gender

For example, men were more typical than women in newsrooms in all 19 countries or territories reporting gender proportions, although in some countries women were almost as numerous as men (New Zealand and Finland), whereas in others women were not (Korea, Algeria, Britain, and Spain). The average proportion of women journalists across these 19 countries and territories was one-third (33 percent), exactly the proportion in the United States in 2002.

Age

Another similarity between the U.S. and the rest of the world as represented here is that journalism is a young person's occupation, with most journalists between 25 and 44 years old. The average age of journalists ranges from 30 to 40 in the dozen places reporting it, with the youngest journalists coming from Hong Kong and Algeria, where the average age is 30, and the oldest living in Canada and Finland, where it is 40.

In most places, journalists are younger on average (35 years old) than is the workforce in general. In Hong Kong, as in other places, many young people become journalists to earn some experience before leaving for more lucrative and stable jobs in other fields, especially public relations. This seems to be a fairly common pattern in many countries.

Education

Although most journalists in the U.S. hold a four-year college degree, this is not the case in a number of countries. The countries with the lowest proportions of college graduate journalists are Australia, Finland and Mexico—all well below one-half. Those with the highest are Korea, Spain, and the United States, with Chile and Ecuador nearly as high. Eleven of 18 countries or territories report more than one-half of their journalists holding a four-year college degree, so it is more common than not for journalists to be college graduates in this group, but the variation is substantial.

It is not typical for journalists to be graduates of journalism programs in college, however. Only three countries reported more than half of their journalists had concentrated on journalism in college—Spain, Brazil, and Chile. In the other 11 countries or territories reporting this proportion, most did not exceed 40 percent, with the lowest figure from Britain (4 percent) and more typical figures hovering in the 30s.

Thus whatever journalistic benefits or evils are attributed to journalism education must be tempered by the fact that most journalists are not graduates of college-level journalism programs in this sample of countries and territories. In fact, the average percentage among the 14 reporting was 41.5. Without including the extremes of Spain, Brazil, Chile and Britain, it was one-third, a bit under the U.S. percentage of 36 in 2002.

Ethnicity

Less than half of the countries and territories represented in *The Global Journalist* study reported a figure for racial and ethnic minority journalists. The reported figures are small at best, ranging from 1 to 11 percent, and reinforcing the conclusion of the 1971 U.S. study by Johnstone *et al.* (1976) that journalists come predominantly from the established and dominant cultural groups in society. This seems to hold true especially in Taiwan, Britain, and Canada, and somewhat less so in Brazil, China, and the United States.

Thus, in terms of demographics, the journalists from the various countries and territories were similar in average age and proportion of minorities, but varied considerably in gender, level of education, and whether they majored in journalism.

Professional values

In *Journalists for the 21st Century*, based on surveys of about 1,800 first-year journalism students in 22 different countries in 1987–88, Splichal and Sparks (1994) argue that even though there is no strict definition of journalism yet, the occupation seems to be moving from craft to profession (although not yet a true profession) because of changes in the education and specialist knowledge of journalists and an emphasis on autonomy and professional ethics.

The conclusion that journalism is not yet a true profession is similar to that by Weaver and Wilhoit (1986, 1991). They wrote at the end of their first American journalist book that U.S journalists are unlikely ever to assume a formal professional status because of their skepticism of institutional forms of professionalism such as certification or licensing, membership in organizations, and readership of professional publications.

Looking across 22 countries, Splichal and Sparks (1994) noted that their initial hypothesis was that similarities across countries should prevail if journalism is really becoming a profession. They concluded in their last chapter that their major finding was a striking similarity in the desire of journalism students for the independence and autonomy of journalism. In addition, they didn't find evidence that journalism education and professional socialization were necessarily a function of politics or dominant ideology.

Based on these findings, they argued that some universal ethical and occupational standards were emerging in journalism, but this conclusion seems to contradict the differences in ethical reporting standards found in surveys of journalists in Britain, Germany, and the U.S., and it may reflect the lack of specific questions about journalism roles, reporting practices or ethical dilemmas in the Splichal–Sparks questionnaire more than the emergence of universal ethical and occupational standards in journalism.

There is no doubt a universal desire for more freedom among journalists in various parts of the world, although our findings on the importance of this job aspect are mixed, but that does not necessarily signal the emergence of any universal standards in journalism, nor is it necessarily anything new. A look at more specific professional roles or values, as well as reporting practices, may help to more precisely define the areas of agreement and disagreement among the 20,000 journalists of the world represented in *The Global Journalist* book by Weaver (1998).

Roles

In their 1992 study of U.S. journalists, Weaver and Wilhoit (1996) found, for the most part, that their perceptions of the roles of the news media were broadly similar to those a decade ago. A majority of U.S. journalists tended to see two responsibilities as extremely important—getting information to the public quickly and investigating government claims. This was still true in 2002, although getting information to the public quickly dropped notably in perceived importance and investigating government claims rose somewhat (Weaver *et al.*, 2003).

Among the 12 countries or territories reporting on the role of getting information to the public quickly, there was also considerable agreement. In most cases, two-thirds or more agreed that it was very important, except in Taiwan and Canada, but even in these places a clear majority agreed.

On investigating government claims (or being a watchdog on government), there was considerably less agreement, however, with journalists most likely to consider this role very important in the more democratic countries of Australia, Britain, and Finland. Those least likely to see this watchdog role as very important came from Taiwan, Algeria, and Chile, where there has not been a long history of democratic forms of government.

But there were exceptions to this pattern. In Germany, which has been a democracy since World War II, there was not any more support for the watchdog role than among Algerian journalists. And in China, which has never had a democratic system of government, there was more support among journalists for investigating government than in France and Canada.

The analytical function of news media—providing analysis of complex problems—remained about the same in the U.S. during the 1980s and 1990s, with about half saying it was extremely important. But among the 14 countries or territories where this role was measured, there were considerable differences, with journalists in Taiwan and France least likely to consider it very important, and those in Finland and Britain most likely to say so.

Another role where there was some disagreement was the extent to which journalists should give ordinary people a chance to express their views on public affairs.

A little less than half of the U.S. sample in 1992 said this was an extremely important role (but this dropped considerably to 39 percent in 2002), with journalists working on daily and weekly newspapers especially likely to say so. Although only six countries reported the importance of this role, there was some agreement among five—Hong Kong, Britain, Finland, Germany, and the United States—but Chinese journalists were notably less likely to see this role as very important. Compared to other journalistic roles, this one was not seen as important by large proportions of journalists in any location. Only in Britain and Finland did slightly more than half of the journalists consider this a very important role.

There was great disagreement on the importance of providing entertainment among the 14 countries or territories reporting this role. Those journalists least likely to consider this very important were from Canada and France (and the U.S. in 2002), whereas those most likely were from Germany and Chile. Clearly, this is one role where national differences in journalistic values are in sharp evidence. It seems that journalists from the Far East and North America were least likely to regard entertainment as an important function of journalism, but in Europe there were huge differences by country, suggesting that this is not a universal Western journalistic role.

There was also disagreement on the importance of reporting accurately or objectively, with those journalists least likely to say so from Britain and the Pacific Islands, and those most likely from Germany, Finland, and Taiwan.

Thus, there was considerable agreement among journalists regarding the importance of reporting the news quickly, and some agreement on the importance of providing access for the public to express opinions, but considerable disagreement on the importance of providing analysis and being a watchdog on government. There was most disagreement on the importance of providing entertainment, and considerable variance in opinions on the importance of accurate or objective reporting.

Clearly, there was more disagreement than agreement over the relative importance of these journalistic roles considered together, hardly evidence to support the universal occupational standards mentioned by Splichal and Sparks (1994). The reasons for the disagreement are difficult to specify for so many possible comparisons, but a secondary analysis of the data from journalists in China, Taiwan, and the United States by Zhu and others suggests that political system similarities and differences are far more important than cultural similarities and differences, organizational constraints or individual characteristics in predicting the variance in perceptions of three roles (timely information, interpretation, and entertainment) by journalists in these societies.

Professional organizations

Another possible indicator of professionalism is membership in organizations that encourage professional standards and values. Only seven studies reported data on this, but among those there was a wide range—from 18 percent claiming to belong to a journalistic organization in Hong Kong to 86 percent in Australia and 83 percent in Hungary, followed fairly closely by Taiwan, Britain, and Spain, with the U.S. in between. Most of these differences are likely explained by the requirement in some countries that journalists belong to a union to be able to work, but the large differences here also call into question whether journalists are becoming more professional around the world.

Ethical practices

Still another measure of how professional journalists are is which reporting methods they consider acceptable. Weaver and Wilhoit's surveys of U.S. journalists included questions about the acceptability of questionable reporting practices that were first asked in a 1980 study of British and West German journalists and also in public opinion surveys in the U.S. during the 1980s.

For example, a majority of U.S. journalists in 1992 and 2002 said that getting employed to gain inside information may be justified on occasion. But a national survey of 1,002 adults done for the American Society of Newspaper Editors (ASNE) in 1985 found that only one-third of the public approved of journalists not identifying themselves as reporters, as did a 1981 Gallup national survey and a 1989 Indiana statewide survey (Weaver and Daniels, 1992). The questions were somewhat different, but it is likely there was a considerable gap between the U.S. press and public on the acceptability of undercover reporting.

Another gap with the public appeared when U.S. journalists' opinions about the use of hidden microphones or cameras were compared with the public's. Less than half of the 1985 national sample of the public and the 1989 Indiana sample approved of using hidden cameras, compared with almost two-thirds of journalists in 1992 and 60 percent in 2002 who said this practice might be justified. Again, the questions were not identical, but a gap seemed likely.

One practice that was approved by fewer U.S. journalists than the U.S. public was paying for information. Only one-fifth of the journalists in the 1992 study and 17 percent in 2002 said this might be justified, compared with about one-third of the 1985 national sample and the 1989 Indiana sample who approved. On this score, then, U.S. journalists seemed less permissive (or more ethical) than the public at large.

If journalists are becoming more professional in a universal sense around the world, we should expect their views on the acceptability of various reporting practices to also become more similar. In an earlier 1982 study of U.S. journalists, Weaver and Wilhoit (1986, 1991) found considerable differences between U.S., British, and German journalists on whether certain practices might be justified. The German journalists were much less likely to approve of badgering or harassing sources, using personal documents without permission and getting employed to gain inside information than were the U.S. and British journalists. The British journalists were especially likely to say that most of the questionable reporting practices could be justified, with the U.S. journalists in between the British and the Germans on most practices.

What about more recent times? Are journalists' views about which reporting methods are acceptable becoming more similar over time?

In the U.S., Weaver and Wilhoit found some large increases from 1982 to 1992 in the percentage of journalists who thought that it might be justifiable to use confidential business or government documents without permission (up from 55 to 82 percent) and to use personal documents such as letters and photographs without permission (up from 28 to 48 percent). But the percentages approving the other methods stayed about the same. There were declines in 2002, however, especially in getting employed to gain inside information (down from 63 to 54 percent), in using personal documents without permission (down from 48 to 41 percent), in claiming to be someone else (down from 22 to 14 percent), and in disclosing the names of rape victims (down from 43 to 36 percent).

When journalists from different areas of the world are compared, there are considerable differences, some very large, on the proportions saying that some reporting methods might be justified, as well as some agreement on other practices.

For example, on revealing confidential news sources, which has been the practice of most agreement (as unacceptable) among U.S. journalists from 1982 to 1992, journalists from 13 of the 14 countries or territories measuring this were very reluctant to say it might be justifiable (10 percent or less said so in Hong Kong, Korea, Taiwan, Australia, Pacific Islands, Britain, France, Germany, Canada, the United States, Brazil, Chile, and Mexico), but 39 percent of the journalists in Finland said it might be acceptable. On this practice, then, there was a high level of agreement among all journalists except those from Finland, suggesting a near-universal professional norm of protecting confidential sources.

On other reporting methods, however, there were some very large differences of opinion. With regard to paying for secret information, the numbers ranged from 9 percent who thought this was justifiable in Canada to 65 percent in Britain and 62 percent in Finland. On undercover reporting (claiming to be someone else), the range was from 7 percent in Canada to 63 percent in Brazil and 58 percent in Chile who might find this practice justifiable. For badgering or harassing news sources, the percentages varied from 12 in Germany to 84 in Hong Kong and 82 in France, and for using personal documents without permission from 11 in Germany to 49 in Britain and 48 in the U.S.

As for using business or government documents without permission, the range of those who might approve ran from 26 percent in Taiwan to 86 percent in Britain, 83 percent in Brazil and 82 percent in the U.S. And, finally, getting employed to gain inside information was seen as possibly justifiable by as few as 22 percent of journalists in Chile and as many as 80 percent in Britain.

Given these very large differences in the percentages of journalists who think that different reporting methods may be acceptable, it seems that there are strong national differences that override any universal professional norms or values of journalism around the world, except in the case of revealing confidential sources, where there is strong agreement that this should never be done.

Aspects of their jobs

Another possible indicator of professionalism of journalists is which dimensions of their jobs they consider most important. Some scholars would argue that salary, job security, and chance to advance are less professional aspects of an occupation than editorial policies, ability to develop a specialty, autonomy, and helping people.

There are wide disagreements among journalists from different countries on which aspects of the job are very important. Journalists in France and the former West Germany were more likely to emphasize freedom on the job than pay, job security, and chance to advance, but this was not the case in Brazil where journalists were more likely to say that pay was very important, followed by freedom and the chance to help people. Journalists in Algeria were likely to think that almost all job aspects were equally important.

Looking at the "non-professional" job aspects, it's clear that Brazilian journalists were most likely to rate pay very important, perhaps because of the very large rates of inflation in that country, followed by former East German journalists. Surprisingly, journalists in Chile and Mexico were least likely to say so. Whatever the reasons for these differences, there is not much agreement across countries on the importance of pay.

For job security, journalists in the U.S. were most likely to consider it very important, no doubt because of the much more competitive job market and the lack of growth in journalism jobs during the 1980s and 1990s, followed by those in East Germany. In 2002, U.S. journalists were slightly less likely to consider job security very important (down from 61 to 58 percent), but still comparable to German and Australian journalists. Those least likely to say so were from Canada and France, most likely reflecting the economic situations in their countries and illustrating a considerable range of disagreement across countries.

As for the chance to advance or to be promoted, those most likely to rate it very important were from Brazil and Australia, again likely reflecting the economies of their countries. Those least concerned about advancement were from Finland and Mexico.

On balance, then, it looks as if the Brazilian journalists were most likely to emphasize the "non-professional" material aspects of the job of journalist, and those from Mexico were among those least likely to rate these aspects very important. There are striking differences in the proportions of journalists from the different countries considering these aspects of their work as very important, suggesting little support for any universal motives of journalists.

Turning to the more "professional" job aspects, journalists from the U.S. and the Pacific Islands were most likely to rate editorial policy as very important, whereas those least likely to do so were from Canada and France. As for developing a specialty, journalists in East Germany and Brazil were most likely to rate it very important, whereas those from France and Canada were least likely.

Even on perceived freedom on the job, a journalistic norm that Splichal and Sparks (1994) identified as strikingly similar among the journalism students from 22 different countries, there were notable differences among the journalists interviewed in the studies reported here. Those from East Germany, Brazil, and France were most likely to say that freedom on the job is very important, whereas those in Canada were least likely (although this was the aspect of their jobs rated most highly as compared to others). There does seem to be more agreement on the importance of this aspect of the job than on others, as Splichal and Sparks argued, but there are still considerable differences between countries.

And, finally, on the journalistic norm of helping people, those journalists most likely to consider this very important were from Brazil and Chile. Those least likely were from Canada, again suggesting a wide range of opinion on this indicator of professionalism.

Images of audience

A final possible indicator of professionalism of journalists is their view of their audiences. Although only six countries included this measure in their studies, there were some striking similarities and differences. About one-quarter of journalists from Algeria, Brazil, and the U.S. strongly agreed that their audiences were interested in breaking news. But only one-third of the journalists in the U.S. (slightly less in 2002) strongly agreed that their audiences were interested in politics and social problems, compared with nearly three-quarters of the East German and Mexican journalists. Nearly one-half of the East German journalists strongly agreed that their audience was gullible, or easily fooled, and the U.S. journalists were the least likely to say so (only 3 percent strongly agreed in both 1992 and 2002).

Again, on these measures of professionalism, there were some striking differences on two of the three, raising the question of whether journalists are becoming more professional around the world.

Conclusion

Whether one thinks that journalists are becoming more professional around the world depends on the definition of professional and the indicators used. But a variety of possible measures of professionalism reviewed here suggest that there are still many differences among journalists from the 21 countries and territories represented in Weaver (1998). Even though these are not a representative sample of all countries, they do include some of the largest and most influential, and they are located in most of the major continents and regions.

Further analysis is needed to uncover some of the reasons behind the differences reported here. Many of them seem to reflect societal influences, especially political system differences, more than the influences of media organizations, journalism education, and professional norms. The patterns of similarities and differences are not neatly classifiable along some of the more common political or cultural dimensions, however, lending some support to the conclusion of Splichal and Sparks (1994) that journalism education and professional socialization are not necessarily a function of politics or dominant ideology. Additional comparative studies of journalists, perhaps using in-depth case studies, might uncover other influences on journalists' views concerning their professional roles and ethics, and document these views in more detail.

As to the question of who journalists are, the findings from our studies of U.S. journalists and of those of journalists in many other countries show that there is a case for journalists of this century being more demographically representative of their larger societies than those of the past century. These future journalists need to be more formally and broadly educated, and they need to know how to report clearly in words and images, given the convergence of various media forms.

The challenge for the news media in various countries will be to provide the resources, support and autonomy for the best and brightest journalists, so that they are not tempted to stray from serious journalism. In this postmodern and hyper-competitive age, when so many boundaries are blurring and so many distractions abound, this will be difficult but vitally important for fulfilling the information needs of various societies.

Note

1 There are exceptions to this generalization. In a 1992 survey of 1,068 Australian journalists, John Henningham (1998) found 44 percent whose fathers had a professional or managerial occupation, 12 percent whose father had a semi-skilled or unskilled occupation and 10 percent who came from an agricultural background, with the remainder split evenly between clerical/sales and skilled trade. Suzanna Layton (1998, p. 130), in a 1992 survey of 164 Pacific island journalists, found a "large cluster of modern middle-class backgrounds," a "smaller cluster of more traditional agrarian backgrounds," and a "very small number of journalists who come from business or blue-collar homes." In a 1995 survey of 726 United Kingdom journalists, John Henningham and Anthony Delano (1998) found 45 percent whose fathers worked in professional or managerial positions, 15 percent who came from unskilled or semi-skilled work backgrounds, and 16 percent from skilled trades occupations. Ari Heinonen (1998), in two 1993 surveys of Finnish journalists, found that more than half identified with the middle class rather than the working or upper

classes. In a 1988 survey of 484 French journalists, Aralynn Abare McMane (1998) found that they were more likely than the French labor force to come from a white-collar background, about as likely to come from an artisan shopkeeper background, and far less likely to come from a family of laborers or farmers. In two surveys of Hungarian journalists, Ildiko Kovats (1998) found that the proportion of those who came from a family in which the father was an intellectual rose from 35 percent in 1981 to 53 percent in 1992.

References

Beam, Randal A. 1990. Journalism professionalism as an organizational-level concept. *Journalism Monographs* 121: 1–43.

Donsbach, Wolfgang. 1983. Journalists' conceptions of their audience. *Gazette* 32: 19–36.

Gaziano, Cecilie and Kristin McGrath. 1986. Measuring the concept of credibility. *Journalism Quarterly* 63: 451–462.

Heinonen, Ari. 1998. The Finnish journalist: Watchdog with a conscience. Pp. 161–190 in D. H. Weaver, ed., *The Global Journalist: News People Around the World*. Cresskill, NJ: Hampton Press.

Henningham, John. 1998. Australian journalists. Pp. 91–107 in D. H. Weaver (ed.), *The Global Journalist: News People Around the World*. Cresskill, NJ: Hampton Press.

Henningham, John, and Anthony Delano. 1998. British journalists. Pp. 143–160 in D. H. Weaver (ed.), *The Global Journalist: News People Around the World*. Cresskill, NJ: Hampton Press.

Johnstone, John W. C., Edward J. Slawski, and William W. Bowman. 1976. *The News People*. Urbana, IL: University of Illinois Press.

Koecher, Renate. 1986. Bloodhounds or missionaries: Role definitions of German and British journalists. *European Journal of Communication* 1: 43–64.

Kovats, Ildiko. 1998. Hungarian journalists. Pp. 257–276 in D. H. Weaver (ed.), *The Global Journalist: News People Around the World*. Cresskill, NJ: Hampton Press.

Layton, Suzanna. 1998. Pacific island journalists. Pp. 125–140 in D. H. Weaver (ed.), *The Global Journalist: News People Around the World*. Cresskill, NJ: Hampton Press.

McLeod, Jack and Searle Hawley Jr. 1964. Professionalization among newsmen. *Journalism Quarterly* 41: 529–538, 577.

McMane, Aralynn Abare. 1998. The French journalist. Pp. 191–212 in D. H. Weaver (ed.), *The Global Journalist: News People Around the World*. Cresskill, NJ: Hampton Press.

Splichal, Slavko and Colin Sparks. 1994. *Journalists for the 21st Century*. Norwood, NJ: Ablex.

Weaver, David H., ed. 1998. *The Global Journalist: News People Around the World*. Cresskill, NJ: Hampton Press.

Weaver, David H. and LeAnne Daniels. 1992. Public opinion on investigative reporting in the 1980s. *Journalism Quarterly* 69: 146–155.

Weaver, David H. and G. Cleveland Wilhoit. 1986. *The American Journalist: A Portrait of U.S. News People and Their Work*. Bloomington, IN: Indiana University Press.

Weaver, David H. and G. Cleveland Wilhoit. 1991. *The American Journalist: A Portrait of U.S. News People and Their Work*. Second edition. Bloomington, IN: Indiana University Press.

Weaver, David H. and G. Cleveland Wilhoit. 1992. Journalists–Who Are They, Really? *Media Studies Journal* 6, 4: 63–79.

Weaver, David H. and G. Cleveland Wilhoit. 1996. *The American Journalist in the 1990s: U.S. News People at the End of an Era*. Mahwah, NJ: Lawrence Erlbaum.

Weaver, David, Randal Beam, Bonnie Brownlee, Paul Voakes, and G. Cleveland Wilhoit. 2003. *The American Journalist in the 21st Century: Key Findings*. Miami, FL: The Knight Foundation. Also on the Internet: http://www.poynter.org/content/content_view.asp?id=28235

Wilke, Juergen. 1998. Journalists in Chile, Ecuador, and Mexico. Pp. 433–452 in D. H. Weaver (ed.), *The Global Journalist: News People Around the World*. Cresskill, NJ: Hampton Press.

Windahl, Swen and Karl Erik Rosengren. 1978. Newsmen's professionalization: Some methodological problems. *Journalism Quarterly* 55: 466–473.

Zhu, Jian-Hua, David Weaver, Ven-hwei Lo, Chongshan Chen, and Wei Wu. 1996. Individual, organizational and societal influences on media role perceptions: A comparative study of journalists in China, Taiwan and the United States. *Journalism & Mass Communication Quarterly* 74: 84–96. (Reprinted pp. 361–374 in Michael Prosser and K. S. Sitaram (eds), *Civic Discourse: Intercultural, International, and Global Media*, Volume 2. Stamford, CT: Ablex, 1999.)

3

JOURNALISM AND THE
MAKING OF A PROFESSION

Howard Tumber and Marina Prentoulis

Classifying the occupation of journalism is never an easy task. From the nineteenth century, when the processes of professionalization began for journalism, until the present, a debate has raged as to whether journalism is a craft, a trade or a profession. In an attempt at classification comparisons are often made with the archetypal professions of medicine and law. People working in these occupations are considered to be a select group of high-status practitioners administering specialized services to members of the community. They generally undergo a lengthy period of tertiary training in their speciality and when admitted to practice normally enjoy a share in a monopoly in the performance of their work (Henningham, 1979: 15; see also Tunstall, 1973: 87).

Unlike the classical professions, the depth of abstract knowledge on which the practice of journalism is based is both limited and less clearly defined, while the emphasis on practical skills brings journalism closer to a craft than a profession. Although journalism has had to face a set of very specific problems inherent in its practice, the sociology of professions and occupations has juggled with providing some stable guidelines on how to characterize professions in general.[1]

The founding fathers of sociology, Marx, Weber and Durkheim, remained relatively vague about the role of the professions, subsuming them under what they deemed the more important categories of their respective theories. Marx's central theme of class struggle left little room for a more detailed account of the professions. The division of society across class lines did not attribute any special role to the professions. In some accounts professions were aligned with the bourgeoisie, in others with the proletariat, and in a third way, treated as bystanders that could align with either side. Subsequent Marxist accounts focused on the role of the professions within the capitalist market, their ability to offer services and to monopolize the administration of services (Dooley, 1997: 7). Similarly, Weber did not pay much attention to the professions as a sociological category in itself. His analysis of work groups and their status centred on the accumulation and manipulation of specialized skills and knowledge that occupational groups began to master. Durkheim, who was interested in the functions of the professions for both their members and society as a whole, did not manage to illuminate the debate. His primary shortcoming was the failure to provide a historical account that captured the particular character of the professions in France, or their development in other parts of the world. He was unable to strike a balance between the specific historical context within which different professions emerged, and a general core illustrating characteristics that all these professions might have in common (Burrage, 1990: 1–2; Dooley, 1997: 7; Dingwall, 1983: 2).

Sociologists tend to emphasize the orientation of the professions in serving the public by applying specialized knowledge and skills. Economists point to the monopolistic character of the professions, the political scientists to their character as 'privileged private governments', and policy makers examine what is good or bad for the public (Freidson, 1983: 19). Scholarly attention paid to occupations and professions can be differentiated between those that examine how certain occupations accumulate professional traits that distinguish them from non-professional groups, and those that try to marry history and sociology by arguing that the development of the professions is related to broader environmental and structural changes (Dooley, 1997: 5).

Trait theories dominated academic analysis during the 1960s and early 1970s. The main problem was how to define a core set of traits, attributes or crucial characteristics that played a decisive role in the distinction between occupations and 'professions'. In reviewing this approach, G. Millerson (1964) identified twenty-three elements that might constitute the various definitions of a profession. As he tried to extract the core elements from the sociological literature, he provided an insight into the problem by pointing out that no single element on his list was accepted by all authors as essential. Some of the most frequently used 'elements' within trait theories include among others: skills based on theoretical knowledge; the provision of training and education; the testing of the competence of the members of the profession; organization; adherence to the professional code of conduct; and altruistic service (Dooley, 1997: 6; Freidson, 1983: 21; Johnson, 1972: 23; Millerson, 1964).[2]

A further problem with trait theory is that it is based on the implicit assumption that there is an 'ideal type', a 'true profession' that can be abstracted from existing occupations. Law and medicine are usually taken as the 'classical cases' (Johnson, 1972: 24). As a result of the theoretical inadequacy of trait theory, the tendency is to accept the definitions of the professionals themselves. Professional rhetoric and codes however, do not necessarily apply in the same way across different sectors of society and while they function as legitimizing devices for the profession itself, one has to question their 'neutral' character *vis-à-vis* the social order (Johnson, 1972: 25–26).

In order to engage with the problems of trait theory, emphasis shifted from the 'static' structure of a profession to a specific account of the historically and culturally dynamic processes by which occupations gain professional status. Furthermore, increased attention was paid to the attempts by practitioners to impose their own definitions of social needs and how these should be fulfilled.

Finally, instead of a search for traits, professions were differentiated according to their claims to abstract knowledge that underpinned the practical technique (Dooley, 1997: 6).

An important forerunner of the more dynamic and historical approach was Everett C. Hughes. Part of the 'Chicago School' in the late 1950s, Hughes moved from questions about what differentiates a profession from an occupation, to questions about the specific circumstances that mark the shift from an occupation to a profession. He focused on the concepts of licence and mandate. Licence carries in it the explicit or implicit acceptance that a group engages in certain activities in exchange for some reward. When the members of a profession group develop a shared identity by virtue of the activity that they carry out, they issue a mandate that defines their own tasks and responsibilities as well as the demands and responses of the public. It was the period of transition from an occupation to a profession that became a focus of sociological research. The historical development of a profession, the wider structural and environmental changes, the interrelation between technological changes, new social movements and institutions, all became important factors in the sociology of professions (Dingwall, 1983: 5–6; Dooley, 1997: 4–5; Hughes, 1958).

Another theoretical trend within sociology sought illumination in the efforts of the professional groups themselves. The creation of professional associations, the formation of boundaries that allowed the empowerment of the professional group and permitted the negotiations with other associated groups, led to a further estrangement with trait theory and a shift to a power model. This approach found its expression in the work of Caplow (1954) and Wilensky (1964), leading to the identification of five stages in the history of professionalism in the United States: the emergence of a full-time occupation; the establishment of a training school; the founding of a professional association; political agitation directed towards the protection of the association by law; and the adoption of a formal code (Dooley, 1997: 6; Freidson, 1983: 21; Johnson, 1972: 28). Despite problems with this approach (see Freidson, 1983; Johnson, 1972), it dispelled previous assumptions about the professions, and recognized them as a social formation tied up with the Anglo-American experience (Burrage, 1990: 4).

The professions and the case of journalism

The original occupations that claimed a 'professional status' in Europe were medicine, law, and the clergy whose university education and disinterested dedication played a part in their development. During the nineteenth century, however, the emerging middle class of Britain and the USA started to demand the same status for a variety of successful middle class occupations as those conferred on the traditionally learned professions. By claming a 'gentlemanly' status, occupations sought to secure a privileged place in the *laissez-faire* economy which would allow them to compete with rival occupations. Control over the training and the credentials of the practitioners was essential for control over employment. The Anglo-American professions gained their distinction from 'their training and identity as particular, corporately-organized occupations to which specialized knowledge, ethicality and importance in society were imputed, and for which privilege was claimed' (Freidson, 1983: 25). The story was quite different in the rest of Europe where the state played a more active role in training and employment. In Germany, professional status was associated with university qualifications and in France with education in one of the *Grandes Ecoles* (Freidson, 1983: 24–25).

Until well after the World War II most British historians focused on the elite professions, often in studies commissioned by the professions themselves. When in 1933 Carr-Saunders and Wilson published their seminal work, they put forth a collective perception of professions as a distinct set of occupations (Burrage, 1990: 6). In their analysis, journalism was examined, even if in a sketchy way, together with other 'liberal' professions such as teaching (Carr-Saunders and Wilson, 1964).

Journalism presented a number of difficulties distinct from other professions. From its beginning it was a much more diverse and undefined activity compared with the 'classic' professions of medicine and law. The first reason was historical. In England since 1476 when William Caxton set up the first printing press, marking the starting point of an overgrowing process of news publishing, and until the development of copyright legislation, copyrights resided with the publisher. Few if any authors made a living by writing and it was only through patronage or additional employment that they managed to survive. The Act of Anne (effective from April 1710) established the right of an author to his/her own property, opening the way to improving the living standards of authors. Through the eighteenth and nineteenth centuries, the writing trade was too small to sustain aspiring writers. In the absence of a dividing line between journalists and writers such as novelists or political theorists, journalistic writing was regarded as part of a wider literary tradition with its practitioners simultaneously engaged in different 'genres' of writing, for example literature, political theory or journal articles. In the nineteenth century, journalism embraced literary figures such as Wordsworth, Coleridge and Dickens, who was a parliamentary reporter and magazine editor as well as a correspondent. Additional employment in areas alien to writing was usually necessary to make ends meet (Bonham-Carter, 1978).

More than two centuries after journalism was recognized as a distinct profession, an undefined line between journalism and other 'literary' professions has developed. Sociology, novel writing and journalism are based on mutual influences and ambitions. Dickens and other nineteenth-century novelists provided important sociological insights on the Industrial Revolution. Ethnographic writing was an integral part of the work of many novelists and journalists. Similarly, contemporary journalistic trends break the barriers between journalism and novel writing. One of the 'hybrid' forms that has emerged for example, is 'new journalism'. Mutual ambitions are expressed in the shared belief among journalists and social scientists that each one is an expert in unveiling the meaning of social life, while both problematize and reflect on their role in observing, reporting and analysing social reality. Research, the founding practice of their analysis, is as much a reality in journalism as in sociology (Strong, 1983: 59–64). The same 'fluidity' is present in the division of labour within journalism itself. In contrast to the 'classic' professions, journalism is marked by the absence of a particular core technique applied to different spheres of activity. Newspapers, for example, are the product of the joint work of a number of individuals specializing in different activities from reporting to sub-editing (Carr-Saunders and Wilson, 1964: 266).

The process of professionalization

Political agitation over freedom of the press during the 1830s in England marked a transitional period from a press tied up in restrictive taxation and censorship to the free-market-oriented news industry familiar today in liberal-democratic societies. The abolition of restrictive legislation which opened the road to the professionalization and industrialization of journalism started in 1825 and was finalized by 1855, when stamp duty, advertising duty and paper duty were repealed (Aspinal, 1949; Curran, 1978; Hollis, 1970). From that time the economic structure of the press underwent a dramatic change. The free market increased the capital investment and running costs of newspapers while at the same time advertising became the primary source of revenue for the industry. This re-structuring was assisted by a number of technological innovations (from the linotype machine to the expansion of the railways and the use of telegraph and telegram that increased the amount of available news) affecting the style and content of newspapers and allowing the progressive commercialization of the press (Curran and Seaton, 1997: 31–32).

Within this new communications environment, the role and position of the practitioners were transformed. The material conditions of the journalists were improved, employment opportunities were enlarged, salaries increased and many more people entered the profession creating the need and conditions for the first professional bodies (Brake, 1988; O'Boyle, 1968; Wiener, 1988).

From the mid-Victorian years the role of the journalist as an educator of the masses became widely accepted. J.S. Mill argued persuasively for the role of 'free discussion' and the 'free press' in promoting the 'truth' and the 'public good'. When the press was industrialized during the second half of the nineteenth century, it assumed a more central role in the political process, taking the status of the 'representative' of the people (Hampton, 2001: 215–217). A group of practitioners, at first predominantly editors and foreign correspondents, started to view their role under the prism of a common responsibility towards the public (Carr-Saunders and Wilson, 1964: 267). The term 'Fourth Estate' exemplified their social responsibility role, while the naming of the newspapers (*The Times,* the *Guardian,* the *Globe,* the *Observer,* and so on) revealed the importance attached to their practice (Strong, 1983: 62).

Journalism is seen as fulfilling the essential need of humans to be informed in order to participate in social and political processes. As an autonomous practice unwilling to compromise its ethic of 'public service' – in order to serve particular interests – journalism makes a strong claim to being a profession (Hallin, 2000: 219). Even if information requirements have changed and socio-political transformations have modified how information needs are perceived, the 'objectivity', 'neutrality' and social responsibility claims of journalism are characteristics that give it a 'professional' grounding and a special role within political and public life (Dooley, 1997: 12; Hallin, 2000: 220).

However, what makes the case of journalism more problematic is the absence of a theoretical and scientific framework that supports the claims to 'truth' and guards against deviations from the duties of social responsibility. In contrast to sociologists, who have a clearly marked theoretical ambition, journalists have always been associated with the performance of a set of tasks that are the product of experience and practice rather than theoretical knowledge (Abbot, 1988: 7–8; Bovee, 1999: 175; Strong, 1983: 64; Trice, 1993: 7, 12). In sharp contrast to the medical profession, which bases its legitimating claims on its body of medical science, or the law profession supported by legal theory, journalism is a mixture of abstract and technical requirements. Furthermore, the subjective nature of tasks such as news writing and editing makes journalism even more vulnerable *vis-à-vis* the classical professions. These two issues, the definition of journalistic work as an altruistic profession fulfilling a particular human need which has an impact on the wider social whole, and the abstract and technical dimensions of their work, are the key ones in understanding where journalism fits into the craft/profession dichotomy (Dooley, 1997: 11–14). One further reason has complicated matters. The industrialization of the press led to its organization as a collective enterprise (Brake, 1988: 10). As a collective effort, newspapers were the product of different practices, and as different considerations underpinned different roles, it became more difficult to isolate a core technique (Carr-Saunders and Wilson, 1964: 266).

Objectivity

Michael Schudson (1978) has examined the occupational ideals of journalists at the end of the nineteenth century. The memoirs of these early professionals reveal a tension between editors and reporters, the former insisting on factual and accurate information, the latter wanting to give more 'colourful' and 'personal' accounts of the events. Their reflections supply evidence of the first different ideological framework under which journalists and editors worked. So, too, does the progressive insistence on factual information that allowed the notion of 'objectivity' to emerge as the founding principle of professional journalism. Julius Chambers (editor of the *New York Herald* and the *New York*

World) remembers his own formative years on the *New York Tribune*: 'Facts; facts; nothing but the facts. So many peas at so much a peck; so much molasses at so much a quart. The index of forbidden words was very lengthy, and misuse of them, when they escaped the keen eye of the copyreader and got into print, was punishable by suspension without pay for a week, or immediate discharge. It was a rigid system, rigidly enforced' (Chambers, quoted in Schudson, 1978: 77). Similarly, Theodore Dreiser remembered his *Chicago Globe* editor Maxwell's insistence on the 'who, what, how, when, and where' rule, the canon for quick and accurate information. Handbooks of journalism such as Edwin L. Shuman's *Steps into Journalism* (1894), although recognizing the role of imagination in re-creating lively accounts that had an ambiguous relationship with factuality, emphasize the importance of keeping news and opinion apart: 'Opinions are the peculiar province of the editorial writer. The spirit of modern journalism demands that the news and the editorials be kept distinctly separate. The one deals with the facts, the other with theoretical interpretations' (quoted in Schudson, 1978: 77–79; see also Barney, 2003).

If theoretical knowledge rests on abstraction, journalistic skills rest on the abstract imperatives defined in the code of journalistic practice. The notions of 'objectivity', 'neutrality' and 'impartiality' (together with their more modern versions of balance and fairness (Chalaby, 1998: 133)), operating in the background of the problems and tasks associated with the profession, provide the abstract system of knowledge that allows the differentiation of journalism from other 'crafts'. The elevation of 'objectivity' to the main ideological commitment of the profession marked the separation of journalism from 'publicity agents' who promoted distorted versions of truth (Bourdieu, 1996: 70; Bovee, 1999: 113; Trice 1993: 7).

Looking more closely at the concept of 'journalistic objectivity', it is possible to identify different claims and objectives inherent in the concept. First, it marks the separation of the press from party politics. In Britain, the end of the restrictive taxation in 1855 allowed editors to distance their newspapers from party patronage, claiming that neutrality and impartiality would be the basis for news provision. This did not necessarily imply that newspapers would not favour one political party or another, but rather that their political affiliation would be the product of independent editorial decision rather than party affiliation or economic considerations (Chalaby, 1998: 130–133). Second, as an ideological ideal, 'objectivity' is interconnected with some notion of 'truth'. This could be an 'objective truth' (Frost, 2000), 'truth' associated with a particular class of journalist, for example war correspondents (McLaughlin, 2002), or as an 'impossible' epistemological claim (Bovee, 1999; Lichtenberg, 2000). Another way of understanding journalistic objectivity is as a 'strategic ritual', that should direct journalistic routines (Tuchman, 1972). Finally, a set of norms related to objectivity, such as truthfulness, factuality, completeness and accuracy, underpinned the claim to objectivity. The publication of all-important facts in a correct fashion and a commitment to the exposition of truth, if not always possible, were the components of this ideal of journalistic objectivity (Chalaby, 1998: 133; Frost, 2000: 36).

Although 'objectivity' became the criterion against which journalistic performance should be judged (Society of Professional Journalists' Code of Practice, cited in Bovee, 1999: 113), the problems of basing professional practice on such an illusive concept have never ceased to challenge. The debate is in many cases based on incompatible arguments that make difficult any definite statement about the possibility or impossibility of objectivity:

> (1) The sincere complaint that a piece of journalism is not objective makes sense only against the background assumption that objectivity is possible (why bother complaining about the inevitable?). (2) The insistence that journalism cannot be objective makes superfluous the view that objectivity is undesirable (why bother denouncing the impossible?). (3) The assertion that objectivity is not desirable makes senseless the complaint that journalism is not objective (what is the complaint?).
>
> (Lichtenberg, 2000: 239)

Professional institutions and codes of practice

For journalists to achieve professional status similar to that of doctors and lawyers, a code of ethics would be essential in ensuring that the distribution of information be regulated and disciplined. In the USA, the American Medical Association founded in 1847 and the American Bar Association, founded in 1878, made the creation of a code of ethics their immediate priority. Walter Lippmann, in his essay 'Liberty and the News', urged journalists to adopt a code of ethics in order to safeguard against abuses while allowing them to regulate their own profession. The continuation of abuses, he warned, and the absence of an ethical framework, could only lead to restrictive legislation. The growing demands for the formalization of the journalistic profession led in the 1920s to the publication of the first books on media ethics. These books discussed journalistic ethics, the social responsibility of the press and journalistic procedure. The American Society of Newspaper Editors (ASNE), founded by editors of daily newspapers in 1922, was the first professional body to adopt a strict professional code. The Sigma Delta Chi, an association of working journalists, created by students at the DuPauw University in Indiana, drafted a Code of Ethics in 1926. Renamed as the Society for Professional Journalists, today it has more than ten thousand members and its code was revised following the Watergate scandal in 1974, and then again in 1987, and in 1996 (Barney, 2003: 677–679).

In the UK, the National Union of Journalists was founded in 1907 with the main objective to improve the material conditions of the members. In 1919 a national agreement established a minimum wage across the different sectors associated with the profession thus ending economic hardship for journalists (Elliott, 1978: 175). However, while the Institute of Journalists made sure that its members abided by the code of ethics, threatening with expulsion any member who ignored it, the NUJ had little to say about professional ethics. It is significant that the NUJ, aiming mainly at the economic protection of the profession, could discipline its members just for protective ends (Carr-Saunders, 1964: 402). As the main organization for journalists, the NUJ had to justify its role according to the regulation not only of the material interests of its members but also in relation to their professional conduct. Only in this way could the professional status of journalism be elevated to that of the medical and legal professions. As a result, the NUJ, despite its ineffective way of regulating the practitioners in terms of their professional conduct, could declare in the report of the first Royal Commission on the Press (1947): 'We seek above all else, as a body of professional men and women, that the industry in which we serve the community should be directed and managed primarily in the public interest' (cited in Elliott, 1978: 176).

Both the creation of codes of ethics and the emergence of formal education and training for journalists fostered a shared culture among journalists. Even if the objectives aspired to by journalists have not been fully met within the actual production of news, the ideal of the social responsibility of journalists to the wider society always remains the standard against which professional practice is measured. This, though, does not free journalism from institutional contradictions. Despite claims to public service and demands for professional autonomy, few belong to professional associations. Studies in the 1970s and 1980s found that, compared to lawyers and doctors, journalists tend to participate less in a shared professional culture that is promoted by professional bodies than other professions (Weaver and Wilhoit, 1986: 127–128).

Education and training

The education of professional journalists, at least for the European and American context, has failed to produce clear professional and pedagogical criteria which would allow journalistic education to achieve a degree of legitimacy and prestige similar to that enjoyed by medical and law studies (Adam, 2001: 315–316). The debate over the education of journalists and its incorporation within academic institutions has a long history and still rages today. One view focuses on market considerations and insists that journalistic skills are more important to the practitioners than any abstract/theoretical knowledge gained in the universities (see discussion in de Burgh, 2003: 97). In this mode, schools of journalism are pushed towards a more 'practical' professional training. An alternative view recognises the benefits of theoretical knowledge but remains internally divided between those who see journalistic education as part of the humanities (see Adam, 2001: 334–335; Carey, 2000), and those who favour a social sciences framework. This dichotomy also extends to the teachers of journalism. Some have experience as practitioners themselves and thus focus on the vocational training of the students. Others come from recognised academic fields such as sociology, philosophy or political sciences and stress a non-vocational agenda, promoting research and intellectual endeavour.

Weaver and Wilhoit divide the history of the development of the field in the USA into four periods: 1700 to 1860; 1860 to 1920; 1920 to 1940; and 1940 to early 1980 (1986: 41–44). During the first period, American journalism was confined to apprenticeship programmes for print. It was only during the latter part of the second period that the development of professional education for journalists became an ongoing concern. During this second period, journalistic education started to be formalized and American colleges introduced courses on journalism into their curriculum. Remaining largely focused on the vocational training associated with printing or as part of English departments, these courses were never fully embraced either by the academy or by the professional community. The first evident changes started in the 1910s when Willard 'Daddy' Bleyer (University of Wisconsin) and Walter Williams (University of Missouri), among others, introduced specific courses in the first Departments of Journalism. The third period in journalistic education was characterized by the dichotomy produced by the different viewpoints of Bleyer and Williams. On the one hand, the creation of independent journalistic schools following the call of Williams in Missouri; on the other, separate departments within colleges of liberal arts following Bleyer's model. A third option appeared at the end of this period with the foundation by Wilbur Schramm of a new field called 'communication', of which the important implications for journalism are discussed in this volume by Betty Medsger. As a broader field of communication studies, this challenged the existing disciplinary boundaries of the period. The formalization of journalistic education was extended during the last period from the 1950s onwards and encompassed advanced degrees such as PhDs in mass communication. During the last period, journalistic education focused on different objectives. For example, during the 1970s and 1980s, journalism schools focused their curriculum on the core practices of writing and reporting while the mid-1980s and 1990s saw a new information age that demanded more reflection on communication theory (Daniels, 2003: 655–659; Schultz, 2002: 224–225).

Within this historical account, special mention should be reserved for the beginning of journalism at Columbia University in 1912. At the beginning of the century Joseph Pulitzer proposed the creation of a College of Journalism at Columbia. His proposals were criticized by many people including journalists. His essay 'Planning a School of Journalism' appeared in the *North American Review* in May 1904 and outlines his main thesis in relation to the formalization of the education of the practitioners. His premise was based on the argument that journalists played a vital role as teachers and critics of society and as such should acquire a wide and deep knowledge. Only this knowledge would give their professional endeavours the moral and intellectual properties that they should exhibit. From the traditional university subjects, the study of jurisprudence and constitutional law seemed the core components of the curriculum that was to enable journalists to fulfil their role in a democratic society. Literature, ethics, economics, history and sociology, among other subject areas, were all important in equipping the students of journalism with a wide intellectual background. At the same time, however, Pulitzer placed a lot of emphasis on the specific needs of the profession. The teaching of the literary art would enable students to have training in writing, press history, and 'principles of journalism'. The critical examination of news cases would also contribute to professional training. All subject areas, traditional and specific to journalism, were to be tailored for the needs of the profession. Pulitzer believed that, in a manner similar to that used for law and business, the teaching of the new subject areas should be based on comparative case studies and reflective criticism that would facilitate the journalistic practice. His efforts led to the foundation of an undergraduate school which opened in 1912 and in 1935 became a separate graduate school strictly devoted to journalism (Adam, 2001: 318–320; Carey, 2000: 15–16).

While Columbia was putting forward the basis for journalistic education, interesting changes were happening in the University of Chicago. Although journalism was not taught there, since Chicago was modelled on the German research universities, the sociologist Everett Hughes developed sociology of place. This trend in sociology focused on local knowledge of the city while at the same time it was closely intertwined with city institutions. According to Carey:

> Chicago sociology was a sociology of communication, transportation, settlement and migration, and the social relations and political institutions built along these fronts of the city. Neighbourhood by neighbourhood, street by street, census tract by census tract, group by group, occupation by occupation, this new urban world, the whole city, was opened up to understanding. This was a sociology very close to journalism.
>
> (2000: 18)

In the late 1940s, further developments led to the independent teaching of journalism. The emergence of a new science of communications aiming at the control and co-ordination of the social structure, recognized journalism as an important social and political channel of control. According to Carey, this new communications field did not have the noble aspirations of Chicago and Columbia. Rather, 'by reading journalism functionally rather than intrinsically, it levelled journalism down to that of a signalling system while not immeasurably increasing our understanding of journalism as a social act, a political phenomenon, and an imaginative construction of the social' (ibid.: 20–21).

Today

This historical account of the development of journalistic education points to a double dichotomy at the heart of journalism. As a cross-disciplinary subject, its professional aspirations can find fertile ground in both the academic fields of humanities and social sciences. Which of the two disciplines benefit the profession more is still open to debate. Furthermore, journalism as both a vocational and intellectual enterprise is subject to influences from both academia and industry. As a result journalistic education has to incorporate both 'idealist' and 'realist' aspirations and both 'practical' and 'intellectual' dimensions.

According to Hartley, journalistic education should contain three aspects: non-vocational education; training; and research. Non-vocational education will illuminate social and political aspects related to democratic practices and the media. Training is defined as 'the traditional focus of journalism schools, devoted to producing employable professionals, whether traditional (violent) or smiling; whether journalists (writers) or redactors'. This will guide the future practitioners in more specific issues related to the profession.[3] Finally, there is research divided into two kinds. First, there is 'research into industry/instrumental matters with the utilitarian/policy orientation directed at the producer/regulator. Second, is social/intellectual research, with the critical/analytical orientation directed at the public' (Hartley, 2000: 46; see also de Burgh, 2003).

Despite the difficulties in combining these three components which do not necessarily sit comfortably with each other, two further questions need addressing: does the contemporary communications environment create new needs and challenges for journalistic education? How influential is the education of journalists on their perception of news reality *vis-à-vis* the socialization processes of the newsrooms?

As an academic subject journalism has an advantage over both social sciences and humanities in that it is a combination of 'reflexive practical and applied theoretical' knowledge. The debate is somehow irrelevant for the employers who consider personal qualities more important than knowledge when recruiting (de Burgh, 2003: 109). Similarly Schultz's secondary analysis of a number of US studies on the education of journalists reveals that, despite the growing number of journalism/communication students who hold a graduate degree, there are no stark differences between graduate and non-graduate students of journalism in terms of their ethical and political orientation and the way they understand their professional role. This can be attributed to the great similarity between college and graduate-school courses, but it is questionable whether further qualifications in research would be likely to change students' perception about journalistic ethics, norms and routines. Even if graduate students are more critical and reflective in relation to their professional role, most of them are going to pursue academic careers rather than ones in the news industry. The questions thus remain: does further education make a difference for the profession? And does graduate education offer something more than a college one? The differences between graduate and non-graduate students of journalism are associated with their employment status. Journalists educated in graduate schools tend to be older and work for larger news organizations than do college journalists. According to Schultz, a possible difference may be that the graduate group puts more emphasis on the interpretative role of the journalist. It is unclear, however, if this is the product of their graduate education, or as Schultz puts it, 'Possibly graduate students are, by a process of self-selection, more likely to emphasize the importance of interpreting and analyzing complex problems to begin with' (2002: 234–235).

As the new communications environment creates new challenges for journalism, a debate about the role of journalists either as straight providers of information, or as interpreters of this information, is gaining new significance (see Tumber, 2001, and Phillips, in this volume). As more outlets have appeared offering unfiltered information, the role of the journalists is changing towards offering guidance and interpretation rather than providing information (see, for example, Bardoel, 1996). It would be misleading, however, to present interpretative reporting as a new phenomenon. In the 1920s and 1930s, for example, Walter Lippmann and Curtis MacDougall argued in favour of this. But while straight reporting was then the norm, today the situation seems different (Hallin, 2000: 226).

Two characteristics of the new communications environment facilitated by the technological changes seem particularly relevant for the shift towards interpretative journalism. First, there is the increase in news providers and the changing nature of news sources as content providers. The Internet has played a decisive role in increasing and diversifying news providers. Yahoo! and Netscape, for example, offer online news and information. Second, owners of content rights such as movie producers and sports-rights owners are now in a position to broadcast directly to their audience, cutting out journalists and traditional media (Chalaby, 2000: 34–35).

The study of political communication suggests further issues. Citizens searching for information and news increasingly use the more direct, 'interactive' possibilities of the new technologies. This, coupled with the increase of horizontal communication among citizens, causes us to question the future of journalism. It is more probable, however, that the journalists will still play a significant role in navigating and interpreting the vast amounts of material that will be available to them in its 'raw' form (Bardoel, 1996: 283–302; see also Tumber, 2001; Tumber and Bromley, 1998).

There seems to be another explanation for this emphasis on the interpretative role of the journalists: with the decline of political authority and the collapse of traditional ideological blocks, journalists feel the pressure to 'fill the void'. As official sources and statements increasingly lose credibility, journalists become more engaged, taking sides, offering more commentary and allowing engagement and subjectivity to be part of their job. As Hallin argues, 'there is also some tendency for the voice of interpretative reporting to change: from the "voice of God" adopted by *Time* magazine or the top Washington columnists of the Cold War era, to the "voice of the people" of tabloid news, or to a more obviously subjective voice' (2000: 227).

The increasing power of journalists may become a problem if the professional culture of journalism is not reinforced. Ethical and normative values in reporting have been less the product of common membership in professional bodies and homogeneous education and more a product of shared practices learned within the newsrooms. Weaver and Wilhoit found that the institutional culture of journalism was weaker in 1992 than it was in the previous decade.

> Compared with other fields, such as accounting, law, university teaching, and medicine, U.S. journalism's formal trappings of institutional vitality were on the decline between 1971 and 1992. Membership in professional organizations and exposure to a common body of critical literature dropped from 1982 to 1992... a professional 'mood' remained in 1992, but the power of its expression rested almost exclusively within individual newsrooms.
>
> (1996: 169–172)

As journalists enter the new technological phase they will be less involved in the routines associated with the editorial desk and more involved in layout and marketing processes. This will have significant impact on the socialization processes traditionally seen as a primary educational process in journalism (Bardoel, 1996: 283–302).

Research suggests that while older journalists tend to be more cautious, younger generations of practitioners are more willing to challenge traditional practices. As we enter this new professional phase, schools of journalism can become more influential in training and in ethical influence (Weaver and Wilhoit, 1996: 168–170). As the shared culture among journalists will be less the product of socialization processes in the future, training and education will have to provide new ethical and practical guidelines, therefore assuming a more central role in moulding the future generations of journalists.

Jeremy Tunstall described journalism as an indeterminate occupation. Comparing it with both law and medicine which are relatively compact, uniform and sharply defined, he described 'journalist' as a 'label which people engaged in a very diverse range of activities apply to themselves' (Tunstall, 1973: 98; see also Tunstall, 1971). This diversity, as we have seen, has increased considerably in the past thirty years and Tunstall's suggestion that 'only occupations which are fairly determinate have any chance of becoming professions' (1973: 98) probably relegates journalism's position even further nowadays from professional status. Tunstall, writing thirty years ago, doubted that journalism 'could ever acquire professional attributes[4] to the extent of, for instance, medicine. A more realistic objective, if the occupation wished to pursue it, would be to make journalism into a semi profession...' (1971: 69).

In a more recent take on the status of journalism, Menand (1995) argues that disinterestedness is now the core value, common to all 'true' professions. While journalism may lack licensing and strict degree requirements, the public views it with the same disdain it holds for lawyers, doctors and professors (cited in Weaver and Wilhoit, 1996: 125). Advocates of public journalism strongly oppose the stance of disinterestedness and at the same time journalism educators are concerned that attempts to professionalize will adversely affect the diversity and robustness of news (Weaver and Wilhoit, 1996: 125–126).

As we enter the twenty-first century, it seems that public criticism, alongside the self-doubts within the 'profession' continue to leave journalism in an uncertain position regarding its status and definition.

Notes

1 The different theoretical perspectives associated with the sociology of professions can also be distinguished as: (a) Functionalist (Durkheim/Parsons); (b) Interactionist (Hughes); (c) Power (Larson); and (d) Systemic Division of Labour (Abbot). For the purpose of this chapter we attempted to demarcate a difference between trait theories and the more dynamic and historical approaches of 'professionalization'.

2 Greenwood (1957) identified five professional characteristics: theory, authority, licence, code of ethics and a professional culture. Tunstall argued that journalism does not meet these criteria but at the same time pointed out that law and medicine, while scoring much higher than journalism, might well score below full points (1973: 89).

3 Journalism as a 'violent' profession is founded on the premise that 'truth is violence, reality is war, news is conflict'. The 'smiling' professions within the media context refers to 'practices associated with TV presenters, lifestyle and consumer journalism, PR, advertising and spin doctors' (Hartley, 2000: 40).

4 Tunstall was referring to Greenwood's characteristics – see note 2 above.

References

Abbot, A. (1988) *The System of Professions*. Chicago: University of Chicago Press.

Adam, S.G. (2001) 'The Education of Journalists', *Journalism*, 2(3): 315–339.

Aspinall, A. (1949) *Politics and the Press, 1780–1850*. London: Home and Val Thal.

Bardoel, J. (1996) 'Beyond Journalism: A Profession between Information Society and Civil Society', in Tumber, H. (ed.) *News: A Reader*. Oxford and New York: Oxford University Press.

Barney, R.D (2003) 'Journalistic Code of Ethics and Conduct', in *Encyclopedia of International Media and Communications*, vol. 2. San Diego, CA: Elsevier Science.

Bonham-Carter, V. (1978) *Authors by Profession*. London: The Society of Authors.

Bourdieu, P. (1996) *On Television and Journalism*. London: Pluto.

Bovee, W. G. (1999) *Discovering Journalism*. Westport, CT: Greenwood Press.

Brake, L. (1988) 'The Old Journalism and the New: Forms of Cultural Production in London in the 1880s', in Wiener, J.H. (ed.) *Papers for the Millions: The New Journalism in Britain, 1850s to 1914*. New York, London: Greenwood.

Burrage, M. (1990) 'Introduction: The Professions in Sociology and History', in Burrage, M. and R. Torstendahl, *The Professions in Theory and History*. London: Sage.

Caplow, T. (1954) *Sociology of Work*, Minneapolis, MN: University of Minnesota Press.

Carey, J.W (2000) 'Some Personal Notes on US Journalism Education', *Journalism*, 1(1): 12–23.

Carr-Saunders, A.M. and Wilson, P.A. (1964) *The Professions*. London: Frank Cass.

Chalaby, J.K. (1998) *The Invention of Journalism*. Basingstoke: Macmillan Press.

—— (2000) 'Journalism Studies in an Era of Transition in Public Communications', *Journalism*, 1(1): 33–38.

Curran, J. (1978) 'The Press as an Agency of Social Control: An Historical Perspective', in Boyce, G., Curran, J. and Wingate, P. (eds) *Newspaper History: From the 17th Century to the Present Day*. London: Constable.

Curran, J. and Seaton, J. (1997) *Power Without Responsibility: The Press and Broadcasting in Britain*. London: Routledge.

Daniels, L. (2003) 'Journalism/Communications Education', in *Encyclopedia of International Media and Communications*, vol. 2. San Diego, CA: Elsevier Science.

de Burgh, H. (2003) 'Skills are not Enough', *Journalism* , 4(1): 95–112.

Dingwall, R. (1983) 'Introduction', in Dingwall R. and Lewis, P. (eds) *The Sociology of Professions: Lawyers, Doctors and Others*. London and Basingstoke: Macmillan Press.

Dooley, P.L. (1997) *Taking Their Political Place: Journalists and the Making of an Occupation*. Westport, CT: Greenwood Press.

Elliott, P. (1978) 'Professional Ideology and Organizational Change: The Journalist since 1800', in Boyce, G., Curran, J. and Wingate, P. (eds) *Newspaper History: From the 17th Century to the Present Day*. London: Constable.

Freidson, E. (1983) 'The Theory of Professions: State of the Art', in Dingwall, R. and Lewis, P. (eds) *The Sociology of Professions: Lawyers, Doctors and Others*. London and Basingstoke: Macmillan Press.

Frost, C. (2000) *Media Ethics*. Harlow: Longman.

Greenwood, E. (1957) 'Attributes of a Profession', *Social Work*, 2 July, 45–55.

Hallin, D.C. (2000) 'Commercialism and Professionalism in the American News Media' in Curran, J. and Gurevitch, M. (eds) *Mass Media and Society*. London: Arnold.

Hampton, M. (2001) 'Understanding Media: Theories of the Press in Britain, 1850–1914', *Media, Culture and Society*, 23: 213–231.

Hartley, J. (2000) 'Communicative Democracy in a Redactional Society: The Future of Journalism Studies', *Journalism*, 1(1): 39–48.

Henningham, J. (1979) 'Journalists and Professionalization', *Australian Journalism Review*, July, 15–20.

Hollis, P. (1970) *The Pauper Press*. London: Oxford University Press.

Hughes, E.C. (1958) *Men and Their Work*. Glencoe, IL: Free Press.

Johnson, T.J. (1972) *Professions and Power.* London and Basingstoke: Macmillan Press.

Lichtenberg, J. (2000) 'In Defence of Objectivity Revisited', in Curran, J. and Gurevitch, M. (eds) *Mass Media and Society. London:* Arnold.

McLaughlin, G. (2002) *The War Correspondent*. London: Pluto.

Millerson, G. (1964) *The Qualifying Associations: A Study of Professionalization*. London: Routledge and Paul.

O'Boyle, L. (1968) 'The Image of the Journalist in France, Germany, and England, 1815–1848', *Comparative Studies in Society and History*, 10, 3 April: 290–317.

Schudson, M. (1978) *Discovering the News: A Social History of American Newspapers*. New York: Basic Books.

Schultz, T. (2002) 'Does Education Matter?', *Journalism*, 3(2): 223–238.

Strong, P.M. (1983) 'The Rivals: an Essay on the Sociological Trades', in Dingwall R. and Lewis, P. (eds) *The Sociology of Professions: Lawyers, Doctors and Others*. London and Basingstoke: Macmillan Press.

Trice, H. (1993) *Occupational Subcultures in the Workplace*. New York: ILR Press.

Tuchman, G. (1972) 'Objectivity as a Strategic Ritual: An Examination of Newsmen's Notion of Objectivity', *American Journal of Sociology*, 77: 660–679.

Tumber, H. (2001) 'Democracy in the Information Age: The Role of the Fourth Estate in Cyberspace', *Information, Communication & Society*, 4(1): 95–112.

Tumber, H. and Bromley, M. (1998) 'Virtual Soundbites: Political Communication in Cyberspace', *Media Culture & Society*, 20: 159–167.

Tunstall, J. (1971) *Journalists at Work*. London: Constable.

Tunstall, J. (1973) 'Journalism as an Occupation', *The Medico-Legal Journal*, Part Three, 87–101.

Weaver, D.H. and Wilhoit, G.C. (1986) *The American Journalist: A Portrait of U.S. News People and Their Work*. Bloomington, IN: Indiana University Press.

Weaver, D.H. and Wilhoit, G.C. (1996) *The American Journalist in the 1990s*. New Jersey: Lawrence Erlbaum Associates.

Wiener, J.H. (1988) 'How New Was the New Journalism?' in Wiener, J.H. (ed.) *Papers for the Millions: The New Journalism in Britain, 1850s to 1914*. New York, London: Greenwood.

Wilensky, H. (1964) 'The Professionalism of Everyone?' *American Journal of Sociology*, 70(2), 137–158.

PART II

JOURNALISM AND LOCATION

4

IS THERE A EUROPEAN MODEL OF JOURNALISM?

Paolo Mancini

Can we talk of a unique model of European journalism that is different from the one that is commonly defined as the "Anglo-American", "Anglophone" or "Anglo-Saxon" model? Does a unique European model exist, or do models exist that differ from country to country? As we shall see, the answer to these questions is neither simple nor unambiguous. It could be articulated following two main contradictory lines. First of all, no, a unique European model of professional journalism does not exist as there are important differences between the different national models of the old continent. Nevertheless, at the same time, there are particular features that are common to professional journalism in most of the continental European countries and that, on the contrary, seem to be missing in the USA and Great Britain where a model of journalism defined as Anglo-American is practised. If the perspective of comparison is privileged, and not the one of unifying characteristics within the old continent, one must affirm that, yes, a European model does exist with several specific characteristics that differentiate it from other models.

The first point that has to be addressed regards the definition of Anglo-Saxon or Anglo-American journalism that refers to a type of journalism practised in the USA and Great Britain and that may be outlined in opposition to the one practised in continental Europe. There seems to be no substantial distinction between the use of one term, Anglo-American, or the other, Anglo-Saxon, and they are normally interchangeable. Since the classic *Four Theories of the Press*, the expression mainly used has been that of "Anglo-American journalism". Siebert *et al.* wrote that "Great Britain, the United States and some of the British Dominions follow a common pattern in what has been described as the "Anglo-American tradition" (1956, p. 57). Starting from the classical texts, among which *Four Theories of the Press* should certainly be numbered, its characteristics have been sufficiently described and discussed: independence from the other powers in whose regard journalism must exercise a function of control, objectivity and existence of professional standards that tend to reinforce the independence of journalism and clearly distinguish it from other professions. Furthermore, its reporting functions are clearly distinct from those of comment and interpretation. Instead of "Anglo-American model", in

Mediterranean countries the term Anglo-Saxon model is often used to identify the same set of characteristics indicated by the other expression to refer to the same countries mentioned above: the United States and Great Britain (Bechelloni, 1982).

Whichever term is used, in many texts on journalism and also in the common vernacular of this profession, a substantial difference is often discussed between a European model, or at least a model traceable to several European countries, and the "Anglo-American" or "Anglo-Saxon" model of journalism. One of the most convincing examples of this contrast was proposed by Jean Chalaby who discussed some of the main features of the "Anglo-American model" and its historical differences with what he defines as the French model (Chalaby, 1996). Following Chalaby, the definition of "Anglo-American journalism" indicates what today is, throughout the whole world, the dominant model of professional journalism. This is the reference model for most of the professionals worldwide and not just in the "Anglo-American countries". This is what, most of the time, journalists indicate when asked about their ethics and their professional routines and procedures (Mancini, 2000). Generally the Anglo-American model of journalism, with all its professional implications, seems to stand out as the only universal model. Starting from this, one can hypothesize alternative or at least different professional models, as I shall attempt to do in this chapter.

But maybe to avoid, at least partially, the simplification inherent in the usual opinion that considers the Anglo-American model as the dominant one, it is opportune to question whether such a model really exists. Are similarities in the professional journalism that is practised in Great Britain and the USA more numerous than the differences that exist between the two countries? And, in like manner, are similarities among the European countries more numerous than the differences?

The main features of the European model: media and politics

Let's see, then, what the most common components are in the professional journalism practised mainly in Western Europe and which do not exist, or at least are very difficult to find, in the Anglo-American model. The main import-ant difference between the USA, and partially Great Britain, on the one hand, and Europe, on the other, is certainly the relationship with politics. The European model of journalism is much more partisan than the Anglo-American one.

As we shall see, in almost every country, European or not, journalism was born with a strong partisan or literary characterization. Indeed, the first sheets that came out were connected with either religious, ethnic or political struggles that bloodied different countries or were the voice of the first economic and social groups founded at the dawn of the new bourgeois societies. The experiences of the first newspapers that were born in Northern Europe fit this trend perfectly. In Holland, the first "corantos" were also, and above all, expressions of economic interests and, what we should call today, political interests. The Thirty Years' War was a time of furious conflicts and, therefore, it was the occasion for the birth and development of propaganda sheets. In the Scandinavian countries, newspapers of the newborn industrial and commercial middle class began to come out that were in opposition to those of the landowners; newspapers appeared of one linguistic group that were opposed to the newspapers of another group (Hadenius and Weibull, 1999). Habermas illustrated the significance and importance of this origin very clearly although it gave rise to doubts and criticism that are well known (Habermas, 1989). Later, Holland offered another important example of the links between newspapers and social conflicts. There, the phenomenon of pillarization[1] came into being, also thanks to the instruments of communication, first newspapers and then television, that cement the relationships among the members of each of the different communities, contributing to the reinforcement of their identities and the struggle against competing pillars (Brants and McQuail, 1992; Nieuwenhuis, 1992).

The events that followed this common origin led to such a precise division that today one can affirm that in European countries the relationship between the mass media and politics is certainly much closer than in Anglo-American ones. This is one of the main important differences between European and Anglo-American journalism, although there are other important distinctions which will be discussed later.

In the Anglo-American countries, with the development of a type of press mainly oriented to mass circulation and conquering markets, its relation with politics has progressively weakened, so much so that in some cases it has completely disappeared, causing a progressive distancing of the Anglo-American model from the European one. In Great Britain and the United States incorporated ownerships, united by inventiveness and entrepreneurship, determined the establishment of a new press model, the so-called popular one, that is no longer tied to political parties but rather oriented exclusively towards selling the journalistic product. The experience of Harmsworth in Great Britain and his creation of a chain of local and national daily papers and periodicals proves this. The great dependence of his newspapers on proceeds from advertising was the basis of the development of a popular press aimed at public spheres that paid ever greater attention to the facts of daily life and which, up to then, had not been taken into consideration. This new press used a simpler and more direct language, distancing the newspaper from its elite and political nature. Harmsworth created the foundations and also the organizational basis for the development of a publishing industry, modernizing the equipment and always giving greater space to the press agencies (Gorman and McLean, 2001).

The American experience was an even greater upheaval; the advent of the penny press in the first half of the nineteenth century, as Michael Schudson (1978) aptly showed, completely revolutionized the behaviour of American newspapers and, in the long run, put an end to political parallelism, giving rise to what would become the key word of modern journalism: objectivity. This was an inevitable necessity for a press aimed at capturing a readership that was as wide as possible. Therefore, the press had to avoid political and ideological associations that might limit the spectrum of its potential consumers.

Very similar phenomena developed in Germany and Austria: the "Boulevardzeitungen" (boulevard press), so called because it was distributed along the streets of Berlin and Vienna, was also based on a type of journalism that was used to deal with everyday facts and less with political life and debate (Humphreys, 1990). The entrepreneurial and political adventure of Alfred Hugenberg, to a large extent linked with the experience of the boulevard press, is a good introduction to the discussion of the differences that exist between the way the Anglo-American model and the European one confront the relation with politics. Indeed, Hugenberg was able very successfully to wed two different needs: commercial penetration and political partisanship. Like Harmsworth in Great Britain, he built a publishing empire based on a solid and, for those times, modern organization in which advertising was the prime mover. At the same time, however, Hugenberg had a very active political life; he was among the founders of the DNVP, the right-wing party that supported Hitler's rise to power. Although his newspapers were part of his political adventure, they launched a new model of journalism that would, over time, create a mass-market press. It is exactly the Hugenberg experience that allows us to present one of the main differences between the Anglo-American model and the European one. Indeed, the European model is a substantially partisan journalism that maintains much closer relations with politics than the Anglo-American one. Even when it is a market-oriented journalism, as in Hugenberg's case, it is often partisan.

In most other European countries the fact that the development both of a press market and, especially, of advertising (its indispensable motor) was slow perpetuated the existence of strong links between the mass media and external economic forces and political organizations. The advent of the mass parties further reinforced the newspapers' tradition of partisanship; Catholic, liberal and, above all, socialist dailies were born, the last of which soon reached the highest circulation of any of the party newspapers. The experience of the Weimar Republic in Germany is symptomatic of the overlapping of mass parties and the press, but the same can be said of what took place in France, Italy, Belgium and the Scandinavian countries. The new-born party structures prospered and grew stronger thanks also to the support they received from the newspapers they controlled. The coming to power of Nazism, Fascism and the dictatorships in Spain and Portugal further strengthened the marriage between the press and mass parties; this union found additional confirmation with the struggle that followed to bring back democracy to these countries. The "Resistance" was helped considerably by the newspapers and even the policy of the Allied Forces, when they arrived in Europe, aimed at ensuring that the new newspapers, that were being set up with the advent of democracy, were in the hands of anti-fascist groups that could use them to promote their ideas. That is what took place in Germany (Humphreys, 1996) and in Italy (Murialdi, 1986).

The model of the party press would affect all professional journalism well beyond the boundaries of party newspapers. Indeed, a type of professional practice spread which meant that journalism had to take a position, defend a cause and fight for it; this even went beyond those who really practised it. Progressively, a professional model inspired by these principles spread, also beyond specific situations and even later when little by little the party papers began to disappear: to be a journalist also meant to take sides. Max Weber has this model clearly in mind when he describes the journalist as a "type of professional politician" (1947, p. 99).

Nevertheless, partisan journalism in Europe presents features that vary in important ways from country to country; in the northern countries it is deeply rooted in the experience of social participation both through party and religious or ethnic organizations and coexists with a rather high level of professionalism. The journalist respects several rules that are common to all those who practise the same profession regardless of their political affiliation. However, at the same time, he takes a position on the various events with which he comes into contact. It is not by chance that, in spite of the high level of partisanship of most of the press, the first professional organizations, sharing professional criteria and standards, were born in northern European countries.[2] These organizations, and the professional criteria linked to them, coexisted with a model of partisan journalism which assumed the form of either party press (that is, the newspapers were owned directly by political organizations or closely associated with them) or partisan journalism that was not directly owned by such organizations but did not hide its own political line which it tended to defend and diffuse.

In the southern countries, the model of partisan press overlapped with the practice of instrumentalization which was widespread in many other fields of social life (Hallin and Papathanassopoulos, 2002). The late development of a press mass market is among the main reasons for the instrumentalization and the politicization of the press: as newspapers were not able to survive on their own revenues from selling and advertising, they found economic resources outside the press industry that started to use the press for their own goals, making room for a tradition that is common even today. The political dimension of the newspaper was often used for instrumental purposes that could comply with a wide range of objectives. It was not uncommon for a newspaper to be used as an instrument of negotiation and even blackmail between groups and persons. In this Mediterranean model of journalism the professional rules are weaker and, in any case, less important for the development of the profession than political and economical links between news organizations and other external organizations.

Therefore, important differences exist in the European model between northern European countries and the Mediterranean ones. In the same way, within what we defined as the Anglo-American model, a very marked difference exists between British journalism and American journalism. Indeed, with the exception (at least partial exception) of the BBC, British journalism, like that in most of the European countries, has always had a rather high degree of partisanship (Curran and Seaton, 1991). It was so in the past and exists even now in both broadsheets and tabloids. The very recent support that Murdoch's dailies gave to Blair is the umpteenth confirmation of this long tradition. Thus, in this regard British journalism is much closer to the European model than the Anglo-American one, even though it takes its name from Great Britain.

Indeed, as stated at the beginning, identifying a European model of journalism is an operation which is more theoretical than empirical. It is an allowable generalization, but with contradictory empirical support. In any case, such a generalization includes considerable differences and important exceptions within it. The relationship between mass media and politics in Great Britain is one of these exceptions. If, at least in theory, in the Anglo-American model there is a complete separation between mass media and politics, in reality such a separation does not exist, or at least is less evident in Great Britain than in the United States, although there are some exceptions in latter as well.

As a matter of fact, frequently, there is no single journalistic model even within the same country; significant differences exist between the professional models of the press and television and differences exist even within the same medium. In this regard, the professional journalism of the BBC represents a search for equilibrium and objectivity that, although frequently criticized (Curran and Seaton, 1991), does not exist in the print press. The BBC shows how, within the same country, politicization of the media coexists with a rather high level of professionalism with canons and standardized and shared procedures that are distinctive characteristics of the Anglo-American model.

The example of the BBC testifies to how the difference in the level of partisanship between the European model and the Anglo-American model is much more evident in television journalism and in the very essence of the public-service broadcasting. In most European countries it was often conceived as being immediately subordinate to the political powers of the government or, in other countries, considered as having to represent the different political voices of society, invigorating that dimension of partisanship that is already well represented in the press.

More precisely, regarding relations between broadcasting and the political system, Humphreys (1996) distinguishes four models: (1) the governmental model in which television is under the direct control of the government; (2) the professional model in which the television journalists have a strong professional autonomy (the case of the BBC); (3) the parliamentary or proportional model in which the contents and organization of television reflect the existing political balances; and (4) the civic or corporatist model in which the relationship between television and the political reality expands to include a plurality of social and cultural groups. The professional model belongs to Great Britain and, at least partially, to the United States while the other three models can be found in different European countries. Just to give some examples: the governmental model is typical of the French phenomenon, the parliamentary one is the Italian situation and the civic one can be found in Germany.

Even today, in most European countries the links between the public broadcasting service and the political system constitute one of the major issues of public debate on mass communications, testifying to how much this problem is still unsolved and represents one of the main issues of democratic life in these countries. By contrast, in the United States, the fact that television is commercialized has impeded political intervention and, consequently, it has rarely been a central theme of public debate. Discussions regarding the First Amendment have essentially been of a juridical nature and have rarely involved party or political views.

The literary roots of the European model

The existence of strong links with literature constitutes another important feature of journalism in many European countries. These links have produced, since their early roots, a journalism that is very much oriented towards commentary and interpretation. Regarding this, Jean Chalaby wrote a very stimulating essay in which he maintains that journalism, as we know it today, is "an Anglo-American invention" and that this is very different from French journalism that for many years has overlapped and identified with literature, so much so as to be considered a sort of secondary sub-brand of the much more prestigious literary profession. The current opinion was that the journalism with the most links with literature and art was the best (Chalaby, 1996). French literature offers numerous examples of such mixing. Lucien de Rubemprè, the hero of Balzac's *Illusions perdues*, is an unsuccessful poet who enters journalism to scrape together a living and must endure all the disgraces, betrayals and compromises of this remedial profession. Similarly, Bel-Ami, the character of Maupassant's homonymous novel, reincarnates the prototype of the fascinating adventurer who becomes ensnared in political blackmail, the life of Parisian salons and their political and artistic/literary discussions. Balzac and Maupassant were themselves both fiction writers and journalists and offer good examples of the overlap that Chalaby points out. This type of journalism is more inclined to comment and evaluation, to interpretation and judgement, and pays more attention to "literary" writing than to the simple and terse telling of the facts that constitutes the essential prerogative of journalism in the modern sense of the term.

In Chalaby's opinion, the origin of the latter trend was different from the French one and was born in those countries where the mix of literature and journalism was less evident, the best examples being Great Britain and the United States. In these countries such practices and structures developed, first of all press agencies and war correspondents, that characterize and constitute the real innovative professional nucleus of modern journalism. Indeed, the task of a war correspondent and a wire-services journalist was to report facts in a terse and essential way. And thus, states Chalaby, "fact-centred discursive practices" were invented; these were discursive practices centred on facts that constitute one of the main features of the dominant professional ideology of modern journalism.

"The literary approach" obstructed and slowed down these discursive practices in France and in other European countries as well. In fact, the literary approach led to comment and interpretation, to a type of writing that strives for beauty and is often pompous in form. Only later would the typical practices of the Anglo-Saxon model spread also in France where a long and hard political struggle (the long-lasting clash between modernism and conservatism, identifiable in the bitter and lengthy French Revolution, and the subsequent events) had accentuated the necessarily polemic and interventionist character of French journalism, distancing it even further from scrupulousness, attention to and conformity with the facts to be told (fact-centred) and from the ideal trend towards objectivity and neutrality that characterizes today's dominant model of journalism. The length of the political clashes, and often their ferocity, led to and facilitated phenomena that were described so well in *Bel-Ami* and *Illusions perdues*. They retarded the birth and development of the real press market and, therefore, those professional practices that today constitute the backbone of modern journalism.

Jürgen Habermas himself emphasizes the importance of the literary gazettes in European journalism (1989). Their birth prefigured a new society, "saloon society", in which aristocrats and members of the new bourgeoisie, who were interested in the arts and sciences, met and discussed the new cultural trends and fashions that accompanied the rise of the new economic order. In these salons, printed sheets that contained extracts from the latest books were circulated and discussed; they were commented on and evaluated just as the latest operas and the performances of the singers were reviewed. Thanks to these sheets, the literature of other countries was discovered and progress and innovations were duly discussed.

The new "public literary sphere" soon resulted in a "public political sphere" in which news and discussions about books and opera widened to include facts regarding the community, its organization and its relations with other communities, in other words, with politics (Habermas, 1989). Thus, the first political sheets, mentioned above, were born and the discussions they promoted within the meeting places of the rising middle class progressively gave body to a new political philosophy that combined both artistic/literary themes and political ones. Following Habermas, the London magazines *The Spectator*, *The Tatler* and *The Craftsman* were among the main actors in this new public sphere.

According to Habermas, with this widening of perspective from literature to politics, the new rising middle class began to explicitly confront the theme of a new political order of society that was more congruent with its needs that were essentially linked with the free circulation of goods and, therefore, the abandon-ment of the constraints that were imposed by an economic system based on the exploitation of the land, which was identifiable with interests within the power system of the absolute monarchies.

For a variety of reasons (slow development of a mass-circulation press, long-lasting political clashes and their radicalization, as well as the late arrival of literacy, at least in some countries, among the less prosperous classes), the effects of the literary origins of journalism have been felt in many European countries until today. Returning to French journalism, and explicitly confirming the hypotheses formulated by Chalaby, Erik Neveu speaks of "tropisme literaire" and of a "tropisme politique" that characterize the history and the recent evolution of journalism in France (2001). "The journalist's job is literary and consists of polemical talent and pyrotechnical rhetoric (Neveu, 2001, p. 14).

In like manner, Asor Rosa speaks of two main trends in the history of Italian journalism: the literary trend and the political one that also consolidate the important role that the clergy plays in Italian culture (Asor Rosa, 1981). The situation has not been very different in other countries. Indeed, Greek newspa-pers were written in a literary language that was quite different from the popular language (Demotike) used in everyday life (Zaharopoulos and Paraschos, 1993).

Literary and political origins merged together because of their inner constituents. First of all, both presuppose that journalism is aimed at an elite public, one having a high level of education and already knowledgeable of the political and social debates. Both imply, as Chalaby rightly observed, discursive practices that are mainly centred on argumentation and oriented towards supporting a point of view regarding a sphere of political matters or that of comment and evaluation on an artistic or literary work. In both cases, dealing with events or situations in purely descriptive terms is considered to be beneath the level of the journalist's task and aspirations. Such writing is considered to be part of a makeshift job.

What we want to emphasize here is that in many European countries, in spite of important differences and the progressive changes that have taken place over time, the effects of the literary origin, like the political one, are still felt today, determining a model of journalism that has a preference for comment, interpretation and evaluation of events and situations. In some cases, such as in German journalism, interpretation and description of events are considered to be separate, although the factual telling of events very often assumes a clear point of view since the political position of the newspaper is very evident in most cases. In many other cases, such as in Italian journalism, but also in Greek and Spanish journalism, the description of the events and their interpretation and evaluation overlap in the same article to such a degree that it is hard to make clear distinctions between them.

The effects of the literary origin of European journalism are felt both when there is a distinction between tabloid and elite newspapers, typical of many European countries, and even when such a distinction is lacking. When both types of newspapers exist, the literary origin influences exclusively the elite ones, determining, along with other factors, their content, structure and way of writing. In such a situation, literary ascendancy is almost completely absent in the tabloids.

However, when such a distinction is lacking, the literary origin is still important. Indeed, in most cases the dominant newspaper model tends to combine the characteristics of the two types of journalism and is almost always still influenced by its distant literary origins and by the tendency to be a model with strong intellectual aspirations. The Italian case is exemplary of this trend: the so-called "omnibus" (addressed to everyone) newspapers (a typology in which today all of the most circulated newspapers can be included), that combine the characteristics of the elite and popular newspapers, even if in an extremely sophisticated form, remain true to their literary origin by offering cultural themes in a writing style that addresses a public with a high level of education. Edmondo Berselli, a well-known Italian journalist, describes the journalistic model of *La Repubblica*, the second biggest-selling newspaper in Italy, in the following way: "an extraordinary mixture of intellectual aristocracy and amusement" which becomes an intellectual way of "giving body to that pedagogic wish that many have criticized in Scalfari's [editor and founder of the daily] newspaper. It wants to be a sort of national conscience which dictates opinions rather than suggests confrontations and discussions" (1999, p. 55).

Let us look more precisely at what the elements are of the literary origins of a considerable part of European journalism that still persist today. The origin and the present literary dimension of journalism imply a substantially elite circulation. The newspaper is written for and addresses a public which is certainly vast but, in any case, is mainly identified with a specific social class that usually has a high level of education and is already familiar with political life.

Second, the literary dimension of journalism is obvious in the choice of subjects and in the selection of news. The choice of a medium-high level readership, at least regarding cultural level and involvement in public affairs, obviously forces journalists to privilege themes that are congenial to it. In general this means limited attention, although it is certainly present, to themes regarding everyday life and strong attention to politics, culture and new and emerging fashions that may interest a class characterized by a high level of education.

Undoubtedly the literary origin of journalism is most felt in the modality of the journalistic discourse. The language used is often rather elaborate, polished and the vocabulary very affected. What counts most, as has been stated more than once, is that comment, interpretation and the evaluation of what has taken place are privileged rather than a simple description of the events. This is due to several reasons. Very often the reader or the television viewer, being a person with a high level of mass-media consumption, already knows what has happened. For this reason he looks for thorough investigation, help and further stimuli and ideas to decode and correctly interpret the facts. At the same time, the journalist himself feels greater gratification by suggesting interpretations and evaluations rather than simply describing what he sees like a passive observer.

In fact, the main aspiration of this type of journalist (fourth characterization) is to be part of the intellectual world and, therefore, to go beyond the work of a simple reporter. According to Chalaby's hypotheses, journalism is considered to be a by-product of literature and is chosen as a makeshift solution by those who have much higher aspirations (Chalaby, 1996). As said, there is continuous overlapping of the figure of the journalist and that of the writer/intellectual. It is not by chance that a high percentage of successful European journalists were and are journalists and writers, or more generally, intellectuals at the same time. And it is not by chance that training in journalism in a considerable number of European countries began rather late compared with the United States and Great Britain (Frohlich and Holtz Bacha, 2003). Above all, it began late in those countries, especially Mediterranean ones, where journalism overlapped the most with other professions, literary or political, and, therefore, did not entail a real and distinct ethical and professional statute.

The role of the state

The role that the state plays in relation to the mass-media system in general and to journalism in particular is another important feature that characterizes European professional models. The importance of the state's role in the mass-media system can be traced back, in a particular way, to the philosophy of the welfare state which is supposed to act to remove any obstacles that might impede greater equality for its citizens and the assurance that they have the best conditions of life. Among the many definitions of the welfare state, the one proposed by Briggs (1961) seems particularly pertinent to our discussion. According to this author, the tasks of the social state can be summarized as follows: (1) modify the goods market; (2) ensure the highest level of solidarity; (3) offer services that are independent of social classes.

Out of this set of objectives come all the interventions regarding the citizens' material life: health, assistance, transport, and also those regarding culture, education, and so on. In order to pursue these objectives, the state also intervenes in the field of mass communication to make it possible for all citizens to get the same level of knowledge, with both equal access to the same sources of news and the same opportunities of expression.

It is well known that the idea of the welfare state marks a major difference between US and European notions of democracy. Indeed, the social state is a typically European notion, more precisely Northern European, while it is much weaker, if not completely absent, in the United States, although it has sometimes been found in certain periods of history. In spite of this, it is exactly at the level of state intervention in the mass media, as we shall see better later, that important differences exist among European countries, just as macroscopic differences exist between the United States and Great Britain in this regard.

According to Gustafsson (1980), the social state can be active in the field of mass communications as owner, funder and regulator. The diffusion of public-service broadcasting in almost all European countries is an exemplary demonstration of the role of the state as owner. European governments were pushed towards the idea of public broadcasting for a variety of reasons. Since both the post and telegraph were under state control, radio, and later television, followed the same road. The second reason concerns national security: it was considered important not to leave control of instruments of communication that were so important to the state's security in the hands of private individuals (Briggs, 1985; Hearst, 1992). But what may have counted most was the philosophy of the welfare state. Instituting a public-service broadcasting was a means of preventing such persuasive and powerful instruments as radio and television from falling under the control of a few economic groups that were interested exclusively either in economic profit or in conquering consensus for private ends. As representing the interests of all citizens, the state could ensure, at least according to the intentions of its promoters, the correct management of the new means of communication, one that respected the needs and rights of all the citizens.

While typical in European countries, the idea of public-service broadcasting brings to light a macroscopic difference within what we have defined as the Anglo-American model. Indeed, historically, the ideal prototype of public-service broadcasting has been identified in the BBC in Britain, whereas in the United States, the other key country of the Anglo-American model, the rule in force is absolute separation between political institutions and the mass media and, therefore, the preclusion of any intervention of the state in the field of broadcasting. The absence of public-service broadcasting in the United States is part of that preclusion, while the exception of PBS with its restricted audience is a confirmation of this attitude.

The British example was subsequently followed by almost all the European countries where, up to the beginning of the 1980s, a system of public broadcasting monopoly dominated in which broadcast journalism was assumed to be oriented towards the values of universalism, objectivity as well as the defence of national values (Blumler, 1992). Although in practice this set of ideal objectives changed in many countries (as seen particularly in countries of the Mediterranean area, including France) into a passive submission of public television to the political system, there is no doubt that in others (above all the Scandinavian countries) such ideals helped to diffuse, also outside broadcasting, the idea of news as a public-interest service oriented towards values of social responsibility (McQuail, 1992). This ideal obviously influenced the profession and its procedures.

In any case, also in the same countries in which the idea of public-service broadcasting became exploited and subaltern to government institutions, the always heated and often very violent discussion around the supposed ideals of the public-service broadcasting and its response to the needs of public interests served to diffuse and widen the debate around the themes of mass communication and news media in particular. Despite what was stated above, rarely did a real practice inspired by needs of universalism and objectivity follow. Anyway, this often heated discussion, which involved many groups and individuals, pushed the various political and social actors towards continuous reciprocal controls which were applied also to the profession, both in the sense of limitations on the journalists' areas of autonomy, which were often subjected to the needs and control of external forces, and also in the sense of an ever clearer consciousness of the social responsibility of the profession.

The second way through which the welfare state is able to intervene in the field of mass media is by funding. Basically this term means economic subsidies to the press. It is well known that this practice began in Scandinavian countries and was subsequently adopted in many other countries, including those in Mediterranean Europe. The practice of press subsidies has always had alternating cycles of great development and successive re-dimensioning. The reason can be stated briefly. Mainly in the sphere of the liberal economy, and also in the political perspective that pertains to it, press subsidies were seen as interventions to shape the way the press market functioned and, therefore, they were opposed. Undoubtedly the main objective of press subsidies was to support newspapers in economic difficulty in that they were the expression of different political, religious, ethnic or linguistic minority groups, and this is the reason that justified the subsidies. It is not by chance that Sweden, and other Scandinavian countries, directed economic subsidies to sustain the "second newspaper in town"; the purpose of this policy was to safeguard political and ideological pluralism by keeping alive the newspapers with the weakest circulation (Gustafsson, 1980). Conservative governments have generally opposed the practice of economic subsidies in that, in their view, it is a distorting element of the market; in any case, today such practices have been reduced also due to the more general process of secularization of society and, contemporaneously, to the commercialization of the mass-media system.

Despite the present reduction in subsidies, the press subsidies system influenced the way of practising journalism; above all it helped reinforce the idea that it is a profession that is not so much oriented towards producing revenue (even if it was and remains important) but rather mainly one that diffuses ideas and points of view. Consequently, the press subsidies system limited the process of commercialization of the press and often limited the exhaustive search for sensationalism, accentuating instead the relationship of the press with particular groups of society and its accountability to them. In other words, it accentuated several characteristics that are typical of European journalism: partisanship, links with social and political groups, attention to comment and interpretation.

The intervention of the state as regulator, typical in a considerable number of European countries, is mainly carried out by the production of legislation regarding mass communication and journalism in particular. It is very evident that this is in complete opposition to the American situation where the First Amendment makes it impossible for Congress to intervene in the field of mass communications. Also in this regard, the British situation differs from the American one, although to a lesser degree than that discussed in the previous points. The regulatory intervention of the state essentially concerns laws that impose the right to reply and the conditions of the election campaign; in this regard precise norms of behaviour exist for television and, in some cases, for the print press. More generally, one can say that intervention by the state as regulator tends to reinforce the concept that information is a "public service" with precise responsibilities entrusted to the journalists, regarding the entire society and, in a particular way, regarding the political system.

Conclusion

As to what has been said so far, it would be difficult to state that a precise differentiation exists between the European model and the Anglo-American model of journalism. Indeed, significant differences emerge that reveal the possibility of different typological aggregations. As a matter of fact, although British journalism is clearly included in what is commonly defined as the "Anglo-American model", it seems that a precise demarcation exists between American journalism and European journalism, British journalism being included in the latter. A rather high level of political partisanship and the presence of a strong and distinguishing public-service broadcasting make the British professional model different from the American one.

In spite of this, the two types of journalism, the American one and the British one, share common features: the existence of "fact-centred practices" is certainly a common characteristic of the two journalisms and, in turn, it differentiates them from many other journalistic practices in Europe.

At the same time, differences exist between the models of journalism of the old continent. Those regarding the level and the quality of state intervention are especially important; in many countries, such intervention is very diffused and strong while in others it is all but absent. This difference can be found essentially in the economic subsidies to the press. Equally important are the differences in the type and in the orientation of the partisanship of the mass media. In the countries of Mediterranean Europe, although with some differences, an instrumental use of partisanship tends to prevail that often becomes an instrument of negotiation if not out and out symbolic blackmail, while it is an occasion and instrument of animation of the public sphere in the countries of Central and Northern Europe. This set of differences within European countries is so great that it seems possible to make a more precise distinction between a Northern European model and a Mediterranean one.

Important differences not only exist within the two hypothesized models, the Anglo-American and the European ones, but also within single countries. The journalism of the broadsheets is substantially different from that of the tabloids just as television journalism is very often quite different from that of the print press.

The comparison between the Anglo-American and the European model points out several ambiguities: there are certainly important differences between the two models. However, it is also possible to find important differences within each model. Therefore, is this comparison useless or over-ambitious? Certainly not, at least for a couple of reasons; first of all, because a comparative analysis, also in the field of mass communication, always allows us to bring to light aspects and functions that would be otherwise difficult to identify. It allows the researcher that distancing from his own socio-cultural context that often leads to important results (Blumler *et al.*, 1992). By comparing the model of journalism practised in European countries with the Anglo-American one, some of its important characteristics can be seen that would be otherwise difficult to reveal: the role of the state, the importance of political aggregations, the strong intellectual characterization of journalism, and so on.

Despite what has been stated up to now, the differences between the Anglo-American model and the European one seem more important than their similarities and the common factors that they share. Also they seem more important than the differences that exist within each model. Indeed, European countries seem to share elements of a common history and a common political culture that influence their professional journalism and determine its structure and operative procedure.

Returning to the initial question of whether or not a European model of journalism exists, it seems possible to state that the factors that are common to the journalism practised in the different countries of the old continent are more numerous, or at least more important, than the differences. On the other hand, Great Britain and the United States are linked by common cultural and historical roots that seem to count as much as, if not more than, their differences.

Our discussion has demonstrated that, in spite of all the limitations, constructing typologies has a significant and important cognitive value and constitutes a valid instrument to organize similarities and differences. At the same time, this chapter is intended to show that putting under the same umbrella different cases and realities is always an operation that tends to sacrifice the complexity of the phenomena observed. Thus, the attempt to define different professional models in journalism, though useful, risks not taking into account the plurality of factors that determine the way this profession behaves.

Notes

1 Pillarization means the division of society into pillars built on religious and political foundations. The pillars (Catholic, Protestant and Socialist) possess their own schools, recreation centres, cultural organizations and means of communication.

2 The first professional organization was born in Norway in 1883; in Holland the first to appear was in 1894; and in Germany a year later. In Sweden a Publicists' Club, uniting journalists and publishers, was founded in 1874.

References

Asor Rosa, Alberto (1981) "Il giornalista: appunti sulla fisiologia di un mestiere difficile", in *Storia d'Italia*, Torino: Einaudi.

Bechelloni, Giovanni (ed.) (1982) *Il mestiere di giornalista*, Napoli: Liguori.

Berselli, Edmondo (1999) "Un giornale tra due fuochi: Ortodossi in politica, eccentrici altrove?", in *Problemi dell'informazione*, Anno XXIV, no. 1, pp. 54–61.

Blumler, Jay (ed.) (1992) *Television and the Public Interest*, London: Sage.

Blumler, Jay, McLeod, Jack and Rosengren, Karl Erik (1992) *Comparatively Speaking: Communication and Culture Across Space and Time*, London: Sage.

Brants, Kees and McQuail, Denis (1992) "The Netherlands", in Euromedia Research Group (ed.) *The Media in Western Europe*, London: Sage.

Briggs, Asa (1961) "The Welfare State in Historical Perspective", *European Journal of Sociology*, II.

Briggs, Asa (1985) *The BBC: The First Fifty Years*, Oxford: Oxford University Press.

Chalaby, Jean (1996) "Journalism as an Anglo-American Invention", *European Journal of Communication*, 11, 3: 303–326.

Curran, James and Seaton, Jean (1991) *Power without Responsibility: The Press and Broadcasting in Britain*, London: Routledge.

Frohlic, Romy and Holtz Bacha, Christina (2003) *Journalism Education in Europe and North America*, Creskill, NJ: Hampton Press.

Gorman, Lyn and McLean, David (2001) *Media and Society in the Twentieth Century*, Oxford: Blackwell.

Gustafsson, Erik (1980) "The Press Subsidies of Sweden: a Decade of Experiment", in Smith, A. (ed.) *Newspapers and Democracy: International Essays on a Changing Medium*, Cambridge, MA: MIT Press.

Habermas, Jürgen (1989) *The Structural Transformations of the Public Sphere*, Cambridge, MA: MIT Press.

Hadenius, Stig and Weibull, Lennart (1999) "The Swedish Newspaper System in the Late 1990s", *Nordicom Review*, 20, 1: 129–152.

Hallin, Daniel and Papathanassopoulos, Stylianos (2002) "Political Clientelism and the Media: Southern Europe and Latin America in Comparative Perspective", *Media Culture and Society*, 24, 2: 175–195.

Hearst, Stephen (1992) "Broadcasting Regulation in Britain", in Blumler, J. (ed.) *Television and the Public Interest*, London: Sage.

Humphreys, Peter (1990) *Media and Media Policy in Germany*, Oxford: Berg.

Humphreys, Peter (1996) *Mass Media and Media Policy in Western Europe*, Manchester: Manchester University Press.

McQuail, Denis (1992) *Media Performance: Mass Communication and the Public Interest*, London: Sage.

Mancini, Paolo (2000) "Political Complexity and Alternative Models of Journalism: the Italian Case", in Curran, J. and Park, M. (eds) *De-Westernizing Media Studies*, London: Routledge.

Murialdi, Paolo (1986) *Storia del giornalismo italiano*, Torino: Gutenberg.

Neveu, Erik (2001) *Sociologie du journalisme*, Paris: Editions La Découverte.

Nieuwenhuis, A. J. (1992) "Media Policy in the Netherlands: Beyond the Market", *European Journal of Communication*, 7, 2: 195–218.

Schudson, Michael (1978) *Discovering the News*, New York: Basic Books.

Siebert, Fredrick, Peterson, Theodore and Schramm, Wilbur (1956) *Four Theories of the Press*, Urbana, IL, and Chicago: University of Illinois Press.

Weber, Max (1947) "Politics as a Vocation", in Gerth, H. and Wright Mills, C. (eds) *From Max Weber: Essays in Sociology*, New York: Oxford University Press.

Zaharopoulos, Thimios and Paraschos, Many (1993) *Mass Media in Greece: Power, Politics and Privatization*, Westport, CT: Praeger.

5

THE US MODEL OF JOURNALISM: EXCEPTION OR EXEMPLAR?

Michael Schudson

American journalism began, like American politics, as a version of British institutions. American printers in the eighteenth century imported their presses, type, and ink from Britain, and borrowed most of their news directly from London papers. For the first half century of American newspapers, readers could find little local news; the American colonies were an outpost of a British world, and the papers demonstrated closer connections to London than to neighboring colonies or even to their own sites of publication.

There is still much that links the British and American models of the press, but there is also much that separates them: the relative importance of news in the capital and in provincial regions; the degree of connection between press and party; a more clearly bifurcated "quality press" and "popular press" distinction in Britain than in the United States; the presence (in Britain) and absence (in America) of a strong tradition of public-service broadcasting; and the greater legal protection American journalism receives than British journalism, thanks to jealously guarded First Amendment privileges.

What follows is an account of how distinctive features of American journalism emerged, particularly professionalization under the banner of objectivity, staunch adherence to the freedoms provided by the First Amendment, and "boosterism," the inclination of newspapers as business establishments to sing the praises, overlook the faults, and promote the economic growth of their home towns. I will reflect on some of the positive and negative consequences of these features for sustaining democratic society, and will consider whether the unique features of the American system of news make it useful or ill-suited as a model for journalism elsewhere around the globe.

Boosterism and the American press

Journalism is not one of the venerable professions. Certainly it was not well established when Benjamin Franklin's older brother James began printing the second newspaper in Britain's American colonies in 1720. James Franklin's friends tried to dissuade him, saying they thought the paper not likely to succeed, "one newspaper being in their judgment enough for America" (Franklin 1961: 32). But James, like so many American entrepreneurs who followed him, plunged ahead nonetheless, driven not by shrewd calculation of "what America needs" but by what personal ambition and ego recommended and what local opportunities seemed to beckon.

Commercial motives propelled American journalism from its beginnings. Still, in the decade before the American Revolution, newspapers became increasingly politicized, and in the first generations of the new nation, political factions and parties came to subsidize or sponsor many leading newspapers. Newspaper editors might preach independence but they generally came to practice partisanship. This included editors like the celebrated Horace Greeley. Greeley began his career on a country weekly in the 1830s but moved to New York to run a literary magazine in 1834. In 1840 he ran the Whig campaign paper, the *Log Cabin*, with a circulation of up to 80,000 for its brief life, and in 1841 began his own commercial paper, the *New York Tribune*. The *Tribune* was among the first of a new breed of cheap, commercially-minded "penny papers" that began to appear in leading cities in the 1830s. This paper, with a circulation of some 10,000 at first, was strongly anti-slavery and clearly showed itself a journal of ideas, reporting on women's rights, socialist experiments, and other topics. Not an advocate of women's rights himself, Greeley nonetheless hired Margaret Fuller in 1844 as the first woman to be a regular staff employee on a major American newspaper. Karl Marx was a European correspondent.

No other newspaper in the country was so cosmopolitan. Few newspapers even dispatched a reporter to the nation's capital. Editors would themselves occasionally visit to do some first-hand commentary but only as politics heated up in the 1850s did newspapers begin to hire Washington reporters, most of whom wrote for half a dozen or more papers and supplemented their salaries with work as clerks for congressional committees or speechwriters for politicians (Ritchie 1991: 4). The occupational world of journalism and politics were not differentiated.

In fact, the metropolitan press at mid-century was practically a subdivision of the political party. Newspapers were fundamental rallying points for political parties. Editors were intimately involved in political patronage. President Andrew Jackson appointed more than fifty journalists to office; as many as 10 percent of the appointments he made requiring Senate approval were journalists (Smith 1977: 90). A generation later Abraham Lincoln followed suit. He rewarded the editor of the Philadelphia *North American*, a pro-Lincoln paper, with federal appointments or Army promotions to four of his sons, not to mention substantial federal advertising directed to his paper. Lincoln appointed editors as ministers, first secretaries of missions, or consuls in fifteen foreign capitals and appointed others to customs house or postmasterships in New Haven, Albany, Harrisburg, Wheeling, Puget Sound, Chicago, Cleveland, St. Louis, and Des Moines (Carman and Luthin 1964: 70–74, 121–128). Newspaper work was not an independent calling so much as one path within the political world of the mid-nineteenth century.

This partisan press was the press that Alexis de Tocqueville judged both vulgar and irreplaceable for American democracy. He wrote that newspapers were a necessity in a democratic society: "We should underrate their importance if we thought they just guaranteed liberty; they maintain civilization" (1969: 517). But de Tocqueville also wrote: "I admit that I do not feel toward freedom of the press that complete and instantaneous love which one accords to things by their nature supremely good. I love it more from considering the evils it prevents than on account of the good it does" (ibid.: 180). De Tocqueville complained of the violence and vulgarity of American journalists. He noted that the greater the number of newspapers and the more they were dispersed around the country rather than concentrated in a capital city, the less influence journalism had. For de Tocqueville, a great virtue of the American press was that its distribution across a vast territory made it weak.

De Tocqueville was impressed by the quantity of American newspapers, as were other European visitors, but he did not understood why there were so many papers scattered across small communities and frontier towns. He took the cause to be the multiple number of responsible governmental units in America. If citizens elected only members of Congress, de Tocqueville suggested, there would not be a need for so many newspapers because there would be so few occasions on which people had to act together politically. The multiplication of governmental units in each state and village "compelled" Americans to cooperate with one another and each one "needs a newspaper to tell him what the others are doing" (ibid.:1969: 519).

In fact, local newspapers in de Tocqueville's America told readers very little about what others in their own communities were up to. Most of the papers printed little local news (Russo 1980: 2). In the 1820s, when an improved mail service brought urban papers more expeditiously to country towns, the country newspapers finally began to run local news in an effort to retain readers with a service the urban papers could not provide (Kielbowicz 1989: 63). In Kingston, New York, where village government was admittedly a modest affair, the press did not mention local elections in the early 1800s and did not cover village government at all until 1845 (Blumin 1976: 126–149).

The multiplication of governmental units that caught de Tocqueville's eye did afford one thing that helped support the press—government subsidy. Getting government printing contracts was a great boon to the newspaper. Demand of a democratic audience for news had less to do with the proliferation of newspapers than supply of government advertising.

Also important in explaining the large numbers of provincial newspapers was a large supply of would-be editors. Entrepreneurs began newspapers in hundreds of small towns in America not because a population demanded them but because the existence of the paper might attract a population. Country crossroads towns established newspapers, small colleges, and grand hotels all on the prospect of future growth (Boorstin 1965: 141). Editors turned their efforts to "boosting" the economic life of their communities. The antislavery leaders who founded the town of Emporia, Kansas, in 1857, for instance, began the *Emporia News* within a few months to help create an image of a prosperous community. Nearly all copies of the inaugural issues were mailed east, hoping to attract emigrants to buy town lots and make the fledgling town live up to its public-relations efforts (Griffith 1989: 14). Like the effort to attract the railroads or to win designation as a county seat or site for a state college, the establishment of a newspaper was a tool of real-estate development. The character of American newspapers has had something to do with their being advertising-supported media, particularly from the 1830s on, but perhaps owes even more to their being through and through a promotional tool of community and urban development.

The revolt against party in US political culture

Americans today seem to believe that journalists are, or should be, a transmission belt of neutral facts about world events. Their passion should be dispassion. To a remarkable degree, it is. American journalists take pride not for writing pieces of advocacy but for being attacked by both left and right for "writing down the middle" (Broder 1973: 235). Playing it down the middle became a cherished professional ideal in the United States—and elsewhere, too, but not so thoroughly nor so long ago as in the US. How did this distinctive brand of American professionalism emerge out of the nineteenth-century partisan press?

What happened was a remarkable transformation of American political culture in the late nineteenth century. In the Progressive era, reformers cleansed voting of what made it corrupt, in their eyes, and compelling, in the eyes of voters. In this Protestant Reformation of American voting, the political party's ability to reward its faithful declined with civil-service reform; its ability to punish voters with social disapproval and reward them with coin and drink faded as the privacy of the voting booth grew secure. Even the party's capacity to attract attention declined as commercial forms of popular entertainment begin to offer serious competition. During the era from 1880 to 1920, liberal reformers began to criticize party loyalty. They promoted new forms of electoral campaigning, urging an "educational" campaign with more pamphlets and fewer parades. At the same time, newspapers became more willing to take an independent stance. By 1890, a quarter of daily newspapers in Northern states, where the reform movement was most advanced, claimed independence of party. It became common and even respectable for party papers to "bolt" from party-endorsed candidates.

By 1896, a reform known as the Australian ballot had swept the country, changing forever the way Americans went to the polls. Until the 1890s, American election days were organized to the last detail by the competing political parties. The parties printed their own tickets and distributed them to voters near the polls. The voter then did not need to mark the ballot in any way—the voter did not need, in fact, to be literate. The voter just took the ticket from the party worker and deposited it in the ballot box.

The Australian ballot symbolized a different understanding of politics. Now the state prepared a ballot that listed candidates from all contending parties. The voter received the ballot from an election clerk and, in the privacy of the voting booth, marked the ballot, choosing the candidates from one or several parties as he wished. An increasingly strident rhetoric prevailed, condemning the corruption of parties and praising forms of governing that transcended party politics.

Voting, in this new context, was transformed. What had been an act of affiliation became an act of individual autonomy. Where it had been standard practice for parties to convey people to the polls, it was now forbidden in many states. Where party workers had distributed tickets, voters now stood in line to receive their official ballot from state-appointed officials. Where parties had mustered armies of paid election-day workers, many states now outlawed the practice. Where electioneering efforts accompanied voters right up to the ballot box, new regulations created a moat of silence within so many feet of the polling station.

With the adoption of the Australian ballot, civil-service reform, corrupt practices acts, voter registration laws, the initiative and referendum, the popular primary, the direct election of senators, and non-partisan municipal elections, politics began to be seen as an administrative science that required experts. Voting came to be seen as an activity in which voters make choices among programs and candidates, not one in which they loyally turn out in ritual solidarity to their party. This new understanding of politics helped transform a fiercely partisan press into an institution differentiated from the parties, with journalists more likely to see themselves as writers rather than as political hangers-on (McGerr 1986; Schudson 1998: 144–187). Turn-of-the-century American reformers succeeded in a more thorough-going set of anti-party reforms than in any other democracy.

This transformation of American political culture was accompanied by an ardent professionalization of journalism. Partisanship endured, but reporters came increasingly to enjoy a culture of their own independent of political parties. They developed their own mythologies (reveling in their intimacy with the urban underworld), their own clubs and watering holes, and their own professional practices. Interviewing, for instance, had become a common activity for reporters in the late nineteenth century. Earlier, reporters talked with public officials but did not refer to these conversations in print. Politicians and diplomats dropped by the newspaper offices but could feel secure, as one reporter recalled, that their confidences "were regarded as inviolate." President Lincoln often spoke with reporters informally but no reporter ever quoted him directly. Not until the 1880s was the interview a well-accepted and institutionalized "media event," an occasion created by journalists from which they could then craft a story. This new style of journalistic intervention did not erase partisanship but it did presage reporters' new dedication to a sense of craft, and new location in an occupational culture with its own rules, its own rewards, and its own *esprit* (Schudson 1995: 72–93).

Interviewing was a practice oriented more to pleasing an audience of news consumers than to parroting a party line. Professionalization and commercialization marched forward hand in hand. Newspapers had become big businesses by the 1880s, with towering downtown buildings, scores of reporters, splashy sponsorship of civic festivals, and pages of advertising from the newly burgeoning department stores. The papers vastly expanded their readership in this growing marketplace; more and more papers counted their circulation in the hundreds of thousands. Accordingly, reporters writing news came to focus on making stories, not on promoting parties. Newspaper circulation leapt forward while the cost of production plummeted with wood pulp as a new source of paper and mechanical typesetting a new labor-saving device. Advertising revenue surpassed subscription fees as the primary source of income as the papers courted new audiences (particularly women). The increasingly commercial orientation of the newspaper certainly helped sustain the innovation of interviewing.

Only after World War I did European reporters adopt the American practice of interviewing—and never so fully as in the United States. In Britain, journalists began to accept the interview after 1900, often through American tutelage. American correspondents, by their example, taught Europeans that their own elites would submit to interviews. The diffusion of interviewing among American journalists seems to have been unaccompanied by any ideological rationale. It fit effortlessly into a journalism already fact-centered and news-centered rather than devoted primarily to political commentary or preoccupied with literary aspirations. It was one of the growing number of practices that identified journalists as a distinct occupational group with distinct patterns of behavior. The growing corporate coherence of that occupational group, generating a demand both for social cohesion and occupational pride, on the one hand, and internal social control, on the other, would by the 1920s eventuate in a self-conscious ethic of objectivity.

The notion that the move from partisanship to objectivity was economically motivated is widely believed. The leading textbook in the history of American journalism puts it this way: "Offering the appearance of fairness was important to owners and editors trying to gain their share of a growing readership and the resulting advertising revenues" (Emery *et al.* 1996: 181). But was it? Readership was growing so rapidly in the late nineteenth century—from 3.5 million daily newspaper readers in 1880 to 33 million in 1920—that a great variety of journalistic styles were economically rewarding. Very likely the most lucrative option remained strident partisanship. Certainly this characterized circulation leaders of the day like William Randolph Hearst's *New York Journal* and Joseph Pulitzer's *New York World*, both enthusiastic supporters of the Democratic Party. Heated political campaigns and the newspapers' ardent participation in them were circulation-builders, not circulation-losers (King 1992: 396–398, 467–468).

The devotion of American journalists to fairness or objectivity could not have emerged before journalists as an occupational group developed loyalties more to their audiences and to themselves as an occupational community than to their publishers or their publishers' favored political parties. At this point journalists also came to articulate rules of the journalistic road more often and more consistently. Rules of objectivity enabled editors to keep lowly reporters in check, although they had less control over high-flying foreign correspondents. Objectivity as ideology was a kind of industrial discipline. At the same time, objectivity seemed a natural and progressive ideology for an aspiring occupational group at a moment when science was god, efficiency was cherished, and elites increasingly judged partisanship a vestige of the tribal nineteenth century (Schudson 2001).

Journalists not only sought to affiliate with the prestige of science, efficiency, and Progressive reform but they sought to disaffiliate from the public-relations specialists and propagandists who were suddenly all around them. Journalists had rejected parties only to find their new-found independence besieged by a squadron of information mercenaries available for hire by government, business, politicians, and others. A new "profession" of public relations emerged and got a great boost from President Woodrow Wilson's attempt in World War I to use public relations to sell the war to the American public. The war stimulated popular public-relations campaigns for war bonds, the Red Cross, the Salvation Army, and the YMCA. By 1920, journalists and journalism critics were complaining that there were a thousand propaganda bureaus in Washington modeled on the war experience (Schudson 1978: 143). Figures circulated among journalists that 50 percent or 60 percent of stories even in the *New York Times* were inspired by press agents. The publicity agent, philosopher John Dewey wrote, "is perhaps the most significant symbol of our present social life" (1930: 44).

Anxious about the manipulability of information in the propaganda age, journalists felt a need to close ranks and assert their collective integrity. By the 1920s, this meant increasingly a scrupulous adherence to scientific ideals. "There is but one kind of unity possible in a world as diverse as ours," Walter Lippmann wrote. "It is unity of method, rather than of aim; the unity of the disciplined experiment." He wanted to upgrade the professional dignity of journalists and provide a training for them "in which the ideal of objective testimony is cardinal" (Lippmann 1920: 67, 82). More than a set of craft rules to fend off libel suits or a set of constraints to help editors keep tabs on their underlings, objectivity was finally a moral code.

Some of the sociological conditions that produced these journalistic norms in America were absent or less pronounced in Europe. The desire of journalists to distinguish themselves from public-relations practitioners was absent in Europe because public relations developed later and less extensively in Europe. The growing anti-partisan nature of American political culture intensified in the Progressive years and went much further than efforts to contain party corruption in Europe. In America, a civil-service tradition had to be invented and emerged as the result of a political movement; in Europe, a degree of bureaucratic autonomy, legitimacy, and professionalism could be taken for granted, so there was less reason for European civil servants to ideologize themselves the way American reformers did. The ideological virtues of a journalistic divorce from party, so readily portrayed in America against this reform background, had no comparable political ballast in European journalism.

It may also be that the cultural space that could be occupied by objectivity as a professional value in American journalism was already occupied in European journalism. Continental European journalists already understood themselves in a publicly successful way—as high literary creators and cosmopolitan political thinkers. They did not have the down-and-dirty sense of themselves as laborers whose standing in the world required upgrading as American—and British— journalists did. If there was to be upgrading, in any event, it was to a literary rather than professional ideal.

This is much too global a generalization about the many different European journalisms, but there is a good case that it applies very well at least to the French experience. Jean Chalaby has argued that British and American jour- nalism experienced a 'unique discursive revolution" and became information and fact-centered in the mid-nineteenth century, but French journalism did not. Until late in the century, when leading British and American newspapers employed numerous foreign correspondents, the French press drew most of its foreign news straight from the London papers. The French were much less concerned than the British and Americans to draw a line between facts and commentary in the news. French journalism was dominated by literary figures and literary aspirations and did not participate in the fact-centered discursive revolution that characterized British and American journalism (Chalaby 1998).

The moral norm American journalists live by in their professional lives, that they use as a means of social control and social identity, and that they accept as the most legitimate grounds for attributing praise and blame, is a norm that took root first, and most deeply, in this journalism and not in others across the Atlantic.

The professionalization of American journalism reached a high point in the 1950s and 1960s, what media scholar Daniel Hallin has called its era of "high modernism" (Hallin 1994: 170–180). In the 1960s and after, criticism emerged inside and outside journalism condemning journalistic professionalism and the norm of objectivity itself as a means of catering to established power, particu- larly governmental authorities. Journalists were judged too polite and too cooperative, too willing to accept Cold War presumptions as their own, too eager to adopt anticommunist ideology and a set of moderate establishment values that took for granted capitalist enterprise, small-town virtues, a two-party system, and other values promoted by political elites (Gans 1979: 39–55).

The criticism had consequences. Propelled by the deep rift in establishment politics that the Vietnam War produced, reporters and editors assumed greater authority relative to their own sources. Vietnam, Watergate, the adversary culture of the 1960s, the revulsion in the media toward Ronald Reagan's photo opportunities and George Bush's cynical flag-waving victory over Michael

Dukakis in 1988 all contributed to a self-consciousness in journalism about both its possibilities and its pitfalls. The practice of journalism has altered significantly, with a more unembarrassed blend of professional detachment, analytic—and hence interpretive—diligence, and market-driven consideration for the passions and interests of the audience than in the immediate past. Yet attachment to a particular vision of journalism—fact-centered, aggressive, energetic, and non-partisan—remains powerful, practically sacred, among most American journalists.

The pluses and minuses of the First Amendment

When journalism operates within a liberal democracy, it may operate in a variety of different ways. "Congress shall make no law abridging freedom of speech, or of the press." This simple, categorical prohibition in the First Amendment (1791) of the Constitution has been the pride of American journalism. And the pride is not misplaced. The press is more free of government restrictions in the United States than in any other nation on earth. However, the First Amendment does not mean exactly what journalists think it means, nor does it resolve all matters of censorship and constraints on expression. In particular, limits on governmental constraints in the United States have made the American news media more vulnerable to censorship by private media companies themselves than media in countries with strong state trusteeship of an independent media, like Britain, or state-subsidized support for media representing diverse and minority viewpoints, as in the Nordic countries. In the views of a growing number of important critics, following the First Amendment rigidly does not provide the best environment for encouraging freedom of expression. The First Amendment is indeed the bulwark of American press liberty, but whether this is to the greater good of press freedom has become an open question.

Consider Pat Tornillo, who in 1972 ran for a seat in the Florida state legislature. The *Miami Herald* wrote a couple of scathing editorials about him. Tornillo asked for space in the paper to respond, citing a 1913 Florida "right-of-reply" statute that required newspapers to provide comparable space for reply, upon request, when the newspaper assails the personal character of any candidate for nomination or for election. When the *Miami Herald* refused to satisfy Tornillo's request, he sued. The Florida Supreme Court held that the right-of-reply statute served the "broad societal interest in the free flow of information to the public". Most democracies around the world would agree. Right-of-reply statutes are commonplace.

The *Miami Herald* believed, by contrast, that a right-of-reply statute abridges the freedom of the newspaper to publish what it pleases. The *Herald* appealed the Florida decision to the US Supreme Court. The case posed a classic problem: could government constitutionally enhance public debate and discussion only by staying out of media regulation altogether? Or could it and should it pass press laws not to abridge but to enhance free expression and to make good what the Court in 1964 in *New York Times v. Sullivan* described as "a profound national commitment to the principle that debate on public issues should be uninhibited, robust, and wide-open"? (*New York Times v. Sullivan* 376 U.S. 270).

On the face of it, a right-of-reply statute would seem a boon to public debate, but the US Supreme Court declared otherwise. Justice Byron White saw in Florida's statute "the heavy hand of government intrusion" that "would make the government the censor of what people may read and know." For Justice White, this is impermissible. If the marketplace is to be the censor, that may be regrettable but it is fully in accord with the Constitution. It is state censorship that the Constitution forbids.

The case here suggests that First Amendment scholar Owen Fiss is correct in referring to dangers of "managerial censorship" in the American press. Some critics, both European and American, distinguish between "government censorship" and "market censorship," the latter referring to the restrictions of free expression that news organizations submit to in a drive to please consumers, advertisers, and investors to improve profits. But it is more accurate to recognize that the market does not automatically censor anyone or anything; human beings make the decisions to include or exclude expression in the news organizations they control. In the Tornillo case, the market was not directly a consideration at all although, surely, the newspaper managers worried about long-term restrictions on their freedom of operation if the government could mandate certain sorts of publication (Fiss 2002: 257–283).

The Court, in the Tornillo case, obviously shied away from having the government tell news organizations anything about what they can or cannot, must or must not, provide the public. The Court has interpreted the First Amendment's prohibition on laws "abridging" the freedom of the press to mean a prohibition on laws "concerning" the freedom of the press.

Obviously, this is a very stringent reading of the role of the government in sustaining a framework for free expression. There is room to disagree about the best legal framework for a democratic media. The US Supreme Court unanimously decided *Tornillo*, but some leading legal scholars think they erred. In their opinion, *Tornillo* fell short of protecting "uninhibited, robust, and wide-open" debate on public issues, the standard Justice William Brennan articulated in the majority opinion in the Sullivan decision (1964).

The Brennan standard suggests that the First Amendment aims not to protect the individual's autonomy of expression (in practice, the individual news organization's autonomy) but to serve the society-wide goal of rich public debate.

If protecting the autonomy of an individual or an enterprise (a newspaper) enlarges free speech and so enhances public debate, then that autonomy is to be devoutly protected—but not for its own sake. If that autonomy itself interferes with rich public debate, then the state should have legitimate means to intervene to preserve robust debate from individuals or enterprises that might hijack it. By this argument, Pat Tornillo should have won his case.

If the Supreme Court is a trustee and interpreter of "a charter of governance that establishes the institutions of government and the norms, standards, and principles that are to control those institutions," as legal scholar Owen Fiss writes, then it is vital to keep the large issue of robust public debate in mind (Fiss 1996: 35). In this view, the protection of individual autonomy of media institutions against the state is a means, not an end, even if it is a favored means.

This doctrine, of course, opens up a vast array of subtle and difficult decisions. It not only makes clear that current American First Amendment law is revisable but suggests also that very different positions in other countries may serve democracy as well or better than the liberal-libertarian First Amendment tradition in the United States.

Is the US model a model for anyone else?

The American model cannot be grafted onto any other system. It emerges out of a unique history and it has been shaped by a relationship to distinctive political institutions and a unique political culture. Even as party loyalty and party-voting patterns are weakening elsewhere in liberal democracies, the American parties' weakness is extreme. A survey of political consultants worldwide found that 80 percent of Australian consultants judged national party organizations "very important" for candidate electoral success, compared with 64 percent of Western European consultants, 45 percent of Latin American consultants, and only 13 percent of US consultants (Plasser 2001: 49). Even with the attractions of the First Amendment, other democracies have found alternative ways to establish expressive freedom that involve, rather than avoid, the exercise of national governmental authority.

Other countries will not—nor should they—accept American-style journalism wholesale, even though they may take some lessons from it here and there. What seems to me worth holding up as an ideal in American journalism is the spirit it exhibits at its best. The political theorist Nancy Rosenblum has suggested in a very different context that nurturing the values that make democracy work should begin at home and that democracies should learn to cultivate in their citizens a set of virtues that people would manifest in everyday life. She lists two virtues or civic "dispositions" as especially important. The first is what she calls "easy spontaneity," a style of civility in which one treats other people identically and easily, without standing on ceremony. Along with this goes the development of "a thick skin," the disposition to make allowances "and to resist the impulse to magnify slights." Rosenblum's second civic disposition is "speaking up," not in cases of life and death but in the most pedestrian instances of everyday injustice. She calls attention here to the value of a person's making at least a minimum response to ordinary injustice, "an iota of recognition when someone is taken advantage of" (Rosenblum 1999: 72–73, 78–79).

Now, there are other dispositions one might recommend for a democracy—say, taking an appropriate interest in public affairs, or willingness to listen and to compromise. The two dispositions that Rosenblum calls attention to, however, seem to me very important—and also, unintentionally, very American. Could Mark Twain's famous character Huckleberry Finn be better defined than by "easy spontaneity" and a willingness to "speak up" about injustices, small and large?

Huckleberry's virtues may also be the virtues of American journalism at its best. The practice of interviewing politicians that Americans developed and to some degree taught to journalists elsewhere in the world is a perfect institutional manifestation of easy spontaneity. Muckraking or investigative reporting is likewise an institutionalization of "speaking up." Neither is essentially related to boosterism, objectivity, or the First Amendment, although there are some obvious connections. But the spirit of easy spontaneity and speaking up are worth holding up for admiration in American journalism. If their spirit spreads, whatever the particular institutional or organizational or cultural apparatus may be in the news practices of other countries, then US journalism has been an inspiration far beyond American shores.

References

Blumin, S. (1976) *The Urban Threshold*, Chicago: University of Chicago Press.

Boorstin, D. (1965) *The Americans: The National Experience*, New York: Random House.

Broder, D. (1973) "Political reporters in presidential politics," in C. Peters and J. Rothchild (eds.) *Inside the System*, New York: Praeger.

Carman, H. J. and Luthin, R. (1964) *Lincoln and the Patronage*, Gloucester, MA: Peter Smith.

Chalaby, J. (1998) *The Invention of Journalism*, London: Macmillan.

Dewey, J. (1930) *Individualism Old and New*, New York: Minton, Balch.

Emery, E., Emery, M., and Roberts, N. (1996) *The Press and America*, Englewood Cliffs, NJ: Prentice-Hall.

Fiss, O. (1996) *Liberalism Divided*, Boulder, CO: Westview Press.

Fiss, O. (2002) "The censorship of television" in L. C. Bollinger and G. R. Stone (eds) *Eternally Vigilant*, Chicago: University of Chicago Press.

Franklin, B. (1961) *Autobiography*, New York: New American Library.

Gans, H. J. (1979) *Deciding What's News*, New York: Pantheon.

Griffith, S. F. (1989) *Home Town News: William Allen White and the Emporia Gazette*, New York: Oxford University Press.

Hallin, D. (1994) *We Keep America on Top of the World*, New York: Routledge.

Kielbowicz, R. (1989) *News in the Mail*, Westport, CT: Greenwood.

King, E. (1992) "Ungagged partisanship: the political values of the public press, 1835–1920," Ph.D. diss., University of California San Diego.

Lippmann, W. (1920) *Liberty and the News*, New York: Harcourt, Brace, and Hone.

McGerr, M. (1986) *The Decline of Popular Politics*, New York: Oxford University Press.

Plasser, F. (2001) "Parties' diminishing relevance for campaign professionals," *Harvard International Journal of Press/Politics* 6: 44–59.

Ritchie, D. (1991) *The Press Gallery*, Cambridge, MA: Harvard University Press.

Rosenblum, N. (1999) "Navigating pluralism: the democracy of everyday life (and where it is learned)," in S. L. Elkin and K. E. Soltan (eds.) *Citizen Competence and Democratic Institutions*, University Park, PA: Pennsylvania State University Press.

Russo, D. P. (1980) "The Origin of Local News in the U.S. Country Press, 1840s–1870s," *Journalism Monographs* 5 (February).

Schudson, M. (1978) *Discovering the News*, New York: Basic Books.

Schudson, M. (1995) *The Power of News*, Cambridge, MA: Harvard University Press.

Schudson, M. (1998) *The Good Citizen: A History of American Civic Life*, New York: Free Press.

Schudson, M. (2001) "The objectivity norm in American journalism," *Journalism* 2, 2: 149–170.

Smith, C. (1977) *The Press, Politics, and Patronage*, Athens, GA: University of Georgia Press.

Tocqueville, A. de (1969) *Democracy in America*, Garden City, NY: Doubleday.

6

THE CONCEPTION OF CHINESE JOURNALISTS

Ideological convergence and contestation

Chin-Chuan Lee

The extension of the press and journalism has historically been an extension of democratic participation. The empowerment of audience as members of the public community is key to any democratic media practice. In this chapter, I shall explore the continuities and discontinuities of three press models that have characterized modern China, with particular reference to their conception of journalists and audience. My historical lineage runs from the turn of the last century when the modern press was first established in China, through the Nationalist rule, to the post-1949 Communist rule (thus excluding the post-1949 press models in Taiwan and Hong Kong). I have summarized these three models in Table 6.1 in terms of their broad historical backgrounds as well as conceptions of journalism, journalists and audience. I do not attempt to construct a grand historical narrative but aim more modestly to extrapolate a rough outline of role conception for modern Chinese journalists in their quest of "national wealth and strength" (*fuqiang*).

Historians have traced the origin of traditional Chinese journalism to the tenth-century official or semi-official gazette (*di bao*) of government activities. But the brief history of modern Chinese press was, as Passin (1963) noted with reference to the Third World, almost exclusively "the result of Western influence" and, more specifically, against the backdrop of Western imperialist invasion. The chief function of the press was enlightenment and propaganda, not provision of information. Passin argued that the early Chinese press was "strongly modernizing, opposing the forces and ideologies based on Confucianism and tradition, and it also opposed the political reality of the country: disunity, warlord control, the delay in the establishment of a modern state system based upon representative government." The Confucian intellectual model forms the background against which other press models will be measured. The Maoist model shares the Confucian emphases of elite responsibility while fighting against them in the name of the "masses." The Maoist "mass line" model is only democratic and anti-elitist in rhetoric but dictatorial in practice. Transposing onto (and absorbed uneasily into) Maoism is the introduction of the previously condemned market economy into dominant media operation and

Table 6.1 Three models of journalism in China

	Confucian liberalism	Maoism	Communist capitalism
Time period	1900s–1940s	1949–present	After the 1980s (especially after 1992)
Role of the media	Enlightenment	Mobilization and propaganda	Dual roles of ideological correctness and commercial profit
Source of income	Small circulation, no or some ads	Party subsidies	Primarily advertising and other market activities
Conception of journalists	Confucian literati	Party cadres and journalists	Information providers; making profit by toeing official line
Conception of the audience	Intellectual elite as educators of the ignorant people	Political masses	Political masses and consuming audience
Methods of audience research	Few codified methods; intellectual critique based on moral precepts	Letters to the editor, focus group and panel interviews, model analysis	Investigative interviews, polls, surveys and other empirical methods, letters to the editors
Exemplary figures	Liang Qichao, Zhang Jiluan, Chu Anping	Deng Tuo, Hu Jiwei	Liu Binyan (1980s); Hu Shuli, Li Yuanjiang (1990s)

culture in the 1990s, making journalists and audience allies of the emerging consumer culture without posing a challenge to the established political power. While the market-oriented press is traditionally associated with the rise of liberal democracy, the media in what Deng Xiaoping called a "socialist market economy with Chinese characteristics" are, in effect, the media in "Communist (and post-Communist) state capitalism with authoritarian characteristics."

My basic argument is that due to the underdeveloped political democracy and market order, the modern Chinese press has not treated the audience as public citizens in a common effort to define their life. The Confucian-liberal model treats the audience as the target of education, guidance, and enlightenment; the Maoist model, as the target of mobilization and indoctrination; and the Communist-capitalist model, as the target of ideological conformity and exploitation for profit. Likewise, the role of the journalist is seen variously as a Confucian-liberal enlightened teacher, a Communist revolutionary cadre, and increasingly a profit-maker in addition to (and in combination with) other ideological roles. Left out in these formulations has been the crucial concern for the democratic public sphere. The democratic concern for public citizenship is rare. Examining the tortured history in the concept formation of journalists and audience is tantamount to tracing the lack of democratic governance in modern China.

Confucian-liberal journalists

With the Qing dynasty in the long process of decay, Confucianism began to lose its unchallenged position and had to compete for legitimacy with other imported social doctrines. In the Confucian discourses, individuals are subservient to the state, personal duty is more important than individual rights, and cultivation of personal virtue and moral education precedes legal or institutional protection (Fairbank, 1979). Many anti-traditional reformists operated within the framework of Confucianism and rebelled against it. To the extent that the Confucian ethos idealized the literati as embracing the masses in their consciences, there was a strong tradition of intellectual advocacy on national reform, modernization, and revolution in the media. Their impulse was Confucian, but their emancipatory imagination was fueled by Western liberalism or socialism.

At the turn of the twentieth century, China's market and industrial economy were so poor that the late-Qing periodicals reached only about 1 percent of national population (Nathan, 1985, p. 147). To escape political persecution, most were published out of treaty ports, foreign concessions, and, notably, Tokyo. Media literati served urban-centered intellectuals, emphasizing the role of nationalist ideology and seeking to reconcile it with their truncated imaginings of Western liberalism as a key to national salvation. They translated the liberal assumption of individual sovereignty into a Confucian ethos of personal duty to serve statist interest. Their journalistic commentaries were largely informed by simple and abstract moral precepts, not based on a concrete understanding of reality through the application of effective empirical methods. No study has come to throw light on the class backgrounds and demographic profiles of Chinese journalists, but I suspect that most of them must have come from port cities and provincial towns instead of remote, impoverished villages. Once incorporated into the lowest echelon of intellectual aristocracy, these journalistic communicators tended to adopt urban orientations while increasingly losing touch with the "audience" they sought to enlighten. The target "audience" must have remained abstract, ambiguous, and vacuous to them.

Although leading intellectuals (from Chen Duxiu to Hu Shi, from Zhou Taofen to Chu Anping) had long relied on magazines as a forum of political discourses, I shall draw on Liang Qichao and Zhang Jiluan—two of the most important newspaper editorialists—along with a short-lived liberal movement, to illustrate the Confucian-liberal model. Liang's relationship with Confucianism is open to interpretations: Levenson (1959) describes him as an "anti-Confucian Confucianist" said to be emotionally attached to the Confucian past but intellectually alienated from it, whereas Huang (1972) regards him as a "Confucian liberal." After the debacle of a reformist movement, the young Liang took refuge in Japan and came into contact with a confluence of Western thoughts. Even though the top-rank Chinese elite despised journalism as a more inferior line of work, Liang firmly believed in the potential of the press for enlightenment. He admired the Western press's variety, richness, and social influence, and turned to journalism to fulfill his failed political ambition. He published a succession of nine short-lived journals that nonetheless came to exert a decisive impact on generations of young minds ranging from Hu Shi, the liberal intellectual leader; to Chen Duxiu and Mao Zedong, leaders of the Chinese Communist Party. The most important journal was the Tokyo-based *Xinmin Congbao* (New Citizen), with a life span of six years and a peak circulation of 14,000 copies that somehow reached 200,000 readers (considered considerable then). The name of the publication suggests that the socially conscious intellectual stratum has the responsibility to educate what Liang had otherwise described as the ignorant and slavish populace.

Nathan (1985) portrays the pre-1903 Liang as an "optimistic Confucian reformer," in contrast to his anti-democratic position afterwards. In the famous 1896 editorial, "On the Benefit of the Press in National Affairs," Liang lamented over widespread public ignorance about the state of affairs in China and in adjacent countries. The press, he envisioned, would enhance solidarity between "above and below" and make both people and government better informed about what today's political scientists would call "modernization" projects: commerce, technology, foreign affairs, and state affairs. To this end, the role of the press was to translate world news, report government activities, analyze foreign relations, and publish important works on political science and arts. In 1902, he opined editorially that the newspaper should act as a watchdog over the government and as a *guide* to the people. After all, he saw nothing but harmony between private interest and public interest (Nathan, 1985); any conflict between them was to be conceptually dissolved by the higher purpose of the collective state. He introduced into China scores of key modern concepts and theories—such as nationalism, social Darwinism, and liberalism—from Meiji Japanese intellectual circles which were infatuated with an influx of Western schools of thought (Huang, 1972). The press was not simply a transmission belt of information, but an intellectual instrument for China to rid itself of widespread ignorance, weakness, and imperialist humiliation.

His journey to the new continent in 1903 produced profound disillusionment with various aspects of American democracy: the anti-Chinese sentiment, the spoils system, the constant electioneering, corruption, and its imperialist impulse (see Arkush and Lee, 1989). When he returned to China, he maintained that given the "slavish mentality" and flaws in Chinese national character, democracy could degenerate China into mob rule. Instead, he advocated "enlightened despotism:" that is, an autocracy should rule in public interest and maintain social order (Chang, 1971; Nathan, 1985). This position made him clash with Republican revolutionary leaders who promoted people's rights. Liang savagely condemned the gentry-literati-official class, but also opposed socialism on account of the fact that class divisions did not exist in the pre-industrial and pre-capitalist China. Official historians of the People's Republic of China (PRC) call Liang a "bourgeois reformer" (Fang, 1992, p. 658).

The second prototypical case of the Confucian-liberal journalism was Zhang Jiluan of *Da Gong Bao*. In the midst of social dislocation from the 1920s to the 1940s, few publications were of political consequence. In the dead silence of big dailies about the most important happenings of the day, as Lin Yutang (1936, p. 141) commented, "even the weak hummings of mostiquoes [press] is a welcome relief." He caricatured the difference between the oldest *Shen Bao* and the most widely circulated *Xinwen Bao*, both in Shanghai, as between "poorly edited" and "not edited at all" (p. 131). Despite its small circulation (35,000 copies, or a third of each of the conservative commercial papers), Lin (1936, p. 131) described *Da Gong Bao* as the "most progressive and best edited paper" and "decidedly designed to appeal to a perhaps *overeducated* public" (emphasis added). A recipient of the 1941 foreign press award from the University of Missouri School of Journalism, it enjoyed unsurpassed reputation for its editorial integrity; the writing of Zhang Jiluan, its soul, from 1929 to 1941 (Zhang, 1944a, 1944b) remains as a model of journalistic excellence. The PRC officialdom used to denounce this paper as a supporter of Chiang Kai-shek, but revisionist historians (Wu, 1994; Jia, 2002) have begun to acknowledge its high professional standard and integrity.

Four outstanding features of *Da Gong Bao* are noteworthy. First, the paper saw itself not as a seeker of power, wealth or fame, but as an organ of political commentary for the literati (*wenren lunzheng*) to serve their country. The investment capital was kept deliberately small and simple to prevent editorial integrity from being compromised by power and money. It was a conscious decision from the outset that if the paper could not stand on its feet with 50,000 *yuan*, it would rather be closed down than take political or commercial donation. Though admiring the Anglo-American free press, Zhang (1944b, p. 126) shared traditional Confucian disdain of money and abhorred money's huge corrupting influence on the Western press. Instead, he staked his paper's independence on intellectual conscience, refusing to be convinced that commercial profit would protect editorial autonomy.

Second, *Da Gong Bao* began to advance a liberal vision of journalism akin, in spirit if not in practice, to the Western concept of professionalism. Its normative standards were embedded in the moral responsibility of Confucian intellectuals, whereas Western media professionalism rose historically from the growth of the market economy (Schudson, 1978). In 1931, Zhang (1944a, pp. 30–31) promulgated four editorial principles: (a) do not align with any political party (*bu dang*), but speak as citizens without bias or prior background; (b) do not trade favor (*bu mai*), accept political subsidies or investment, or be swayed by money; (c) do not serve private or selfish ends (*bu si*), but make the paper the eyes and ears of the public; and (d) do not be blinded by ideology or emotion (*bu mang*). To be editorially independent, *Da Gong Bao* did not hire any known party members; but as a liberal paper, it was tolerant of reporters and writers with divergent political leanings (Wu, 1994, p. 101; Fang, 1996, p. 474). The literati were to exercise the influence of the pen from an intellectual "conscience," without the corruption of power and money. If the western press relied historically on the imperatives of profitablity to foster diverse accounts that complement and check on one another in the "marketplace of ideas" (Schudson, 1978), Confucian literati were largely ignorant of or even hostile to the market forces. To put it in Gouldner's terms (1976, p. 173), they were members of the "cultural apparatus" congenial to social utilitarianism, rather than agents of the "consciousness industry" in pursuit of individualistic and market-based utilitarianism. As social teachers, the literati pride themselves on proffering expert opinions, while Western media professionals separate news from opinions to attract the widest mass audiences (Schudson, 1978).

Third, *Da Gong Bao* acknowledged the central role of news reporting, noting with sadness that China's urban-centered politics and enterprises had left 90 percent of the rural and agrarian population unheeded. Therefore, it sent a small contingent of roving correspondents to take the pulse of people's sufferings around the country (Wu, 1994). In one instance, after publishing reports about the devastating conditions in several northern counties, the paper lashed out at the indifferent authorities for failing to take care of these poor people or to eradicate their poverty and ignorance (Zhang, 1944a, pp. 6–7). Its "news net" (Tuchman, 1978) was not systematically institutionalized enough to cover the huge and underdeveloped China. But staff correspondents contributed to half of its two-page "important news," while peer newspapers relied almost exclusively on the provision of news agencies (Fang, 1996, p. 475). Many of these reporters—Xu Zhucheng, Fan Changjiang, and Xiao Qian—achieved national renown and supported insurgence against the Nationalists, only to be purged by the Communists later.

Fourth, the paper exhibited a strong statist orientation. During China's war with Japan, the paper willingly submitted itself to military censorship to prevent the leaking of national secrets. National survival overrode the professional autonomy it had long advocated. The paper had no quarrel with the need for wartime news censorship, but took issue with censors' bad attitudes and backward methods. In times of national survival, the paper urged that the entire country, even the Communist insurgents, should rally around Chiang Kai-shek as the undisputed national leader (Wu, 1994; Fang, 1996).

The 1940s, amidst the civil war, saw the sudden beginning and ending of a short-lived Chinese liberal movement. Very loosely organized, several hundreds of university professors and intellectuals, many of them having been educated in the United States and the United Kingdom, rallied around key editorial outposts—including *Da Gong Bao* (under Wang Yunsheng, who succeeded Zhang Jiluan), *Wenhui Bao*, and the *Observer* magazine—to advocate a "third way," separate from the Guomindang and the Communist Party (Zhang, 2002). The tenet of their visions for China bore a strong imprint of Western political liberty and Fabian economic equality. They opposed Chiang Kai-shek's authoritarianism. They were then gradually attracted to Mao Zedong's call for "new democratic doctrine" (*xin minzhu zhuyi*), even though one of the leading members, Chu Anping, editor of the *Observer*, presciently proclaimed in 1947: "To be honest, under the Nationalists our fight for freedom is really over the question of 'how much freedom.' If the Communists come to power, the question is going to be 'Will we have freedom at all?' " (quoted in Dai, 1989).

It is a sad chapter to recall that almost none of these liberal intellectuals could later escape the fate of Communist persecution. During the "Hundred Flowers Movement" in 1956, many intellectuals were moved to tears when Chairman Mao Zedong implored them to speak out and criticize the party. Chu Anping took advantage of this invitation to castigate the Communist Party for forgetting that only the people, not the Party, were the "true masters of the country." As the going got rough, Mao abruptly decided in 1957 to retaliate without mercy and purged 550,000 intellectuals as "anti-Party, anti-Socialist rightists." Chu died, and the reason for his death remains mysterious.

Why did Chinese liberalism fail so miserably? Five postulates can be given (Zhang, 2002; Lee, 2004, pp. 72–73):

1) If Barrington Moore (1967) is correct in pronouncing "No bourgoisie, no democracy," then it is clear that the Chinese society had not gone through capitalist development and there were no significant middle classes to speak of.

2) Several hundreds of liberal intellectuals, most unorganised, were a drop in the bucket of the Chinese population. Unorganized, some of them turned to the Communists as anti-Guomindang allies, but eventually were gobbled up by the Communists.

3) They preached on the high platform of abstract democratic ideals, but they did not have concrete strategies and were out of touch with the common people.

4) They spoke without legal or institutional protection.

5) Their relationship to the powers that be is ambiguous: even anti-Confucian liberals are heirs to the cultural heritage of Confucianism. While critical of powerful authorities, they tend to regard it as their responsibility to serve their leader cum nation when opportunities arise. Otherwise, how could Wang Yunshen of *Da Gong Bao* claim to be "born again" by deciding to follow the Communists, having only spent a few sleepless nights after receiving a personal letter from Mao?

Communist journalists

Fairbank (1979) has called Maoism "Confucianism in Leninist garb." Both Maoism and Confucianism stress the pivotal role of ideology; both Confucianism (intellectuals) and Leninism (party cadres) share the elitist and statist orientations. Mao and his anti-Confucian peers retained strong Confucian legacies, into which they selectively absorbed Marxist-Leninist influences to form a core ideological framework. These similarities aside, they differ sharply. First, while the Leninist vanguard party's role is compatible with Confucian suppositions about the harmonious unity of private and state interests, Communist cadre-journalists' party discipline has taken the place of Confucian literati's "conscience." Second, in contrast to the elitist orientations of Confucian literati and Leninist party cadres, Maoism promotes the cult of the masses as the embodiment of revolutionary ideals. Third, Confucian literati dedicated themselves to educating the people, but Maoist journalists wanted to do more in mobilizing the masses within the party-state apparatuses and remolding them though a common ideology and absolute power.

Declaring that "politics takes command," Mao embellished the Leninist view of the press and journalists in the context of "democratic centrism" (Schram, 1976, pp. 11–12). But he gave it a more populist, radical, and voluntaristic character that tended to undermine political stability. Mao claimed that thought determined action: if the masses were imbued with the "correct" thought, they would act "correctly." The media must create social impact closely related to the grand ideology and political lines. In pursuit of permanent revolution, Mao exalted the human will to its extreme; he despised bureaucratic regularization, role differentiation, and professional expertise. In the name of "mass-line journalism," he purged tens of thousands of "reactionary bourgeois liberal" journalists and sent them to remote villages and factories in order to receive re-education from revolutionary masses and amateur ideological enthusiasts. Mao's policy did not go uncontested. But he eventually defeated Liu Shaoqi, whose position was closer to the Bolsheviks in encouraging long-term cultivation of national culture and consciousness through the persuasive efforts of propaganda organizations and professional ideologists (Lee, 2001). Despite the power and policy rifts, Liu never developed a press theory at variance with Mao's tenet of the "mass line," criticism, and self-criticism (Dittmer, 1973, 1974).

Inasmuch as the "mass line" policy aims to align party discipline with mass will, Mao (1979) declared, "No investigation, no right to speak." Even if an investigation is conducted, journalists still don't have the right to speak if they get "bogged down in narrow empiricism" without coming to grips with the principal contradictions of class conflict. Once a policy is set, cadres must gather views from the masses and submit reports to party committees for consideration; they also take instructions from the central authorities back to the masses (Dittmer, 1974). Liu Shaoqi (1998) echoed mass-line journalism in a celebrated 1948 talk by urging journalists to reflect the voices of the masses and to obey the party secretary's leadership. Also, he insisted that journalists use Marxist class conflict and dialectical materialism to analyze concrete phenomena.

How far could the mass-line journalism go? As a top party propagandist, Deng Tuo was intellectually attached to the new socialist order, but as a man of high culture he was also emotionally alienated from the party's abuses and vulgarization of daily life by the "proletarian culture" (Cheek, 1997). He was, in this sense, a Confucian Leninist. In the 1950s he brought the concept of "key reporting" to the *People's Daily*: that is, framing all writings—news, correspondents' reports, essays, and editorials—in the light of current policy. All letters to the editor should be answered. Reporters were encouraged to live among the masses, who were invited to write for themselves, and local activists were recruited as informants. The paper also synthesized the themes of local papers to identify national problems or patterns. Despite these efforts, he was berated by Mao in 1957 as leading "a bunch of dead men" in the *People's Daily* which, in Mao's view, did not do enough to propagate his Hundred Flowers policy. Deng was dismissed and later took his own life.

Mao conceded his power temporarily to Liu Shaoqi after mass famine claimed 30 million lives from 1959 to 1961. Declaring class struggle in the PRC to be over, Liu was determined to harness the media to further socialist economic reconstruction and integrate the entire population instead of only servicing the proletarian classes. Having previously borne the brunt of Mao's wrath, the *People's Daily* now fell under Liu's sharp lash for manufacturing falsehood that contributed to the colossal calamity of the Great Leap Forward campaign. Condemning the party organ as "a lifeless loudspeaker" rather than "a brainy mouthpiece" (Hu, 1989, p. 100), Liu proclaimed that "having a lying paper is worse than having no paper" (p. 98). In 1961, the *People's Daily* staff followed Liu to his native Hunan province to learn how to conduct rural investigations among local peasants. Liu told journalists not to "stick theoretical labels" on people, especially those with views deviating from party policy. He urged the journalist to listen to "gossips" ("grievances") from their relatives and friends, preferably in private and out-of-town to avoid pressure from local cadres. On this basis, journalists could generalize from what they heard to broader mass opinions.

Liu's promulgation of "serving the readers" was soon to be vehemently denounced as "revisionist" during the Cultural Revolution. Mao's personality cult and ideological conformity reached an apex. Revolutionary rhetoric turned out to be a tool for rationalizing the established factional power interests, even between Mao and his erstwhile closest allies. Political agitation was so intense that Pool (1973) observed that China offered "something like a laboratory test of limits of what propaganda can do." As power struggles led to unpredictable policy reversals and personnel purges, the media constantly contradicted their own rhetoric.

Communist politics regards investigations, letters to the editor, criticism, and self-criticism as key methods of collecting opinions. When letters to the editor reappeared, the *People's Daily* received more than 3,000 letters per day in October 1978, all vividly exposing past atrocities of the radical left (Chu and Chu, 1983). The published letters were foregrounded by the editor's note to present "model cases," which supports policy aims and highlight ideological significance by dramatizing the attributes of heroes and villains. They enforce behavioral compliance of party and mass opinions while encouraging them to identify with certain desired goals (Rosen, 1989).

These crude methods of opinion collection originated in the oral- communication environment of early Communist bases that relied on small-group meetings with illiterate peasants (Dittmer, 1974; Zhu, 1988). Hostile to Western representative institutions, Chinese Communists view direct contact between cadres and masses as an instrument of eliciting political participation and keeping political leaders in touch with popular demands. Mao (1979) stressed that journalists, in conducting fact-finding, should not only pose questions but also produce solutions. When they go to a community, according to Mao, they should investigate two or three people from each of the class strata designated as politically advanced, average, and backward. This semi-anthropological and semi-clinical approach is likened to "dissecting a sparrow:" despite its small body, it presumably reveals all the characteristics and connections of vital organs. However, the ideologically assigned class distinction fell into widespread abuse. The old thermometer of mass opinion in the simple and homogeneous guerrilla base becomes wholly inadequate for a much more complex and heterogeneous population (Zhu, 1988).

The real problem of "mass line" is not limited to where and how to survey the opinion. More seriously, there are no legal or institutional mechanisms to resolve the dialectical contradictions between democracy and centralism, between mass opinions and party policy, and between participation and mobilization. Journalists serve two masters: party leaders and the masses. Potential conflicts inherent in the unequal power between these two masters may be harmonized at the level of abstract theorization (by making an *a priori* claim, for example, that the vanguard party represents the masses), but not in practice. Even the "revisionist" Liu Shaoqi seemed acutely aware of the practical dilemma when he noted the dilemma of "obeying the party secretary" and "daring to reflect problems and raise opinions" to the party secretary (Hu, 1989, p. 110). He advised that journalists should not fear reprisal because "if your report is accurate and you get expelled [from the party], that's your honor." Liu (1967) took an absolutist position toward what constituted a "good Communist:" the person must go through a long process of revolutionary remolding and "unconditionally subordinate" personal interests to the interests of the party. To Liu, personal virtues are more important than institutional mechanisms in guaranteeing that the press is responsive to mass opinions. As if to mock this circular rhetoric, Mao later ruthlessly persecuted Liu to death.

Hu Jiwei, Deng Tuo's deputy, shepherded the *People's Daily* into being a leading party voice of reform from the 1978 to 1983. Despite his liberal image, Hu (1989, p. 326) could do no better than urge the victims of reprisal and institutional injustice to keep up their faith in the party which would "become more and more democratic." Or else, "so be it, should you suffer from personal misfortune!" Hu implored that the party secretary grant free discussion on critical issues either openly in the press or, alternatively, within internal reference channels. He suggested that if journalists improved their political and professional consciousness, they would be in a position to fathom the party secretary's intention and earn his confidence. But if the party secretary should decide to prohibit publication of critical issues, Hu thought it "not a bad thing" to withhold them (p. 333). This twisted argument seems to accommodate all sides but satisfy none, proving how doomed reformist party journalists could be in trying to work a way out of the rigid Communist framework. Hu himself was purged from the party organ in 1983.

The boundaries between journalists and the party secretary are arbitrary, in flux, and not at all rules-based. Journalists can only draw on personal faith and political experience to imagine what the party secretary may want. To rely on party secretaries and journalists to be morally virtuous typifies what Benjamin Schwartz calls "a new version of the traditional Chinese conception of 'moralizing the holders of power'" (quoted in White, 1983). In this power equation, who is the guardian of power, and who guards the guardian? Both moralizers and moralized are "enmeshed in the same state apparatus and subject to the same logic of hierarchical stratification" (White, 1983). All measures of opinion gathering are conducted within the intra-bureaucratic framework without legal and institutional protection. They stress the personal courage and morality of party journalists, but do not address the basic structural problems of power and protection. Journalists were virtually at the mercy of the whims of the party secretary.

Communist-capitalist journalists

The Communist-capitalist media negotiate, paradoxically, between Communist ideological control and quasi-capitalist market operation. Two caveats are in order. First, the motif of the 1980s was political reform, whereas that of the 1990s was marketization. Although media advertising began to be introduced at the embryonic stage of Communist capitalism in the 1980s, it was not until after 1992 that media marketization gathered its momentum and ushered in an era of post-Communist capitalism. Second, there is no longer Communism in China; all that remains is a gigantic Communist Party emptied of revolutionary idealism with a monopoly on tremendous coercive power and resources. Nor is there the kind of market transparency and discipline that presumably exist in a "healthy" capitalist society. Private capital is denied media ownership; all journalists are virtually state employees. Suffice it for my purpose to call this peculiar model of development "market Leninism" or "Communist (and post-Communist) authoritarian state capitalism."

The tortured contours of this model emerged as a response to profound disillusionment with Maoist dictatorship, necessitating and providing impetuses for China's much needed economic and journalism reforms since the 1980s. When Deng Xiaoping returned to power, he showed little patience with Maoist class struggle and, instead, heralded economic reform agendas. He showed still less tolerance of ideological challenge to his power, intent on harnessing the media to uphold, not weaken, the legitimacy of Communist power. Deng opted for economic modernization to forestall popular pressure for political reform in China, whereas Gorbachev failed to solve economic problems through political reform in the former Soviet Union. But throughout the 1980s China's pathway to economic liberalization was ferociously contested between proponents of greater market incentives and orthodox advocates of a Soviet-style centrally planned economy. The media were caught up in rounds of factional warfare.

Deng installed two of his protégés, Hu Yaobang and Zhao Ziyang, to launch reform projects, but eventually sacrificed them when factional power struggles lost critical balance. Media policy saw highly unstable pendulum swings between the push of economic liberalization and the pull of rigid ideological control. Hu courageously used the media to fight against the ideological ortho-doxy of the Maoists in the late 1970s to advance reform agendas (Goldman, 1994). But at one point he retreated under pressure to concede that while literary writers could choose subjects and develop themes with "completely comradely suggestions and advice" from the Party, journalists should primarily propagate the Party's achievements. Zhao's position was no less hesitant, dubious, or contradictory. While discouraging media autonomy by espousing neo-authoritarianism, he propounded the concept of "supervision by public opinion" (*yulun jiandu*) to enhance government transparency and introduce a media watch on bureaucratic wrongdoing (Polumbaum, 1990). Despite the oscillating political winds, Deng quelled dissent and opposition by resorting to the state apparatuses rather than to mass mobilization from below. The state's retreat from mass campaigns and its de-emphasis on revolutionary ideology made it possible for more varied cultural genres, livelier media entertainments, and ideologically less loaded materials to flourish as long as they did not pose a threat to state power (Lee, 1990). The reform intiatives survived the challenges of the short-lived Anti-Spiritual Pollution Campaign (1983) and the Anti-Bourgeois Liberalization Campaign (1987) but were, in the end, tragically undermined by the Tiananmen Square crackdown (1989).

Deng's marketization of political management called for more and better information to improve managerial, financial, and technological infrastructures, as well as for "emancipation of the mind" among intellectuals. To the extent that official ideology was organized around a revolutionary praxis and full of internal contradictions, reformist intellectuals and journalists sought to accen-tuate the less authoritarian aspects of Marxist, Leninist, and Maoist interpretations in order to promote socialist democracy, "socialist press freedom," policy transparency, and "supervision by public opinion" (Lee, 2000). They were emboldened to raise taboo questions such as the public's right to know and the role of public opinion in policy-making process. Media laws were drafted. Zhao's advisory group, according to an insider's chronicle (Wu, 1997), even deliberated behind closed doors a wide range of options for structural reform, including Western-style multiparty systems, popular elections, and greater press freedom. From 1986 to 1989, Shanghai's *World Economic Herald* ventured to the edge of the permissible by pushing elite-defined political reform agendas with the technique of "hitting line balls" (*cha bian qiu*)—aiming for the very edge of the ping-pong table where a ball is almost out of bounds but remains a fair hit (Goldman, 1994).

The momentum for journalism reform was unprecedented, partly encouraged by the more activist and tolerant political climate of the 1980s and partly responding to social dislocation arising from the vast changes. In a major survey study, Polumbaum (1990) discovered widespread dissatisfaction with the press among the leaders, the readers, and the journalists. Journalists were particularly dissatisfied with the dilemmas of having to serve two masters (the party versus the audience) and with various layers of control mechanisms. They pointed to the lack of journalistic autonomy and initiative as the foremost concern, and aspired to "lean on the side of the people" by offering more critical, investigative, and diverse reports. The People's University Public Opinion Research Institute conducted a series of five large-scale surveys from 1987 to 1988, similarly mirroring strong elite aspirations for political and journalism reforms (Yu, 1993; Yu and Liu, 1993). Several secondary analyses of audience and media data collected in the 1980s (Zhu *et al.*, 1990; Zhu and Rosen, 1993; Zhao *et al.*, 1994) also provide much evidence of a burning concern for reform.

The experience of Liu Binyan (1989), China's premier investigative journalist, illustrates the severe limits to which the reformist party press could go. In the early 1980s he played a surrogate role of justice, receiving victims of power abuse who traveled from afar in vain hope of seeking media redress. Loyal to his party, Liu was determined to expose injustice and promote good officials through his investigative efforts. Reporters of his stature exercise "quasi-official, always unwritten, investigatory rights" on behalf of the party (Nathan, 1985, p. 156). After a brief period of success, he was accused of "wrecking stability and solidarity" by powerful provincial party secretaries. He pleaded his case to the reformist leader Hu Yaobang via an internal channel, but Hu was under too much political pressure to look after his protégé. Liu was expelled from the party in 1987.

The market mechanism was beginning to intervene in media management in the 1980s but its full force would not be felt until after the 1990s. To lift China out of international isolation and domestic stagnation, resulting from the Tiananmen Square crackdown, Deng reignited the flame of market liberalization in late 1992, which caused an "epistemological break" for the media. Since then they have jumped into "the ocean of raging commercialization" instead of continuing to rely on state subsidies, and have one by one profited from the phenomenal growth in advertising. Making money is no longer a sin as long as you don't defy the party-state. Calls for greater economic freedom and cultural pluralism have replaced those of political reform and intellectual enlightenment. No longer do the media advocate grand political reform. They have learned to improvise a variety of editorial or marketing strategies—which span the gamut of non-routine news genres, formats, and techniques—to cater to the market without violating official bounds (Pan, 2000). He (2000) describes these schizophrenic market-oriented media as "a capitalistic body" that wears "a socialist face." He argues that China's Party press is being transformed from a strict mouthpiece of the government into what he calls the "Party Publicity Inc." to promote Party images and legitimacy rather than to brainwash people.

Surveys and opinion polls came into being in the early 1980s, only after arduous struggles to justify them as a legitimate part of "mass line" rather than "bourgeois" practice; they were chiefly geared toward aiding political reforms (Womack, 1986; Chen and Mi, 1989). Facing arguably the most open environment for political discourses in the late 1980s, as noted earlier, surveys displayed a prevailing mood of frustration among journalists with lack of professional autonomy and with the party-state's meddling in their day-to-day newswork (Polumbaum, 1990; Yu and Liu, 1993). In contrast, political discourses grew more restricted in the 1990s as the universe of social discourses was broadened; surveys reported that 60 or 70 percent of journalists enjoyed "a great deal of job autonomy" (Chen et al, 1998). Material gains provide a major explanation for this psychological role transformation; the wealthier journalists become, the less politically engaged they are. Now polling agencies have mushroomed like a cottage industry to serve the market needs; the *People's Daily* reports close to 1,000 such outlets in Beijing alone (Yu, 1996). The Maoist-style panel interviews have largely been abandoned. Many media organizations (notably CCTV) have organized audience surveys as a marketing and public-relations tool, first to tap into people's lifestyles for sale, and secondarily to reflect their voices in a circumscribed way. Market surveys have primarily served the fledging consumerism rather than democratic citizenship.

The implications of marketization on the media have been paradoxical. First, media autonomy has gained only precarious ground, but marketization has brought about what I call "demobilized liberalization" (Lee, 2000). The media enjoy greater "negative freedom," both chipping away at state commandism and ushering in increasing supremacy of the commercial logic. The non-political range of media discourses has expanded—often to the benefit of urban professional and buying classes at the expense of peasants and workers (Lee, 2003; Zhao, 2003)—but political coverage remains highly controlled. Journalists have greater latitutde in reporting economic issues as long as the money trail does not lead to high-ranking officials and their families (Keatley, 2003).

Second, Pan and Lu (2003) postulate that journalists use various discursive resources in everyday practice as "tactics" to evade, appropriate, and resist the controlling "strategies" imposed by those with power. They take whatever official rhetoric can offer selectively to justify what they wish to achieve in the market. Many media outlets imitate one another in producing highly popular and thus lucrative programs to "swat the flies, but not beat the tigers," bolstered by the legitimating claims of marketized media professionalism and Communist mass-line rhetoric. Bearing a clear trace of American influence, Hu Shuli is a leading example of a financial muckraker who has weathered political pressure to expose serious cases of stock manipulation and corporate irregularities, which implicated so many ranking local officials that *Business Week* dubbed her "China's most dangerous woman" (CJR, 2003). Investigative journalists were found to consciously model themselves after the heroic colleagues in CBS's *60 Minutes*. Renewed attention given to audience interest, thanks to market appeal and rapid diffusion of the Internet, has served to deconstruct the dominant party media power.

Marketization has a third implication of being liberating in some cases but ethically dubious in other cases. Compared with the 1980s, rampant media corruption has almost become a way of life. Media conglomerates are organized under the party-state patronage and control, manifesting a strange collaboration of power and money; as part of state capitalism, the state adopts a corporatist strategy to expend economic favors in exchange for media loyalty (Zhao, 2000; Lee, in press). They compete for advertising dollars and run business enterprises (such as hotel and tourism) unrelated to their core missions in professionally and ethically dubious manners. Li Yuanjiang's example may be dramatic but not alone: having built the *Guangzhou Daily* into being China's first, largest, and richest press group, he was sacked on account of embezzlement, corruption, and misbehavior. Tragic lessons from the Tiananmen Square crackdown and the enticing power of money have consigned socialist idealism to marginality. The crippling state-led marketization has engendered various brutal and distorted consequences, without developing the norms of business discipline, fair play, or civic participation. Worse, the media have catered primarily to urban, professional, and commercial classes at the expense of peasants and workers (Zhao, 1998).

Conclusion

Despite the seemingly irreconcilable differences, the three press models—Confucian liberalism, Maoism, and Communist capitalism—all conceive of the press as an instrument of China's century-old quest for national wealth and strength. The concepts of democracy and press freedom were not introduced into China until the 1900s; what's more, they were not valued as ends, but as means to national modernization. When democracy failed to prove an effective panacea, however, it could be dropped as easily as it was picked up. An early press advocate of democracy, Liang Qichao retreated to favor "enlightened despotism" in 1903. The radical anti-traditional iconoclasm of the May Fourth Movement in 1919 sought to uphold Western democracy and science as twin methods to build a strong China free from imperialist humiliation, even if such values assumed a different normative order in the Western context. Amidst the Japanese invasion of China in the 1930s, many leading members of the US-educated intellectual circle who had been democracy's strong allies suddenly turned their backs on democracy. Arguing as Liang had done 30 years before, they did not believe that China was prepared to have democracy, and thus called for some form of "enlightened dictatorship" to bring about national unity and industrialization with the aid of Western science and technology (Zhang, 1987, pp. 167–201). During one of the PRC's most relaxed periods in the late-1980s, Premier Zhao promoted "neo-authoritarianism" to justify China's pursuit of economic growth under iron-fisted control. The motif of "national wealth and strength" has remained unchanged, at the sacrifice of individual sovereignty or democratic citizenship, despite large-scale regime transformation from Qing, Nationalist, to Communist rule.

Most "ideological priests" in today's China follow what Cheek (1994) calls "the mandarin vocation": patriotic toward the state, receptive to patronage toward superiors, peers, and subordinates, and paternalistic and elitest in self-expression. However, the media have also been a site of ideological contestation and accommodation, derived from the ambiguities and contradictions between the revolutionary rhetoric of Communism and the practical discourses of marketization. This active process of everyday struggle is waged around what Williams (1977) calls the "dominant structure" of Communist ideology (party propaganda) in relation to the "residual structure" of Confucian ethos (intellectual ethics) and the "emerging culture" of imported media professionalism in tandem with the market logic.

In many ways, "audience" is an unfortunate term for it evokes the image of a mass of passive receivers of messages. In the Chinese context, the audience has been enlightened, mobilized, or sold for profit, all in the name of serving national interest. They are not seen as free citizens who take part in democratic discourses in the public sphere. Individuals are objects, not subjects; means, not goals; or part of the collective goals. The Confucian-liberal model is perhaps the most benign of the three, while the Maoist model is most penetrative and authoritarian despite rhetoric to the contrary. Some of the Maoist elements have been weakened by the market forces, which have nonetheless produced a different set of problems. In a mature democracy, the dialectic of consumer and citizen has always been a focal point of concern for intellectual scholars ranging from J. Dewey to J. Habermas (Dahlgren, 1995). This consciousness has been conspicuously absent in today's public or private discourses in China, where the rise of consumer culture in the 1990s has been tinged with nationalist fervour, which is an anti-liberal backlash in the context of globalization (Huang and Lee, 2003; Lee, 2003). The current stage of primitive capital accumulation in

China represents a radical pendulum swing in a short span of time from decades of material asceticism to material fetishism where money is everything if not the only thing, with little regard for justice, fairness, or democracy.

Acknowledgements

The author gratefully acknowledges the financial support of the Competitive Earmarked Research Grant (CityU 1246/03H) awarded by the Research Grants Committee of Hong Kong. Thanks are also due to Dr. Yu Huang, who provided earlier feedback on the manuscript.

References

Arkush, R. D., and Lee, Leo Oufan (Eds.) (1989). *Land Without Hosts: Chinese Impressions of America from the Mid-Nineteenth Century to the Present*. Berkeley, CA: University of California Press.

Chang, Hao (1971). *Liang Ch'i-ch'ao and Intellectual Transition in China, 1890–1907*. Cambridge, MA: Harvard University Press.

Cheek, Timothy (1994). From priests to professionals: intellectuals and the state under the CCP. In Jeffrey N. Wasserstrom and Elizabeth J. Perry (Eds.), *Popular Protest and Political Culture in Modern China* (2nd ed., pp. 184–205). Boulder, CO: Westview.

Cheek, Timothy (1997). *Propaganda and Culture in Mao's China: Deng Tuo and the Intelligentsia*. Oxford: Clarendon Press.

Chen, Chongshan and Mi, X. L. (Eds.) (1989). *Zhongguo chuanbo xiaoguo toushi* [Perspectives on Communication Effects in China]. Shenyang: Shenyang Press.

Chen, Chongshan, Zhu, Jianhua, and Wu, Wei (1988). The Chinese journalist. In David Weaver (Ed.), *The Global Journalist* (pp. 9–30). Cresskill, NJ: Hampton.

Chu, Godwin C. and Chu, Leonard L. (1983). Mass media and conflict revolution: an analysis of letters to the editor. In Godwin C. Chu and Francis L. K. Hsu (Eds.), *China's New Social Fabric*. London: Kegan Paul International.

CJR (*Chinese Journalism Review*) (2003). Hu Shuli: chanying he laohu, huaide dou xiangda [Hu Shuli: no matter they are flies or tigers, (we) beat them as long as they are bad]. http://www.cjr.com.cn (February 26).

Dahlgren, Peter (1995). *Television and the Public Sphere*. London: Sage.

Dai, Qing (1989) *Chu Anping yu 'dang tianxia'* [Chu Anping and 'Party Monopoly Over the Heaven']. Nanjing: Jiangsu Literary Press.

Dittmer, Lowell (1973). The structural evolution of "criticism and self-criticism," *China Quarterly* (56), 708–729.

Dittmer, Lowell (1974). Mass line and "mass criticism" in China: an analysis of the fall of Liu Shao-ch'I, *Asian Survey*, 13, 772–792.

Fairbank, John K. (1979). *The United States and China*. Cambridge, MA: Harvard University Press.

Fang, Hanqi (Ed.) (1992, vol. 1; 1996, vol. 2). *Zhongguo xinwen shiye tongshi* [History of Chinese Journalism]. Beijing: People's University Press.

Goldman, Merle (1994). The role of the press in post-Mao political struggles. In Chin-Chuan Lee (Ed.), *China's Media, Media's China* (pp. 23–36). Boulder, CO: Westview.

Gouldner, Alvin W. (1976). *The Dialectic of Ideology and Technology*. New York: Oxford University Press.

He, Zhou (2000). Chinese communist party press in a tug of war. In Chin-Chuan Lee (Ed.), *Power, Money, and Media: Communication Patterns and Bureaucratic Control in Cultural China* (pp. 112–151). Evanston, IL: Northwestern University Press.

Hu, Jiwei (1989). *Xinwen gongzuo lunshuoji* [Essays on Journalistic Work]. Beijing: Workers' Press.

Huang, Philip C. (1972). *Liang Ch'i-ch'ao and Modern Chinese Liberalism*. Seattle: University of Washington Press.

Huang, Yu and Lee, Chin-Chuan (2003). Peddling party ideology for a profit: media and the rise of Chinese nationalism in the 1990s. In Gary Rawnsley and Ming-yeh Rawnsley (Eds.), *Political Communication in Greater China: The Construction and Reflections of Reality* (pp. 41–61). London: RoutledgeCurzon.

Jia, Xiaohui (2002). *Da Gong Bao xinlun* [A New Treatise on Da Gong Bao]. Tianjin: People's Press.

Keatley, Robert L. (2003). The role of the media in a market economy. China Policy Series, No. 19. Washington, DC: National Committee on United States–China Relations.

Lee, Chin-Chuan (1990). Mass media: of China, about China. In Chin-Chuan Lee (Ed.), *Voices of China: The Interplay of Politics and Journalism* (pp. 3–32). New York: Guilford.

Lee, Chin-Chuan (2000). China's journalism: the emancipatory potential of social theory, *Journalism Studies*, 1, 4, 559–576.

Lee, Chin-Chuan (2001). Servants of the Party or the market: media and journalists in China. In Jeremy Tunstall (Ed.), *Media Occupations and Professions* (pp. 240–252). Oxford: Oxford University Press.

Lee, Chin-Chuan (2003). The global and the national of the Chinese media: discourses, market, technology, and ideology. In Chin-Chuan Lee (Ed.), *Chinese Media, Global Contexts* (pp. 1–31). London: RoutledgeCurzon.

Lee, Chin-Chuan (2004). *Chaoyue xifang baquan: Chuanmei yu zhongguo de xiandaixing* [Beyond Western Hegemony: Media and Chinese Modernity]. Hong Kong: Oxford University Press.

Lee, Chin-Chuan (in press). Globalization, state capitalism, and press conglomeration in China. In David Finkelstein (Ed.), *China's New Media Milieu: Commercialization, Continuity, and Reform*. Armonk, NY: Sharpe.

Levenson, Joseph (1959). *Liang Ch'i-ch'ao and the Mind of Modern China* (2nd ed.). Berkeley, CA: University of California Press.

Lin, Yutang (1936). *A History of the Press and Public Opinion in China*. Chicago: University of Chicago Press.

Liu, Binyan (1989). *Liu Binyan zizhuan* [Autobiography]. Taibei: China Times Press.

Liu, Shaoqi (1967). How to be a good Communist? In Franz Schurmann and Orville Schell (Eds.), *Communist China* (pp. 68–76). New York: Random House.

Liu, Shaoqi (1998). Dui Huabei jizhetuan de tanhua [Talk to the northern China press corps], *Xinwen Zhanxian* 12, 4–10. (Original work published 1948.)

Mao, Zedong (Jan. 5, 1979). On constructing rural surveys, *Beijing Review*, 12–15. (Original work published 1941.)

Moore, Barrington (1967). *Social Origins of Dictatorship and Democracy*. Boston: Beacon.

124

Nathan, Andrew J. (1985). *Chinese Democracy*. New York: Knopf.

Pan, Zhongdang (2000). Improvising reform activities: the changing reality of journalistic practice in China. In Chin-Chuan Lee (Ed.), *Power, Money, and Media: Communication Patterns and Bureaucratic Control in Cultural China* (pp. 68–111). Evanston, IL: Northwestern University Press.

Pan, Zhongdang and Lu, Ye (2003). Localizing professionalism: discursive practices in China's media reforms. In Chin-Chuan Lee (Ed.), *Chinese Media, Global Contexts* (pp. 215–236). London: Routledge.

Passin, Herbert (1963). Writer and journalist in the transitional society. In Lucian W. Pye (Ed.), *Communications and Political Development* (pp. 82–123). Princeton, NJ: Princeton University Press.

Polumbaum, Judy (1990). The tribulations of China's journalists after a decade of reform. In Chin-Chuan Lee (Ed.), *Voices of China: The Interplay of Politics and Journalism* (pp. 3—32). New York: Guilford.

Pool, Ithiel de sola (1973). Communication in totalitarian societies. In Ithiel de Sola Pool and Wilbur Schramm (Eds.), *Handbook of Communication*. Chicago: Rand McNally.

Rosen, Stanley (1989). Public opinion and reform in the People's Republic of China, *Studies in Comparative Communism*, 22(2/3), 153–170.

Schram, Stuart (Ed.). (1976). *Mao Tse-tung Unrehearsed*. Harmondsworth: Penguin.

Schudson, Michael (1978). *Discovering the News*. New York: Basic.

Tuchman, Gaye (1978). *Making News*. New York: Free Press.

White, G. (1983). The postrevolutionary Chinese state. In V. Nee and D. Mozingo (Eds.), *State and Society in Contemporary China* (pp. 27–52). Ithaca, NY: Cornell University Press.

Williams, Raymond (1977). *Marxism and Literature*. New York: Oxford University Press.

Womack, Brantly (1986). *Media and the Chinese Public*. Armonk, NY: Sharpe.

Wu, Guoguang (1997). *Zhao Zhiyang yu zhengzhi gaige* [Zhao Ziyang and Political Reform]. Hong Kong: Pacific Century.

Wu, Tingjun (1994). *Xinji Da Gong Bao shigao* [A History of Da Gong Bao]. Wuhan: Wuhan Press.

Yu, Guoming (1993). *Zhongguo xinwenye toushi* [Perspectives on China's Journalism Enterprises]. Henan: Henan People's Press.

Yu, Guoming (1996). Fanrong yu kundun: lun jiushi niandai zhongguo minyi cheyan de fazhan [Prosperity and setback: the development of China's public opinion polls in the 1990s], *Chuanmei toushi* (Media Digest), Hong Kong, December, 2–5.

Yu, Guoming and Liu, X. Y. (1993). *Zhongguo minyi yanjiu* [Public Opinion Research in China]. Beijing: People's University Press.

Zhang, Jiluan (1944a, vol. 1; 1944b, vol. 2). *Jiluan wencun* (Vol. 1 and Vol. 2) [Collected Writings]. Taibei: Wenxin Press. Reprinted 1962.

Zhang, Yuren (2002). *Ziyou de lixian: Zhongguo ziyou zhuyi xinwen sixiangshi* [The Trajectory of Freedom: History of Chinese Liberalism's Press Thought]. Yunnan: Yunnan People's.

Zhang, Zhongdong (1987). *Hushi wulun* [Five Essays on Hu Shi]. Taibei: Yunchen.

Zhao, Xinshu, Zhu, Jianhua, Li, Hairong and Bleske, G. (1994). Media effects under a monopoly: the case of Beijing in economic reform, *International Journal of Public Opinion Research*, 6(2), 95–117.

Zhao, Yuezhi (1998). *Media, Market, and Democracy in China*. Urbana, IL: University of Illinois Press.

Zhao, Yuezhi (2000). From commercialization to conglomeration: the transformation of the Chinese press within the orbit of the party state, *Journal of Communication*, 50, 3–26.

Zhao, Yuezhi (2003). Enter the world: neo-liberal globalization, the dream for a strong nation, and Chinese press discourses on the WTO. In Chin-Chuan Lee (Ed.), *Chinese Media, Global Contexts* (pp. 32–56). London: RoutledgeCurzon.

Zhu, Jianhua (1988). Public opinion polling in China: a descriptive review, *Gazette*, 41, 127–138.

Zhu, Jianhua, and Rosen, Stanley (1993). From discontent to protest: individual-level causes of the 1989 pro-democracy movement in China, *International Journal of Public Opinion Research*, 5(3), 234–249.

Zhu, Jianhua, Zhao, Xinshu, and Li, Hairong (1990). Public political consciousness in China: an empirical profile, *Asian Survey*, 30(10), 992–1106.

7

ADAPTING TO
GLOBALISATION
The changing contours of journalism in India

Daya Kishan Thussu

This chapter examines the impact of media globalisation on journalism in India. The entrance and expansion of the mainly Western-based transnational media corporations into the Indian media market have transformed the country's media landscape and significantly affected journalistic practice.

Profound changes have taken place in Indian news media during the late 1990s, particularly in broadcasting, which has grown from a state-controlled monopoly to a multiplicity of private television channels, in what used to be one of the world's most protected broadcasting environments. The chapter examines the evolution of journalism in India – the world's largest democracy – and analyses how Indian journalists are adapting to a news environment influenced by Western media practices and whether this has affected their professional journalistic values.

In studies exploring the impact of media globalisation in India (Pendakur and Kapur, 1997; Gupta, 1998; Melkote *et al.*, 1998; Farmer, 2000), the issue of how it has affected news professionals has largely been ignored. In the Western world, and within it the dominant Anglo-American media research tradition, the sociology of journalism is a well-developed area of academic inquiry. Among the major studies examining attitudes of media professionals, one of the most notable is the seminal work by the US sociologist Herbert Gans, based on extensive interviews with journalists and observation of media activities at *CBS Evening News*, *NBC Nightly News*, and the two agenda-setting news weeklies, *Newsweek* and *Time* (Gans, 1979). Another significant US study by David Weaver and G. Cleveland Wilhoit, first published in 1986, detailed the profile of media workers in the US, based on demographic, educational, class, race and gender categories (Weaver and Wilhoit, 1991). In Britain, one key study is that conducted by British sociologist Jeremy Tunstall (1993) about television producers. In an international context, the first major survey of journalists in more than 20 countries, published in 1998, did not include journalists from India (Weaver, 1998). This chapter includes the initial results of research undertaken in 1999–2000, part of a larger ongoing project on Indian media to examine the impact of Western television on Indian journalists.

The evolution of Indian journalism

Journalism in India has deep roots in the nationalist movement: during British colonial rule many nationalist leaders, notably Mahatma Gandhi, 'the Father of the Nation', were actively involved in journalistic work. This legacy of anti-colonialism has continued to influence Indian media even after Independence from Britain in 1947, when India inherited from the British the combination of a private press and a government-controlled broadcasting system (Chatterjee, 1991). In the newly independent country, by and large the Indian press acted as a fourth estate in the fledgling democracy, with many journalists taking a critical stance on national and international issues. However, journalists working for the state-controlled electronic media – first All India Radio (AIR), a key instrument of mass persuasion in a hugely illiterate country, and, after 1959, Doordarshan, the state-run television network – saw their role, more often than not, as information bureaucrats disseminating government information and contributing to what came to be known as 'nation-building'.

This sentiment was in evidence even in the privately owned newspaper industry. In a detailed study of the Indian-language press, Robin Jeffrey observes:

> The content of successful Indian-language newspapers was subtly local and rarely dull. In some circumstances, to be sure, they could powerfully propel political parties and movements opposed to the central government of the day. But the overall thrust of their news-gathering and dissemination was to propagate subliminal ideas about the existence and legitimacy of an *Indian* state and an *Indian* nation.
>
> (2000: 9; italics in original)

The media and the public sphere

As in many other developing countries, most journalists in India saw their task as following a developmental agenda set by an activist state. For its part, the government subsidised news agencies, newspapers and magazines by providing them with cheap newsprint and public-sector advertising, thus indirectly affecting even the privately owned and diverse press. However, despite such interference by the government, the relative autonomy of the private print media significantly contributed to the evolution of multi-party democracy in India. It helped create and then sustain a public sphere within which a democratic discourse could flourish.

In many respects, India, the so-called 'functioning anarchy', was a unique case among the countries of the global South. Parliamentary democracy took root in the country despite a profoundly unequal social system, with its caste hierarchies and class barriers.

The composition of India's political leadership in the early years of independence under the Prime Ministership of Jawaharlal Nehru may have contributed to the success of parliamentary democracy, underpinned by a free press. Nehru, himself a journalist during the anti-colonial period, was keen that the managerial and editorial control of the British-owned newspapers in India such as *The Statesman*, *The Mail* and *The Pioneer* should pass into Indian hands. The first Press Commission in its 1954 report supported this line of argument. Unlike most of the developing world, Indian newspapers were Indian owned and run.

A democratic polity ensured that the government tolerated criticism on the editorial pages of the national press. This tolerance provided the arena in which Indian journalists – most coming from an urban middle-class milieu – were able to develop high professional standards and the opportunity to engage in critical debates on socio-political and economic issues. More importantly, the pro-active and often adversarial role of journalists contributed to the evolution of an early-warning system for serious food shortages and thus a preventive mechanism against famine (Ram, 1990). With the growing population and an increasing, albeit slowly, rate of literacy, the print media experienced unprecedented growth – demonstrable in the daily circulation of newspapers which showed nearly a fourteen-fold rise over four decades (see Table 7.1).

According to *The Hindu*, India's most respected newspaper:

> The long-term Indian press experience, set in larger context, suggests a set of functions that serious newspapers have performed with benefit to society. These are (a) the credible-informational, (b) the critical-investigative-'watchdog', (c) the educational, and (d) the agenda-building functions.

Summarising its own principles, the newspaper said in a special editorial to mark its 125th anniversary, in August 2003:

> *The Hindu* has worked out for itself a set of five principles as a template for socially responsible and ethical journalism. The first is the principle of *truth telling*. The second principle is that of *freedom and independence*. The third component of the template is the principle of *justice*. The fourth principle is that of *humaneness*. The fifth principle is that of *contributing to the social good*.
>
> (*The Hindu*, 2003; italics in the original)

Table 7.1 Indian daily newspapers circulation: 1956-1996 (figures in millions)

	1956	1966	1976	1986	1996
Population	400	493	617	754	932
Daily circulation	2.9	6.8	9.3	21.5	40.2

Source: Based on Jeffrey (2000)

Though most newspapers did not measure up to the exacting standards of *The Hindu*, the principle of freedom and independence did tend to influence journalism across the country (Ram, 1990; Jeffrey, 2000). By the end of the 1990s, the media had become a major industry (Chandrasekhar, 2003). According to the 2002 National Readership Survey, the print media reached 242 million Indians, television 329 million and radio 174 million citizens across the vast country (Bunsha, 2002). However, there remained significant regional variations in media use, especially print media, given that growth in newspaper and magazine circulation has a close relationship with literacy levels. The southern state of Kerala, which boasts near-total literacy, claims that more than 74 per cent of the population read at least one newspaper or magazine, while in Bihar, one of India's poorest states – with half the population illiterate – just over 15 per cent of the population read newspapers or magazines.

Barriers to broadcasting

Unlike the press, the radio and television monopoly broadcasters were little more than government mouthpieces. Indira Gandhi, Prime Minister for 14 years during the 1970s and 1980s, was unambiguous about the role of broadcasting in a new democracy, arguing that unlike her counterparts in the rest of Asia and Africa, she did not own any newspapers. Thus the government, so went her argument, needed to control the airwaves – during her premiership All India Radio was rechristened by her critics as 'All Indira Radio'. Television news too was equally Indira-centric, almost daily showing the photogenic prime minister opening conferences and meeting foreign dignitaries. Her government was instrumental in creating a satellite network across the country – satellite television came to India in 1982, six years before Rupert Murdoch launched Sky network, heralding satellite revolution in Europe.

Accelerated by the combined impact of new communication technologies and the opening-up of global markets, Indian broadcasting experienced profound changes from the early 1990s onwards. Economic liberalisation, deregulation and privatisation contributed to the expansion of Indian media corporations, facilitated by joint ventures with international media conglomerates. Such developments have revolutionised broadcasting in what used to be a heavily protected media market, one of the most regulated among the world's democracies. Gradual deregulation and privatisation of television have transformed the media landscape in the country, evident in the exponential growth in the number of television channels, from 1991 when Doordarshan was the sole government-run and rather bland network, whose programmes were seen to be 'insipid and uninspired' (Gupta, 1998: 31), to more than 100 channels in 2003. Out of these, more than 20 were in Hindi or English and therefore national in reach, while others catered to regional audiences in their own languages. Most of these new channels were entertainment-oriented, though some had dedicated news and current-affairs operations.

The privatisation of broadcasting encouraged many Western transnational media players to enter the 'emerging market' of India – potentially one of the world's biggest English-language television markets. Not least of the attractions were the existence of a huge middle class – estimated between 200–300 million – with aspirations to a Western lifestyle; a well-developed national satellite network, linking the vast country, and a fast-growing advertising sector – in 2002, television accounted for 52 per cent of the total media outlay, followed by the print media's share at 33 per cent (Chandrasekhar, 2003).

Since its inception in the late 1950s as a government propaganda organisation, television was seen as a means of disseminating state policies, and its main aim was to foster a feeling of national identity. The ethos was based on the public-service model of broadcasting, with clear emphasis on education and information at the expense of entertainment (Chatterjee, 1991). Borrowing the best traditions of the BBC, the broadcasting of high and 'authentic' Indian culture, in the form of classical dance and music, was encouraged to raise the audience's cultural tastes and values in preference to popular or populist forms of television (Gupta, 1998).

The entry of global media conglomerates into India opened up a new window for Indian journalists – first through the live coverage of the 1990–91 Gulf crisis by the Cable News Network (CNN) and later through Hong Kong-based Star (Satellite Television Asian Region) TV, part of global media magnate Rupert Murdoch's News Corporation. The rapid growth in advertising revenues ensured that cable and satellite television extended their penetration of Indian market substantially – from 1.2 million homes having cable and satellite television in 1992 to nearly 40 million cable TV homes by 2003. Among the main channels were major transnational broadcasters – CNN, Disney, CNBC, MTV, Star, Sony Entertainment Television, BBC – and scores of Indian channels, operating both at regional, national and provincial levels.

The emergence of a hybrid media culture

It has been argued that the globalisation of Western culture is producing 'heterogeneous disjunctures' rather than a homogenised global culture (Appadurai, 1996). The global–local interaction also appears to be leading to a hybrid media culture, one that blurs the boundaries between the modern and the traditional, the national and the global (which in essence means US-dominated Western) culture. Ronald Robertson coined a phrase for such a phenomenon, 'glocalisation', characterised by cultural fusion as a result of adaptation of Western media genres to suit local languages, styles and cultural conventions, using new communication technologies (Robertson, 1992).

A prime example of this cultural hybridity can be found in the case of India, where television news networks have appropriated Western, or, more specifically,

American TV programme formats and Indianised them to suit local tastes and languages, creating a new model of hybridisation. This global–local media interaction has contributed to the emergence of Hinglish – a mixture of Hindi, the most widely used language in India, though predominantly spoken in northern India, and English, the medium of international communication and global media. Though largely neglected in academic discourses, the emergence and unprecedented growth of a new mediated language, Hinglish, appear to have benefited the northern-based journalists. Indian television software companies such as Television Eighteen made English-language informational programmes for transnational broadcasters such as the *India Show* on Star Plus or the *India Business Report* on BBC, increasingly using a mixture of Hindi and English, reflecting the market for Hinglish (Datta, 1999).

The growing popularity of this new media language has earned the disapproval of language purists, while critical analysts view it as yet another example of the media and cultural imperialism that the West, led by the United States, exercises over the developing world. Those subscribing to a postmodernist view of the world see this as a positive sign, arguing that Western television networks operating in India have had to adapt to Indian conditions, exemplified by the growth of Indian-made programmes in Indian languages, broadcast on foreign-owned satellite channels. Table 7.2 lists some of the main bilingual channels operational in 2003.

Given its domination of global media, commerce and communication, English has emerged as an important vehicle for the globalisation of the US version of capitalism. This unrivalled domination has a historical context, as noted by David Crystal:

> The present-day world status of English is primarily the result of two factors: the expansion of British colonial power, which peaked towards the end of the 19th century, and the emergence of the United States as the leading economic power of the 20th century. It is the latter factor which continues to explain the position of the English language today.
>
> (1995: 106)

Table 7.2 The main bilingual channels in India

Channel	Type	Languages
MTV India	Music	Hindi/English
Channel V	Music	Hindi/English
Disney	Animation	Hindi/English
Star Plus	General	Hindi/English*
Discovery	Documentaries	Hindi/English
Star Sports	Sports	Hindi/English
SET MAX	Sports	Hindi/English
Zee Network	General	Hindi/English*

Note:* Only a few programmes are in English.

Table 7.3 Top five newspapers (in millions)

Publication	Language/type	Readership
Dainik Jagran	Hindi daily	14.0
Dainik Bhaskar	Hindi daily	13.5
Malyalam Manorama	Malayalam weekly	9.2
Daily Thanthi	Tamil daily	8.8
Eenadu	Telugu daily	8.0

Source: Indian Readership Survey 2002

In a multi-lingual country like India (400 languages are spoken across the country, while the Indian Constitution recognises 18 languages), language is a crucial element of cultural self-expression. Reflecting its colonial history, English remains the link language in India – of national judiciary and bureaucracy, higher education and corporate sector – while Hindi, with its regional variations, is the most widely spoken language. It is also the language of India's main film industry. Though spoken by a tiny minority as a first language, English carries a disproportionate degree of social and intellectual prestige. The usage of English in India signifies a particular social class, with its attendant power and influence, perhaps a reflection of the colonial hangover, prompting some to view English as hegemonic (Kachru, 1996). Competence in the language privileges the user in the most important social areas – for example in acquiring top jobs in government and commerce, especially with transnational corporations. It has also been argued that the language of the colonial powers has been Indianised to the extent that it has become an 'indigenous language and therefore available to all Indians' (D'Souza, 1999: 103).

Despite the influence of the English language in India, the biggest media growth is in regional languages – the 2002 National Readership Survey in India showed that not one English-language publication could be found in the top five daily or weekly newspapers in terms of their readerships (see Table 7.3).

According to the Registrar of Newspapers for India, more than 40,000 newspapers and magazines were in operation with a total circulation of more than 80 million, in 19 principal languages and 100 other languages and dialects. One reason for such diversity is the size of the regional media market, segmented into geo-linguistically formed readerships in such major languages as Tamil, Telugu and Bengali. The changing contours of national politics, with regional parties taking centre stage, have given a new impetus to newspapers in Indian languages and contributed significantly to the growth of regional language television channels. According to the Indian Newspaper Society, newspapers and magazines in Indian languages sell four times more than the English language publications.

Impact of media globalisation on journalists

The opening up of the media sector in India has had a major impact on the journalism profession as many more opportunities have emerged, especially as transnational media corporations are increasingly investing in Indian-language media outlets. The pilot study investigated whether the availability of new technologies and a relatively liberal working environment had changed the professional output of the media personnel and asked whether the proliferation of private TV companies has led to a market-driven journalism. Does the foreign ownership of media organisations affect their editorial priorities? How do journalists see their role as providers of public information in a country where nearly half the population still cannot read or write?

The main aim of the study was to assess how the journalists were reacting to the changed media landscape. The study was conducted both among the elite English-language media personnel – often the beneficiaries of globalisation – and among journalists working for Indian-language publications and television channels. More than 150 survey questionnaires were sent to various media organisations – news agencies, newspapers and magazines, radio and television networks – reflecting the types and geographical distribution of the media: 70 responses were received from news journalists. As Table 7.4 indicates, the response reflected a range of media category, gender and editorial position of media personnel.

Table 7.4 Characteristics of journalists responding (total number 70)

Characteristics	Percentage
Media category	
Newspapers	50
Magazines	15
Television	15
News agencies	15
Radio	5
Gender	
Male	75
Female	25
Age	
< 25	2
25–35	35
35–45	39
45–55	12
> 55	2
Editorial position	
Senior level	40
Middle level	50
Lower level	10

Of the 70 responses received, 50 per cent belonged to newspapers – both national and regional; 15 per cent worked for news magazines; 15 per cent were employees of national news agencies, while 15 per cent were television journalists and 5 per cent were working for radio. The preponderance of print journalism can be explained from the fact that the Indian press is huge and diverse, that there was very limited professional broadcast journalism before globalisation and that it was only in the 1990s that many journalists moved from press to broadcasting.

The sample was chosen with a view to examine how the transformations in the media scene were affecting journalists from the regional language press, as well as from the internationally oriented English-language national media. In terms of gender, 75 per cent of all those who filled in the survey questionnaire were male. The 25 per cent of females who responded reflected the fact that the majority of women reporters/journalists work on non-news media, such as magazine sections of the newspapers, focusing mainly on consumer affairs or lifestyle journalism. The majority of the sample was aged between 25 and 45. Only 2 per cent of respondents were under 25, while the biggest age group – 39 per cent – was 35–45, in middle-level journalistic jobs. The second biggest group aged 25–35 accounted for 35 per cent of the sample while 12 per cent each were in the age groups 45–55 and over 55.

In terms of seniority, the majority of the respondents belonged to middle-level journalism – senior correspondent, assistant editor, and so on, accounting for 50 per cent of the sample. Some 35 per cent of top editorial people were also included in the study, while the junior staff consisted of merely 15 per cent.

Of all the journalists examined, 40 per cent said they had professional qualifications. Most of these were in the lower age brackets. Only one of the journalists over 55 had a professional qualification in journalism, although they were almost all graduates. Apart from a very few, all journalists included in the survey had higher degrees, and many had post-graduate qualifications – in subjects such as politics, history and English literature.

Attitudes towards media liberalisation

The journalists were asked whether globalisation had affected the working environment for news professionals. Most agreed that globalisation had opened up more career opportunities in media industries, with greater promotion and better salary prospects. Journalists working for the English-language publications or television networks seemed to be more enthusiastic about the entry of global media players into India. However, journalists employed by the regional language newspapers and magazines, though largely agreeing that there were more career opportunities, thought that only a few transnational broadcasters were interested in their expertise. To the question of whether the opening-up of media had brought more freedom of expression as a journalist, a large proportion of them – 70 per cent – agreed with the proposition. There was overwhelming support – 88 per cent – for the proposition that opening up the media to competition was a positive development.

Table 7.5 Top five English-language publications

Publication	Type	Readership
Times of India	Daily newspaper	6.1 million
India Today	Weekly news magazine	3.0 million
The Hindu	Daily newspaper	2.8 million
Filmfare	Weekly film magazine	100,000
Reader's Digest	Monthly general magazine	100,000

Source: Indian Readership Survey 2002

Foreign ownership of the media

When it came to questions about foreign ownership of the media, opinion was more divided: though the majority disagreed with the proposition that foreign ownership of the media was a positive development, 40 per cent did agree. The opposition to foreign ownership of the media is partly explained by the fact that the mainstream press has traditionally had a left-of-centre leaning, influenced in no small measure by Nehruvian socialism, the staple ideological diet of independent India for over 40 years. The efforts of London's *Financial Times* to start a new business daily with *Business Standard* of Calcutta and *Time* magazine's plans to produce an Indian edition in collaboration with Living Media group, publishers of *India Today*, India's best-known news magazine, had been thwarted by state regulation.

The debate over foreign ownership of the Indian press had often been very bitter. Unlike many developing countries, most newspapers in India are run by Indians, who feared a loss of identity if foreign media were allowed majority ownership (Ram, 1994). Given the power of US-dominated Western media, there was concern that competition would drive Indian national newspapers out of the market, or at least reduce the rich diversity of a press that represents a multiplicity of interests and political opinions, with New Delhi alone having more than a dozen daily newspapers. The major media houses have traditionally dominated newspaper circulation, with the top ten newspaper groups accounting for nearly half of the total national newspaper circulation (Jeffrey, 2000). As Table 7.5 shows, only one foreign publication (the Indian edition of *Reader's Digest*, one of the world's most widely read general-interest monthly magazines) figures among the top five English-language publications in India.

In 1955 a Cabinet Committee headed by the then Prime Minister Jawaharlal Nehru adopted a resolution prohibiting the entry of foreign investment in the media industry. The decision was taken in the wake of the recommendations of India's first Press Commission which opposed 'any attempt to bring out Indian editions of foreign periodicals dealing mainly with news and current affairs'. The second Press Commission suggested, in 1982, a legal provision against foreign ownership of newspapers: 'there should be a specific legal provision under which no newspaper undertaking should have any foreign ownership either in the form of share or in the form of loans' (quoted in Katyal, 2000).

In the mid-1990s, and under the pressures of Western governments, a Cabinet committee was set up to suggest how foreigners may be allowed to own Indian newspapers and magazines. However, it failed to produce a unanimous report. In 2002, the right-wing Bharatiya Janata Party-led coalition government reversed the traditional policy on foreign ownership of the print media and allowed foreign companies to own print media in India, though their share of ownership was capped at 26 per cent, prompting much criticism from many journalists. Said *The Hindu*, in a 2002 editorial: 'an ill-advised decision that will have disturbing implications for the quality of democratic discourse in the country.' Kuldip Nayar, one of India's best-known journalists, wrote:

> The print media is one of the pillars of our democracy, and a nation buffeted by disruptive forces can't take chances by opening its print media to those who are capable of stoking the fires of separatism and parochialism. Foreign companies are already an economic force in the country; their share in the print media can give them a political clout which no outsider should wield.
>
> (Nayar 2002)

In an era of globalisation and proliferation of private television news networks and the Internet, it was argued that foreign investment in the print sector was inevitable and restricting it when almost all other sectors of media and communication are being privatised, was meaningless. Although the President of the Indian Newspapers Society asserted that a majority of its 700 members opposed to foreign investment in the print media, major newspapers and news magazines such as *India Today, Indian Express, Business Standard* and *The Pioneer* welcomed the entry of foreign money, technology and editorial expertise.

Public-service role of the media

The media, newspapers in particular and lately television and on-line media, have performed a watchdog function in India which has included exposing government inefficiencies, mismanagement and corruption. Among the key examples are Chitra Subramaniam of *The Hindu* reporting on 'kickbacks' in defence deals with Swedish arms company Bofors in 1980s during the prime ministership of Rajiv Gandhi; the reporting from eastern drought-ridden Orissa state about starvation deaths, in the face of persistent official denials by Sampad Mahapatra of New Delhi Television (NDYV); and the exposé of corruption at highest places by Tarun Tejpal's news portal Tehalka.com, leading to the resignation of the President of the ruling BJP in 2001 (Verghese, 2003).

In the survey, opinion over whether privatisation and globalisation were threatening the public-service role of the media was evenly divided, with 43 per cent agreeing and 42 per cent disagreeing (the rest were neutral). And yet a large majority of respondents – nearly 70 per cent – thought that competition had led to an emphasis on infotainment.

There was an interesting correlation between journalists working for private television networks, who seemed to believe that private television was not posing a threat to public broadcasting: they were more likely to think that the public-service role of the media was not under threat, in comparison to journalists working for newspapers and autonomous news agencies.

A general perception among many journalists, especially those belonging to regional newspapers, was that the English-language media seemed to increasingly overlook the growing disparity between the rich and the poor (UNDP, 2003). Though by 2003, Doordarshan was operating 21 channels, and claiming that the total number of viewers who watch its programmes at least once a week to be around 500 million, it is under constant commercial pressure to provide entertainment at the expense of educational programmes. Most journalists agreed that news professionals were increasingly adopting 'Western' practices and values and apart from a few cases it was not seen as a problem. In fact, most Indian journalists seemed to admire the professionalism of Western media workers.

Media use

Journalists were asked what television news channels they watched on a regular basis (daily or weekly). Of the two main Western news channels – CNN and BBC World – the majority watched BBC World regularly. Among the Indian channels the two most popular were Doordarshan and Star News – all three were in English. While the BBC was seen as representing high professional standards, Star News (which also has a daily Hindi edition) was considered as the most professionally produced Indian news network. The high use of Doordarshan news reflects traditional attitudes towards the national broadcaster – as it is the government's public information channel and given the important role of governments in setting the media agenda (despite premature reports of the death of the state), most journalists feel they need to be in the know. The widespread following of the BBC – even among those journalists who are not working for English-language publications or networks – shows the esteem in which British broadcasting is still held in India. Only 28 per cent said they watched CNN regularly. The majority of respondents watched a combination of BBC, Doordarshan and Star News.

Conclusion

The findings from this pilot study show that globalisation of the media has generally been well received by Indian journalists. It has contributed to opening up new career opportunities and improvements in professional standards, especially in broadcast journalism. However, there are also concerns among a sizeable section of the journalists surveyed about the consequences of foreign ownership of media, especially the print media, on its diversity and independence. Although the Hindi language journalists seem to have benefited hugely with the availability of pan-Indian news channels, such as Star News and international news networks such as Zee News, journalists working for regional-language press and broadcasting organisations have yet to feel the impact of globalisation on their professional output.

Since the study, major media corporations such as Zee have launched four regional channels under its Alpha umbrella – Alpha Marathi, Alpha Gujarati, Alpha Punjabi and Alpha Bengali. In addition, the network also has a round-the-clock, free-to-air news channel Zee News (Zee Network website). This should ensure that regional journalists will have more revenue to make programmes. Also, some new players have entered the news arena. *Aaj Tak*, part of India Today group and launched only at the end of 2000, has emerged as a leader in Hindi news, accounting for more than 40 per cent of audience share in satellite and cable homes. Since April 2003, Star News has gone native – it now broadcasts news only in Hindi. Other round-the-clock news networks such as NDTV 24/7 (in English), NDTV India (in Hindi) and Sahara Samay (in Hindi) show the pre-eminence of national language in television news discourses.

The globalisation of the Indian media industries themselves – Zee now reaches a South Asian diaspora audience spread across all six continents, while Star too is prominent in Britain – is likely to affect journalism in India (Jacka and Ray 1996; Thussu, 1998; Power and Mazumdar, 2000; Shedde, 2000). Therefore, there is need for further research on how journalists operate in an increasingly global media environment, especially with the growing use of on-line media. Media globalisation has provided new opportunities and challenges for journalists in India. It is fair to say that by and large they have adapted well to Anglo-American norms of journalism, embodying 'global' news media. Given the internationally comparable professional standards of the journalistic output of networks such as NDTV which for five years (1998–2003) provided news content to Murdoch's Star News operations in India, it is not inconceivable that News Corporation might utilise its expertise in conjunction with its two other major international news outfits –– Fox News in the United States and Sky News in Europe, to rival CNN's domination of global television news. This may open up a new arena for the critically informed, English-fluent, Internet-savvy Indian journalists.

References

Appadurai, A. (1996) *Modernity at Large: Cultural Dimensions of Globalisation*, University of Minnesota Press, Minneapolis.
Bunsha, D. (2002) 'The Rise of Print', *Frontline* 19/14, July 6–19.

Chandrasekhar, C. P. (2003) 'Media: More Business, Less Diversity', *The Hindu*, August 30.

Chatterjee, P. C. (1991) *Broadcasting in India*, Sage, New Delhi.

Crystal, D. (1995) *The Cambridge Encyclopaedia of the English Language*, Cambridge University Press, Cambridge.

Datta, N. (1999) 'Switch on TV-18 for handsome returns', *The Financial Express*, December 18.

D'Souza, J. (1999) 'Indian English: Some Myths, Some Realities', *English World-Wide*, vol. 18, no. 1, pp. 91–105.

Farmer, V. (2000) 'Depicting the Nation: Media Politics in Independent India', in Frankel, F., Hasan, Z., Bhargava, R. and Arora, B. (eds) *Transforming India*, Oxford University Press, New Delhi.

Gans, H. (1979) *Deciding What's News*, Vintage Books, New York.

Gupta, N. (1998) *Switching Channels: Ideologies of Television in India*, Oxford University Press, New Delhi.

Hindu, The (2002) 'An Indian Institution Under Threat', editorial, June 27.

Hindu, The (2003) 'The Hindu', special editorial, August 27, web edition available at: http://www.hinduonnet.com.

Jacka, E. and Ray, M. (1996) 'Indian Television: An Emerging Regional Force,' in Sinclair, J, Jacka E and Cunningham, S. (eds) *New Patterns in Global Television: Peripheral Vision*, Oxford University Press, Oxford.

Jeffrey, R. (2000) *India's Newspaper Revolution: Capitalism, Politics and the Indian Language Press 1977–1999*, Hurst and Co., London.

Kachru, B. B. (ed.) (1996) *The Other Tongue: English Across Cultures*, Oxford University Press, New Delhi, second edition.

Katyal, K. K. (2000) 'Protect the Press', *The Hindu*, October 23, web edition available at: http://www.hinduonnet.com.

Melkote, S., Shields, P. and Agrawal, B. C. (eds) (1998) *International Satellite Broadcasting in South Asia: Political, Economic and Cultural Implications*, University Press of America, Lanham, MD.

Nayar, K. (2002) 'The Sovereign Word', *Outlook*, February 18, web edition available at http://www.outlookindia.com

Pendakur, M. and Kapur, J. (1997) 'Think Globally, Program Locally: Privatisation of Indian National Television,' in Bailie, M. and Winseck, D. (eds) *Democratizing Communication? Comparative Perspectives on Information and Power*, Hampton Press, Cresskill, NJ.

Power, C. and Mazumdar, S. (2000) 'Bollywood Goes Global', *Newsweek*, February 28, pp. 88–94.

Ram, N. (1990) 'An Independent Press and Anti-Hunger Strategies: The Indian Experience,' in Dreze, J. and Sen, A. (eds) *The Political Economy of Hunger*, Vol. I, Clarendon Press, Oxford.

Ram, N. (1994) 'Foreign Media Entry into the Press – Issues and Implications', *Economic and Political Weekly*, October 22, pp. 2787–2790.

Robertson, R. (1992) *Globalisation: Social Theory and Global Culture*, Sage, London.

Shedde, M. (2000) 'Damp Ammunition – Quixotic Vision of an ICE Boom', *The Times of India*, 19 June.

Thussu, D. K. (1998) 'Localising the Global – Zee TV in India', in Thussu, D. K. (ed.) *Electronic Empires: Global Media and Local Resistance*, Arnold, London.

Tunstall, J. (1993) *Television Producers*, Routledge, London.

UNDP (2003) *Human Development Report 2003: Millennium Development Goals: A Compact among Nations to End Human Poverty.* United Nations Development Programme, Oxford University Press.

Verghese, B. G. (ed.) (2003) *Breaking the Big Story: Great Moments in Indian Journalism*, Penguin, London.

Weaver, D. (ed.) (1998) *The Global Journalist: News People Around the World*, Hampton Press, Cresskill, NJ.

Weaver, D. and Wilhoit, G C. (1991) *The American Journalist: A Portrait of U.S. News People and Their Work*, Indiana University Press, Bloomington, IN, second edition (first edition published in 1986).

Zee Network website (2003): http://www.zeetelevision.com.

8

THE CHANGING DYNAMICS OF ARAB JOURNALISM

Naomi Sakr

Where governments come to power by means other than the ballot box and remain there without public endorsement, they have a problem of missing legitimacy on their hands. One way to manufacture this vital asset is to delegitimise past regimes by casting them as rogues and traitors or, at least, inept and corrupt (Shaaban 1990: 61–2). Another is to smear current opponents as a threat to national security and stability (Sakr 2003). Such a process of false legitimisation, all too obvious in the Arab world, wreaks havoc with both historiography and news reporting. Accounts of the past are either suppressed or turned to the incumbent regime's advantage, while public records of the present are distorted to extol the supposed virtues of those who control access to the reporting process. In these circumstances the essentialist suppositions and ill-informed assumptions that have become entrenched in Western media coverage of Arab societies (Said 1981) have been able to circulate globally with no credible challenge or rebuttal mounted by Arab media or historians (Karim 2002: 106).

Where do Arab journalists stand in this sorry state of affairs? Scholars familiar with the extent of censorship in key Arab countries stress its all-pervading capacity to condition and structure the entire field of journalistic endeavour (e.g. El Khawaga 2001: 149). Yet, as testified by human rights groups' regular alerts, Arab journalists go into battle daily against censorious regimes, often at great personal risk to themselves and their families (Arab Press Freedom Watch 2003). While analysis of structures is clearly indispensable to an understanding of trends in Arab journalism, it is equally important to assess the individual contributions of journalists who, by contesting these structures, have altered them in some way. Journalists may fashion their output in accordance with the exigencies of organised production (Golding and Elliott 1979: 114–23, 206–11) but it is misleading to suggest that they do not sometimes resist (Phillips 2003). Acknowledging influences in both directions, this chapter starts from the premise that history has given rise to particular structures in the Arab news media, within which the practice of journalism has been confined and constrained. Since structures and practices evolve, the study's main concern is with the key factors and forces in that evolution. It begins by reviewing journalistic norms that predated satellite television's disruptive impact during the 1990s and goes on to examine aspects of that impact, taking account of other changes in journalism already under way and examining journalists' use of the new technology. Insofar as a normative position underlies the analysis, it is one that favours pluralistic media systems capable of maximising scope for free expression of diverse perspectives and conflicting views.[1]

Structures, norms and resistance

'Advocacy journalism' and 'mobilisation press' are phrases sometimes linked to dominant styles of Arab journalism in the second half of the twentieth century. Such terms are used not only in contradistinction to the ideals of impartiality and objectivity urged upon journalists in some other settings, but also to highlight fundamental differences in roles assigned to the press. 'Unlike American journalists', wrote Tom McFadden, 'the majority of Arab editors place little emphasis upon the informing role of the press in society. There is a striking amount of agreement that fighting for causes is primary and informing is secondary' (1953: 14). McFadden did not believe that Arab journalists were motivated by different impulses from those elsewhere. Indeed, his research led him to conclude that 'at least as many Arab journalists [were] sincerely and unselfishly trying to serve the public interest' as would be found anywhere in the world. His point was that they served the public interest 'according to their understanding of it' (ibid.: 17). This understanding was based on a consensus on causes that should be promoted by the press and on the ranking of those causes. McFadden's discovery of a consensus can be viewed in the historical context of the time. Israel had been established in 1948 in what was previously Palestine. Arab nationalism was meanwhile gathering momentum in the aftermath of the Second World War, which had left the main colonial powers, Britain and France, in a weakened state. Thus, in the early 1950s, struggles against imperialism and Zionism were deemed priority causes, followed by the promotion of Arab unity. Next on the list were fighting government corruption and promoting reform and modernisation (ibid.: 14–15). Significantly, however, consensus was lacking over the crucial matter of precisely how any of these five causes should be advanced. This in turn contributed to a highly partisan press serving a multiplicity of minority political groups (ibid.).

It is not surprising that anti-imperialism topped journalists' agendas. Two respected authorities on development in Arab states have recently concluded that the 'tradition of external intervention in the region' has been a bigger factor than religion or culture in defining the political attitudes and actions to be found there (Henry and Springborg 2000: 8–10).[2] Demonstrating the globally un-paralleled scope of external intervention in the Middle East in terms of its length (two centuries), intrusiveness (e.g. oil exploitation) and multilateral nature, these authors note that the great powers were generally too busy competing with each other to establish responsible local government institutions (ibid.). If, for example, the rise of the Egyptian press in the late nineteenth and early twentieth centuries is viewed against a backdrop of colonisation, the origins and antecedents of the journalistic attitudes described by McFadden become clearer.

The Egyptian Khedive Ismail encouraged a transformation of the press in the expectation that this would buttress his efforts to assert independence from the seat of Ottoman power and from his European creditors, Britain and France (Kelidar 1993: 3). The nascent Egyptian newspaper industry was invigorated by the welcome extended to Syrian publishers who moved from Beirut to Cairo during the 1870s and 1880s. As European control over Egypt tightened, different titles became associated with groups for and against that control, including a growing but divided nationalist movement. Rapid expansion in the number of publications went hand in hand with expansion in the size of the reading public (Ayalon 1995: 54). By the early twentieth century a range of nationalist viewpoints were represented in the press. But they were represented in a way that enabled political parties to grow out of specific newspapers, because papers distinguished themselves from each other by proposing different policies and courses of political action *vis-à-vis* independence from Britain (Kelidar 1993: 16–17).

By the time William Rugh drew up his classic typology of the Arab press in the 1970s, the political environment had changed dramatically, compared with either the early 1900s or 1950s. Moreover, television had arrived on the scene alongside newspapers and radio. But the convention of using news media outlets to pursue narrow political agendas remained. Rugh himself identified three types of press in Arab countries, attaching to them the labels 'mobilisation', 'loyalist' and 'diverse'. He found that, in the wake of military coups and large-scale nationalisation in key countries, media systems aimed at mobilising the masses behind their national governments had replaced previously 'diverse' or 'loyalist' systems in several Arab states (Rugh, 1987: 165). 'Loyalist' in this definition referred to newspapers found to be consistently loyal to the regime despite being privately owned (ibid.: 71). 'Diverse' meant that newspapers were 'clearly different from each other in content and apparent political tendency, as well as in style' (ibid.: 89). As can be inferred from this typology, it was rare for any single newspaper or broadcasting station to seek to provide information that was sufficiently copious, sensitive or critical to support a range of political views.

A prime example of a mobilised press in Rugh's account was to be found in Egypt, where Gamal Abdel-Nasser, who became president in 1954, nationalised the press in 1960 after failing to elicit routine approval from newspaper editors. From then on editors were subjected to dismissal, banning, imprisonment and exile, while readers increasingly turned to sources other than newspapers for news (Dabous 1993: 108–10). At the same time, Egypt's state-run broadcaster promoted Nasserist ideology on its pan-Arab radio station, Voice of the Arabs, and supplied free programmes to emerging television networks in other Arab states (Dajani 1980: 108). This process prompted reactions from Arab governments criticised by Nasser's media machine. In particular, the Saudi ruling family was jolted into launching domestic radio broadcasting to compete with hostile Egyptian radio propaganda (Boyd 1999: 146–7).

Thus began a prolonged Saudi campaign to control the Arab press and airwaves. Flush with oil revenues after oil prices skyrocketed in the mid-1970s, ruling elites in Saudi Arabia and other Gulf states, notably Iraq, were suddenly able to spend large amounts in support of media ownership and control. Whereas Cairo and Beirut were the main centres for Arab newspapers circulating beyond national borders before the oil boom, after the boom Gulf countries were able to attract Egyptian, Lebanese and Palestinian journalists to work on publications based in Gulf cities or outside the Arab world altogether, in London and Paris. Two additional factors reinforced this trend during the 1980s. One was Lebanon's civil war from 1975 to 1990. Lebanese journalists had been targeted for assassination before 1975 (Dajani 1992: 53) but the war put them in ever-greater peril. The torture and murder in 1980 of a leading publisher, Salim al-Louzi, apparently by Syrian agents, had an effect so terrifying and long-lasting that a Lebanese lawyer later drew an analogy with the Hiroshima bomb (Article 19, 1998: 76). A second factor, this time diverting media business away from Cairo, was the Arab League's ten-year boycott of Egypt, which began in 1979, after Egypt signed a peace treaty with Israel.

All these developments in the evolution of media institutions had profound implications for journalism. Before Arab satellite television started to inject major new stimuli during the second half of the 1990s, the vast majority of journalists employed by Arab-owned media were either working for government-controlled broadcasting monopolies or for newspapers closely allied to governments or political interest groups. In Egypt, Law No. 40 of 1977 had reintroduced political parties and, with them, political party newspapers, published under strict controls. To all intents and purposes, even after so-called independent papers started to be allowed in the mid-1990s, a dualism persisted between government-owned newspapers on one hand and *al-sahafa al-mu'ardha* (the 'opposition press') on the other. Journalists in both camps, however, worked under tight restrictions. In the non-government press they were denied equal access to sources or equal representation on the sole legally recognised national journalists' union. Journalists writing for government organs meanwhile worked to pre-set agendas that hardly required any proactive newsgathering at all.

In Lebanon, the power-sharing formula adopted to end the civil war was reflected in media organisations tied to the country's leading confessional groups (Maronite Christian, Greek Orthodox, Sunni Muslim, Shia Muslim) and power-brokers, notably Syria. In Saudi Arabia, the Basic Law of 1992 preserved the status quo by authorising members of the ruling family to play an equally prominent role in both government and media (Sakr 2001a: 41). It fostered a built-in tendency for power struggles among ruling family members to be played out in the competing political agendas of Saudi-owned media outlets. One of the journalists best known for his work in the Saudi press of the 1980s and 1990s is Jihad Khazen, a Palestinian-born Lebanese, who edited two London-based titles launched by sons of senior Saudi princes. He started with *Asharq al-Awsat* and moved to *Al-Hayat*. Prince Khaled bin Sultan bin Abdel-Aziz used *Al-Hayat* to maintain prominence in pan-Arab affairs after heading the joint Arab forces in the 1991 Gulf War. To this end he allowed Khazen an unusually free hand. But Khazen himself was clear about how far his editorial freedom went. A difficult balance had to be struck, he said, between making *Al-Hayat* interesting enough to maximise circulation and advertising income but uncontentious enough to be allowed to circulate in the Saudi market. Whereas being banned in the kingdom for a day could be good for sales, because it demonstrated independence and credibility, being banned for a month could cause the paper to fold. For that reason, Khazen openly admitted, he was prepared to commit sins of omission. He once declined to publish a story on Saudi mistreatment of an Egyptian doctor rather than run the inevitable risk of upsetting one or other of the governments involved (Atwan and Khazen 1996: 52–3). Khazen's admission gives an idea of the scale of omissions in newspapers with less liberal owners. The Iraqi gas attack on the Kurdish town of Halabja in 1988 went unreported in the Gulf press until after the 1991 Gulf War (Milhem 1993: 19).

Examples like these demonstrate the practical impact of government paranoia on the gathering and dissemination of news. Silenced journalists cannot hope to command respect or prestige. Newspapers promoting narrow group interests co-exist in a fragmented market rather than competing with each other across a diverse and demanding readership. Limited sales mean limited profits. Lack of profit means resource constraints, which in turn means limited salaries and lack of job security for editorial staff, who thereby become further exposed to pressure to follow stories for reasons other than newsworthiness. In the case of government-owned papers, copies are distributed in bulk whether or not they are read or returned, while staff have tenure, provided they toe the line. Toeing the line means practising what local critics call 'receive and see-off journalism' (Qassem 2003). This consists of reports on the meeting and greeting of heads of state and top officials, devoid of any information about what is discussed. As one journalist has noted, it is as if the country's ruler heads the media institution, with his intelligence chief occupying the editor's chair (Fouda 2001).

When credible local or national stories are deliberately suppressed and investigative reporting is all but unknown, media space ends up being filled with international news, syndicated columns and acres of local commentary and opinion, often mixed in with news reports. This creates a vicious circle in which journalists find themselves cut off from news sources, because officials have no incentive to talk to them, except for propaganda purposes. They are also cut off from local audiences; Arab audiences learned long before the advent of satellite television to rely on foreign radio stations such as the BBC Arabic service or Radio Monte Carlo Moyen Orient. A sense of the contempt and suspicion attached to mainstream journalism in the region is evident in the explicit attempts of a few editors to promote a 'new type of quality journalism' that would be distinguished by its separation between fact and commentary and its readiness to publish stories suppressed elsewhere (Kraemer 2001: 59–60). Such an initiative should be seen as indicative of pockets of resistance across the region to the limits imposed on journalism, and a reminder that resistance can take many forms. It is beyond the scope of this article to identify the many Arab journalists who took up opportunities to work abroad, including for public-service broadcasters in Europe and Japan, or who worked for foreign media as best they could in their home countries, within the limits of local laws.[3] Nor is there space for the list of journalists jailed or threatened for reports considered critical of ruling elites. The next section, however, in tracing the changing dynamics of Arab journalism in the age of transnational television takes account of journalists' actions as well as structural change.

Initiatives and opportunities after 1990

It was suggested earlier that formative influences on Arab journalism could be viewed in two phases: before and after the rise of satellite television. Convenient as such a chronological approach might be, adopting it too simplistically would be a mistake. For one thing, although the arrival of the first general Arab-owned, Arabic-language satellite channel can be dated precisely to December 1990, the process whereby a very small group of satellite broadcasters introduced new journalistic standards started gradually some time later. Second, attempts at media liberalisation predated the spread of satellite channels. Algeria and Yemen provide examples from either end of the Arab world. A new constitution and information law in Algeria in 1989–90 opened the way to a proliferation of non-government newspapers there, even offering financial incentives for journalists from the state-run media to join them. But the opening-up was short-lived, as the army intervened in 1992 to abort the electoral process and declare a State of Emergency. Meanwhile, unification of North and South Yemen in 1990 was followed by elections and more freedom for the Yemeni press. Again, however, the process was reversed, by a combination of civil war and a new institution designed to muzzle journalists. As these examples illustrate, media liberalisation is not irreversible. It could even be said that transnationalisation of television journalism frightened Arab governments into retaliating ever more harshly against locally based print journalists.[4]

In purely technical terms, major change in the Arab media was triggered by Iraq's invasion of Kuwait in 1990 and the US-led war to free Kuwait in 1991. Egypt's state broadcaster swung into action to send programming by satellite to its troops and other viewers in the Gulf. In their continuing bid for regional media superiority, influential Saudis responded in kind. Having learned the lessons of CNN's widely viewed reporting from Baghdad, they determined to create an Arabic rival to CNN (Sakr 2001a: 45, 84). The immediate aim was to provide a credible news-led general channel that would appeal to Arabic-speaking viewers by being newsworthy and relevant but, at the same time, avoid criticism of the Saudi government or its friends and allies. The result was Middle East Broadcasting Centre (MBC), which started in London in 1991 with Westerners involved in management, including the direction of news programming. MBC set some noteworthy precedents in Arab journalism. Its international network of correspondents was more extensive than that of any other regional media institution hitherto and enabled the channel to at least claim it was competing with global media giants in providing direct first-hand reports of world events (MBC 1997). Occasionally these would be sensitive events in Arab states (Alterman 1998: 20) but not in Saudi Arabia or its immediate region (Ayish 1997: 482).

By creating new job opportunities while also aiming for credibility, Saudi-financed *émigré* ventures such as MBC and *Al-Hayat* contributed to a perceptible development of Arab journalism. They accepted what viewers, readers and frustrated journalists already knew, that credible journalism requires 'legwork' in search of exclusive stories and interviews. What they had more trouble accepting was a form of journalism that routinely reports — within the same outlet — on sharply conflicting political views relating to issues close to the proprietors' own interests (Ghareeb 2000: 402, 413). The next milestone along this particular road came with the setting up of another Saudi-owned satellite network, a pay-TV operation called Orbit. Orbit took two important steps. First, in 1994, it signed a contract with the British Broadcasting Corporation (BBC) for a regular supply of Arabic-language news. Orbit did not go far along this path. It terminated the contract in 1996 in protest at BBC reporting on human-rights abuses in Saudi Arabia and the activities of Saudi dissidents in London. Orbit's second step was a sideways move. Instead of persevering with Arabic-language news, it built up a political talkshow and phone-in programme inspired by CNN's *Larry King Live*. Hosted by Imadeddin Adeeb, Egyptian editor of the newspaper *Al-Aalam al-Yawm* (The World Today), the live phone-in talkshow called *Aala al-Hawa* (On the Air) featured controversial political personalities as guests.

Orbit's experiments had important repercussions for the direction taken by Arab journalism — both in broadcasting and print — from then on. The new ruler of the small Gulf state of Qatar watched Orbit's current affairs coverage and resolved to set up a satellite channel that would follow suit.[5] When the BBC Arabic news service folded, Qatari officials set about recruiting its redundant members of staff, thereby forming the nucleus of what was to become Al-Jazeera Satellite Channel, broadcast from Qatar's capital, Doha, with effect from the end of 1996. It is relevant that the outgoing BBC employees had not been waiting passively for other employers to seek them out. They held rallies, picketed BBC headquarters and lobbied Parliament to save the service (*Journalist* 1996: 27). One group found alternative funding and tried to negotiate a buy-out. When all these efforts failed, the 90 journalists and 100 others who had worked for the now-defunct service went their separate ways, taking with them their experience of following BBC norms and practices and the radicalising impact of having lost their jobs – even in London – for respecting the public's right to know. Those who joined the embryonic Al-Jazeera valued their BBC background and suspected they would face a different environment in Doha. It had been both a dream and a challenge, talkshow presenter Sami Haddad told a media awards ceremony in June 2003, to move from reporting the world 'from the viewpoint of London' to meeting the 'real needs' of Arab viewers from inside the Arab world, through 'facts not propaganda, different views not sanitised views, appeals to their intelligence, not insults to their intelligence' (Haddad 2003). Cairo correspondent Hussein Abdel-Ghani described the process as 'peel[ing]' away from the BBC model, so that Al-Jazeera might establish its own 'persona, style and standards' (Abdel-Ghani 2003).

Al-Jazeera, left mostly to the direction of journalists as opposed to politicians, became a driving force in Arab print and broadcast journalism from around 1998 onwards, mainly because its distinctive and largely uncensored approach attracted audiences from across the Arabic-speaking world.[6] This is not to say that all other media instantly copied either its style or substance. On the contrary, as already stated, restrictive media laws continued to be invoked to keep the lid on public discussion of corruption or unpopular policies. Jordan's government brought in new legislation in 1998 to quell the cacophony of weekly papers that grew up under the country's mildly liberal Press Law of 1993. Magdi Hussein, editor of Egypt's Islamist paper *Al-Shaab*, was repeatedly tried and jailed between 1998 and 2000 for publishing sensationalist exposés targeting named government ministers. Nevertheless, despite these clampdowns, many new satellite channels were encouraged to enter the market in response to rapid growth in satellite viewership. These players, as well as the existing government-controlled media outlets, were all forced to give an appearance of putting some bite into their journalism, simply to create a veneer of credibility in an enlivened market.

For example, Egypt's state broadcaster mounted a campaign dubbed 'media nationalism' to woo back personalities who had made names for themselves on the new satellite channels. Hamdi Kandil, who returned to Egyptian terrestrial television in 1998, had particular success in boosting viewership with stinging criticism of US policy in his weekly programme *The Editor* (Hammond 2001). While some saw the scope allowed to Kandil as deliberate government manoeuvring vis-à-vis Egyptian public opinion and Washington policy-makers, Kandil seized what he saw as an opportunity to push back the 'red lines' of censorship (ibid.). Likewise, with Al-Jazeera applying its own news values, critical events could no longer be hushed up indefinitely. In 1989, Hisham Milhem, a journalist with *Al-Safir* in Beirut and *Al-Qabas* in Kuwait, had been unable to get either publication to publish his report of the shooting down of an Egyptian fighter plane during an airshow in Iraq – an incident that was kept secret in both Egypt and Iraq (Milhem 1993: 17). A decade later, in 1999, when EgyptAir Flight 990 crashed inexplicably into the Atlantic, staff on Egyptian state television again took the 'safe' route of not reporting it all initially. But after relatives of the victims learned what had happened from satellite channel correspondents who descended on Cairo airport (Negus 1999: 13), the risks of silence became all too apparent.

Al-Jazeera, meanwhile, was not only covering news stories according to internationally accepted criteria of newsworthiness, but probing them in a regular slot for investigative journalism called *Top Secret* and bringing guests into the studio to debate them in talkshows whose very titles – *More than One Opinion* and *The Opposite Direction* – highlighted the ingredients missing in other media. Faisal Qassem, the long-standing presenter of *The Opposite Direction*, believes that allowing opinions to clash in public is necessary if societies are to reach a consensus (Qassem 2003). In his view, stormy exchanges are not divisive in the long run. Qassem, a Syrian who holds a PhD in English literature from a British university, has insisted on several occasions that no-one interferes with his controversial choice of debating topics. He has said he tackles issues he 'never even dreamed of covering' during his time at the BBC (e.g. El-Nawawy and Iskandar 2002: 97). Foreign journalists who have visited the studio confirm that *The Opposite Direction* goes out live and that phone-calls from viewers are not filtered or time-delayed (Whitaker 2003). The contribution made by Qassem and his colleagues in boosting Al-Jazeera's ratings can only be explained by reference to the strong demand for open discussion among ordinary people in the Arab world. Respected journalists in other media were regularly urging a more forthright approach to sensitive issues when Al-Jazeera was still just emerging onto the scene. Khaled Maenna, interviewed as editor of Saudi Arabia's English-language daily *Arab News* in 1997, made a point that came to sound highly prophetic after 15 Saudis took part in the September 2001 suicide attacks in the US. Arguing that openness about 'shortcomings' could actually 'forge cohesion', he said: 'The Saudi people are not fools. They have hopes, aspirations, fears. We should address them all. We cannot sweep them under the carpet or some day Pandora's box will open up' (Gulf Marketing Review 1997: 22–3).

Ironically, as Al-Jazeera gained publicity beyond the Arab world by covering the US bombing of Afghanistan that followed the September 11th attacks, it found itself accused of inciting the very unrest that people in the Arab world had warned was being stoked by censorship. Before Al-Jazeera and a few other channels started to break with taboos, public fury at undemocratic Arab regimes and their Western backers had no legal means of being expressed, let alone communicated to politicians in the West. But lack of expression was no proof that fury did not exist. It was only when Arab journalists started to work for uncensored media in Arabic that public perceptions of being 'caught between domestic oppression and foreign injustice'[7] finally found an international voice. Journalists involved in conveying such perceptions won acclaim from ordinary people, who turned to them as they might to ombudsmen.[8] In contrast, some in authority in Arab countries and the West took exception to both the message and the messenger. Arab governments launched a smear campaign against Al-Jazeera, saying that its practice of interviewing representatives of Israel and the US meant it must be a Zionist channel paid by the CIA. In the USA, press commentators accused the channel of fanning the flames of anti-Americanism by screening tapes of the Saudi-born dissident Osama Bin Laden, airing Palestinian accounts of Israeli military offensives and filming American soldiers captured by Iraqi troops. Al-Jazeera journalists defended their reporting on the grounds of enabling audiences to see all aspects of current events, including those not shown elsewhere.[9] Their approach, partly emulated from 2000 by Abu Dhabi TV and from 2003 by Al-Arabiya, stood in stark contrast to an Arab media tradition of overtly selective reporting that now seemed (despite having been discredited in the eyes of a growing number of Arab journalists) to be spreading beyond the Arab world. As a British journalist noted in April 2003, during the US-led war on Iraq, a multi-sided approach distinguished Al-Jazeera from the US-based Fox News. 'While Al-Jazeera interviews senior US officials as much as it does Iraqi ones', he wrote, 'Fox appears unable to accommodate the Arab point of view – whether government or public' (Butt 2003: C4).

The prominence of Al-Jazeera, Abu Dhabi TV and Al-Arabiya, combined with the move towards credibility among competing print and broadcast media, as well as the intensified physical hazards of reporting in the West Bank, Gaza and Iraq, all served to raise the profile of individual Arab journalists during 2002–3. Media owners and managers became increasingly aware that certain correspondents – male and female[10] – were capable of attracting public attention or trust, with the result that the balance of power between journalists and organisations started to undergo a small shift. Valued journalists began to have more say in their conditions of employment and in some cases kept their jobs despite editorial disputes. Al-Arabiya hired Salah Negm, who was previously editor-in-chief at Al-Jazeera. Negm, having also worked for the BBC Arabic service, knew how to pick his team. In all, Al-Arabiya reportedly approached 15 members of Al-Jazeera staff, offering to double or treble their salaries.[11] In the past, journalists who criticised Arab leaders too trenchantly would be removed, whereas in the new era that was no longer guaranteed. Faisal al-Qassem went off the air for a few weeks after referring to Arab leaders as 'bastards' (*awlad zinna*), only to return after the fuss had died down. Jamal Khashoggi, editor of Saudi Arabia's widely read reformist national newspaper *Al-Watan* (The Homeland), was sacked from his post under pressure from powerful anti-reformist elements in May 2003, after publishing editorials and cartoons implying a link between dogmatic clerics and the terrorist leanings of Saudi followers of Osama Bin Laden. Yet he remained close to *Al-Watan* management, who seemed ready to countenance his eventual return to the editorship.

For every such example, however, there were dozens of others in which Arab journalists continued to be dismissed, penalised and obstructed, with few shows of solidarity from their colleagues. Staff at the Saudi-backed station Al-Arabiya apparently made no call for a ban on Al-Jazeera crews entering Saudi Arabia to be reversed. Those with Al-Jazeera seem not to have objected to the tit-for-tat bar on Al-Arabiya crews attending press briefings on the Iraq war at US Central Command in Doha. In the absence of any new, independent, transnational body to protect Arab journalists' collective interests, this task was left to the region's existing national journalists' syndicates. These are monopoly bodies with many restrictions on membership.[12] Filled by employees of government-run newspapers, they have traditionally concerned themselves more with material perks for members than with tussles over freedom of speech.[13] Indeed, the syndicates have on several occasions censured their own members for communicating with Israelis, denouncing such acts as 'normalisation' with the enemy. They have also helped to police government rules for journalists, which governments describe as 'codes of ethics' but which actually protect officials from public scrutiny or criticism. Such intervention contravenes international norms for media regulation, whereby journalists collectively decide their own ethics and codes of practice.[14]

Some signs could be found, however, of unions asserting a greater degree of independence from their paymasters. One example was the 2003 election to replace Ibrahim Nafie as chair of Egypt's Press Syndicate. Nafie, editor of *Al-Ahram* and a close associate of the country's president, Hosni Mubarak, had served his maximum two consecutive terms. Instead of electing Nafie's own appointed proxy in his place, syndicate members rebelled and chose a Nasserite, Galal Aref, who campaigned on a platform of change. Another example emerged in the long-delayed multiplication of links between Arab unions and the International Federation of Journalists (IFJ). The IFJ helped in establishing syndicates for Palestinian and Algerian journalists in 1998 and 1999 respectively. Yet, by 2003, it still had only four affiliates in Arab countries out of a possible 17. It was therefore something of a breakthrough when the IFJ managed in April 2003 to hold its first meeting with the regional representative body, the Federation of Arab Journalists. The following month, the IFJ joined with the Egyptian Press Syndicate and London-based Arab Press Freedom Watch to hold a workshop on Ethics in Journalism in Cairo.

Events like that accord with the orthodox view that, after decades of repression, training is the most urgent requirement for Arab journalists. Rapid growth in the number of broadcasters has been followed by the mushrooming of training centres in places such as Cairo, Bahrain and Dubai. Western grants have helped to pay for courses in independent and investigative journalism on the basis that a good way to make the Arab media more pluralistic is to upgrade the skills of Arab journalists. But there is a feeling in some quarters that focusing on individuals is missing the point. According to this view, the priority is to establish independently viable media structures that can survive on their own merits without subsidies tied to political agendas. Hisham Qassem, then editor of the weekly *Cairo Times*, told a workshop in Alexandria in May 2003 that the more urgent need was for media managers to understand financial spreadsheets and know how to restructure their operations to boost sales income and cut costs. Until that happens, he said, journalists would receive training 'only to be thrown to the wolves'.

Conclusion

This account of the making of Arab journalists has been predominantly an account of restrictions. But it has also shown that, while multi-layered censorship shapes journalism, it cannot neutralise journalists. Clearly, many have been complicit in controls blocking the dissemination of information that both the public and policy-makers in Arab countries need in order to make informed choices. But, at crucial points of structural development in news reporting in the Arab world, whether these resulted from the rise of the *émigré* press, short-lived attempts at media liberalisation, or the application of satellite technology, there were journalists who seized the opportunities and, by doing so, helped to push structural change forward. Their actions highlight the extent to which structures of ownership and financing in the Arab media have limited, and continue to limit, the potential for journalists to develop professionally and act in solidarity with each other to protect their interests against ruling elites. Whereas satellite channels and pan-Arab newspapers have opened the way to more incisive coverage of pan-Arab affairs, it cannot be said of national or terrestrial media that they have moved equally far towards probing issues affecting a specific locality or community. Meanwhile, as shown by the adverse reactions of some influential groups in the West, moves to represent Arab perceptions of reality via transnational media can be unwelcome. Events before and after the US-led invasion of Iraq suggested that internal obstacles to free reporting within Arab countries were being augmented by external ones.

Notes

1 The literature cited in the chapter comes mainly from outside the Arab region. According to Ayish (1998: 49–53), seminal theoretical work on the subject in Arabic is lacking.
2 It might be argued that the collective experience of external intervention has in fact become an integral part of Arab culture.
3 Good connections to foreign media in Damascus did not save Ibrahim Hamdi from being jailed from December 2002 to March 2003 on a charge of publishing 'false news' about Syrian contingency plans to accommodate Iraqi refugees. Hamdi was released with the original charge, which carries a three-year jail sentence, still hanging over him. Mohammed al-Jassem, editor-in-chief of the Kuwaiti newspaper *Al-Watan*, who has close connections to *Newsweek*, *Foreign Policy* and the *International Herald Tribune*, was charged in June 2003 under a 1970 law that prohibits 'abusive statements' against the emir of Kuwait. Jassem had allegedly talked to a private gathering

about reports of interference by members of Kuwait's ruling family in the outcome of the country's July 2003 elections. He was freed on bail but could face a five-year prison sentence if convicted. Releasing defendants in this way is common practice in Arab countries, as it makes those released extremely cautious about future transgressions.

4 See Note 3 for examples.

5 According to Salah Negm, who worked with the BBC Arabic news service and was recruited by Qatar to play a leading editorial role in Al-Jazeera (Negm 2000).

6 Annual statistical surveys published by the satellite operator Eutelsat show that total satellite access across eight populous Arab countries (Algeria, Egypt, Jordan, Lebanon, Morocco, Saudi Arabia, Syria and Tunisia) increased by an average of 21.5 per cent per year between 1998 and 2002, to reach 12 million households by mid-2002 (*www.eutelsat.com/products/2_1_3_2.html*).

7 *Arabs Caught between Domestic Oppression and Foreign Injustice* is the title of a collection of commentaries published by the Cairo Institute for Human Rights Studies in 2001.

8 An elderly lady telephoned MBC's Jerusalem office in 2002 to ask the station to help secure severance pay for her son who had lost his job. MBC correspondent Nabil Khatib later said the call was typical of the way local people had come to regard Arab satellite channels as 'ombudsmen' (Khatib 2002).

9 Asked to respond to the British and US governments' outrage that it had shown corpses of allied soldiers, Al-Jazeera editor-in-chief Ibrahim Hilal told the BBC:

> What we are doing is showing the reality. We didn't invent the bodies; we didn't make them in the graphics unit. This is the war. ...The viewer has to judge whether war is the most suitable way to solve problems. If I hide shots of British or American people being killed, it is misleading to the British and American audience. It is misleading to the Arab audience if they imagine that the only victims of this war are the children and women of Iraq. They have to know that there are victims from both sides.

(BBC 2003)

10 For more on contemporary Arab women journalists, see Sakr (2001b) and Abu-Fadhil (2004).

11 According to Ibrahim Hilal (Shadid 2003).

12 An Egyptian court sentenced Hussein al-Mataani to three and a half years in prison with hard labour for attempting in 1998 to form an alternative union called the Syndicate of Independent Journalists (Reuters 1999).

13 Candidates for elections to the presidency and council of Egypt's Press Syndicate in 1999 promised the following in return for votes: apartments, holiday homes, computers, cell phones, cheap loans, cut-price travel and sports club membership (Shehab 1999).

14 UNESCO's January 1996 Sanaa Declaration states: 'Guidelines for journalistic standards are the concern of the news media professionals. Any attempt to set down standards and guidelines should come from the journalists themselves' (UNESCO 1996: 60).

References

Abdel-Ghani, Hussein (2003) 'The development of Arab satellite TV channels: case study of Al-Jazeera'. Paper presented to a workshop on The Image of the Other in the Media, organised by the Swedish Institute in Alexandria: Alexandria, May 26–27.

Abu-Fadhil, Magda (2004) 'Straddling cultures: Arab women journalists at home and abroad', in N. Sakr (ed.) *Women and Media in the Middle East*, London: I B Tauris, pp. 180–201.

Alterman, Jon (1998) *New Media, New Politics? From Satellite Television to the Internet in the Arab World*, Washington DC: Washington Institute for Near East Policy.

Arab Press Freedom Watch (2003) *The State of the Arab Media 2003: The Fight for Democracy*, London: Arab Press Freedom Watch.

Article 19 (1998) *Walls of Silence: Media and Censorship in Syria*. London: Article 19.

Atwan, Abdel-Bari. and Khazen, Jihad (1996) 'In the Saudi pocket', *Index on Censorship* 2: 50–5.

Ayalon, Ami (1995) *The Press in the Arab Middle East: A History*, Oxford: Oxford University Press.

Ayish, Muhammad. I. (1997) 'Arab television goes commercial', *Gazette* 59 (December): 473–93.

—— (1998) 'Communication research in the Arab world: a new perspective', *Javnost/The Public* 5 (1): 33–59.

BBC (2003) 'Al-Jazeera defends war reports'. Online at www.news.bbc.co.uk: 24 May.

Boyd, Douglas. A. (1999) *Broadcasting in the Arab World: A Survey of the Electronic Media in the Middle East*. 3rd edition, Ames: Iowa State University Press.

Butt, Gerald (2003) 'Contrasting war coverage', *Middle East Economic Survey* XLVI/14 (7 April): C3–4.

Dabous, Sonia (1993) 'Nasser and the Egyptian press', in C. Tripp (ed.) *Contemporary Egypt through Egyptian Eyes*, London: Routledge, pp. 100–21.

Dajani, Karen. F. (1980) 'Egypt's role as a major media producer, supplier and distributor to the Arab world: an historical descriptive study', unpublished PhD thesis, University of Michigan, Ann Arbor.

Dajani, Nabil. H. (1992) *Disoriented Media in a Fragmented Society: The Lebanese Experience*, Beirut: American University of Beirut.

El Khawaga, Dina (2001) 'Sisyphe ou les avatars du nouveau journalisme égyptien', *Egypt-Monde Arabe* 3/1: 149–65.

El-Nawawy, Mohammed and Iskandar, Adel (2002) *Al-Jazeera: How the Free Arab News Network Scooped the World and Changed the Middle East*, Boulder, CO: Westview.

Fouda, Yosri (2001) 'Here we stand: we cannot do otherwise', *Transnational Broadcasting Studies* 6 (Spring/Summer). Online at www.tbsjournal.com.

Ghareeb, Edmund (2000) 'New media and the information revolution in the Arab world: an assessment', *Middle East Journal* 54/3 (Summer): 395–418

Golding, Peter and Elliott, Philip (1979) *Making the News*, London: Longman.

Gulf Marketing Review (1997) 'Interview with Khaled Maenna', *Gulf Marketing Review* (June): 22–3.

Haddad, Sami (2003) 'Al-Jazeera came at the right time to fill a vacuum', *Independent*, 16 June.

Hammond, Andrew (2001) 'The rise of Hamdi Kandil', *Middle East International* No 664, 7 December. 23.

Henry, Clement and Springborg, Robert (2000) *Globalization and the Politics of Development in the Middle East*, Cambridge: Cambridge University Press.

Journalist (1996) 'Arab TV journalists "not good enough for Arabic radio"', *Journalist* (June/July): 27.

Karim, Karim (2002) 'Making sense of the "Islamic peril": journalism as cultural practice', in B. Zelizer and S. Allan (eds) *Journalism After September 11*, London: Routledge, pp. 101–16.

Kelidar, Abbas (1993) 'The political press in Egypt, 1882–1914', in C. Tripp (ed.) *Contemporary Egypt: Through Egyptian Eyes*, London: Routledge, pp. 1–21.

Khatib, Nabil (2002) 'Case study: Palestine'. Paper presented to the conference on New Media and Change in the Arab World organised by the Konrad Adenauer Foundation, Amman: 27 February–1 March.

Kraemer, Gilles (2001) *La presse francophone en Méditerranée*, Paris: Servedit/Maisonneuve & Larousse.

McFadden, Tom J. (1953) *Daily Journalism in the Arab States*, Columbus, OH: Ohio State University Press.

MBC (1997) *Background Information*, London: Middle East Broadcasting Centre Public Relations and Promotions Department.

Milhem, Hisham (1993) 'Politics and media in the Arab world' (interview), *Middle East Report* 180, January–February: 16–19.

Negm, Saleh (2000) Personal communication, Cairo: September 16.

Negus, Steve (1999) 'Season of disasters', *Middle East International* No 612, 12 November, pp 12–13.

Phillips, Angela (2003) 'Ethnic minority journalists in mainstream newsrooms', paper presented to the symposium on Cultures of Journalism at Goldsmiths College, University of London: 24 April.

Qassem, Faisal (2003) 'The Opposite Direction', paper presented to a conference on Broadcasting in the Arab World – Challenges and Prospects. University of Westminster, London: June 10.

Reuters (1999) 'Rights group protests jailing of Egyptian journalist', Cairo: 22 June.

Rugh, William. A. (1987) *The Arab Press: News Media and Political Process in the Arab World*, Revised 2nd edn, Syracuse, NY: Syracuse University Press.

Said, Edward (1981) *Covering Islam*, London: Routledge and Kegan Paul.

Sakr, Naomi (2001a) *Satellite Realms: Transnational Television, Globalization and the Middle East*. London: I B Tauris.

—— (2001b) 'Breaking down barriers in the Arab media', *Nieman Reports* 55/4 (Winter): 108–10.

—— (2003) 'Freedom of expression, accountability and development in the Arab region', *Journal of Human Development* 4/1: 29–46.

Shaaban, Boutheina (1990) 'The Arab woman journalist in the first half of the twentieth century' [in Arabic], in N. Saadawi (ed.) *International Seminar on Women's Journalism in the Arab World*, Cairo: Arab Women's Solidarity Association, pp. 61–72.

Shadid, Anthony (2003) 'Rivalry for eyes of Arab world', *Washington Post*, 11 February.

Shehab, Shaden (1999) 'The heat is on at the Press Syndicate', *Al-Ahram Weekly*, Issue 435, 24–30 June.

UNESCO (1996) *Final Report of the Seminar on Promoting Independent and Pluralistic Arab Media*. (CII-96/CONF.702/LD.1) Paris: United Nations Educational, Scientific and Cultural Organisation.

Whitaker, Brian (2003) 'Battle station', *Guardian*, 7 February.

9

AFRICAN JOURNALISM AND THE STRUGGLE FOR DEMOCRATIC MEDIA

Helge Rønning

Journalism in Africa is faced with many problems and obstacles. The most serious are threats to journalists' safety, and attempts to curb the freedom of the press. There are daily reports coming out of the continent of journalists being arrested, beaten up and even killed by both governments and by criminals.[1] According to the 2003 report by Reporters Sans Frontières (RSF) about 180 journalists were detained in Africa during 2002, and more than 80 news media were censored in Africa during 2002.[2] Some parts of the continent are worse than others. The situation on the Horn of Africa is particularly difficult. In Eritrea journalists are detained continuously. The Committee to Protect Journalists[3] has singled out the country as one of the ten worst places in the world to be a journalist. But it also applies to the situation in Ethiopia and Somalia. In other parts of the continent the situation in Zimbabwe is of special concern.[4] Here journalists are arrested regularly. The government constantly attacks the independent press, and the country's only independent daily *The Daily News* was banned in September 2003, it was allowed to publish again in January 2004 after a lengthy undecided court case, to the vehement protests of government, only to be banned again later after a split ruling in the supreme court. In June 2004 yet another newspaper, the weekly *Tribune*, was banned in Zimbabwe. The Media Monitoring Project Zimbabwe reported that the paper was closed by the government-appointed Media and Information Commission (MIC) for allegedly violating sections of the Access to Information and Protection of Privacy Act (AIPPA). The MIC accused the publishers of the paper, Africa Tribune Newspapers (ATN), of not notifying the commission of material changes such as change of ownership, the masthead, trade name and title of the paper as required under section 67 of AIPPA. MIC also cited the hiring of an unaccredited journalist as another reason for cancelling the paper's licence.[5] The international press has, to an increasing degree, been prevented from reporting from inside Zimbabwe. For example, in February 2005 three Zimbabwean journalists working for the international press fled the country after serious threats from the police and security forces.

To ban a newspaper

The history of the banning of *The Daily News* is, while it is particular to Zimbabwe, also illustrative of many of the problems facing independent and critical journalism in Africa as a whole. *The Daily News* was started in April 1999 under the editorship of Geoff Nyarota, a courageous Zimbabwean journalist and editor who over the years has constantly practised independent investigative reporting, exposed corruption, and stood for the principle of freedom and independence of the press. As editor of *The Daily News* he was arrested several times. The offices and the press of the paper were bombed. When the infamous AIPPA, which requires that all media and journalists in Zimbabwe register with the MIC, was introduced, Geoff Nyarota and a journalist on *The Daily* News were the first reporters to be arrested under the law. The background was an article on the murder of an opposition politician, which the government alleged was a publication of falsehood and thus punishable under the new law. The two journalists defended their case while their lawyers challenged the relevant provision of AIPPA in the Supreme Court. The Court ruled in favour of the two journalists and the case was dropped. In the wake of the new law the climate for free media in Zimbabwe deteriorated. There were many arrests and cases. Due to the difficult economic situation in the country, the independent press also suffered economically, and new shareholders came into the company that owned the paper, Associated Newspapers of Zimbabwe (ANZ). They sacked Nyarota at Christmas in 2002, in a situation of great controversy. While the rest of the independent press decided upon registration as a tactic, but to challenge AIPPA in court, *The Daily News* did not register and this gave the government an excuse for banning it in September 2003. There is speculation that this action by the owners of *The Daily News* was in reality a provocation intended to have the paper stopped. It is quite clear, however, that to break the ranks of the independent press in Zimbabwe as *The Daily News* did seriously weakened the situation of the free media in the country. In an account of how he sees the history, Nyarota concludes:

> What prompted the majority of independent publishers and journalists, who otherwise fiercely opposed AIPPA, to opt for tactical registration was the real threat of being totally disbanded by a desperate regime if they failed to register in terms of a law lambasted by maverick Zanu PF politician Eddison Zvobgo as "the most calculated and determined assault on our liberties guaranteed by the constitution". ANZ management gambled on a matter of principle and relied solely on a suicidal battle against a regime notorious in recent years for its determination not to uphold the rule of law.
>
> (Nyarota 2003)

The history of *The Daily News* illustrates the complicated challenges of a legal and economic kind that the independent press faces in many parts of Africa.

Geoff Nyarota took on the Zimbabwean government for the first time in 1988 when he, as the editor of the government newspaper in Bulawayo, *The Chronicle*, exposed corruption in the government. This led to the resignation of six ministers and to his being sacked as editor. Since then he has been harassed, arrested, sacked, exiled and persecuted constantly, at personal risk and leading to great economic trouble. One may wonder what makes him and other equally courageous journalists in Africa take on the battles that they do. Maybe part of the answer can be found in what he once wrote to me about the need and obligation of a journalist to try to tell what happens in a society in a truthful manner in order not "to conceal the truth from the same public that we sacrificed so much to keep informed" (Nyarota 2003), and that a journalist must be prepared to suffer for the sake of principles. Because Nyarota is a brave man, he suffered in the Zimbabwean situation where it often is very difficult to decide whose side who is on, and which forces support the government, and who acts as agent for whom. In such a situation it is extremely difficult to maintain journalistic integrity and it often forces people with such principles to endure, as Nyarota writes, "deprivation and humiliation in silence in what I believed was the national interest".[6] In February 2005, the ruling ZANU (PF) party published a booklet titled *Traitors Do Much Damage to National Goals*, in which the party named Zimbabweans whom they saw as traitors, and of course, Geoff Nyarota had the honour of being on that list.

Journalism and government intervention

In the parts of the continent where there are civil wars and armed conflicts, journalists are constantly under threat and several have been killed. This is the case for among others Liberia. In the Ivory Coast two journalists were killed in 2003 – one Ivorian, one French. The murderer of the French journalist Jean Hélène was sentenced to 17 years imprisonment in January 2004. The situation in the Democratic Republic of Congo is very serious, with regular reports of journalists being persecuted, arrested and beaten up, and papers and radio stations being shut down. One example is the case of Bamporiki Chamira, a journalist with the daily *La Tempête des Tropiques*, in the capital Kinshasa, who has spent a year in prison without any form of trial, accused of plotting to kill President Joseph Kabila and trying to overthrow the government. .

Particularly worrying is that the situation has deteriorated in countries that for many years were free of interventions and threats to press freedom – examples of this are Senegal[7] and Niger,[8] and also to a certain degree Botswana[9] and Namibia,[10] where new restrictive media laws are in the process of being implemented.

The situation outlined here may be seen as result of what one of the veterans of African journalism, the Ghanaian journalist and professor Paul A. V. Ansah (1938–1993), identified in 1991 as three major crises of the media in Africa: namely the crisis of power, the crisis of ownership and the crisis of resources (Ansah 1991).

The crisis of power has two sides. One is related to the weakness of the African states and the other is related to the weakness of the media themselves. Weak states are particularly suspicious of media as these are seen as tools for the sowing of dissent, and consequently perceived as a threat to the survival of the government as well as the cohesion of the state. The result is that states have tried to control the media through a variety of techniques ranging from outright censorship and oppression to more subtle means, which often combine state ownership of the media with a system of economic awards to journalists who tow the line, and reprisals against those who do not. African states are by and large characterised by having low legitimacy, and the state apparatus is often dependent on various forms of clientelism often combined with authoritarian practices to uphold social cohesion. This contrasts fundamentally with the practice of democratic states with strong legitimacy where political and social cohesion is upheld through consensus building. In these processes independent media play a central role by *media*ting between views and opinions. This way of using the media contrasts with the manner often employed in societies with weak states, where the media are linked directly to the state apparatus, and where they are often used to promote various forms of personality cults of the head of state and other prominent politicians.

It is particularly in the state broadcasters that this form of journalism is prevalent. The consequence of this is that public radio and television are seen as a means to spread government policy to the exclusion of the interests of civil society interests, and the agenda of the state is merged with that of the ruling regime. The interests of government are presented as being the same as public interest. Thus the ruling party and its president become synonymous with the state and opinions, or events that may be seen to oppose the government are not reported, as this is assumed not to be in the interest of the public. This form of journalism consists of endless news reports in all media of all occasions where the president is present, regardless of how insignificant these events are. As may be imagined, these reports often border on the sycophantic. An outspoken veteran of African journalism, the Zimbabwean Willie Musarurwa (1927–1990), once characterised this form of journalism as "minister and sunshine journalism", typified by the following formula: "The sun was shining and the minister spoke."

The clearest expression of this form of reporting can be witnessed in the way elections are being covered by African state broadcasters. The many reports on media coverage of elections on the continent testify to this. But in countries where the state also controls a sizeable portion of the print media, the same pattern is found there. The ruling party and its candidates are given wall-to-wall coverage, and everything good that happens is attributed to them. The opposition, on the other hand, are excluded from or allocated the minimum coverage possible, and its views are often misrepresented. Even paid or sponsored election campaign advertisements are not guaranteed airtime and have been considered subversive. One of the worst examples of this form of election reporting was found in Zimbabwe in the parliamentary elections in 2000 and the presidential elections in 2002 (Media Monitoring Project 2004) (Waldahl 2004). Combined with widespread election rigging, this ensured the victory of ZANU (PF) and President Mugabe in spite of the fact that independent observers believe there is little doubt that the opposition otherwise would have won. The same media scenario, though less blatant, was played out in Zambia in December 2001 and in the Kenyan elections in December 2002. In the latter case, the opposition nevertheless managed to win after having twice before tried to unseat the government, but lost in fraudulent elections. This situation typifies how journalism often functions as a form of propaganda rather than critical coverage, and furthermore it is indicative of the close relationship between politics and media in Africa, where state media are stronger than private media, not least because the state controls the national broadcasters, which are the most important news media. It is also over the control of public broadcasters that the fiercest struggle between the ministries of information and the independent media interests take place. In the reforms to the Zambian media laws that were passed in 2003, the state kept control of ZNBC, and did not transform it into a proper public broadcaster. The result of this situation is that journalists in government media often act more like state information officers than journalists.

The difficult relationship to the state is one indication of the crisis of African media; the other is that the press is weak compared to the national broadcasters due to low penetration of society, as newspapers only reach a small proportion of the population. Particularly the independent press finds itself in a more or less permanent crisis because the market it serves is small. This is due to a number of factors. One is economic in that the majority of the population cannot afford to be regular newspaper readers. Another has to do with lack of education and illiteracy. A third has to do with underdeveloped infrastructures and distribution systems, which means that newspapers are urban, and only in addition reaches communities along the main highways. The independent press thus has little opportunity to present its case in times of crises as there are few parallel media outlets, and they cannot count on support from the state media in their struggle for independence and professional standards, which would be the case in societies with a fully developed media structure. In addition, the professional press organisations are weak.

Owners and donors

The crisis of ownership has two aspects. One is that the media in Africa, as discussed above, to a large degree in some way or other are owned or economically controlled by the state. This is the case also in many of the new multiparty states that have come into existence since the democratisation process started in the early 1990s. The second is that professional owners or media investors are few. The exception is South Africa where there is a concentration of power in five newspaper groups: Independent Newspapers, Johnnic Publishing, Nasionale Media, New Africa Publications and CTP/Caxton. The country's newspapers, however, are based mainly on separate control of the editorial and management departments, and thus are run according to international professional standards. In other parts of the continent the role of regional conglomerates is the exception. One of them is the Nation Group in Kenya, which has cross-media ownership interests in East Africa. It has been claimed that the most important non-government newspaper in Uganda – *The Monitor* – has become less critical of the Museveni government after the Nation Group bought it.

African newspapers and private media are in general owned by indigenous business ventures, which are often undercapitalised and usually in financial difficulty. In addition, because of a weak financial basis they are often unable to withstand onslaughts in the form of legal or economic attacks. The so-called alternative media are often owned by small trusts which again are controlled by a small group of allies and friends, or are totally dependent on one person's dedication. They are faced with being economically weak due to low penetration and because they cater for special interests, have little access to advertising and lack proper distribution systems. In addition they may to a certain degree be dependent on donor funding from foreign sources, such as religious organisations, international NGOs and donors.

In these cases the relationship between the local media and their international backers may raise serious issues of independence. The case of religious media is maybe the most clear-cut, but here also there are different scenarios. Many of the non-state radio stations, and not an insignificant number of publications, are linked to powerful international religious movements, many of them of a fundamentalist kind – both Christian and Muslim. They range from radio stations with a clear and aggressive message such as that put out in radio and TV -stations run by the originally Brazilian sect Igreja Universal do Rei Deus in Mozambique, to the publications and radio stations run by the Catholic Church, which in many cases have been important in the democratic struggles on the continent.

The international NGOs are of many kinds and they want their message and point of views and interests put forward in the media they partly support and to a certain extent exercise control over. Here the agendas of the international NGOs may come into conflict with the interests of the local groups. The problem in this context is linked to donor funding for media. Many Northern donors have provided substantial support to African media, as part of their interest in furthering democracy and transparency. This raises at least two problems. It may create dependency upon the donor, whether editorial or financial. Donor countries may have a different agenda than the media they support; they may for instance want a more cautious line when criticising the authorities, in order not to endanger the relationship between the donor country and the African government. Second, because media as a rule are also businesses, supporting them raises the question of donor support for national business ventures.

The influence of the donor community on the press in Africa's new multi-party states is based on the understanding that liberal democracy demands that the press should play the role of the Fourth Estate and act as the classical watchdog. The main driving force behind the influence of NGOs, opposition parties and governments over the media is itself traceable to the donor support these organisations receive. For NGOs, oppositional groups and governments are in different ways beneficiaries of external funds, and are influenced by donors' ideas about what the press in a multiparty democracy should do and be. These ideas again form the background for demands for press reform. The NGOs in particular are even given funds by the donors which are specifically meant to directly or indirectly influence the philosophy and approach of the press (Kasoma 2000b).

This situation does not serve as an incentive to efforts to be economically viable, and on the other hand it makes the press vulnerable both to shifts in donor policies, and economic and political changes which the media have no possibility of controlling or influencing. Furthermore, such a situation is no encouragement to developing an independent and critical journalism. On the contrary it often leads to a form of journalistic coverage that plays up to the interests of advertisers and economic and political forces that may secure the finances of the enterprise in the short run. There have also been quite a few cases of journalists accepting bribes for giving favourable coverage to companies and politicians. This has been reported to be particularly the case in West Africa – Nigeria, Ghana and Cameroon. And in 2003 there were charges brought against senior journalists in South Africa for plagiarism.

In the 1970s and 1980s, in the period of one-party states in particular, solutions to the crises of power and ownership were sometimes sought through the establishment of organs, such as press councils and media trusts, intended to provide a compromise between direct state control or ownership and private ownership. One of the most elaborate structures of this kind is the Zimbabwe Mass Media Trust which was set up at independence of the country in 1980 and controls among others the majority of shares in the country's largest newspaper group (Zimpapers), the national news agency, a local newspaper project, and the country's largest chain of bookstores and stationers. In theory, the trust is independent, but in practice the Minister of Information controls it. Structures such as this point to dangers inherent in a situation where the dividing lines between government interests and media independence are unclear.

This is a type of conflict that arises over and over again, especially in relation to the precarious balance between state control and independence. One area where this is the case is the many elaborate media laws that are designed to regulate ethical standards, and that have been used to suppress the press – for example, as a pretext for banning *The Daily News* in Zimbabwe. And it has also led to serious conflicts over proposals to set up press councils, which often have been proposed to function as a form of semi-state or civil-society institution. This is the case in Zimbabwe, where the council has served as a willing tool for the Minister of Information. Many governments, and those who uphold democratic principles, are sceptical about the establishment of voluntary media councils. The official position seems to be that such councils amount to creating a situation where journalists become a law unto themselves. While governments have been suspicious of the setting up of voluntary and independent councils, there have been several suggestions for the creation of official organs to ensure that the media uphold ethical standards, for instance in Zambia and Tanzania. These proposals have often consisted of creating a kind of mixed organisation with members appointed by press organs as well as by government and civil society. What can be said in favour of such a system is that government approval gives the council a form of official legitimacy, but on the other it may be argued against this set-up that it also implies an undermining of the independence of the idea of an ethical council. An example of this is that in 1997 the National Assembly in Senegal passed a law that instituted a press code that emphasises ethics and responsibility, while requiring publishers to report print-runs. This code has been used to attack the press for breaking ethical rules, when in reality it was conducting perfectly acceptable political and economic reporting. Thus the Senegalese experience is a good example of how ethical codes passed by the state may serve as a pretext for curtailing press freedom.

Markets and ethics

The crisis of resources pertains to all levels of the media. The experience and education of media personnel in Africa are by and large low by international standards, so the professionalism of the products cannot compete with international products. This is particularly problematic when it comes to areas where international competition is strong, such as the electronic media. But it is also a problem as regards journalistic competence and self-confidence, which again make the press more susceptible to pressure. The generally low competence, the low wages experienced by journalists in general and the lack of economic resources have an impact on the ethical standards of reporting in many parts of Africa. In order to create high immediate circulation figures there are many examples of sensationalist stories being printed that are often based on nothing but rumours, and in other cases are closer to fiction than truth. Many such stories involve the reporting of witchcraft, sorcery and non-natural phenomena.

One example was that in relation to the solar eclipse in Southern Africa in 2002. There were newspaper stories all over the region (also in serious papers) about how this phenomenon could cause all sorts of disasters and unnatural phenomena, like babies born with two heads. The practice of checking and double-checking a story and trying to obtain different sources is hampered by costs and time pressure as well as by the reluctance of sources to come forward, partly because they are afraid of being revealed at a later stage.

The weak economic situation of African news media results in television news being dependent on the big international news operations, so that often local news stories are not reported properly and given sufficient room. To illustrate this point: in a discussion about news agendas in Africa, an Angolan journalist from Angolan TV once told me that at the same time as a terrible massacre had taken place in the civil war in the country, the top news story illustrated with footage from CNN on Angolan TV news was the conflict in Bosnia, and a massacre there, and the Angolan terror only received a minor mention.

There is a general shortage of material resources, which hamper the development of the media but also make them vulnerable to political and economic pressure. Even if new information technologies are being developed in Africa to a substantial degree, they are still very much a minority phenomenon and while many African newspapers now have electronic editions (with all 54 African countries now having Internet access), this does not mean that they reach more than a very limited part of the population. The information and media gap between the information-strong and information-weak parts of the world is not going to disappear despite optimistic pronouncements of the Internet creating a new era of democratic communication in the near future.

On the one hand the emergence of a global information society may be a powerful democratising force. Yet on the other hand there are tendencies that threaten the very public space of dialogue that the media open up. This is linked to the struggle over control of the media between authoritarian states on the one hand and civil society on the other, and there are dire warnings in many parts of Africa that governments want to control the Internet, and thus also control independent critical journalism reaching international audiences. The right to privacy of Internet users is being attacked for different reasons in Africa: in each case governments claim to be acting in the interests of protecting their citizens from what is called "moral corruption", "terrorism" or "cybercrime". This is achieved through the constant surveillance and registration of Internet users, the banning of Internet publications, the use of Internet filters and/or the imprisonment of publishers. Governments often use old provisions such as law and order maintenance acts to survey and censor Internet use. In some countries, such as Zimbabwe, repressive media laws are being developed by authoritarian governments to attack individuals who publish their content on the Internet. In June 2004 the government in Zimbabwe demanded that all Internet service providers in the country should open their servers for government control. Another example is that in Tanzania the Zanzibar government in December 2003 threatened to take legal action against the editorial board of the banned weekly *Dira* if it attempted to publish the newspaper on the Internet. To do so was declared to be contrary to the government's order, which banned the newspaper throughout the United Republic of Tanzania.

With the exception of the very big papers (particularly in South Africa), newspapers in Africa suffer from lack of fully developed modern production and editorial technology, and the printing presses often produce very poor quality material. This varies tremendously from country to country, and between the papers within one country. But in general it is fair to say that the technological standard in African journalism is below that found in other parts of the world, an additional challenge to add to the many others that face journalists in Africa.

Let me illustrate this point with my impressions of the situation at *The Zambia Daily Mail*, which is one of the two government-owned daily newspapers in the country. It is a broadsheet paper with a circulation estimated at between 10,000 and 15,000. Its newsrooms, print works and administration departments are very poorly equipped. The computers that the paper has are few, in general, old and not sufficient to alleviate the problems the company faces when it comes to producing a modern newspaper. It seems that the shortage of computers and on-line connection also makes the coverage of African and international news difficult. The print works are adequate but outdated and suffer frequent breakdowns. The printing quality is not good, particularly affecting the quality of the pictures, which is obviously linked to poor reprographic equipment. The paper has distribution problems in that it is dependent upon street sales and has serious problems distributing outside the capital Lusaka.

The small markets served by the media constitute another serious problem. Newspapers and television cater mainly to an urban and middle-class audience, whereas the majority of the population lives in the rural areas. With widespread poverty, few outside the elite can afford to regularly purchase a newspaper. There exists widespread illiteracy, even if this varies from country to country. It has been pointed out that those who are literate may act as channels of communication to others, and that it is not the size of the readership which decides the influence of the press. However, growth in literacy rates does appear to be associated with increased demand for newspapers. Because of the uneven development and bifurcation of the African societies the rural population will have access only to a very limited variety of media. It has been claimed that the poor will only find themselves featured in the media when they do bizarre things, such as rape, murder and other crimes. The implication is that the interests of the African poor, who constitute the vast majority of the population, are treated only as exceptional stories, rather than as legitimate social and political concerns. Even when newspapers want to report on the grievances of the poor, they are often constrained by their size and lack of professional staff to report on them. The achievements and interests of the elite, on the other hand, are significantly highlighted.

The private press to an even greater degree than the official press tend to be more urban in their audience and driven by advertising and therefore not aimed at the poorest populations. The result of these serious social contradictions may funnel conflicts between elites and the masses, and particularly in situations of social anomy threaten the common identity of belonging to a greater community of citizens, and have an inherent possibility of falling back on primary identities. In several instances this has been utilised by irresponsible media to create conditions of widespread violence and genocide. Of course, the most serious example is in Rwanda and the activities of Radio-Télévision Libre des Mille Collines (RTLM) (Prunier 1995, 1997; Berry and Berry 1999; Carver 2000). But also during the civil war in the Ivory Coast the broadcasting media and the press have been guilty of inciting hatred.

The possibility of a viable, independent press is affected by the amount of wealth in the society. The prevalence of poverty will restrict potential readership, advertising revenue and likely investors. The markets for consumer goods are limited, and as modern communication media are linked both to the existence of mass consumption and mass democracy, this represents a severe obstacle to the development of democratic media, particularly on a local level. Poor infrastructure and communication impede the distribution of newspapers and magazines outside the cities and larger towns. Largely as a result of these constraints, privately owned newspapers and magazines suffer from under-capitalisation. They have limited print runs and low advertising revenues. The multifaceted economic woes of the African press still undermine the development of independent and professional journalistic media.

Let me use the situation in Zambia in 2003 as an example of the challenges facing the press in an African country. The most striking characteristic of the current media situation in Zambia is that the print media are in a situation of crisis and underdevelopment, and this applies to all types of papers, which seem to be in dire economic straits with a small and even dwindling circulation. There are three dailies, two of which are government-owned: *The Times of Zambia* and *The Zambia Daily Mail*. Both papers have Sunday editions, and the *Mail* also has a business edition. The first is published in Ndola in the Copper Belt, the second in Lusaka. *The Times* is the bigger of the two: its circulation was estimated to be 20,000 in 1996, but it is probably down by 5,000 now; the *Daily Mail* had 12,000 in 1996, but is probably a bit lower now.[11] The crisis of the dailies comes out clearly when looking at circulation figures for 1983 when *The Times* had 63,000, and *The Mail* 35,000. The independent daily is *The Post*, which developed out of the weekly and later bi-weekly *Weekly Post*. Its audited circulation in 1995 was 20,000; although it is difficult to estimate, it is probably down to around 15,000 now. The main weeklies, except the Sunday editions of the government papers, and *The Financial Mail*, are independent papers. *The Monitor* (bi-weekly) had an estimated circulation in 1996 of 30,000; it is now down to under 10,000. *Today* is a weekly with a circulation of 4,000, with the *National Star* probably about the same. The *National Mirror*, which is the oldest independent paper with a base in the Christian community, had a circulation of 10,000 in 1983, down to 5,000 in 1996, and probably the same now. There are also some local smaller newspapers. Thus on an average day the total circulation of newspapers in Zambia in one day is approximately 55,000 copies. The low circulation is a reflection of the cost of the papers – between ZMK 1,500 and 2,500 – which means that they are a luxury item that few people can afford. Copies therefore tend to be passed around from one person to the next. If we assume that a maximum of 15 people read each copy (the audited figures from *The Post* readership estimate in 1995), then there are a maximum of 825,000 newspaper readers in a population of 10 million people. But the low circulations indicate that most of these papers are in dire financial straits, and that they face problems in relation to advertising, production and distribution.

Even in the most developed country on the continent in terms of the media and the press, the situation demonstrates the relatively weak position of print journalism. Of all adults in South Africa (the population is in the region of 45 million), only 18.1 per cent are reached by a newspaper. Circulation of the seventeen dailies is in excess of 1.2 million. The two biggest, *The Star* and *The Sowetan*, have respectively 164,364 and 154,747 readers. The four Sunday newspapers have just a circulation of just one million, of which the biggest, the *Sunday Times*, accounts for 504,295, and the Afrikaans paper *Rapport* 338,702. The non-dailies, of which there are 104, reach in excess of 1.6 million. Furthermore 151 free sheets have an average circulation of over 3 million.[12] An interesting development in South Africa was the launch in October 2003 of a new daily newspaper *This Day*, which is owned by Nigerian media capital, and is reported to have a circulation of approximately 30,000. The owner of *This Day*, Nduka Obaigbena, decided in October 2004 to suspend the publication of the newspaper after it failed to attract advertisers, in spite of the fact that it was popular among upmarket readers. This is indicative of the fiercely competitive media market in South Africa.

Power and corruption and one courageous journalist

The core of a democratic society is public debate, so that choices made by the power holders can be publicly scrutinised and contested. The public scrutiny of decisions that affect the political, social and cultural life of a community is essential to the development of society. The problem in Africa is that a large portion of the population has no possibility of taking part in such a process of scrutiny, nor even to be informed about it. Thus the political process often takes the form of rumours, disgruntled grumbling, or the falling back on primary identities which either express themselves as uncritical or more often reluctant support for the powers that be, and participation in ritualised rallying at election times. These observations should not, however, lead to the conclusion that people are not informed, and have no knowledge of what goes on; the problem is that they have no, or very underdeveloped, media where they can voice their concerns and which represent their interests properly.

Journalistic media in Africa are politically vulnerable because of the weak basis they often have in a wider society, and this is of particular importance in relation to the safety of journalists. When journalists really uphold their watchdog role, they may be in real danger of their lives, as reported by the international NGOs that supervise violations of press freedom. Politicians everywhere have power but usually not wealth. They are therefore often tempted to translate the one into the other. Given the power–wealth gap in Africa, it might be argued that temptations are even greater than usual on this continent than elsewhere. This politics of corruption increasingly characterises politics in Africa. Neither government nor opposition bothers to pretend that significant principles are at stake in their debates. This situation encourages a growing reliance on those in power to decide on issues, which should be left to democratic political contestation, and a passive relationship between the governed and the governing develops. And it fails to deal with the difficult business of building political alternatives to government policies.

This is the situation that is often the outcome of what has been dubbed the victory of illiberal democracy in apparently relatively free elections. Many experiences in Africa show that elections do not guarantee democracy based on transparency and a real development of political alternatives. The opposition won the elections in Kenya 2002, but the victorious alliance consisted of many former politicians from the previous ruling elite. And in many countries former military rulers and one-party presidents were returned in democratic elections. The game of politics and wealth has not really changed. There are no strong opposition parties to provide a voice for the angry and alienated, or to suggest political, economic or social alternatives to the problems of society. Unsurprisingly, many people have become cynical. They are ready to put the knife into those who are seen to have responsibility for the mess in which ordinary people have to live. In many countries the crusade against corruption has transformed the political landscape. The reputation of politics can no longer merely be restored by a change of government. In the absence of genuine political differences, personal morality becomes the only basis on which politicians can be tried. In such a situation the press may be the voice of those who want change and feel disenfranchised. Through campaigns around issues of corruption and personal rectitude the media may change the nature of politics. The importance and dangers of such journalism in Africa can be illustrated by the role played by the Mozambican journalist Carlos Cardoso in uncovering corruption and oppression.

Cardoso was assassinated on 22 November 2000, while he was investigating the theft of fourteen million dollars from Mozambique's largest bank, Banco Comercial de Moçambique (BCM). The fraud was a result of the privatisation of the banking sector in the country. In 1996 and 1997 the two state-owned commercial banks, BCM and Banco Popular de Desenvolvimento (BDP) (later renamed Banco Austral), were sold to private investors, without any proper audit undertaken. And the history of the two banks since they were privatised is one long series of events involving fraud, corruption and murder. The case has many ramifications and is so full of complicated details that this is not the place to go into them. The full story of it reads like crime fiction, though it is brutal fact (Fauvet and Mosse 2003). In many parts of the continent the structural-adjustment programmes and the liberalisation politics that involved the selling off of public property have increased the corruption of African political and economic elites. These politics that the IMF and the World Bank imposed on the majority of Sub-Saharan African countries since the early 1980s consisted of privatisation and an attack on state spending. Given the high level of dependence of the African elite upon the state, this further frustrated their advancement. Western obsession with good governance, conducted in the name of anti-corruption, was a frontal assault upon the networks that were necessary for the ruling elite to rule.

What Cardoso did was diligently to follow up the story of the two banks and try to find out who were responsible for the corruption and the fraud, and put this in the wider context of the politics of structural adjustment. When Cardoso took on the case of BCM, it was consistent with his whole journalistic career, but it is also an exemplary history that can illustrate one side of the relationship between journalism and politics in Africa – the heroic side. Carlos Cardoso became a journalist just after the Mozambican revolution in 1975. He was a strong, but also critical, supporter of the ruling party Frelimo. He had studied in South Africa and had been expelled from the apartheid state, and came back to Mozambique when most Mozambicans of Portuguese descent, including his own family, were leaving the country. He started his journalistic career in the weekly news magazine *Tempo*, which was the most independent-minded and journalistically conscious organ in the early Frelimo years. From there he moved to the national news agency, where he served as director for a period. He was arrested once, in 1982, for having published an article comparing the situation in Angola and Mozambique – both countries were involved in a civil war – which the government perceived as breaking the rules. He was released after a while, but the situation for independent-minded journalists in the 1980s was not easy, with conflicts between the journalists and the party.

After Samora Machel's death in 1986 and the intensification of the civil war, Cardoso became ever more dissatisfied with the way Mozambican journalism functioned, as well as with the deteriorating moral fabric of the country. He knew that everywhere in the country people were speaking about the war, but this was not reflected in the media, which downplayed the seriousness of the situation. In the late 1980s many Mozambicans started campaigning for a change in the media climate. And in 1990 162 journalists signed a petition demanding full press freedom. In July 1991 the new press law was passed, and it contained virtually everything the petitioners had asked for. Early in 1992 Carlos Cardoso was one of the founding members of a journalists' cooperative whose first operation was to start a fax newspaper *Mediafax*, and later in 1994 a weekly newspaper *Savana*. But *Mediafax* was Cardoso's paper, and he ran it based on a formula of critical independent investigative journalism, particularly focusing on corruption and abuse of power, and was critical of the IMF's and World Bank's restructuring policies in the country.

During this period Cardoso made many enemies among the powerful in Mozambique, but he was also highly respected because his stories were well researched and sourced, and he could not be accused of any form of corrupt practices, something that was uncommon among journalists. In 1997 there was a serious conflict over principles in Mediacoop and Cardoso left both the cooperative and *Mediafax*, and in June 1997 he started a new fax newspaper called *Metical* (the name of the Mozambican currency), especially dedicated to critical economic and political journalism with a particular focus on corruption. In so doing he attacked very powerful people in Mozambican society including the President's family, ministers, high officials, wealthy businessmen with international connections and the World Bank.

170

Cardoso's journalism was always marked by high ethical standards and outspoken opinions. There was never any doubt about his integrity. He also had a very deep understanding of the society that he was part of, and he argued that the importance of critical journalism in any society, but particularly in Mozambique, must be based on credibility. As a result, many whistleblowers turned to Cardoso with their stories, and he protected their anonymity and checked and double-checked the stories. Thus he also contributed to breaking to a small degree a culture of secrecy and fears of reprisals. But this also led to his death. When he was killed, ordinary people in the streets of Maputo said: "Who is now going to speak up for us?"

On 31 January 2003 six people, found guilty of conspiring to murder Cardoso, were sentenced to long prison terms.[13] There is little doubt that the accused expected to escape, on account of their connections, but there was an international campaign, heavy pressure on the authorities and also a rift in the party over the case. The hunt for others who may have been involved continues; among those mentioned is the son of President Chissano.

The Cardoso story shows how one journalist working together with other dedicated people can at great personal risk take on the politically and economically powerful in society, and contribute to a certain degree to more openness and honesty. But it is also a story of the dangers of challenging the political and economic elite in an African country. And even if there is more openness in Mozambique now, the culture of secrecy, corruption and fear is still strong. The relationship between the independent journalists and the government continues to be uneasy.

It is difficult and dangerous for journalists in Africa to challenge political and economic power, and it is the journalists who in general are weak and the politicians who are strong. There are many cases on the continent where journalists are being threatened, particularly when they step too close to the sensitive combination of political and economic corruption. Intimidation of journalists is widespread, and the role of being a watchdog is a difficult one. As the alerts posted by the Committee to Protect Journalists and Reporters sans frontières testify, journalism remains a difficult profession on the continent, with adverse government policies, and widespread intimidation both from politicians and corrupt businesses. There are many other examples of African journalists who have been murdered because of their investigations into corruption and power abuse, including the Nigerian editor and journalist Dele Giwa, who was bombed in 1986, and the Burkinabe journalist Norbert Zongo, who was assassinated in 1998.[14]

The official press and the independent press

Zimbabwe may be contrasted with Mozambique. Here the journalists in the government-controlled newspapers and broadcasting do not undertake independent journalistic activities, but follow the government line in all their political reporting. There are many reasons for this. One is the strict control that government ownership through the Zimbabwe Mass Media Trust implies, which means that journalists and editors run a constant risk of being sacked – something that has happened frequently. Another aspect is the way that news stories and opinions are being vetted inside the media organisations that are closely linked to the office of the Minister of Information. A third is the serious political crisis in the country, which has led to the closure of the main independ-ent daily, arrests of independent journalists and editors, and a climate of confrontation between the remaining independent press and the government media. More than anything this situation has resulted in the widespread practice of self-censorship among journalists in government media. This is not unique to Zimbabwe, but prevalent in many parts of Africa.

The situation in Zimbabwe in 2004 is extreme, but my many discussions with practising journalists in Africa have convinced me that there is a widespread assumption that there exist far more stringent limitations to what may be written than is really the case, and that the media organisations themselves have found that this is an easy way out of the dilemmas raised by modern, hard-hitting critical journalism. It is not the political powers that be that restrict so much of African journalism and make it fall back on "ministerial speech reporting"; it is rather internalised assumptions of what is expected of the media. It is of course also a far simpler form of journalism to practise than proper reporting. This again is linked to the poor training which many journalists have received and their often low social standing. By this I am not indicating that self-censorship is not often based on a very real fear of reprisals from government and other powers, as may be the case in Zimbabwe. The intention is to illustrate how self-imposed regulations emanating from real or imagined threats often function as efficiently as formalised forms of censorship. The example of what happened to Carlos Cardoso is also revealing in this perspective. On the one hand his courage was remarkable, but on the other his death may have served as a warning to others who dared to step too close to the interests of the powerful.

What an independent press entails has in the current debate in Africa come to mean only independence from the government. Thus the problem of whether it is possible for any media to be truly independent of interest groups and be objective has faded into the background. The distinction between independence and impartiality has only been brought up to a limited degree. Thus both sides in the debate concentrate on the concept of independence. The government maintains that the non-government press is oppositional, and consequently not independent, because it chooses a different angle or position than the one found in the government-controlled press. The independent press claims that it is independent because it is not associated with government or political parties. But both the government-controlled and the independent press are of course partial in their reporting. It is the discovery that the press in Africa may hold other opinions than those of the ruling party

which has led to the attacks on the non-government press for being oppositional. However, using Kenya as an example, the private media have been able
to carry divergent views across the political divide. The government media
often portray criticism in the independent press of the way affairs are
conducted as sabotage, but the public is able to read between the lines and
see the implications. This came out clearly in the Kenyan election campaign in
2002. The mainstream newspapers did dedicate space to news covering rural,
political, social and economic concerns. The worrying aspect of these attacks
by governments on the independent press is not so much that they are
accused of sabotaging the politics of the government, but that this is often
done in the form of more or less direct threats against the principle of the
freedom of expression. What is often at stake is that political leaders are
unwilling to let themselves be subject to legitimate public scrutiny, which is an
essential part of journalism. Thus instead of attempting to create a climate for
an open debate, the state uses authoritarian laws to stifle the valid interest of
the public through the press to get an insight into how government works,
and what roles politicians play in the often shady relationships between
government and private businesses. Many of the arrests of journalists on the
continent have sprung from such circumstances.

The best kind of answer from journalists to such government action is one
such as the editor of *Zimbabwe Independent*, Iden Wetherell, produced when he
and three of his colleagues were arrested in January 2004. Iden Wetherell
answered:

> We expected something of this sort but not from this story. We are
> going to be targeted. We are the only outspoken voice remaining, and
> this action was inevitable. We were prepared for that but did not know
> what form it would take. The government is hostile to media pluralism
> and freedom of speech. It is frightened of free speech because it
> exposes Mugabe's misrule. Do not forget that criminal defamation is a
> relic of empire. It was used by colonial governments to suppress critical
> voices. So we should not be surprised to find it lurking in the govern-
> ment's arsenal of repressive laws. Zimbabwe has a long history of
> attachment to its colonial laws.[15]

On the other hand, very often the answer may be one of compliance. The
threats and arrests instil a sense of anxiety among journalists, and they stop
writing critical stories about governments and officials.

There are a number of reasons behind the concern in Africa over the role of
the media in relation to the democratic process and regarding the interest in the
issue of the relationship between the state and the media. They pertain to more
general political trends, but they are also a result of developments more
narrowly confined to the media themselves. In a more general political perspective it is easy to point out that the fall of one-party regimes since the 1990s, and

the development of multiparty systems, combined with a demand for more democratic structures, will involve questions of the need for independent and critical media that can play a role as the vehicle for the exchange of ideas and information. In Africa one aspect of this new media situation is the many new newspapers and magazines which have sprung up all over the continent in the wake of the demise of the one-party regimes.

The struggle for democracy

In the debate over the role of the media in the democratic process in Africa over the past years too much emphasis has been put on the role of the state, and the solution to state control has invariably been seen as privatisation and a complete opening-up to market forces. This is again a result of many years of strict government control with the media, often in the form of direct ownership. Thus the problematic role of the market in relation to the media has been underplayed, and consequently too little attention has been paid to a discussion of media in relation to citizens' rights. It is not surprising that this has been the case. The really big players in the international media scene have not yet really entered Africa, and the continent has not been seen as a viable market for the strongly commercialised international media.

African critics of the official media have felt that strong state control only can be met by introducing market forces, and in this strong international interests and trends have supported them. The arguments for free-market media are strong in a situation where the state exercises direct or indirect control with the media. On the other hand governments who see their influence of their media threatened and fear that they will lose control over the flow of information have had a tendency to regard all forms of independent media, be they commercial or alternative, as mouthpieces for political opposition.

Analysing the experiences of the role of the media in relation to democratisation processes in Africa or in the voicing of protests against authoritarian forms of government, it seems that the media have had less of a leading role and more of a mediating role. The history of the political role of the African press goes back to colonial times, and during the struggle for independence, which was termed the first wave of democratisation of the media, the press played a role as the mouthpiece of nationalism (Hydén and Okigbo 2002). And in the first period after independence it was claimed that African journalism created a new discursive realm that consisted of an important debate of what development path the new African states should follow. During the years of military dictatorships and one-party states from the late 1960s and till the 1990s this potentially democratic discursive realm deteriorated and in general yielded to a press ideology of developmentalism and uncritical support of the state, the party and the national leader, and widespread repression of the press. In the second wave of the development of a democratic African press, the role of the press in both representing multiple voices in society and serving as a watchdog against power abuse has been essential.

Often the process of political change has come about through a combination of pressure from outside forces, and internal popular pressure from below; the media have often been caught in a situation where their links to the different actors in the political game to a large degree have decided their role. Thus the official or state-controlled media have either played down the pressure for change, or explicitly fought it. There are few examples of the media playing a triggering role in the movements of political change. They, and particularly the independent press, have, however, contributed to the change in two significant ways. First, by exposing abuses of power and corruption, and by reporting about protest against the authoritarian order, the press has kept an influential and active part of society informed about the issues at stake. Second, in a situation in which popular protest or opposition demands were already beginning to mount, the media created new and strengthened existing awareness of issues at stake. In addition, by placing events in a broader perspective and providing comments, they contributed to a wider understanding of the developments. The media, and particularly the press, as the broadcast media were often more strictly controlled, contributed to the further mobilisation and expression of popular protest. This deepening and accelerating political communication contributed to the pressures put on the authorities. Thus it is reasonable to maintain that the press did not really instigate political change, but that in the second part of processes for democratisation the press did play a significant role as interpreter of events, and in communicating information to the public about the situation.

It is of course necessary to analyse the situation in each country on the basis of the individual histories and conditions there, but there are many examples of how the media have contributed to the democratic processes in Africa. One example is how the independent press and a variety of civic groups in Zimbabwe successfully opposed the introduction of the formal one-party system, and there was a very lively debate on the issue in the country in the late 1980s. In Kenya the private press and a number of papers were advocating multiparty politics quite some time before the government gave in to the demands for political change, and elections were held, and finally the regime of President Moi was replaced. The situation in both Malawi and Tanzania before multiparty elections took place was characterised by the sudden growth of a plethora of independent and new newspapers of varying quality and sustainability. They contributed significantly to the pressure for the creation of a more transparent and accountable political system.

The growth of the independent press is clearly related to the increased popular interest in politics. The new and reconstructed press chronicled and agitated for a transition to democracy. Even in countries which lacked much of a critical journalistic tradition, private newspapers and magazines appeared. Also in this connection Malawi is a good example. Another example is the situation in Cameroon, which otherwise is not an easy place for independent journalism. The country's most popular newspaper *Le Messager* has been a thorn in the side of government since it was founded in 1979, and its editor Pius Njawe has been constantly persecuted and arrested several times. He was once instructed to disseminate "healthy, dispassionate, and less controversial information". Nevertheless more than 50 private newspapers came into being between 1990 and 1995, many to fold relatively soon (Kale 1997). Pius Njawe's radio station Radio Freedom was banned in May 2003, and in December 2003 more than a dozen independent broadcasters were shut down, apparently in preparation for planned presidential elections in 2004.

In Tanzania in 1988, the government allowed the first independent press to be published since the mid-1960s as part of its controlled political liberalisation. The privately owned newspapers such as *Business Times*, *The Express* and *Majira* established themselves as an alternative press, often seen by both the government and the public as opposition. They became a forum for criticism of the government and the ruling party. From the 1990s there has been a flourishing of the Kiswahili and English press, and a growing independence of view in the state-owned newspapers and the organs of the formerly CCM-dominated mass organisations. This has continued after the election of the new CCM government under President Benjamin Mkapa.

In contributing to the beginnings of a democratisation process, the press has often acted in some sense on its own account or at least as instruments of political forces opposed to an incumbent authoritarian regime; the situation of the new independent press in Malawi and Zambia is a good example. But we should not forget that in those cases where the process of democratisation has originated with a decision by the governing regime to allow a limited transition, controlled from above, the media have been called in to assist the political authorities in this task. This has been the role of the official media in Tanzania, for example.

While the media have rarely constituted the actual cause or served as the direct catalyst for the democratic process, both the mainstream media and the journalists based within them and the new and alternative media have often been a source of direct pressure and demands for democratisation and a watchdog in relation to governmental malpractice. In this perspective the role of *The Post* in Zambia is very illuminating. In the last period of the Kaunda regime the paper served as a vocal and consistent voice for the demands for a change of system and multiparty elections. After the victory of MMD the paper continued its independent and critical role in relation to the new Chiluba government, something which angered the new president considerably and led to more than one hundred charges of different press violations being issued against the editor Fred Membe during the Chiluba years. *The Post* has continued its critical role after President Levy Mwanawasa replaced Chiluba (Kasoma 2000a).

Both national and international media have contributed to the different stages of the democratisation process. Vicky Randall (1993) has argued that democratisation processes in the Third World may be analysed as going through three phases. It could be argued that the international media were most import-ant in creating the initial impetus for the democratisation of the press in Africa in the early phase. But there is no doubt that, in a majority of the countries, sections of the national media have contributed to the preservation of a critical tradition, often against very difficult odds through periods of one-party states and military dictatorships. The new independent media with a democratic agenda did not emerge from a vacuum when they started appearing in the late 1980s; indeed there was also critical and independent voices in the media in Africa in the period of one-party rule, and criticism was voiced even in the official press. An important part of this tradition has its roots in the anti-colonial struggles. A privately owned and independent and nationalist press emerged along with the nationalist movement in colonial Africa, especially in the British colonies. This was especially the case in West Africa, but also the history of the press in Southern Africa features examples of courageous and critical and democratic newspapers. A famous case in point is the role played by the Catholic weekly *Moto* in the Zimbabwean liberation struggle. And in South Africa there is a long tradition of alternative journalism critical of the apartheid state. In this context it is also important to remember the very important and brave role that the Nigerian press played during the Babangida and Abacha dictatorships.

In contributing to the beginnings of a democratisation process, the media and particularly the press often acted in some sense on their own account or at least as instruments of political forces opposed to an incumbent authoritarian regime. The regular and the alternative media have supplied crucial channels to communicate and interpret information during the various stages of the democratisation process, both in the initial stages by voicing dissatisfaction, exposing malpractices and abuse of power, and in the transitional phase by serving as mouthpieces for the variety of groups involved in the period before the election. Especially in the cases where national, official media have remained constrained and strictly government-controlled, the alternative media have functioned as an additional source of pressure.

In the transition phase to democracy in the early 1990s the media responded to the new democratic openings and opportunities. In the consolidation phase, the challenges to the media lay in expanding their democratic role by maintaining their critical and independent role both in relation to the new government and the new market liberalism. Even if democratic change has taken place, experience from new democracies in many parts of the world show that fears about lingering authoritarianism are not unfounded. In the realm of the media this is particularly pronounced in relation to the broadcast media. Governments are often reluctant to yield control over broadcasting, or to permit alternative radio and television stations. It is a clear feature of this process that the broadcasting companies have been the last media organisations to open up, and also the ones that have been least likely to provide alternative information. The task of opening up the publicly funded broadcasting networks is going to be one of the most difficult and essential struggles for the creation of democratic forms of communication, and here the question is not so much of allowing commercial broadcasting as creating the basis for true public-service broadcasting, particularly as regards news and current-affairs reporting. This is the reason why the Southern African regional independent media organisation the Media Institute of Southern Africa (MISA) has made the freeing of the airwaves a primary objective of its advocacy campaigns, calling for the establishment of a three-tier broadcasting structure consisting of editorially independent public broadcasters, private broadcasters and community broadcasting.

The relationship of the state to the media has been the central concern of MISA since its foundation in 1992. There seems to be mutual antagonism between governments, both towards newly elected and old ones, and the independent press. The new Kenyan government has already started to act in a repressive manner to the alternative press in the country, arresting journalists and preventing the street sale of papers. To a lesser and greater degree ministers, officials and even presidents condemn the press for what they perceive as and call misrepresentations, irresponsible reporting, sensationalism and outright lies. The accusations from government sources tend to centre on reports about the activities of government, and often there are veiled threats in the attacks, which are sometimes put into practice. The relationship between the press and government should ideally be one of critical distance, but not necessarily of hostility. At the moment, it seems as if in many African countries there is a situation where the official media maintain an over-close and uncritical relationship with government, while the independent press often has a tendency to be sensationalist and rumour-mongering.

It could be said that there are no truly independent media, but there are degrees of dependence, and that at the core of a democratic society is the presence of a public debate about the distribution and execution of power, so that choices made by the power holders may be publicly scrutinised and contested. The public examination of decisions that affect the political, social and cultural life of a community is essential to the development of society. For their physical survival people need certain basics such as food, shelter, healthcare and social welfare that are part of the social dimension of human rights. Human dignity is dependent on principles that are intrinsic to true democracy. Freedom of expression and conscience, based on reason, responsibility and mutual respect are unthinkable without mediated forms of communication. A prerequisite for democracy and respect for human rights is the democratisation of communication, broad access to representative media, which in turn requires the empowerment of both a variety of interest groups and the individual citizen. Africa is a long way from achieving this, but the continent's many brave journalists are making a contribution against very difficult odds to realise this ideal.

Notes

1 For a running report on political and social issues from Africa, including media and freedom of expression, see: http://www.pambazuka.org/
2 See http://www.rsf.org/
3 See http://www.cpj.org/ and also: http://www.cpj.org/Briefings/2003/Joshua/war_words.html
4 The media situation in Zimbabwe is being monitored and reported on by the Zimbabwe Media Monitoring Project. See http://www.mmpz.org.zw
5 MMPZ weekly media update 7–13 June 2004.
6 Geoff Nyarota in e-mail to me on 15 Oct. 2003.
7 See http://www.cpj.org/attacks02/africa02/senegal.html
8 See http://www.cpj.org/attacks02/africa02/niger.html
9 See http://www.cpj.org/attacks02/africa02/botswana.html
10 See http://www.cpj.org/Briefings/2002/Namibia_oct02/Namibia_oct02.html
11 There is no proper audited information on the circulation of Zambian newspapers.
12 See http://www.cpu.org.uk/focus_africa.html; and *http://www.southafrica.info/ess_info/sa_glance/constitution/news.htm*
13 The man called Anibalzinho who actually shot Cardoso escaped from prison, or rather was helped to escape in May 2004. He later surfaced in Canada where he applied for political asylum, but was extradited to Mozambique early in 2005, and now faces a retrial for his involvement in the Cardoso murder. The question is, of course, who helped him escape from the country's maximum-security prison, and why?
14 For an overview of the case, see Reporters sans frontières: http://www.rsf.org/article.php3?id_article=8793
15 http://www.worldpress.org/Africa/1765.cfm

References

Ansah, Paul A.V. (1991) "Blueprint for Freedom", *Index on Censorship*, Vol. 9.
Berry, John A. and Berry, Carol Pott (eds) (1999) *Genocide in Rwanda: A Collective Memory*, Washington DC, Howard University Press.
Carver, Richard (2000) "Broadcasting and Political Transition. Rwanda and Beyond", in Fardon, Richard and Furniss, Graham (eds) *African Broadcast Cultures: Radio in Transition*, Oxford, James Currey.
Eribo, Festus and Jong-Ebot, William (eds) (1997) *Press Freedom and Communication in Africa*, Trenton, NJ, Africa World Press.
Fardon, Richard and Furniss, Graham (eds) (2000) *African Broadcast Cultures: Radio in Transition*, Oxford, James Currey.
Fauvet, Paul and Mosse, Marcelo (2003) *É proibido pôr algemas nas palavras: Carlos Cardoso e a Revolução Moçambicana*, Maputo, Ndjira. English version: *Carlos Cardoso: Telling the Truth in Mozambique*, Cape Town, Double Storey Books.
Hydén, Goran; Leslie, Michael and Ogundimu, Folu F. (eds) (2002) *Media and Democracy in Africa*, Uppsala, Nordic Africa Institute.
Hydén, Goran and Okigbo, Charles (2002) "The Media and the Two Waves of Democracy", in Hydén, Goran, Leslie, Michael and Ogundimu, Folu F. (eds) *Media and Democracy in Africa*, Uppsala, Nordic Africa Insitute.
Kale, II, MacDonald Ndombo (1997) "Deconstructing the Dialectics of Press Freedom in Cameroon", in Eribo, Festus and Jong-Ebot, William (eds) *Press Freedom and Communication in Africa*, Trenton, NJ, Africa World Press.

Kasoma, Francis P. (2000a) "Press and Politics in Zambia", in M'Bayo, Ritchard Tamba, Onwumechili, Chuka and Nwanko, R. Nwafo (eds) *Press and Politics in Africa*, Lewiston, Edwin Mellen Press.

Kasoma, Francis P. (2000b) *The Press and Multiparty Politics in Africa*, Tampere, University of Tampere.

M'Bayo, Ritchard Tamba, Onwumechili, Chuka and Nwanko, R. Nwafo (2000) *Press and Politics in Africa*, Lewiston, Edwin Mellen Press.

Media Monitoring Project Zimbabwe (2004) *Media under Siege: Report on the Media Coverage of the 2002 Presidential and Mayoral Elections*, Harare, Media Monitoring Project Zimbabwe.

Nyarota, Geoff (2003) "Death of the *Daily News* – Telling It Like It Is", article sent to me by e-mail, then published in the *Zimbabwe Independent*.

Prunier, Gérard (1995, 1997) *The Rwanda Crisis: History of a Genocide*, London, Hurst.

Randall, Vicky (1993) "The Media and Democratisation in the Third World", *Third World Quarterly*, Vol. 14, No. 3, London, Carfax.

Waldahl, Ragnar (2004) *Politics and Persuasion: Media Coverage of Zimbabwe's 2000 Election*, Harare, Weaver Press, and Oslo, Unipub Forlag.

10

FROM LAPDOG TO WATCHDOG

The role of the press in Latin America's democratization

Rosental Calmon Alves

Over the past two decades, Latin America has experienced an unprecedented period of political stability and consolidation of democratic regimes. Long gone is the proliferation of military dictatorships, frequent *coups d'état* and lifetime dicta-tors. It has not been an easy process and there is still a long way to go regarding the strengthening of democratic institutions, but the fact is that all Latin American countries, except Cuba, are ruled by elected governments. During the democratization period, journalism has evolved throughout the region toward an independent and aggressive style, more attuned with the role of the free press as a fundamental tool with the checks and balance necessary for a working democracy. This chapter will focus on five representative cases of newspapers emblematic of that evolution. The papers analyzed here had a leading role during the political transition in their countries, not only contributing to democratization, but also as driving forces of modernization of the rest of the media in their countries.

During the period of political instability and authoritarian regimes, the Latin American press was by and large muzzled or developed a *modus operandi* char-acterized by an automatic alliance with whoever had taken charge of the government. The media companies benefited from such lapdog behavior, espe-cially in countries where the state was the main economic power and the largest advertiser. The wave of democratization of the 1980s and 1990s went way beyond politics, including the economic neo-liberalism imposed by globaliza-tion. Privatization of thousands of state companies meant a significant shrinking of the size and the purchasing power of the state, which helped to change its relationship with the media.

Waisbord studied the evolution of investigative journalism in South America and noticed "watchdog reporting was relegated to marginal, nonmainstream publications during democratic periods, and to underground, clandestine outlets during dictatorial periods." But he observed a significant change in the media landscape in the region: "There are unmistakable signs that a journalism who [*sic*] prizes the sniffing out of wrongdoing has become more visible and legitimate in the region" (Waisbord, 2000: xiii). In fact, any attempt to trans-form the lapdog press into a watchdog press in the past would have been severely punished and the media outlet destroyed by economic means, if not by violence. The violence against journalists persists even today, under democratic regimes. The Inter American Press Association recorded the assassination of 140 Latin American journalists between 1993 and 2003 (IAPA, 2004). Although violence on the part of governments or public officials seems to have diminished considerably, it is now perpetrated by those such as drug traffickers and other criminals.

The watchdog journalism that was introduced in many parts of Latin America for the first time during the democratization processes of the last decade is not without risk. The five newspapers analyzed faced very different circumstances and difficulties in introducing into their countries a style of journalism that breaks with tradition. The results were different in each case, but there were striking common traits, including their trust in democratization and their influence on other media outlets.

Mexico: *El Norte/Reforma*

The media have not been immune to a social disease that attacks most Latin American countries in epidemic proportions: widespread corruption. However, there is no country in Latin America in which the press has been as openly involved in corruption as in Mexico. The media not only have supported the one-party authoritarian regime that has ruled Mexico for 70 years, but have become part of the corrupt regime itself. The media institutionalized their own practices of corruption: Payments of bribes to journalists and media companies became so common and acceptable that they were not even disguised, as elsewhere.

It was considered "normal" for reporters to receive a cash payment from a public official or politician they were assigned to cover. The payments even have special names, called *embutes* when they are weekly or monthly payments or *chayote* when they are occasional gifts. In addition, it was a common practice to publish *Gacetillas*, press releases disguised as regular news, which cost the client (usually a politician or public officer) "two or three times the going advertising rate" (Keenan, 1996: 42). The owners of the media companies not only were aware of this situation, they even counted on it to ensure the profitability of their operations. Besides receiving direct money in disguised advertising, they also felt no obligation to pay better salaries for journalists, since they could go after other sources of revenue.

These are only some of the characteristics that Alejandro Junco de la Vega found back home, when he returned to Monterrey in 1971 after graduating from the School of Journalism at the University of Texas at Austin. Junco was only 24 years old when he and his brother inherited the newspaper *El Norte* from his grandfather. Slowly he began to modernize the newspaper, trying to model it on the US style of a profit-oriented and politically independent company. Junco recruited and trained young journalists, and sent some of them to UT-Austin. In addition, he imported one of his journalism instructors from Texas. For about two decades, Professor Mary A. Gardner spent every summer in Monterrey training reporters and editors.

Junco was determined to break with the tradition of media corruption, and especially with the unconditional support that was given to the government at all levels, in exchange for all sorts of favors. In 1973, *El Norte* criticized the way the authorities had dealt with the kidnapping and murder of a Monterrey businessman by leftist guerrillas. The government's response was strong: PIPSA, the state-owned company that had a monopoly on newsprint and was part of the government's official arsenal against the Mexican press, stopped supplying *El Norte*. "By October, we had received only 17 percent of our annual quota," recalled Junco. This was a clear attempt by then-President Luis Echeverria to shut down the paper, which reacted by dramatically shrinking its editions and buying newsprint on the black market.

Not only did Junco survive the boycott, but he also succeeded in transforming the small newspaper into a sort of pioneer of the modernization process that the media are now undergoing in Mexico. The company created the tradition of paying journalists much higher salaries than the ones paid by other newspapers, and prohibited them from receiving *embutes* or *chayotes*. *El Norte*'s circulation jumped and soon Monterrey became too small for Junco's company. He eventually expanded to Mexico City, where he launched the newspaper *Reforma*, in November 1993, despite the high-risk operation and some political opposition. The first obstacle was the government-leaning union that has controlled newspaper distribution in the city for decades. The *voceadores*, as they are known in Mexico, were accustomed to dictating the rules for the papers, like the prohibition of circulation on certain holidays. Junco defied them and so far *Reforma* is the only one among Mexico City's 24 daily papers that is not sold in newsstands. It had to create its own distribution system, including home-delivery subscriptions.

Substantially different from the other papers of the capital, *Reforma* came with multiple sections, extensive use of color, and a strong opinion page with some of the most respected Mexican columnists of different political tendencies. As in *El Norte*, *Reforma*'s editorial line is politically independent, which allows the frequent publication of consistent investigative reporting pieces. The style and tone of the exposés printed in *Reforma* followed the model the company had developed in Monterrey for several years, but they were quite new for Mexico City.

Perhaps Alejandro Junco's biggest achievement has been to prove it was possible to build a news company in Mexico that is profit-oriented and independent from the government, with a firmly declared commitment to serving the community. Junco showed in a crystal-clear way to other publishers in Mexico that the dream was not only possible, but could produce positive financial results. For other publishers in Mexico, Junco's journalistic enterprise became a model.

It was no surprise when other media companies began to change their journalism practices in search of more independent and aggressive reporting. Such is the case of the 88-year-old *El Universal*, the leader in classified advertising in Mexico City and a paper that had been seen as tied to the government. It was after *Reforma*'s arrival and clear success that *El Universal* hired the American Press Institute to help in a redesign and started an impressive modernization program that included changing its political line substantially toward a position that is more critical and independent of the government. As soon as the results of that modernization started, the government reacted. On September 12, 1996, the paper's headquarters was surrounded by dozens of heavily armed police officers. The mission was to arrest the publisher, Juan Francisco Ealy Ortiz, for tax evasion. The absence of an arrest warrant and the use of excessive force in the operation prompted claims that it was a blatant act of intimidation.

It could also have been a warning to other newspaper publishers that might be attracted by the same editorial changes. *New York Times* correspondent Julia Preston wrote that the case "comes at the time of shifting relations between the Mexican government and the press," and pointed out the changes in *El Universal*: "For years the paper was staunchly pro-Government. But recently Mr. Ealy Ortiz hired a young editor-in-chief, some hard-driving investigative reporters and several columnists known for their criticism of President Zedillo" (Preston, 1996). The owner of *El Universal* eventually turned himself in to a judge and posted bail, while the tax-evasion accusation was resolved.

Junco's experience influenced several traditional newspapers in Mexico's countryside. *Siglo 21,* launched in November 1991 in Guadalajara, is a significant example of that. A businessman hired Jorge Zepeda Patterson, a sociology professor who took two years to learn journalism abroad, and became the editor-in-chief. Zepeda followed "the *El Norte* model" and formed the newsroom with "a staff that, for the most part, had little prior journalistic experience. He focused on energetic young people with writing skills and curiosity" (Fromson, 1996: 135). The result was a vibrant and modern newspaper, able to investigate and publish world-class stories.

Unfortunately, the businessman who owned the paper had second thoughts regarding the principles of independent journalism. Zepeda left the newspaper and was followed just a few weeks later, in August 1997, by more than 100 *Siglo 21* employees. In an extraordinary move, the entire newsroom personnel, outraged with the owner's behavior, joined Zepeda in a project of a new newspaper that would follow the original principles of *Siglo 21*. *Publico*, the new paper, was launched on September 8, 1997. Along with its pledge of independent and honest journalism, *Publico* printed in its first issue a pie chart, outlining the ownership of the newspaper's company stocks. It showed that 52 percent of the shares belonged to the 155 journalists who worked for the paper. "This newspaper is owned by everybody, and by nobody in particular," said the article on *Publico*'s ownership. The competition with the old newspapers and, ironically, with a new one launched in Guadalajara in 1998 by Alejandro Junco forced the journalists to sell *Publico* and Zepeda moved to *El Universal*, in Mexico City.

Although *El Norte/Reforma* are used here as the best example of newspapers at the vanguard of the modernization and democratization of the press in Mexico, there have been other cases of pioneers that challenged the authoritarian regime. In the late 1960s and early 1970s, *Excelsior*, which was the most important and one of the oldest newspapers in Mexico City, tried to free itself from government control, but could not resist the government reaction. Another outstanding case is that of the weekly magazine *Proceso*, created in November 1976 by Julio Scherer, a respected journalist who was forced to leave the newspaper *Excelsior* because of his insistence on practicing independent journalism. *Proceso* has been a combative opponent of the corrupt political system, and the true leader in investigative reporting and exposés of malfeasance and human-rights abuses.

When the 71-year-old authoritarian regime changed in Mexico with the victory of the opposition in the 2000 presidential election, the media landscape in Mexico was quite different. Besides the modernization of the newspapers, pioneered by *El Norte*, the changes had finally reached television and, especially, *Televisa*, for decades a virtual monopoly and one of the pillars of the political system. Newspapers, such as *Reforma* and *El Universal*, did not stop their efforts towards the consolidation of democracy in Mexico and led a civic mobilization to demand more transparency in the government. Thanks to the campaign that they initiated and extended to other sectors of the civil society, in 2002 Mexico passed a transparency law similar to the Freedom of Information Act of the United States. The reinvigorated Mexican press started immediately to use the law to break into one of the most secretive of bureaucracies.

Guatemala: *Siglo Veintiuno*

Guatemala had been embroiled in a bloody civil war for more than 30 years when 14 businessmen decided in 1990 to invest in a very risky venture: a modern newspaper that would promote democracy through its independence, aggressive reporting, and openness to a plurality of opinions. When *Siglo Veintiuno* (21st Century) was launched later that year, the stockholders received flowers at their homes, but it was not to congratulate them. They were funeral wreaths with a threatening note, showing that the risk they had taken was not only financial. It was a life-and-death risk, without any exaggeration, as was demonstrated by decades of unpunished political assassinations in Guatemala. Scores of journalists have been murdered or attacked. The civil war ended in December 1996, after almost 36 years and more than 100,000 deaths. By that time, *Siglo Veintiuno* was the second largest newspaper in circulation and advertising, but the first to set the standards by which to modernize the press in Guatemala.

Since its inception, *Siglo Veintiuno* tried to distance itself from the other five newspapers in Guatemala City that had established a history of partisanship or automatic alliance with whoever was in charge of the government. The main goal of the new company was to create an independent and economically sound newspaper. The publisher Lionel Torriello Najera explained the immediate success by saying, "the time was ripe for a new newspaper." He added, "In the kingdom of the blind, the one-eyed man is a king. The state of the press was dismal. We were different in that we were committed to changes that the society desperately needs. We present a position that is unabashedly pro-democratic and pro-free market. We discovered that a lot of people liked this approach" (Bogart and Giner, 1997: 100).

Siglo Veintiuno became a leader of more critical and investigative journalism and was followed by other papers, despite constant threats, assassinations, kidnappings, harassment and even bombings. The leading Guatemalan paper *Prensa Libre* responded to the new competition by changing its traditional line of automatic alliance with the government, regardless of whether it was legitimate. The shift was noticed during the administration of President Jorge Serrano Elias (1991–1993), when it became evident that *Siglo Veintiuno*'s editorial line had boosted circulation.

Influenced by military groups, Serrano carried out a *coup d'état* on May 25, 1993, dismissing the Congress and the Supreme Court. But he faced strong opposition from the press, led by *Siglo Veintiuno*. After four days of not publishing for refusing to submit to government censorship, *Siglo Veintiuno*'s editor cheated the censors and produced a historical edition. They changed the name of the paper on the masthead to *Siglo Catorce* (14th Century) on a blacked-out front-page, with only one sentence explaining that the country had entered "The Dark Ages." Journalists and other employees of the paper distributed the edition on the streets.

Two other papers, *La Hora* and *El Grafico*, joined *Siglo Veintiuno* in the resistance against censorship. However, the leading newspaper *Prensa Libre* surrendered to the dictatorship. The owners agreed to self-censorship and Editor Sandoval resigned in protest, putting an end to his nine-month effort to resist.

Serrano was ousted by the military and, amid an outcry for a civilian and democratic solution, the congress elected Ramiro de Leon Carpio as provisional President. De Leon, who was the president of the Human Rights Commission, immediately re-established freedom of the press and governed the country under constitutional rules until the beginning of 1996. He paved the way for his successor, Alvaro Arzu Irigoyen, elected in 1995, who strengthened democracy by ending the longest war in the history of the Americas and dramatically reducing the size of the armed forces. The kind of modern and independent journalism that *Siglo Veintiuno* introduced in Guatemala had a lot to do with the current progress toward the consolidation of democracy. And it clearly pushed other media companies to follow that new style.

When Serrano launched his coup, *Siglo Veintiuno* was still a very young paper, only two-and-a-half years old. Nevertheless, it had already become "Guatemala's most independent newspaper by far," according to the *Los*

Angeles Times (Wilkinson, 1993). Two months before Serrano's attempt, the same reporter published a story integrally dedicated to the introduction of independent journalism in a country which at that time had "enjoyed only 17 years of press freedom in its 172 years of independence" (Buckman, 1993). The story, printed on March 16, 1993 in the *Los Angeles Times*, described how

> armed men arrived in the middle of the night, sweeping simultaneously into seven distribution centers of the feisty Guatemalan newspaper *Siglo Veintiuno*. By the time they finished, the men had burned thousands of copies of the next day's edition and terrified vendors who peddle the paper on Guatemala's street corners.

It added that,

> *Siglo Veintiuno* took on once-taboo subjects ranging from army human rights abuses to government corruption and official complicity in drug trafficking. And as a result, the paper's editor contends they've received death threats, and two reporters have been physically assaulted on the job. A funeral wreath was sent anonymously to the home of one *Siglo Veintiuno* editor.

After Serrano's failed self-coup, *Siglo Veintiuno* continued to take on once-taboo subjects, and gained more international recognition, including some awards. The New York-based Committee to Protect Journalists (CPJ) gave its International Press Freedom Award to Siglo's editor Jose Ruben Zamora in 1995. In its annual report Attacks on the Press in 1995, CPJ pointed out several cases of violence against journalists and media outlets in Guatemala, including one assassination. But it rejoiced that "the muckraking *Siglo Veintiuno* provided Guatemalan reporters with an encouraging role model of how they could effect change." The report added that *Siglo Veintiuno*

> continued to break ground in reporting on corruption and human rights violations, despite the ongoing attacks and threats against its reporters. The paper's continued financial success also proved to its competitors and other Central American newspapers that good and bold journalism can be good business too.
>
> (CPJ, 1996)

Despite attempts on his life, Zamora started a new newspaper called *elPeriodico* in December 1996, repeating the same independent and aggressive style he introduced in Guatemala with *Siglo*. In 2003, Zamora's residence was invaded by 11 heavily armed men and women, who kidnapped him and his family for a few hours, humiliated him and simulated his execution several times, in front of his children, his wife and house employees. Zamora's own investigation led to the identification of some of the attackers as members of the government security forces and direct subordinates to the president of Guatemala (Zamora, 2003). Publication of the newspaper's investigation of this was delayed until January 2004 and the presidential inauguration, after which the Supreme Court intervened and the suspects were arrested (*elPeriodico*, 2004).

This episode shows that, despite all the progress of democracy and the end of the civil war, the Guatemalan press probably enjoys more liberties now than previously, but dangers persist.

Panama: *La Prensa*

After three years of exile, Roberto Eisenmann was flying back to Panama in 1979 when he decided to build a powerful weapon against General Omar Torrijos' dictatorship: a newspaper. A young businessman with an MBA degree from University of Pennsylvania's Wharton School, Eisenmann could have had a successful career managing his family's companies, but instead he decided to fight for democracy. "I became obsessed with the political system in my country and dedicated myself full time to overthrowing the dictatorship," he explained to *Editor & Publisher* magazine (Luxner, 1992). Eisenmann invited five people to help build the newspaper, each one from a different party or political movement. Each one put up $5,000 and agreed to work part-time every day on the project. No one had previous experience in journalism, so they gave themselves one year to learn the business. They soon got help and encouragement from foreign newspapers such as *The Miami Herald*, Costa Rica's *La Nación*, and Puerto Rico's *El Nuevo Día*. A *Herald* employee drafted a business plan, and said the group needed $1 million to go ahead with the project.

At first, the estimate alarmed the group, and they thought that was the end of the dream. Suddenly, however, Eisenmann had a brilliant fundraising idea:

> One day I saw the light: The way is to gather many people who each put in a little money because the dictatorship will not destroy the project by hitting one person. We will share the risk and we will have a newspaper without an owner, independent from all powers. Six months later, we had collected the million dollars, and we started the crazy thing.
>
> (Eisenmann, quoted in Guerrero, 1996)

There were 759 stockholders, and none of them investing more than $5,000. University of Southern Louisiana Professor of Communication Robert Buckman notes that this format prevented "the possibility that Torrijos could single out a particular owner for harassment, as he had done with three privately owned papers in 1968" (Buckman, 1990).

This was the start of *La Prensa*, currently the leading newspaper in Panama, which had a pivotal role in opposing the military regime, and in the country's transition to democracy. Today it retains the same "ownerless" structure, with about 1,300 stockholders, including all the journalists and other employees who reap the company's profits. *La Prensa* has been a very successful newspaper, both in the editorial aspects and on the business side. *La Prensa* entered Panamanian history as a kind of hero in the pro-democracy fight and has been a role model, pushing the other papers and media outlets to modernize and take a more democratic editorial line.

Eisenmann was told that the dictator let the newspaper be established only because he was convinced it had no chance of surviving:

> One month before our start, Omar Torrijos asked his staff how much *Editora Revolucionaria* [the official press] had in losses, and he was told that it was $1.2 million. Torrijos answered: 'Let them open it. They will lose double, since they do not have government advertising, and we will be allowed to say that here there is freedom of expression.' What Torrijos did not know was that from the one million we had collected, $250,000 was set aside to cover the losses. We did not panic because we knew that we were about to lose for a year and a half. Only in the 19th month did we start to make money.
>
> (Eisenmann, quoted in Guerrero 1996)

The first edition was published on August 4, 1980. From issue number one, the paper differed from the others, which had been tamed by the dictatorship. Torrijos died a year later in an airplane crash, and the new strongman of the military regime, General Manuel Noriega, had little patience with *La Prensa*'s criticism. He shut down the paper three times, the last time so violently that the soldiers destroyed everything they found inside the building.

The government's first invasion of the paper was in 1982 and the shutdown lasted only a few days, but troops used acid to destroy the printing press. The soldiers returned to the paper in June 1987, and sealed the building until January 1988, when there was an amnesty and, surprisingly, *La Prensa* was allowed to restart, only to be violently shut down again a month later. The reopening occurred about two years later, in January 1990, after the US military invaded Panama and overthrew Noriega's regime.

When Eisenmann returned to Panama in early January 1990, the newspaper building was protected by American troops against Noriega's "dignity battalions," violent paramilitary groups. At least one sniper was repelled (Buckman, 1990). The biggest problem, however, was inside the building, where equipment had been destroyed. It took some days to fix or improvise the minimal equipment necessary to put together the first edition of a new era for *La Prensa* on January 8, 1990. "Today's paper is the first *La Prensa* that we have ever published without a threat, without being under the gun," Eisenmann told the *New York Times* (Pitt, 1990).

That first issue was marked also by unexpected commercial success. The team had planned an eight-page issue, but the amount of advertising was such that they had to expand to a 24-page issue. This advertising success was a sign that *La Prensa* was not only able to recover its status as the leading paper, despite the two-year shutdown, but it had a good chance of becoming a profitable and fast-growing company, which eventually happened. The biggest challenge, however, was the political adaptation to the new era, because after all the paper was created as a combative and crusading medium with the stated goal of over-throwing the dictatorship. How would it adapt to democracy?

La Prensa's friends, comrades from the hard fight against the military regime, formed the new administration. Three members of the presidential cabinet, including the nation's vice-president, were among the paper's share-holders who were asked to step down because of an evident conflict of interest. The board of directors bought Eisenmann's idea that the newspaper had to continue in the same line of independent journalism it had respected since its inception. Eisenmann later described the paper's editorial line to *Editor & Publisher*: "*La Prensa* is really an independent newspaper, tolerant of all opinions, contrary to the typical Latin American newspaper that is born as an instrument of a political party or interest" (Luxner, 1992).

When his old friends approached the newspaper to demand support for the government, Eisenmann was firm in his refusal:

> I told them that the mandate given by the shareholders was to create an independent and free newspaper, and that this one would be an independent and free newspaper. And that meant that we would be very critical although it was a government of friends.
>
> (Eisenmann, quoted in Guerrero 1996)

Six months after *La Prensa* achieved its mission of overthrowing the dictator-ship, a *Boston Globe* correspondent observed that the newspaper found itself "in an awkward new role: criticizing the democratic leaders it sought to place in power and arousing the wrath of newly installed officials who assumed it would become their mouthpiece" (Constable, 1990).

The first big battle started when the paper became very critical of the way the military forces were being reorganized and the lack of punishment for offi-cers accused of human-rights abuses. Ricardo Arias, the first vice-president of the Republic, and one of the three cabinet members among the founders of *La Prensa*, was the one responsible for reorganizing the military. He disagreed with the criticism and had a very different interpretation of the real mission of the paper he had helped to organize ten years earlier. When a cartoon showed him socializing with guerrillas, Arias decided to launch a campaign to persuade the shareholders that they had to fire Eisenmann. When Arias called on *La Prensa*'s stockholders to oust Eisenmann in early May, Miguel Antonio Bernal, a Panamanian Professor of International Relations at Lehigh University, wrote on the *Chicago Tribune's* op-ed page: "Imagine President Bush urging stock-holders of US newspapers to fire editors for printing Doonesbury." He concluded:

> As we struggle for liberty and justice in Panama, I shall also remember the words of Thomas Jefferson: "The price of liberty is eternal vigilance." And I shall maintain my conviction that a government that respects criminals more than it respects freedom of expression can never deserve the support of its people.
>
> (Bernal, 1990)

Eisenmann survived Arias's onslaught, which eventually backfired. The paper grew even more zealous in defense of its editorial independence. It was "virtually the only source of constructive criticism" in those months after the Noriega's regime, "since the political parties were in shambles due to years of dictatorship" (Constable 1990) and the other papers remained pro-government.

In adjusting to the new regime, *La Prensa* stressed its independence even more and improved its journalism, including investigative reporting. An example of the results was *La Prensa's* probe of a drug trafficker who had donated thousands of dollars to President Ernesto Perez Balladares' electoral campaign. The government reacted by threatening legal action but, just a few days after its complaints, Balladares had to admit that *La Prensa* was right.

That exposé occurred a few months after Roberto Eisenmann had stepped down from his position as editor and publisher of *La Prensa*. Aged 58, 15 years after the paper opened and precisely when it was being consolidated as the leader in the Panama market, he decided it was time to retire:

> Our experiment is one of a medium without an owner. Since the struggle was so hard, people began to identify *La Prensa* with myself. They started to say that the story of no owner was Bobby's joke. I thought it was very negative and I knew that the experiment needed more institutionalization, and for that to happen I had to leave.
>
> (Eisenmann, quoted in Guerrero 1996)

Chile: *La Epoca*

Like *La Prensa* in Panama, *La Epoca* was founded in the midst of a military dictatorship and had the declared goal of fighting for democracy. Founder Emilio Fillipi had previously started the successful magazine *Hoy* in 1977, four years after Augusto Pinochet's *coup d'état* against the Allende government. Fillipi, a Christian Democrat, was initially sympathetic to the coup as a way of ending the chaotic situation under Allende. But, like many other Chileans he soon became disappointed with the brutality of the military regime and with Pinochet's determination to hold onto power for a long period.

When the violent coup occurred on September 11, 1973, Fillipi had been for five years the editor of *Ercilla*, the top newsmagazine in Chile. He left *Ercilla* along with most of his colleagues because it was sold to a group of Pinochet supporters. With his team, Fillipi put together *Hoy*. "The news magazine was an instant success, the only news medium that was both independent and generally objective, neither a pro-government sycophant nor an opinion organ like *Análisis* or *Mensaje*" (Buckman 1990).

In the 1980s the dictatorship became more tolerant of the press, although it provoked self-censorship. A host of opposition magazines, some of clear leftist political leaning, were tolerated, mainly because they had very small circulation and helped to give some appearance of freedom of the press. The Chilean newspapers had played an important role in the efforts to destabilize Salvador Allende's administration, participating in the collusion organized by the US Central Intelligence Agency. It later was made public that Chilean newspapers even got cash payments from the CIA, including $1,665,000 to the leading *El Mercurio* alone (Pierce, 1979: 60).

Despite the press's sympathy, the military government imposed a strict censorship in the first months and demanded a severe purge of journalists considered leftists (the newspapers complied with no known resistance) and then issued informal reporting guidelines to the publishers and editors, who substituted for the censors. But Emilio Fillipi, encouraged by the success of *Hoy*, became obsessed with the idea of creating an independent newspaper truly committed to democratic principles. It took him two years, a lawsuit and a Supreme Court decision to have a license to open *La Epoca* on March 17, 1987.

The money came from Fillipi himself and 24 investors led by Juan Hamilton, a prominent Christian Democrat politician. The first issue of *La Epoca*, on March 18, 1987, proclaimed in an editorial that, "This newspaper will bet on democracy as the best system to ensure a peaceful, stable and just society for Chile." Explaining why a new paper was necessary, the editorial said that the Chilean public deserved "not just one side of the coin," in an indirect reference to the other papers' alliance with the dictatorship.

The news about *La Epoca* echoed around the world as a real breakthrough for democracy. "For the first time since the military took power 13 years ago, a daily newspaper identified with the opposition to President Augusto Pinochet went on sale today in the kiosks of the Chilean capital," announced the *New York Times* (Christian, 1987). A *Los Angeles Times* correspondent reported:

> Amid chaos on the sixth floor of a downtown office building here [in Santiago], a few dozen young Chileans are editing an audacious new newspaper called *La Epoca*. Each day their product, which is not political partisan but of frankly democratic cast, is testing the limits of one of the hemisphere's toughest dictatorships.
>
> (Montalbano, 1987)

In a letter to his staff in 1987, Fillipi said, "Chile lacks a newspaper with four basic characteristics: professional, independent, pluralist and democratic. These are indispensable qualities for a different kind of newspaper. Without them, *La Epoca* would have no reason for being" (Montalbano, 1987). Fillipi tried to separate himself from the political partisan opposition against the regime, but he was also convinced that the role of an independent and professional press was even more important for democracy than party politics. He told *Los Angeles Times* correspondent William Montalbano:

> Our job is more important than that of a political party. We offer access to ideas of all kinds: left, right and center, resisting identification with one of them. This kind of newspaper is essential for Chile if democracy is to return. Explain the options and let people decide for themselves. That's what good newspapers do all over the world.
>
> (ibid., 1987)

One of *La Epoca*'s first big journalistic strikes on the competition seems to epitomize what Fillipi meant by using the label "independent" rather than "opposition." A few weeks after the launching of the new newspaper, Pope John Paul II visited Santiago. The biggest Chilean newspaper, *El Mercurio* announced proudly that it had two journalists on the plane with the Pope but curiously neither of them noticed that, during an interview on board, John Paul II called the Pinochet government "dictatorial." And there was no language barrier, because the Pope repeated it in seven languages. The next day, the Pope's statement was the leading story in newspapers around the world, including *La Epoca*'s headline front-page story, based on wire services. *El Mercurio* blatantly ignored the news because of its allegiance to the dictatorship. This kind of difference in content was more and more noticeable, and eventually drove the other newspapers to change, slowly, their editorial line.

La Epoca's style clearly influenced other newspapers, helped along by the fact that some news magazines had become even more aggressive against the regime, taking advantage of the political openness. Chile and Paraguay were, at that time, the only two countries in South America governed by military dictators. Six other countries (Argentina, Bolivia, Brazil, Ecuador, Peru and Uruguay) had jumped from dictatorships to democratic regimes in recent years.

La Epoca soon emerged as a key player in the campaign for the plebiscite General Pinochet scheduled for October 1988, in an attempt to gain people's support for him to stay in government until, at least, 1997. The newspaper supported the campaign for the "no" answer that would oust Pinochet. The dictator eventually lost the referendum with a vote of 55–43 percent, despite his strategic advantage in manipulating the mass media and other forms of pressure available.

Less than a year after it started, the paper was on the brink of shutting down because of lack of funds. The staff took "drastic pay cuts in order to try to help the paper survive," the circulation was smaller than anticipated and advertisers did not come through (Ungar, 1988). "Indeed, some corporations and businesses pay *La Epoca* for their advertisements, but then ask the newspaper not to publish that, out of a fear of political consequences," (ibid.).

In 1992, *La Epoca* started a series of financial and commercial maneuvers in a desperate attempt to survive, including selling stocks to other media companies. At that point *La Epoca*'s own independence was being questioned. Other papers, including *El Mercurio*, had adapted their editorial line to the democratic times, improving the quality of their work, although keeping the general "don't rock the boat" style, pretty different from the more aggressive press in neighboring countries (Heuvel and Dennis, 1995: 119). *La Epoca* was frequently accused of being a mouthpiece for President Patricio Aylwin of the Christian Democrat party, who was elected to replace General Pinochet. The paper received vital support from the Christian Democrat administration. The more *La Epoca* accepted direct or indirect help from the government, the more it was distancing itself from the independent, non-partisan line Fillipi had promised to follow. From the vanguard of democracy, *La Epoca* moved to a less prominent place, taking a back seat to other media. It was the beginning of the end. "Deprived of its one big issue—Pinochet himself—the former opposition press has fallen on hard times," a *Washington Post* correspondent wrote (Robinson, 1991).

Before 1995, though, "*La Epoca* changed the practices of the Chilean press," because it forced the other papers to cover issues and actors that they had previously vetoed and, since it came just before the plebiscite, it became an active tribune for the "no" against General Pinochet (Cavallo, 1997). *La Epoca* was the first newspaper in Chile to separate the political section from the national, to have a cultural section (apart from entertainment) and to have a foreign desk instead of just publishing wire services dispatches. There were only 64 journalists on the staff, yet Cavallo believes that their impetus pushed the rest of the press in Chile toward a more democratic openness and toward a more professional style.

Among *La Epoca*'s outstanding achievements during its heyday was an investigative reporting story, printed in 1990, that resulted in the reopening of the investigation of the assassination in Washington, DC, of the former Chilean foreign minister Orlando Letelier. Some of those involved in the conspiracy were to be convicted. Since then, investigative journalism, such as that of *La Epoca*'s has been rare in Chile, raising suspicion that a certain dose of self-censorship still persists, along with a fear of disrupting the country's stability and jeopardizing the unfinished democratization process (Heuvel and Dennis, 1995).

Argentina: *Pagina/12*

After a period of brutal political repression, a veritable genocide, with estimates of the number of victims ranging from 9,000 to 30,000, among them almost

100 journalists, the Argentine press reached its nadir in 1982. It sank along with the bloody military dictatorship, by which it had been victimized like many other civilian institutions in the country, even though the major news organizations initially supported the *coup d'état* of 1976.

Although in very different ways, dictator and media were all brought down by the same culprit in 1982: military defeat. As a foreign correspondent there at that time, I was shocked by the way the media went along with the military's lies about the war. That defeat was surprising and humiliating because the media had acted as a propaganda mouthpiece. The self-esteem of journalists fell to unprecedented depths, following the rest of the nation into a general depression. On top of the war problem, there was the terrible legacy of the recent genocide in the country and the shameful behavior of most media outlets during that bloody nightmare, from which the country was waking up. Argentine journalist Oscar Raul Cardoso (1995) found this way to explain this complicated situation:

> The straight cooperation and complacency of local major news organizations with the military regime, openly sympathetic to the coup d'état even before it materialized, and the fear of editors and reporters of becoming—or having a relative, a friend or a lover become—a desaparecido [missing person] and another unaccounted prisoner in the dungeons of pain and death of the juntas made the Argentine press a silent partner to the national tragedy, a ghost that still haunts the media.

The "ghost" mentioned by Cardoso was still haunting the country in the first years of the democratization process that succeeded the military regime debacle of 1982. However, the media made successful efforts to regain prestige by telling the truth about what really happened in the Falklands War as well as in the so-called dirty war, the mass assassinations committed by the military. *Clarin*'s journalists published a series of truly investigative reporting of good quality about the war with Great Britain that eventually became a book (Cardoso *et al.*, 1983: 440). Dramatic exposés about the human-rights abuses during the military regime finally made the pages of mainstream newspapers.

The main problem, however, was that Argentina lacked the good quality journalism it certainly deserved as one of the richest and most educated nations of this hemisphere. Despite their huge circulation, many times larger than average for the rest of Latin America, newspapers lacked professionalism and modern journalism techniques. Styles from news-story writing to page layout used in Argentina in the 1980s were very similar to the international trends for newspapers in the 1940s or 1950s. Investigative reporting was extremely rare even in major newspapers.

But in a decade, the situation changed dramatically. It is hard to recognize the same Argentine media outlets today. Investigative reporting is routinely practiced by newspapers and magazines, which have become so aggressive that some analysts consider its doses excessive and dangerous. Foreign consultants helped to update the newspapers, from page design to news writing and techniques.

One of the most important factors in provoking the change of tone of Argentine press coverage was created in Buenos Aires, in May 1987. The name of this catalyst was *Pagina/12*, which means simply "page 12." The newspaper was named after one characteristic of the poor conditions surrounding its launch: the first issue had only 12 pages, the maximum size editor Jorge Lanata, co-editor Ernesto Tiffenberg, and investor Fernando Sokolowisky thought they could afford (McCullough, 1991). Sokolowisky was a young businessman who believed in the creation of a left-of-center alternative newspaper, and invested the money necessary to start the operation, becoming the company's only owner.

The public's response to the new daily was better than the editors expected. They printed 35,000 copies, expecting to sell 5,000 or 6,000. It sold 27,000 and some people went to the newsroom to get a copy when many newsstands had run out of papers. Despite that success, *Pagina/12* was not taken seriously by the mainstream media or by the elected government that succeeded the military regime. The first impression the newcomer made was one of an opposition paper, another alternative, left-wing press experiment, inexorably condemned to die after a short period of relative success.

Indeed, its name, its satirical political style, its photomontage mocking authorities on the front-page every day, and its emphasis on humor seemed to lead to the conclusion that *Pagina/12* would never be taken seriously as a major newspaper. If people at that time had foreseen the tremendous influence that the little 12-page tabloid would have on the lazy Argentine press, they would have been called crazy.

Its histrionic and mocking traits were very important, but it was for other reasons that *Pagina/12* began to gain prestige and recognition. What made this possible was a strong knack for investigative reporting, muckraking and getting government sources to leak information. Soon, *Pagina/12* became the third most important newspaper in the country. The first was *Clarin*, a 50-year old daily, the largest circulation in the world for a paper in the Spanish language (over one million on Sundays), and the second was the centennial *La Nación*, considered by the elite "the paper of record."

Even without appropriate quantitative research, it is possible to conclude that most of the biggest political scandals that shook Argentina in the 1990s came from *Pagina/12*. Almost all of those investigative pieces had the same byline: Horacio Verbisky. In a story dedicated to that extraordinary reporter in May 1992, the fifth anniversary of the newspaper, *Columbia Journalism Review* summarized Verbisky's achievements:

> At fifty, an age when most American journalists are wrestling with
> burnout or moving into management, Argentina's Horacio Verbisky is

just hitting his stride. In the last year, the celebrated columnist for Argentina's alternative daily *Pagina/12*, has: (1) brought down a top advisor during the celebrated "Swift-gate," an alleged attempt by officials of the [President Carlos Saul] Menem government to solicit bribes from the Swift meat-packing concern; (2) exposed corruption in the sell-off of the army's steel works, Somisa, which had been losing more than $1 million a day while officials approved sweetheart deals to dump cheap steel abroad; and (3) discovered that health officials were permitting unsanitary conditions in the production of dairy products, including the alleged contamination with human waste of cheese at a mozzarella factory—"Milk-gate."

(Millman, 1992)

In that same story, Verbisky takes the initiative to point out the impact *Pagina/12* had already had on other Buenos Aires newspapers:

Verbisky dismisses his rivals. "*Pagina/12* is the first," he says with a wave of his hand. "*La Nación* comes out a day or two later to mention that this infamy has been alleged, and they will check it out. *Ambito Financiero* accuses us of lying, then they end up printing the same thing. *Clarin* ignore us altogether." Verbisky proudly calls *Pagina/12* Latin America's first leftist newspaper also read by the right. He wants to put an end, he says, to the Argentine media's tradition of "extreme moderation," and he provides a working example of what Argentina's institutions offer to investigative journalism. "It's not that I am so good," he says with a smile. "It's that they are so bad."

(Millman, 1992)

At that point, it was no longer possible to ignore *Pagina/12*. The little, irreverent paper was growing and influencing the others, forcing them to go after their scoops. The international recognition for *Pagina/12*'s economics started to come from the most unexpected sources, such as *The Financial Times*:

How is it that a muckraking, strident anti-establishment newspaper launched on a shoestring five years ago has become one of Argentina's best selling and most influential newspapers? *Pagina/12* is now required reading among businessmen, diplomats and politicians as well as its target readership of professionals, students and left-wingers. It has built up an average daily circulation of 110,000 with a diet of punchy news, investigative journalism, opinion and cultural columns.

(quoted in Barham, 1992)

The same British correspondent concluded, "*Pagina/12*'s success reflects the growing maturity of Argentine society." He quoted editor Jorge Lanata in an obvious effort to reinforce the impression that the paper was distancing itself from its political and ideological origin of a classical alternative leftist publication. "We are not left or right wing newspaper. I say we are a liberal newspaper. The left attacks us for belonging to the new right and the right attacks us for being on the left," said the editor. *The Financial Times* also observed the influence of *Pagina/12* on the other big Buenos Aires papers. "The competition is having to react to *Pagina/12*'s success. For instance, the tabloid *Clarin*, Argentina's best selling newspaper, has promoted younger and more aggressive editors, who have begun to outflank *Pagina/12* with exclusive articles of their own" (Barham, 1992). The second-largest paper, *La Nación*, took more time to respond but eventually followed *Clarin* with the same kind of changes.

The result of the modernization of the Argentine press was a series of exposés of malfeasance during President Carlos Saul Menem's administration. The Argentine civilian society gladly reconciled with its media. A study done by pollster Graciela Romer from December 1993 to mid-1995 revealed that almost 50 percent of the people polled considered the media to be "reliable" and "very reliable." It was an outstanding result, especially when compared with the low confidence levels obtained by labor unions (6 percent), political parties (20 percent), the judicial system (22 percent), the Congress (22 percent), and the Armed Forces (35 percent) (Cardoso, 1995).

Despite the corruption found by press investigations in his government, Menem was re-elected on May 15, 1995, mainly because of the extraordinary success of his economic policy in getting rid of hyperinflation. A few hours after his victory had been recognized, Menem declared in a television interview: "I've beaten the opposition candidates, but that is inconsequential, really. What is important is that I've beaten the press" (Cardoso, 1995). At that point, it was not *Pagina/12* but the whole press that Menem considered adversarial.

The violence against journalists, however, never stopped. Argentineans were especially shocked to learn that photojournalist Jose Luis Cabezas had been assassinated on January 25, 1997. He was handcuffed in his car, shot in the head and burned. Cabezas was involved in investigations about police corruption. His death had enormous repercussions in the country, sparking demonstrations of thousands of people who went on to the streets of Buenos Aires demanding justice. Even after this episode, President Menem did not stop his criticism against free press. According to CPJ's 1997 Report,

> On June 17, during a press briefing for foreign correspondents, Menem described Horacio Verbisky as "one of the biggest terrorists in Argentina." And on September 8, President Menem was quoted as proposing that the *Ley de Palos* ("The Law of the Stick") be used against journalists (he later said he was joking).

The investigative reporting wave started in Argentina by *Pagina/12* has survived all the government pressures and even the criticism of some exaggerations.

Journalist Oscar Raul Cardoso says that investigative reporting has had its "bright moments," but points out that "a major judicial conviction is yet to arise from a journalist's exposé." He warns about the decline in the quality of journalistic investigations, saying they have "slowly been shifting toward an articulated variety of mostly unconfirmed gossip" (Cardoso 1995).

Even with some mistakes and exaggerations, the introduction of investigative reporting as a main trait of the Argentine press has contributed to the improvement of its quality and put it in a better position to pursue its role as a watchdog of democracy. Despite serious financial problems, *Pagina/12* has survived and is still an influential newspaper that competes on a daily basis with others that it helped to wake up from their lapdog style.

Conclusion

Newspapers, such as those analyzed here, have tried to emulate the US watchdog press, even when and where the political and legal circumstances were adverse. Soruco and Ferreira showed, for instance, that

> Unlike that of the United States, constitutional laws in Latin America usually prescribe a free but responsible press, giving state authorities powers to regulate and guarantee its legitimate exercise. Hence, if the U.S. federal media system is institutionally arranged to be suspicious of the government, the Latin American countries have been structurally designed to trust the state as defender of the public good.
>
> (1994: 339)

The newspapers studied here are good examples of how the press is defying even an adverse legal system to assume its watchdog role. In many cases, journalists and media companies in Latin America act as if they had laws guaranteeing their rights to be suspicious of the government. They tend to ignore the fact that the nascent democracies kept intact the legal apparatus of the recent dictatorships. Sometimes, the elected governments are too embarrassed to use that legacy and have problems imposing their own regulations to limit freedom of the press. In other cases, however, they not only use all legal means against journalists and newspapers, but also they do their best, implicitly or explicitly, to muzzle the press.

Analyzing investigative reporting in South America, Waisbord (1996) explains the press in that region "has never fit[ted] neatly within the two paradigms that have dominated Western democracies, the 'independent' model, commonly synonymous with US journalism, and the 'partisan' model, typical of many European countries." He also tries to find reasons why journalism in South America (it is certainly the case in all Latin America) differs from that in the United States:

In summary, none of the factors that originated the emergence of professional and objective journalism in the United States can be found in South America. The mass market was not as weighty for press economies as it was for U.S. newspapers. Dailies had their economic antennae tuned to state rather than market signals. Nor did any cultural movement determined to purify politics from partisan politics or to imprint journalism with a more impartial character ever surface. Additionally, and perhaps most dramatically, military juntas gave the "kiss of death" to journalism *à là Americaine* by firmly controlling the press and persecuting critical journalists.

(Waisbord, 1996).

Nevertheless the process of building democracy and the simultaneous emergence of a form of capitalism imposed by globalization are creating conditions for an independent journalism *à là Americaine* throughout Latin America. Certainly, none of the factors that helped create professional, "objective" journalism in the United States could be found in Latin America. But those factors are now emerging, along with the new political and economic environment.

Among our five cases, *El Norte/Reforma* in Mexico and *La Prensa* in Panama are the best examples of an extraordinary business success combined with a kind of independent journalism clearly copied from the United States. Journalism *à la Americaine* is by far the predominant model these days in Latin America, but it is not the only style. Guatemala's *Siglo Vientiuno* and *La Epoca* found their model in Europe, trying to emulate Spain's *El País*, with success in the first case and failure in the second. The fifth newspaper, *Pagina/12*, chose to create its own model, instead of getting inspiration from abroad.

La Epoca's disaster, however, has nothing to do with its model. *El País* was created just after the end of the 40-year-old dictatorship of Francisco Franco, and became one of the best and most successful independent newspapers in the world. It indeed fits very well the model of a watchdog newspaper. The *El País* model worked very well in Guatemala and has influenced several other newspapers in Latin America.

Beyond mismanagement and lack of capital, what really killed *La Epoca* was a disease that could very well be called "partisanitis acutis"—acute partisanship. The fatal bout of the disease occurred in the very beginning of the post-dictatorship period. Newspaper friends (and some of the owners) took over the government, through democratic election, and count on *La Epoca* as an ally, not as an independent paper ready to test in democracy the same principles of independent watchdog journalism it had practiced during the dictatorship. Pressured by its unremitting financial problems, the paper delivered what the Christian Democrats expected.

The same occurred with Panama's *La Prensa*, with the opposite result. In keeping its promises of non-partisan, independent, watchdog journalism, *La Prensa* not only survived the disappearance of the dictatorship it was created to fight against, but it also prospered in a brilliant way. Had Roberto Eisenmann delivered the lapdog journalism the old comrades of the anti-dictatorship struggle demanded, perhaps *La Prensa* would have suffered the same fate as *La Epoca*.

Despite its fate, *La Epoca* remains one of the group of newspapers that fought for democracy and for watchdog journalism in Latin America. It introduced forgotten or unknown concepts of modern and independent journalism in Chile, shaking the media out of their lethargy. If it was an important booster for the pro-democracy movement, it also had a tremendous impact on the other newspapers.

This capacity to influence other media is among the main characteristics of these five cases. By pioneering a form of aggressive and independent journalism, they all introduced standards that would be followed by the competition. They set the agenda for the new order.

References

Barham, John. Survey of Argentina. *Financial Times*, London, May 14, 1992.

Bernal, Miguel Antonio. Panama's fight for free expression. *Chicago Tribune*, May 29, 1990.

Bogart, Leo and Giner, Juan Antonio. *Achievements and Challenges: The State of the Newspaper Industry in Latin America: 32 Profiles*, regional survey report of the Innovation International Media Consulting Group for the World Association of Newspapers (FIEJ), 1997.

Buckman, Robert. Free at last: the rebirth of Panama's *La Prensa*. *The Quill*, March, 1990.

Buckman, Robert T. Guatemalan press withstands throwback to dictatorship. *Editor & Publisher*, July 31, 1993.

Cardoso, Oscar Raúl. In Argentina, contradictions abound. *Nieman Reports*, Fall, 1995.

Cardoso, O. R., Kirschbaum, R. and Van der Kooy, E. (1983). *Malvinas, la trama secreta*. Buenos Aires: Sudamericana/Planeta.

Cavallo, Ascanio. Interview with the author by e-mail, May 13, 1997.

Christian, Shirley. Opposition paper launched in Chile. *New York Times*, March 19, 1987.

Constable, Pamela. Dissident paper retains its independent voice. *Boston Globe*, July 9, 1990.

CPJ's Report: Attacks on the press in 1995. Published by the Committee to Protect Journalists, New York, March 1996.

elPeriodico, Guatemala, January 20, 2004: http://www.elperiodico.com.gt

Fromson, Murray. Mexico's struggle for a free press. In Cole, Richard R. (Ed.) *Communication in Latin America: Journalism, Mass Media, and Society*. Wilmington, DE: Jaguar Books on Latin America, no. 14, 1996.

Guerrero, Alina. Roberto Eisenmann Jr: El aprendizado de Bobby. *Pulso del Periodismo* magazine, no. 25, January/March, 1996.

Heuvel, Jon Vanden and Dennis, Everette E. *Changing Patterns: Latin America's Vital Media*. A report of the Freedom Forum Media Studies Center at Columbia University, New York, 1995.

IAPA (Inter American Press Association) Cases of murder of journalists, http://www.impunidad.com/statistics/stats15_4_04E.htm (accessed July 18, 2004).

Keenan, Joe. La Gacetilla: How advertise masquerades as news. In Orme Jr., William A. (Ed.), *A Culture of Collusion: An Inside Look at Mexican Press.* Miami, FL: North South Center Press, University of Miami, 1996.

Luxner, Larry. Elusive concept: *La Prensa*'s Eisenmann continues battle for press freedom in post-Noriega Panama. *Editor & Publisher*, December 26, 1992.

McCullough, Ed. Argentine daily makes impact: Irreverent paper scores with scoops, editorial cartoons.*Chicago Tribune*, November 11, 1991.

Meyer, Philip. E-mail message to the author, December 3, 1996.

Millman, Joel. Argentina, a fix on corruption. *Columbia Journalism Review*, May, 1992.

Montalbano, William D. Young newspaper tests limits of Chile's dictatorship. *Los Angeles Times*, May 17, 1987.

Pierce, Robert N. *Keeping the Flame: Media and Government in Latin America.* New York: Hasting House, 1979.

Pitt, David E. The US and Panama: The press; paper Noriega crushed is reborn as a watchdog. *New York Times*, January 10, 1990.

Preston, Julia. Mexican publisher arrest on tax fraud charge. *New York Times*, September 14, 1996.

Robinson, Eugene. Awaken Chile media is failing back to sleep. *Washington Post*, December 1, 1991.

Soruco, Gonzalo and Ferreira, Leonardo. Latin America and the Caribbean. In Merrill, John C. (Ed.) *Global Journalism: Survey of International Communication.* White Plains, NY: Longman, 1974.

Ungar, Stanford J. How Chile muzzles its press. *Washington Post*, January 3, 1988.

Waisbord, Silvio. Investigative Journalism and Political Accountability in South American Democracies. *Critical Studies in Mass Communication*, vol. 13, no. 4, December 1996.

Waisbord, Silvio. *Watchdog Journalism in South America: News, Accountability, and Democracy.* New York: Columbia University Press, 2000.

Wilkinson, Tracy. Press freedom carries a price in Guatemala: upstart newspaper is raided after it takes on once-taboo subjects. *Los Angeles Times*, March 16, 1993.

Zamora Marroquín, José Ruben. Interview with the author in November, 2003, in Austin, TX.

Part III

JOURNALISM AND THE FUTURE

11

THE EVOLUTION OF JOURNALISM EDUCATION IN THE UNITED STATES

Betty Medsger

During more than a century of existence, journalism education in the United States has been defined in numerous ways, shaped and reshaped to suit numerous purposes. In the beginning, it was a discrete field of study designed to improve the quality of journalism. Recently, it has been a confusing field. In some universities, journalism education, like hundreds of journalists during the war against Iraq, is embedded. It is embedded with public relations, advertising and assorted other disciplines that together are considered a generic form of communication. Like the embedded journalists, embedded journalism education at times is uncertain about its priorities.

Journalism education started to become rooted in American higher education in the early twentieth century, but there is general agreement that the first plan for future journalists to receive a college education was created by the losing general in the Civil War, Robert E. Lee. Immediately after the war, Lee became president of Washington College, what would later become Washington and Lee College, now Washington and Lee University, in Lexington, Virginia. Educated journalists were needed, thought Lee, to help rebuild the South (Mirando 1995: 14). Under his widely publicized plan, the college offered scholarships for men to study journalism, business and agricultural chemistry. It was a radical idea, not only because no college in the nation had offered courses in journalism, but because then, as now, Washington and Lee, like most colleges then, was known for its basic liberal arts education, not professional education. Records at Washington and Lee do not indicate how many people studied journalism in response to Lee's call, but it is known that the scholarships, originally offered in 1869, lasted only a few years (ibid.: 24).

Like journalists in many countries, well into the twentieth century many US journalists believed that the best way to become a journalist was by being an apprentice to an experienced journalist. Skepticism about journalism as an academic discipline has been expressed since the first journalism courses were offered. At first, there were editors and reporters who thought such an education would be a waste of time. This was tough work, went that view; it was closer to ditch-digging than to teaching or preaching, professions that found homes in American universities from the beginning. Until the 1960s, many if not most journalists came from working-class families, and they did not have college degrees. By the 1960s, a bachelor's degree became a minimum qualification for being hired as a journalist. In the 2002 American Journalist survey—conducted every 10 years by researchers at the School of Journalism at Indiana University—only 11 percent of journalists working for news media in the United States did not have at least a bachelor's degree (Weaver and Wilhoit 2002). By the late twentieth century, when most journalists had degrees in journalism, ironically the major skeptics of the discipline were university administrators and communication-theory scholars, many of whom think of journalism courses as 'mere nuts and bolts' instruction in simple writing rather than as an intellectual pursuit.

At the time of President Lee's initiative, most newspapers, especially small ones, were owned and operated by editors who were also printers. The enthusiasm of printers for the invitation to study journalism at the college is evident in an 1869 letter to Professor Johnston from John Plaxton of the Nashville Typographical Union. "We look upon this action of Washington College as a very important step toward raising American journalism from the slough of venality, corruption and party subservience into which it has too notoriously fallen to the high position it should occupy" (Mirando 1995: 31).

Journalism education was first created to accomplish two interrelated goals: to improve the minds of journalists and to improve the image of journalism. A. Ross Hill, President of the University of Missouri, expressed those goals upon the opening in 1908 of the University's School of Journalism (the first school of journalism in the U.S., indeed, in the world):

> I believe it is possible for this school to give dignity to the profession of journalism, to anticipate to some extent the difficulties that journalists must meet and to prepare its graduates to overcome them, to give prospective journalists a professional spirit and high ideals of service, to discover those with real talent for the work and discourage those who are likely to prove failures in the profession, and to give the state better newspapers and newspapermen and a better citizenship.
>
> (Farrar 1998: 140)

"Protect society and government against ... unscrupulous journalists"

Willard G. Bleyer, founder of journalism education at the University of Wisconsin in 1912, creator of the first doctoral research program in journalism and an early proponent of accreditation of journalism education programs, speaking in 1905, put a very heavy burden on the study of journalism. The graduates of journalism schools, he declared, are "necessary to protect society and government against immature, half-educated, unscrupulous journalists" (Rogers and Chaffee 1994: 14).

Bleyer and others believed that journalism education would transform the reputation of journalism. The image of rough drunks in the newsrooms would be replaced by an image of thoughtful, educated journalists. Journalism schools would be, in part, the finishing schools of journalism.

James W. Carey, of Columbia Graduate School of Journalism in New York, discussed the founders' motives in a 1992 address to the Columbia faculty. "Reporters were not educated men and most assuredly thereby were not men of letters," Carey said. "They were an unlikely collection of itinerant scribblers, aspiring or, more often, failed novelists, ne'er-do-well sons of established families and, most importantly, the upwardly mobile children of immigrants with an inherited rather than an educated gift of language, without much education and certainly without much refinement." Some newspaper publishers and editors, Joseph Pulitzer among them, believed that education would "improve" reporters. The leaders of journalism, Carey said, were not alone at that time in "believing that university education might domesticate this unruly class, turn them into disciplined workers and end their flirtation with socialism and trade unions." To varying degrees, the universities themselves welcomed the opportunity to make "the quest for knowledge and professional standards" available to those preparing to enter journalism and other professions (Carey 1992: 5).

Pulitzer, owner of the *New York World* and *St. Louis Dispatch,* focused more sharply on the need to improve the minds of journalists than on the need to smooth journalists' rough edges. When Pulitzer proposed endowing a school of journalism at Columbia, he had to work hard to sell the idea. While many journalists had no interest in embellishing their work with a degree from a university, Ivy League colleges were not enthralled with the idea of adding mere professional studies, especially journalism, to their curricula. To some extent, the colleges' attitude was elitist, but their administrators also believed strongly that an education in liberal arts and the sciences, rather than in studies geared toward specific professions, was the ideal education for anyone.

Columbia accepted Pulitzer's offer, but only after a public debate took place over several years, with influential journalists and educators participating in it. Responding to critics who said a journalism education was ridiculous because news instinct must be born, not taught, Pulitzer wrote a 1904 article in *North American Review* magazine that expanded his vision of journalism education:

> If news instinct as born were turned loose in any newspaper office in New York without the control of sound judgment bred by considerable experience and training, the results would be much more pleasing to the lawyers than to the editor. One of the chief difficulties in journalism now is to keep the news instinct from running rampant over the restraints of accuracy and conscience. And if a "nose for news" is born in the cradle, does not the instinct, like other great

qualities, need development by teaching, by training, by practical object lessons illustrating the good and the bad, the Right and the Wrong, the popular and the unpopular, the things that succeed and the things that fail, and above all the things that deserve to succeed, and the things that do not – not the things only that make circulation for today, but the things that make character and influence and public confidence?

(Pulitzer 1904: 22)

Pulitzer believed that journalism education would help future journalists develop minds that would be filled with knowledge and curious about everything. He put more emphasis than other journalism-education founders did on the non-journalism subjects a student would study than he did on the study of journalism.

Each of the principal visionaries of journalism education—Bleyer at the University of Wisconsin, Walter Williams at the University of Missouri School of Journalism and Pulitzer at Columbia University—looked beyond the immediate goal of educating journalists and improving newspapers. The larger goal to which they aspired was to produce a more informed citizenry through better journalism. Pulitzer was especially eloquent in expressing that goal:

While it is a great pleasure to feel that a large number of young men will be helped to a better start in life by means of this college, this is not my primary object. Neither is the elevation of the profession which I love so much and regard so highly. In all my planning the chief end I had in view was the welfare of the Republic. It will be the object of the college to make better journalists, who will make better newspapers, which will better serve the public.

(Pulitzer 1904: 58)

At Wisconsin, after establishing undergraduate courses in journalism, Bleyer pioneered graduate-school journalism education. He stressed that research about journalism should be as important a part of journalism education as preparing students to enter the profession. The two scholarly functions would coexist side by side and enrich each other, as Bleyer saw it: teaching the skills of journalism and, additionally, studying journalism as an institution to be examined—its history, how it is practiced, its impact on society and on democracy. He was instrumental in the creation of two pillars of the journalism education establishment in the United States: the Association of Journalism Education Administrators (now known as the Association of Schools of Journalism and Mass Communication) and the accrediting body for journalism programs (now known as the Accrediting Council on Education in Journalism and Mass Communication).

Journalism education marked by fragility

A remarkable characteristic of journalism education in the U.S. is the fact that it always has been fragile. In many universities, it has had trouble defining itself in ways that convince university officials it belongs there as a discipline. It has been diminished by other disciplines. Its fragility has been increased by the fact that while it started out as a brainchild, in most instances, of leaders of journalism, throughout its history many journalists thought there was no need for journalism education. Surely no other field of higher education that prepares students for entry to a profession has suffered such ignominy as has journalism.

Some of the reasons for the fragility of journalism education can be traced to the culture of journalism, and other reasons can be traced to the culture of universities. The journalist-is-born-not-educated attitude is part of the long-held assumption held by many journalists that news falls from the sky (which may account for the mediocre quality of some journalism). Such an approach leads them to behave as though showing up for work is nearly the only work-related fact over which they have much control. They approach journalism as though their minds are absent from the process. It's an attitude that is expressed by even some of the brightest journalists. They do not seem to see the key role played by their minds and, therefore, by their values and assumptions, in the numerous decisions they make in all stages of the journalistic process, from story idea to completed story. The journalists-are-born concept also undoubtedly has contributed to the anti-intellectual attitude that has been part of the fabric of American journalism through most of its life (Medsger 1999: 64).

This anti-intellectualism probably contributed mightily to journalists and journalism educators who have backgrounds as journalists being unable to make the case adequately for the place of journalism in universities when dramatic change began roaring through their programs in the 1950s. By then a new force was taking root in some journalism-education programs. Eventually, it would permeate most journalism-education programs in the U.S. This new force—communication studies—would radically rewrite the rules governing who should teach journalism, and it would lead to changes and confusion that continue to dog journalism education in the U.S. and in many other countries (Medsger 1996: 56).

The uniting of communication studies and journalism education grew, in substantial part, out of a mix of bureaucratic expediency and a lack of understanding of journalism by university administrators. The union did not result from an altruistic desire for new philosophical understandings about journalism and/or a new commitment to academic or professional excellence on behalf of the improvement of journalism.

Scholars had studied the impact of communication for many years in the United States and in other countries, but the scholars who studied various communication problems did so from their bases in other disciplines, such as psychology, sociology, history, political science or anthropology. At mid-century, Wilbur Schramm, the person who would become the chief architect of communication studies, thought the time had come for it to be a separate discipline, with its teachers bearing the title of "communication professors." There is wide agreement with the claim made by Rogers in *A History of Communication Study* (1994) that Schramm, head of journalism education at Iowa shortly after World War II and later the founder of communication research institutes at the University of Illinois and Stanford University, was "the founder of the field, the first individual to identify himself as a communication scholar." Schramm created "the first academic degree-granting programs with communication in their name; and he trained the first generation of communication scholars ... Schramm set in motion the patterns of scholarly work in communication study that continue to this day," wrote Rogers (1994: 29), of the University of New Mexico.

The development of communication studies in the twentieth century probably was inevitable. As technologies expanded the size of the audience for various kinds of communication, it was natural that some scholars of human behavior would feel compelled to study what a mass audience was and how it behaved, how mass media behaved, and what impact mass media had on various demographic groups as well as on the overall population. There were political and commercial interests eager to understand and use whatever could be learned about—or could be done to or for—the masses. In addition to serving scholarly purposes, communication scholars served commercial and political interests in their research on communication issues.

During World War II, Schramm spent a year in the federal government's Office of Facts and Figures. With other scholars, he designed projects to sell the war effort to the American public and to analyze the effectiveness of various ways of communicating to the public. It was there, in those intense propaganda experiments, which were going on at the same time in Germany among that country's early communication scholars, that Schramm got the idea that communications should be a distinct discipline. In 1943 Schramm returned from Washington to the University of Iowa, where earlier he had established the much respected Writers Workshop. He wrote "Blueprint for a School of Journalism" for the administrators at the university. Creating a new academic discipline can be a difficult bureaucratic task, given the reluctance, or at least slowness, of universities to adopt new structures. Schramm decided to avoid that hassle by grafting communication studies onto an existing discipline, journalism. He chose journalism at Iowa, as he would later at Illinois and Stanford. Not until he was at Stanford, beginning in the early 1960s, did he fully achieve his goal. There Schramm and his scholarly descendants would develop communication studies as a discipline and Schramm would create most of his voluminous body of writing on communication studies. During those years at Stanford and later at the University of Hawaii, Schramm traveled to developing countries to conduct research and also to encourage the development of communication studies at universities in those countries (Rogers 1994: 460). "Most media scholars are heavy users of Wilbur Schramm's great organizing principles, his scholarly output and his instincts for institution building," wrote Dennis. "He gave our field what Tom Wolfe would call 'a rocket boost of energy' and a good deal more" (1989: 161).

One result was the beginning of the institutional marriage that would be replicated repeatedly at US campuses and that exists today in the majority of journalism-education programs. Though Schramm and the graduate students he and other communication studies scholars sent into the field made their home in journalism education, it was a home they eventually rebuilt, with journalism education in a considerably diminished position and no longer in charge of its destiny.

Schramm and the other early communications scholars originally found it useful to piggyback on journalism programs, but fairly early they found the association also posed a significant disadvantage. As Rogers wrote, scholars from other disciplines "would be less likely to participate in communication study if such research were headquartered in a school of journalism, which other disciplines were likely to perceive as irrelevant to their research interests" (1994: 27). Schramm addressed that problem by establishing "institutes" of communication studies. They were within the journalism programs, but they had enough autonomy to appeal to academics from other fields. These scholars could say they were working with the institute rather than with the journalism-education program, thus saving them the shame of being associated with journalism.

Journalism lecturers were supposed to be grateful for this marriage, though to them it may have felt more like a divorce. In exchange for providing the base for such institutes and for hiring the new communication-degree faculty members, Schramm felt he was giving journalism-education programs an opportunity to enhance their standing. "A communication research institute could serve as a source of prestige for a school of journalism that may have been looked down upon by academics in other fields because of the perceived trade school nature of journalism training," Rogers noted (1994: 27).

When Schramm established his doctoral degree-granting programs in the late 1940s and 1950s, Rogers wrote, he "went one step beyond Bleyer of Wisconsin. He established a doctoral program in mass communications, not in journalism as Bleyer had at Wisconsin." He did so, in large part, wrote Rogers, because, unlike Bleyer or Pulitzer, Schramm did not see journalism as an intellectual activity. He had very little interest, in fact, in preparing students to become journalists. Those who studied under Bleyer had been journalists, and their primary interest remained journalism. Those who studied under Schramm had found the infrastructure of journalism education a convenient base for their discipline, but their interest in journalism was secondary, if even that.

Within a decade of Schramm establishing communications studies as a discipline, many of the newly minted PhDs in communication studies fanned out to take positions at universities around the country. The stage was set for establishing a PhD, usually one in mass communication, as the minimum qualification to teach in journalism education programs. They soon added "communication" or "mass communication" to the names of their programs, and some of them subtracted "journalism."

Originally, prospective candidates for doctoral studies in communication were required, as a condition of admission to doctoral programs, to have, as Rogers wrote,

> several years of experience in the mass media, ideally in newspaper journalism. An unstated reason for this requirement was so that when these students completed their Ph.D. degrees, they would be considered for employment in schools of journalism. By the mid 1960s, the media experience requirement was changed officially in graduate school catalogs to "or equivalent," and finally it was dropped.
>
> (1994: 480)

Despite eliminating professional experience as a qualification for teaching in journalism programs, Rogers noted, communication lecturers "must teach their students, especially undergraduates, the practical skills of communication: effective public speaking, newswriting, film-making, how to design and pre-test advertising messages" (ibid.).

According to a survey conducted in 1995 by the Roper Center at the University of Connecticut for the study *Winds of Change: Challenges Confronting Journalism Education*, the notion that expertise in journalism is not needed to teach journalism skills has become commonplace in journalism-education programs. The survey was conducted only among full-time faculty who taught at least some journalism courses. The findings include these (Medsger 1996: 73):

- 67 per cent of journalism faculty members had doctoral degrees (66 percent of faculty in accredited programs compared with 71 percent in non-accredited programs).
- The portion of journalism faculty members with doctoral degrees had doubled among those who began teaching in the decade that began in 1985—42 percent of those who had taught more than 10 years had doctorates, but 84 percent of those who had taught 10 or fewer years had them.
- 48 percent of journalism educators had doctoral degrees in mass communication, 4 percent had doctoral degrees in law, and 15 percent had doctoral degrees in other areas of study.
- 17 percent of journalism faculty members never worked as journalists. They included 13 percent of those 60 and older, 15 percent of those 45 to 59, and 23 percent of those 44 and younger.

- An additional 47 percent of journalism faculty worked 10 or fewer years as journalists.

Although two of every three journalism educators as of 1995 had doctoral degrees, only one in seven (14 percent) strongly agreed that journalism educators *should* have doctoral degrees (23 percent mildly agreed, 22 percent neither agreed nor disagreed, 18 percent mildly disagreed, and 22 percent strongly disagreed).

Of those with doctoral degrees, only 22 percent said they strongly believed journalism educators should be *required* to have them. Among those who had worked 10 or fewer years as journalists, 21 percent strongly agreed, compared with 5 percent of those who worked as journalists more than 10 years.

Some programs have established a doctorate in *any* discipline as appropriate for meeting minimal degree requirements to be recruited to the permanent staff. Nearly half—48 percent of journalism educators who have doctoral degrees, though, have mass-communication doctorates. That's not surprising given the fact that that degree is the one granted by the doctoral degree-granting journalism and mass-communication programs. What is surprising is the attitude of doctoral degree-holding journalism education academics about whether the degree in mass communications should be required. A very small portion of journalism educators—only 5 percent of all full-time journalism educators and 9 percent of those who *have* doctoral degrees—agreed that journalism educators should have a doctoral degree in mass communication (Medsger 1996: 87). This finding suggests that there is a great deal of ambivalence about the value of the communication doctoral degree even by those who have earned it.

Typically, a communications program that includes undergraduate majors and minors in journalism, public relations or advertising relies for most of its financial footing on undergraduate student enrollment in those courses. In other words, without these students the programs could not exist. The academic needs of these students, who have enrolled because they want an education that will prepare them to become journalists, are given secondary importance while the needs of communication scholars to have faculty positions is given highest priority. As an observer of similar trends in Latin American universities wrote in 2003, not only is communication theory an ever larger part of journalism education programs, but the basic skills courses are being taught theoretically by people who have little or no experience as a journalist (Gaunt 1992: 127). Some programs, recognizing the need for the journalism and other professional courses to be taught by practitioners, hire large numbers of experienced professionals to teach these courses as part-time lecturers. Invariably, in the United States these lecturers are paid at very low levels. Consequently, in addition to saving the programs considerable money, these lecturers make it possible for the tenured and tenure track faculty to have time and money to pursue research and teaching agendas that, unfortunately, may be unrelated in substance to the courses that make up the heart of the programs and serve most of the students.

Journalism schools same as schools of trailer-park management

As journalism educators watched their discipline being radically reshaped in the 1960s and 1970s, few of them had much hope of retaining full citizenship in their discipline as its infrastructure was taken over by communication studies scholars.

For those who relied on their expertise as journalists as their major qualification for teaching journalism, the timing of the rise of communication studies could not have been worse. The years when communication studies academics were taking over journalism education programs were the same years that American universities were growing and competing to be recognized as major research institutions. Mere expertise in a discipline was not enough in this national race for prestige. Institutional reputations were being built, in part, by counting the number of doctoral degrees on one's faculty rather than by creating academically enriching undergraduate and master's degree programs in professionally related disciplines as well as the liberal arts and sciences.

The younger communication scholars with doctoral degrees "won the intellectual revolution in the schools bit by bit," wrote Rogers. University administrators "were previously somewhat puzzled by their vocationally oriented schools of journalism." He noted that Wayne Danielson, an academic descendant of Schramm and the former Dean of the College of Communication at the University of Texas, once said that journalism schools were regarded by university administrators as "something equivalent to a school of trailer park management" (Rogers 1994: 462). The administrators may have had that perception because the communication scholars were eager for administrators to see journalism that way. Some of the communications academics even regarded journalism issues as an inappropriate area for research by doctoral candidates and discouraged doctoral candidates from focusing their research on journalism issues.

Eventually, said Rogers, the younger generation of scholars outlived the journalism educators who had been journalists, "which settled their dispute on an actuarial basis at most schools of journalism in the United States" (1994: 464). As his analysis makes clear, the takeover of journalism education was cold-blooded. There seems to have been little concern for whether this dramatic change would improve or damage journalism.

Important impacts as journalism is submerged

One significant impact of the submersion of journalism that took place at many universities has been that it has become increasingly difficult to find teachers whose key expertise and major interests are in journalism. There are few journalism education programs in the United States devoted primarily to educating students who want to become journalists. It probably is possible for a motivated student to find a teacher at most programs who is highly qualified to teach journalism and who can be an excellent teacher of skills and ethics. It is probable that the educator is not on the permanent faculty, or, if so, may be on the bottom rung of the academic ladder and may have been there a long time.

Another impact has been the development of generic communication skills courses. These courses prepare students not for specific fields (journalism, public relations, and advertising) but for those fields and others all at once. Advocates of such teaching say they are training students to be communicators rather than training them for any one of the fields of communication (Blanchard and Christ 1993: 47). Opponents of this generic approach say that the values of journalism are antithetical to some of the values of the other two fields.

Perhaps the most profound impact of the takeover of journalism education by communication studies at mid-century has been the loss of a half century of research about journalism that could have led to increased criticism, improvement and maturation of journalism as a profession. The field of journalism education, thanks to early founders and their successors, had reached a point of development by mid-century that could reasonably be interpreted to mean that, if left on its own to develop, journalism education probably would have evolved into a mature discipline whose teachers could have established a tradition for journalism educators to engage in research about journalism while also being excellent teachers (Medsger 1996: 61). Imagine the possible outcome. If journalism educators had not been suppressed and had recognized their own ability to engage in depth research and had made the case to university administrators for the practice of journalism being an intellectual process, they could have started building a body of work that by today would better inform journalists, students, other academic colleagues and the public about the historical issues and contemporary problems in journalism. Journalism as a field has had many serious problems in the past 50 years. Unlike other professions that have academic programs—such as law, medicine, business—the journalism profession has not been able to expect, let alone rely on, its academic counterparts to explore the issues and problems of journalism by using either quantitative or qualitative research methods. Communications-studies academics did a great deal of research in that half-century, but very little of it was about journalism issues. In fact, such research was actively discouraged at many universities.

In the absence of research about journalism in the academy, in the past 20 years the most significant research about journalism has been done by two organizations outside universities. One, the Project for Excellence in Journalism, was created in the early 1990s by journalists who were alarmed at the lack of clarity about core values in journalism. PEJ usually conducts short-term studies of current journalism practices. Its research has revealed important information to news organizations about their weaknesses and their strengths. The results of the studies, widely published, have led to widespread discussion about journalism inside and outside the profession and have led to change in policies and practices. The other organization, the Media Studies Center, was a program of The Freedom Forum, a foundation. The Center provided fellowships for academics and journalists to conduct research for a year. Numerous books about journalism issues were published as a result of these fellowships before the Center was closed after less than a decade

The lack of research about journalism by faculty members in journalism and mass-communication programs helps explain how journalists and journalism educators grew apart. This was reflected vividly in responses of newsroom recruiters and supervisors during a survey (Medsger 1996). Only 3 percent of them strongly agreed that journalism educators are on the cutting edge of journalism issues and have a strong influence on change in the profession. The same small portion agreed that people in their news organizations often ask journalism educators for advice on newsroom issues (ibid.: 92).

Though the accreditation review process has continued to involve professional journalists working with educators to review journalism and mass-communication programs, faculty members who see scholarly research as a chief or only measure of faculty adequacy often dominate the review process. Reports by teams that visited programs and made recommendations regarding accreditation seldom included comment about some of the aspects of journalism education that concern newsroom employers the most. The review of the most recent six-year cycle of the accreditation evaluations of all accredited journalism education programs during *Winds of Change* revealed 50 percent of the reports included no comment about ethics instruction, 74 percent included no comments about the quality of writing instruction, no reports included comments about the quality of student writing and 78 percent included no comments about the quality of campus student publications or broadcast outlets. In 26 percent of the reports, the committees that evaluated programs urged programs to accept only scholarly research, not journalistic research, as appropriate faculty research. While a majority of these reports suggested that faculty needed to engage in more traditional scholarly research, none suggested faculty should engage in more depth journalistic research (Accrediting Council on Education in Journalism and Mass Communications 1986–96).

During the last century, there were many issues that would have been appropriate subjects for research by journalism educators, issues on which journalists and journalism educators could have collaborated or which journalism educators could have investigated and analyzed independently as critics. Very little such research occurred, and both journalism and journalism education suffered in various ways from that failure to conduct research.

An example is racial and ethnic diversity. No issue in the last 30 years has been as important or perplexing to American journalism. Most news organizations have failed to expand coverage to be inclusive of diverse segments of communities and to develop and hire a diverse workforce. The original impetus for noticing this issue came in the aftermath of the 1967 race riots. Surveys conducted for the National Advisory Commission on Civil Disorders revealed that African Americans believed that journalists relied exclusively on official versions of events, that in stories about blacks there was an absence of context, selective coverage that unfairly ignored white violence and illegal official behavior, including police brutality, and an overlooking of positive black activities (de Uriarte *et al.* 2003: 28). "Along with the country as a whole, the press has too long basked in a white world, looking out of it, if at all, with white men's eyes and a white perspective ... They must make a reality of integration—in both their product and their personnel" (U.S. Riot Commission Report 1968: 389).

This important issue has many facets, each of which would have been an appropriate area for research, some of which could have contributed to finding solutions to a problem that still persists in many news organizations. The problem was not confronted until 10 years after the Commission's report was published. In 1978, in response to a proposal by the late Robert Maynard, a very talented journalist who became the first African American to own a metropolitan newspaper (the *Oakland Tribune*), the American Society of Newspaper Editors set a goal for diversification: by 2000 the ethnic and racial makeup of newsroom staffs should be approximately the same as the ethnic and racial makeup of the country. Yet in 2004, according to the American Society of Newspapers, 40 percent of all newspapers in the United States had *no* ethnic minority people on their staffs (American Society of Newspaper Editors 1995–2003).

And, also as of 2004, despite the continuing critical need of the profession for more diverse journalists, only a few journalism education programs had made a point of recruiting for diversity. In this matter, as in others, the serious disconnect between news organizations and journalism education has impeded progress for both fields.

In the best programs, research *and* teaching flourish

As journalism education programs have shifted in emphasis, sometimes dramatically, at a few universities a strong emphasis on journalism has stayed in place, even deepened. Key among these programs are: Columbia University, University of California at Berkeley, Northwestern University, University of Maryland, University of Missouri, New York University, San Francisco State University, Washington and Lee University, Arizona State University, and University of Arizona.

It is striking that while dozens of lesser known universities, even some community colleges, refuse to hire full-time journalism educators who don't have doctoral degrees, one of the most prestigious universities in the world, the University of California at Berkeley, has no problem hiring, promoting and granting tenure to the excellent journalists hired by its prestigious Graduate

School of Journalism. Highly regarded for its research, the university as a whole—not just the School of Journalism—embraces with equal respect various types of research. This policy makes it possible for permanent faculty in the performing arts, journalism and other disciplines to conduct research that is closely related to the nature and needs of the professions in which they have their expertise. In the case of the journalism educators, this means that they may engage in depth journalistic research that examines either issues in journalism or societal issues. It also means that they are given the same promotion and tenure opportunities that are offered to traditional scholars (Medsger 1996: 168).

Most of those working in journalism education would prefer this. Surveyed, 79 percent said they thought they should be permitted to engage in *either* traditional scholarly research and writing or depth journalistic research and writing as part of the hiring, promotion and tenure processes. That desire for flexibility included 78 percent of the academics who have doctoral degrees (Medsger 1996: 87).

Perhaps it is not surprising that the expertise of teachers seems to have a significant impact on whether journalism students become journalists. In 1996, among all accredited programs, 49 percent reported that 10 or fewer journalism graduates were working as journalists three years after they graduated. Two programs had none. Eight—7.6 percent of all accredited programs—reported that 50 percent or more of their graduates who majored in journalism (print or broadcast) were working as journalists three years after they graduated. Among these eight programs that had more students entering journalism, the portion of their tenured and tenure-track faculties with doctoral degrees ranged from 9 percent to 55 percent, most of them well below the 68 percent average for all accredited programs (Medsger 1996: 51). Though this suggests that students are more likely to excel at journalism if they are taught journalism by people with extensive experience as journalists, the trend in the United States and in many other countries is to hire fewer people with such experience.

Journalists inadvertently have contributed to their second-class citizenship in American universities. Journalists and journalism educators have been rather inarticulate about the true nature of their work. Asked to describe what they do, even the best journalists may say their work is *just* finding and telling stories.

Given the complexity and sophistication of the various processes involved in creating depth journalism articles or books, journalism education administrators should be able to articulate the qualifications and accomplishments of journalist-scholars in terms that are parallel to the analysis that is provided to personnel review committees and university academic officials for the writing and research of traditional scholars. If journalist-scholars were analyzed in that way, from hiring to tenure, it is likely that university leaders would see, as academic officials at UC Berkeley and a few other universities have, that journalists are just as capable as are traditional scholars of contributing to a university's mission to create new knowledge, to engage in productive research. The way in which journalists can use clear expression to describe even very complex information can conceal the sophistication of the research that was involved in the gathering and organization of material. Ideally, students would collaborate with academics on their research projects. As a result of this collaboration, some students would be ready, like students in some other professional disciplines, such as architecture, to enter the profession not only as beginning journalists but as new journalists who have cutting-edge ideas about journalism that could infuse new energy and innovation into the news organizations they enter.

This is not to say that research and writing should replace fine teaching, long considered by journalism educators with a professional background as the only thing they should do. But research cannot be ignored. "A mania for credentials … has spanned this century [twentieth]," said Thomas C. Leonard, historian on the journalism faculty at UC Berkeley and now university librarian. "The research model has triumphed in higher education since World War II. It has seemed far more important to expand knowledge than to polish students' skills or to nurture them" (Medsger 1996: 46). Leonard makes the case for meaningful research as a way to improve the situation:

> I've seen instances of hunkering down and defensiveness [by journalists who become academics]. I'd understand this if the challenge was to fill the *Journalism Quarterly* [a scholarly journal]. But at the universities that will count distinguished reporting as tenure-worthy, the failure to produce does journalism education real harm. Modern universities and colleges just aren't set up to reward the dedicated teaching of fundamentals. There is a powerful argument behind this: A professional's skills and experience may be superb now, but in time they will grow stale. The best guarantee of distinguished teaching over time is continual production that is reviewed and judged by the best people in the field and compared with work in other academic departments.

One foundation has recognized the critical need for excellent journalists to be hired as teachers in journalism education. The John S. and James L. Knight Foundation has endowed 18 chairs, each with a special emphasis, such as environmental reporting, at that many schools (Knight 2004). Those appointed to them are expected to engage in research and become catalysts between journalism and other disciplines related to their reporting specialty. By funding these chairs, the foundation has added an infusion of journalistic excellence into the schools where the chairs are based. Ironically, most of them would not be hired at most journalism education programs because of the requirement that permanent staff must have a PhD.

Waiting for Columbia

During the 2002–2003 academic year, the eyes of many journalism educators were on Columbia University. In Pulitzer's school, it seemed as though a crisis

219

might be brewing. People were shocked in July 2002 when the university's new President, Lee C. Bollinger, announced before settling into his new office—and before he met the journalism faculty—that he would reject the finalists for Dean of the School selected by a search committee and instead would assemble a task force of prominent journalists and academics to help him decide what the School should become (Bollinger 2002).

For a School long regarded as one of the great journalism schools in the world, the President's words were alarming to some of the School's constituents. Faculty members there were accustomed to occasional public controversies about whether, by continuing to teach the skills of journalism, they were standing in the way of progress or they were keeping the barbarians from the door. They were concerned about what Bollinger meant when he wrote in his bombshell letter, which was reported in the *New York Times*:

> There is a yawning gulf between the various visions of what a modern school of journalism ought to be ... We live in an age in which the system of communications is widely understood to be undergoing revolutionary changes and, at the same time, is the critical element in forging democracies, markets, culture and the phenomenon of globalization. To teach the craft of journalism is a worthy goal but clearly insufficient in this new world and within the setting of a great university.
>
> (Bollinger 2002)

In addition to his questioning the teaching of craft, Bollinger's use of the "c" word, "communications," caused concern among the School's natural constituents—the faculty, the graduates of the School and many of the editors and news directors who hire the School's graduates. University administrators in South Africa, Hong Kong, Europe and elsewhere read his announcement and told journalism education program heads they were "waiting to see what happened" at Columbia. It was a tribute to the University and to the School that the president's public doubt about the School would have such a wide impact, but the reaction was frightening for journalism education leaders who feared the impact Columbia's decisions, depending on what they were, might have on their programs. Would this be the death knell to the few all-journalism programs?

The waiting ended in April 2003. Answering the question he had posed a year earlier, Bollinger wrote an eloquent statement at the end of his search for a vision of what the School should become. He acknowledged that "students must receive an introduction to the skills and craft of writing and reporting which are the foundation of the profession." He also said students must

> acquire an intellectual ability to deal with new situations, as knowledge and working conditions shift over time or as their own knowledge proves inadequate ... Students ought to become familiar with how

their profession developed ... What are the trends at work now and where are they leading the profession? ... Students must acquire a sense of an identity as a professional, which includes the moral and ethical standards that should guide professional behavior.

(Bollinger 2003)

He laid out his philosophy of journalism education and his general vision for the additional elements he wanted the faculty to create with a new dean:

I start from the premise that journalism and a free press are among the most important human institutions of the modern world. Democracy, civil society and free markets cannot exist over time without them ... A great journalism school within a great university should always stand at a certain distance from the profession itself. Its faculty should be made up of leading practitioners of the profession who, in the manner of other university faculty, both teach and actively explore, in their ongoing work, the greatest possibilities of journalism. The faculty should also reflect on the profession—drawing attention to important issues, engaging in research to assist in their resolution and communicating these findings to students, the profession and the interested public.

(Bollinger 2003)

To lead the faculty in making changes at Columbia, Bollinger appointed Nicholas Lemann as dean in 2003 (Bollinger 2003). Well known for his depth articles in the *New Yorker* magazine, Lemann is also the author of books on race and on the testing required for admission to many American universities. Like his counterparts at the leading schools of journalism in the US—Orville Schell at the University of California at Berkeley, Loren Ghiglione at Northwestern University and Tom Kunkel at the University of Maryland— Lemann's body of writing is considered both journalism and history.

At his first faculty meeting as dean in fall 2003, Lemann told his new colleagues he thought students at the Graduate School should experience in a disciplined way "what is available here at this great university, and available nowhere else, that will be helpful to them as journalists throughout their careers." That remark forecast his eventual plan, endorsed by Bollinger, for the School to expand from providing only a one-year curriculum to adding an optional second year that would include study in other disciplines. The faculty pressed him that day to answer the question that journalists and journalism educators have been asking for 50 years in the US and in other countries: What comes first? His answer pleased them: "Finding and reporting the facts so a clear and accurate expression of current events can be provided to the public." That, said the new dean, has always been the bedrock, the first priority at Columbia, and "I will do nothing to change that" (Lemann 2003).

Other questions to consider

When examining the state of journalism education, an overarching concern should be whether the education stimulates the intellectual development that makes it possible for a student to have the qualities of the best journalists, chief among them a lively mind that explores subjects deeply, and writes about them with clarity and eloquence. There probably would be general agreement that such a person should have a keen sense of what citizens need to know, a strong love of justice and a desire to find and reveal the truth about matters of importance and deep interest. What educational backgrounds are most likely to nurture such qualities?

Over the past 25 years, it was widely assumed by journalists and journalism educators in the U.S. that nearly all beginning journalists hired each year had majored in journalism. For even longer, it has been assumed that a major in journalism at either the undergraduate or graduate level should be the educational background of the typical journalist. There was, however, no systematic effort to determine the educational backgrounds of the journalists who did not study journalism or of the best journalists. The survey conducted for *Winds of Change* found that the majority of journalists had, indeed, studied journalism. It also revealed that 27 percent of the new journalists, people who had been in the profession one to 11 years as of the summer of 1995, not only didn't hold degrees or minor in journalism, but had never taken a journalism course (Medsger 1996: 111).

A closer analysis of the data regarding those journalists, coupled with additional research, revealed that by a number of measures the minority of journalists who did not study journalism are the best journalists. Contrary to some expectations, this minority of "best" journalists whose majors are in other disciplines—a majority in literature and history, with others studying in a wide range of majors, but none of them in communications studies—are not from elite eastern schools. Instead, they graduated from a wide variety of universities across the nation and were working at a wide variety of news organizations, not just large metropolitan newspapers and broadcast outlets (ibid.: 29).

To try to determine the educational backgrounds of journalists who reasonably could be considered representative of the best journalists in the US today, records of the most prestigious journalism award winners and of those who received two of journalism's most prestigious fellowships were reviewed. It was found that in the previous 10 years:

- 59 percent of print journalists who won Pulitzer Prizes never studied journalism;
- 75 percent of broadcast journalists who won Alfred I. Du Pont Awards never studied journalism;
- 58 percent of journalists awarded Nieman Fellowships at Harvard University never studied journalism;
- 51 percent of journalists awarded Knight Fellowships at Stanford University never studied journalism;

- 27 percent of the people who entered the profession recently (those who had been in the profession one to eleven years as of the summer of 1995) never studied journalism at any level and, by various measures, were doing better in the profession than their colleagues who had studied journalism.

A larger portion of the new journalists who never studied journalism earn higher salaries and have greater job satisfaction than those who studied journalism. The same portion of those who never studied journalism advance to leadership roles as do those who have undergraduate degrees in journalism, and a much larger portion of those who never studied journalism than those with master's degrees in journalism become newsroom managers. In all categories, half of the journalists who didn't study journalism studied either literature or history (Medsger 1996: 29).

Unlike news organizations in the United Kingdom, Australia and many other countries, some American news organizations offer short internship programs but do not have organized apprenticeship programs. That seems to mean that most of the journalists who are excelling in journalism without studying it at universities are learning to be fine journalists through informal but very effective mentoring.

Could it be that journalism education as a major or minor deprives students of the opportunity to take the courses in the liberal arts and sciences where they would be more likely to learn the knowledge and habits of mind that would better inform them and better prepare them to explore more deeply and more broadly as journalists?

Could it be that at the undergraduate level journalism education experimental programs should be created in which journalism is neither a major or minor but is instead an intensive introduction to journalism? Such programs could recruit students from many parts of a university who have excelled in their majors. In their senior year, students could enroll in journalism courses that introduce them to the skills, history and ethics of journalism. Such programs could also include courses that would introduce other students, not just ones interested in becoming journalists, to the role of journalism in a democratic society and how they as citizens could use and critique journalism.

Similar concerns about journalism education arise throughout the world. While programs in developing countries worry about a lack of resources, current articles indicate they also are often caught up in the same dilemma regarding who is qualified to teach journalism, and what combination of skills, survey and theory courses should be taught. Many of them live in the shadow of firsthand examples of the sacrifices journalists have made when the truth they reported endangered their lives. Do they know what made that courage possible?

Given the poor performance of many US news organizations in covering some of the most important news events of the first years of the twenty-first century, the questions about what education journalists should have may be more important than ever. American journalists were excellent at finding and telling countless moving personal stories about people who survived or died after the attacks of September 11, 2001. But as the plans for war in Iraq emerged, and as the war has been carried out, many critics felt the quality of American reporting was inadequate. What made US journalists, especially broadcast journalists, "protect" Americans from seeing the worst impact of the war in Iraq, while broadcast journalists in Europe and in some other countries broadcast much more complete accounts of the war? What caused reporters and editors at the *New York Times* to drop their skepticism and accept government claims at face value? The errors of commission and omission were so significant that the *New York Times*, in a very rare action, ran an unsigned essay from "the editors" on May 26, 2004, acknowledging, but not apologizing for, the weaknesses in its Iraq coverage. It might be helpful to find out what gives journalists the wisdom and courage to want to search for and tell the stories that powerful people—sometimes their own bosses, sometimes government officials—do not want told, but that if told might empower people to make better decisions as citizens. The American people might have reacted less enthusiastically to plans for war if journalists in the US had provided a more complete forum of opinions and investigated more carefully the claims that were the basis of the US decision to go to war. We need to learn more about how journalism can be taught in ways that motivate students to conceptualize and execute important stories that either are not immediately obvious or require that courage.

In the interests of contributing to the development of better journalism, more needs to be known about the range of ingredients most likely to produce the values and the will to engage in fine journalism. To what extent does education—journalism education and/or other education—play a role in inspiring courage and commitment to searching for and revealing the truth? If it does not, how could it?

References

Accrediting Council on Education in Journalism and Mass Communications (1986–96) "Visiting committee reports and other files," University of Kansas, Lawrence.

Adam, G. (1993) "Notes toward a Definition of Journalism – Understanding an Old Craft as an Art Form," *The Poynter Papers: No. 2*, St. Petersburg, FL: The Poynter Institute for Media Studies.

American Society of Newspaper Editors (1995–2003) *Newsroom Employment Census.* Available online: http://asne.org.

Blanchard, R. and Christ, W. (1993) *Media Education and the Liberal Arts: A Blueprint for the New Professionalism*, Hillsdale, NJ: Lawrence Erlbaum Associates.

Bleyer, W. Collected papers, University Archives, University of Wisconsin, Madison

Bollinger, L. (July 23, 2002) "Columbia President Plan to Review What Journalism School Should Be." Available online: http://www.jrn.columbia.edu/news/2002–07/bollinger.asp

Bollinger, L. (April 2003a) "Columbia President Issues Statement on Journalism Education." Available online: http://www.jrn.columbia.edu/news/2003–04/taskforce.asp

Bollinger, L. (April 2003b) "Columbia President Appoints Nicholas Lemann Dean," Columbia Graduate School of Journalism. Available online: http://www.jrn.columbia.edu/news/2003–04/lemann.asp

Carey, J. (Oct. 14, 1992) "Where Journalism Education Went Wrong," remarks, Columbia University, New York. Available online: http://www.mtsu.edu/~masscomm/seig96/carey/carey.htm

Christ, W. (ed.) (1994) *Assessing Communication Education: A Handbook for Media, Speech and Theatre Educators,* Mahwah, NJ: Lawrence Erlbaum.

Cleary, J. (Spring 2003) "Shaping Mexican Journalists: The Role of University and On-the-Job Training," *Journalism & Mass Communication Educator,* Columbia, SC: AEJMC.

de Burgh, H. (2003) *The Chinese Journalist: Mediating Information in the World's Most Populous Country,* London: Routledge.

Dennis, E. (1989) *Reshaping the Media: Mass Communication in an Information Age,* Newbury Park, CA: Sage Publications.

de Uriarte, M., Bodinger-de Uriarte, C. and Benavides, J. (2003) *Diversity Disconnects: From Classroom to Newsroom,* New York: The Ford Foundation.

Farrar, R. (1998) *A Creed for My Profession: Walter Williams, Journalist to the World,* Columbia, MO: University of Missouri Press.

"From the Editors: The Times and Iraq" (May 26, 2004) *New York Times.*

Gaunt, P. (1992) *Making the Newsmakers: International Handbook on Journalism Training,* Westport, CT: Greenwood Press.

Knight Foundation Chairs in Journalism. Available online: http://www.knightfdn.org

Lemann, N. (2003) remarks at October 1, 2003, faculty meeting, Graduate School of Journalism, Columbia University, New York.

Leonard, T. (1995) *News for All: America's Coming-of-Age with the Press,* New York: Oxford University Press.

Medsger, B. (1996) *Winds of Change: Challenges Confronting Journalism Education,* Arlington, VA: The Freedom Forum.

Medsger, B. (March 1999) "Thoughts Without Thinkers," *American Journalism Review.* Available online: http://www.ajr.org/Article.asp?id=3315

Mirando, J. (1995) "The First College Journalism Students: Answering Robert E. Lee's Offer of a Higher Education," AEJMC Conference Papers. Available online: http://msu.edu/cgi-bin/wa?A2=ind9602d&L=aejmc&F=&S=&P=3820

Pulitzer, J. (1904) "Planning a School of Journalism—the Basic Concept in 1904," *North American Review,* vol. 178, May.

Radio and Television News Directors Foundation (1995) *The Future of News, Defining the Issues,* Washington, DC: RDNDA report.

Rogers, E. (1994) *A History of Communication Study: A Biographical Approach,* New York: The Free Press.

Rogers, E. and Chaffee, S. (December 1994) "Communication and Journalism from 'Daddy' Bleyer to Wilbur Schramm," *Journalism Monographs,* vol. 148.

Schramm, W. (1957) *Responsibility in Mass Communication,* New York: Harper & Brothers.

Simpson, C. (1994) *Science of Coercion: Communication Research and Psychological Warfare 1945–1960,* New York: Oxford University Press.

U.S. Riot Commission Report (1968) New York: Bantam Books.

Weaver, D. and Wilhoit, G. (1996) *The American Journalist in the 1990s: U.S. News People at the End of an Era*, Mahwah, NJ: Lawrence Erlbaum.

Weaver, D. and Wilhoit, G. (April 10, 2002) "The American Journalist Survey: Methodology of the Study." Available online: http://poynter.org/content/content_view.asp

Weaver, D. and Wilhoit, G. (2003): http//poynter.org/content/content_view.asp?id= 28778.

12

WHO'S TO MAKE
JOURNALISTS?

Angela Phillips

This chapter explores the dilemma at the heart of journalism education: are we educating young people to hold power to account or are we merely training them to fill jobs in the communications industries? Can we balance these two requirements, the political and the industrial, and if so what is the best way of ensuring that the demands of public interest will be balanced with the demands of industry?

Although virtually all journalists, in Europe and the USA, are educated to degree level and in nearly 50 per cent of cases, beyond that (Journalism Forum 2002; Medsger 1996; Stephenson and Mory 1990), journalists are still arguing as to whether journalism is a skill or a profession and whether or not journalists need higher education at all. Universities are often seen, not as the natural place for educating future journalists, but as the enemy of journalistic authenticity. In a paper on journalism training in Latin America, Alves (2003) observes:

> Companies rarely, if ever, attempt to establish strategic alliances with local universities who have had journalism programmes in place for decades. In fact the old antagonism between journalists and schools of journalism is still alive and well in Latin America.

So it is necessary to start this chapter by establishing whether or not journalists actually need to be educated. I will then go on to look at whether/if that education/training should be organised and controlled by educators or by the industry and ask whether journalism education should serve the interests of employers, the 'public' or the students. Can all three interests be addressed together and, if so, what is the best structure to adopt? Although I will be looking at models across the world, the main example I will be using is that of the system in the UK which, because it is currently very much in flux, provides useful examples of the possible effects of competing methods and interests.

Learning to think

It is rare to read journalists writing in praise of their own education. Where they mention journalism education at all it is usually to hark back to a golden age when the job was all about truth and the reporting of facts, and reporters started their trade in the post room. In many ways the disparaging of journalism education mirrors a similar attitude to Media Studies. Indeed, newspaper journalists very often confuse the two, assuming that the only aim of anyone interested in the media must be to become a newspaper journalist. In reality, newspaper journalism is a relatively small part of journalism, and journalism is only one possible route into the media industries.

Barker (2001: 213), examining newspaper attacks on Media Studies between 1993 and 1999, discovered five common positions for these attacks. In four out of five there was what I call the 'John Humphrys'[1] critique: 'it isn't a real subject and anyone doing it must be an intellectual pygmy while anyone teaching it is a charlatan.' The fifth position suggests that it is vocationally inadequate, as Michael Hann suggested in an article in Media *Guardian*: 'In their desire to gets bums on seats and fees in accounts, too many colleges and universities are running courses that do not provide students, even after three years, with the skills they need to get a job' (Hann, 2001). Many of the letters replying to Hann came from students who pointed out that they wouldn't have been able to get his piece past their course tutors based, as it was, on one anecdote and a single interview.

The most common complaint from journalists (even those actually teaching journalism) is that there is too much 'theory' and that there is a contradiction between the teaching of the practice and theory of journalism, as though it would be like teaching philosophy to someone who only needs to fix the toilet. As one ex-editor (now a journalism educator himself) put it: '[Students] wax lyrical about bias and semiotics but seem to know nothing about intros and contacts ... I have nothing against studying the media ... but one area is about learning to be a journalist, to do journalism; the other is learning to apply critical theory to the products of journalism' (Cole 1996).

Listening to many journalists who write about journalism, or come into the colleges to talk to young people, one might imagine that they had never been educated at all. Andrew Marr, then editor of a UK national newspaper (the *Independent*), told assembled students that his degree (from Oxford) had been completely useless to him as a journalist and that all that was really required was shorthand and law. Listening to Marr (now at the BBC) it is impossible to imagine this erudite, intelligent analysis coming from a completely untrained mind. Marr and many others like him seem to have so completely internalised the lessons of their broad, liberal education that they can no longer disentangle the effects of it from what they take to be their own, innate, intelligence. Robert Samuelson, writing in the *Washington Post* (2003), demonstrates that this 'anti-intellectualism' is not simply a British phenomenon:

> Journalism is best learned by doing it. Mostly, an aspiring reporter needs a job, preferably for an exacting editor. You try to be accurate, clear, quick, perceptive and engaging. These are not abstract skills

learned in a classroom. At best, journalism schools are necessary evils. They provide basic training—usually through mock newsrooms—that most papers and broadcast stations won't. Some get this training on college papers and stations. Journalism school is an alternative. But keep it brief. In general, universities are sheltered places.

It seems to me astonishing that anyone who practises journalism (let alone anyone who employs journalists) would seriously suggest that they do not need 'abstract skills'. Personally I can see no reason why a plumber shouldn't benefit from philosophy even if it has no direct relationship to the trade. I think journalists need critical theory not just because it will make them better thinkers, but also because it will make them more critical journalists, and I think that the job of a journalist is to think critically, not merely to report. As Andrew Gilligan, then a BBC senior correspondent, put it:

> Journalists are seen as holding power to account. But many actually find themselves allies of the powerful – transmitting their spin, accepting their assumptions, rarely enquiring beneath the surface. This is not usually because evil Tory/New Labour proprietors order them to brown-nose the ruling class – but because too many journalists lack skills and inclination to question or analyse effectively.
>
> (seminar with Goldsmiths students, October 2002)

A university education gives students the time, and should give them the tools, with which to question and analyse effectively. The UK Higher Education Funding Council's quality guidelines for media degrees suggests that 'the fostering of employability requires the development of students' creative, intellectual, analytical and research skills' (QAA 2001). I would suggest that these are the skills that should be basic to any first degree and are absolutely central to the education of young journalists. The following description of the objective of a literary education would pretty much describe what I would want to see as part of any journalist's education too: '[to] expand their range of human awareness and sympathy; to enlarge their imagination beyond the limits of their own class and country; to show them that our problems and obsessions are part of a larger pattern of human experience' (Hough, in Woods and Barrow 1988).

My own inclination would be to add the learning of theories relating to how power is used – and abused. While I would not reduce such understanding to the question of 'bias' I do think that any young journalist needs to have an understanding of the issues at stake because, as Castells observes:

> [Media] ... has a fundamental effect on politics. In all countries, the media have become the essential space of politics. Not all politics takes place through the media, and image making still has to relate to real

229

issues and real conflicts. But without significant presence in the space of the media, actors and ideas are reduced to political marginality.

(1997: 398)

Of all the attributes mentioned, the question of power, who holds it and how they use it, is the one that is least likely to be encouraged in local newspaper training. Indeed, it was a representative of the Newspaper Society (the organisation for UK local and regional newspapers) who told a meeting of journalism educators in the mid-1990s that graduates entering the newsrooms of local newspapers had 'the wrong attitude'. I would like to think that something that universities should do well is to foster the 'wrong attitude' and to encourage journalists to be a thorn in the side of power rather than its bedfellow.

The wrong kind of thinking

The attacks on journalism education don't only come from those who think university education is unnecessary to the practice of journalism. Cohen, writing in the *New Statesman* (1998), is concerned that we are teaching the wrong kind of thinking. He blames what he describes as 'the death of liberal journalism' on 'the preposterous but dominant intellectual fashion of postmodernism'. He writes:

> When great writers and causes, texts, genders and institutions are dismissed as false constructs, the personal and confessional can seem the last refuge of authenticity. People who blurt out their most intimate secrets at least appear to be truthful, even though the emotionally honest are often the biggest liars of all.
>
> (Cohen 1998)

If asking students to think about the way in which ideas are constructed is wrong, then I must plead guilty. When students arrive at Goldsmiths College, where I teach journalism, they often say that they want to 'tell the truth' about the world. One of the first things we do is send them to a court in order to spend a day discovering how many different versions of truth can co-exist – not just in the courtroom but in their own summaries of the events. It is just the start of a process in which the secure foundations of belief about facts and truth, impartiality and objectivity will be tested and questioned. Is such questioning rightly a part of a journalist's education? Or should we merely be teaching would-be journalists a few tricks of the trade so that they can be recruited into the industry knowing how things are done – rather than questioning the rules?

I would argue that a very important part of journalism education requires us to question those great shibboleths. An editor may well train new recruits to recognise 'a good news story'. A university should point out that news values are not handed down by God, they are created by the cultures we live in and shaped both by those who work in newsroom and those who employ them. That mythical 'nose for news' is in fact a finely tuned understanding of the culture and the particular power nexus in the subject, or geographical area in which we work. If Cohen was attending a good university, he might be asked to consider why newspapers used only to report the words of the people in power whereas now they are more likely also to represent the thoughts and opinions of the powerless, or the popular. He might also ask himself whether this tendency is dumbing down or democratising? Understanding how news is constructed might make the job of a journalist harder but it should also make for better, more sophisticated thinkers.

For those journalists who seek to change the status quo in the newsrooms and challenge prevailing assumptions about what constitutes 'liberal news', a recognition of the way in which language creates a sense of belonging (or alienation) is hardly redundant. Indeed, it is such an understanding which may help this young reporter to resist being forced into the racist discourse of the newspaper for which she (currently) works and will almost certainly ensure that she doesn't reproduce it when it is her turn to edit: 'We went through a phase of doing black crime, black crime, black crime every day; muggings, car-jackings: if there was a crime with a black face, we published it and that made me just think "what am I doing here?"' (Phillips 2003).

While I have sympathy with Cohen's concerns that easy comment is pushing out longer investment in investigation I very much doubt that postmodernist theory is to blame. Commercial pressure combined with marketing theory is more likely to be the cause (oddly enough the very things that Samuelson (2003) thinks journalism courses should be more aware of). Confessional journalism and opinion pieces sell rather well and are much cheaper to produce than investigations. Certainly we teach our students how to produce them but I doubt that they would be wasting their time, or undermining their usefulness as future journalists, if they were also encouraged to use the work of Foucault, Giddens or Judith Butler to question that interest and ask why people might wish to construct their life stories in a particular way.

Samuelson (2003) retorts in his *Washington Post* article that many journalism graduates will be spending their time writing reports of their local sports teams rather than thinking of 'abstract' matters. But this is an absurd objection. In every field of work it is necessary to start at the bottom but surely we should aim to provide students with the sort of education which will ensure that they don't remain there. Many (if not most) respected national journalists started their careers on local newspapers or local radio doing just such mundane reporting jobs but it was their ability to see beyond the local and to understand how their culture was changing which allowed their careers, and their status, to grow. In my own experience, students graduating from an MA in Journalism rarely last more than 18 months in their first job.

Of course not all our journalism students will end up working for news organisations. Today people with journalism training are to be found every-where: they produce magazines and research talk shows, they write internal company bulletins and create new products for companies at the cutting edge of the communications industries. Employers in these fields are also looking for people with imagination, flair and the ability to make unexpected connections rather than simply re-produce what has been done before:

> Its about creativity, it's about cross-functional thinking, cross-functional acting. You are more likely to get that skillset from people who have a broad range of skills, not a particular core competency in a subject matter, whether it is mathematics or humanities. I don't think university is about going after a particular job. I think it is about how you round yourself out as an individual so you are prepared for a multiplicity of opportunities ... the key is to get a very well-rounded education.
> (Bill Nuti, Cisco Systems, Europe, BBC Analysis, 20 April 2000)

How should journalism education be delivered?

While journalists argue about whether they need anything other than a know-ledge of shorthand and law to do their jobs, those who employ journalists have been gradually pushing up the entry qualifications. It is clear from employment figures that most employers, when faced with the choice, will opt for a candi-date with a degree (and increasingly post-graduate qualification too) rather than a school leaver. According to a recent British survey (Journalism Forum 2002: 22) in the UK, 95 per cent of working journalists have first degrees and a further 43 per cent have post-graduate qualifications. A survey of American journalists (Medsger 1996: 97) found an identical proportion amongst those under the age of 36. Degrees are also the norm in the rest of the EC (Stephenson and Mory, 1990: 27) and increasingly in the rest of the world. In Brazil, for example, a university education is mandatory (Hume 2000).

There is no way of teasing out information as to what kinds of degrees students are undertaking. In the UK a minority will have first degrees in jour-nalism. Most will have done a degree in another subject followed by either a post-graduate qualification or training course. There are many advantages to this arrangement (Gaber and Phillips 1996). De Burgh (2002) has written in favour of specialist journalism degrees which combine a broad humanities education with specific study of the skills required for journalism. Stephenson and Mory (1990: 31), commenting on this debate, pointed out that in the UK, and in most of Europe, the role of universities has been 'the perpetuation of academic excellence and the enhancement of academic knowledge'. Journalism is not a traditional academic subject and therefore did not sit well with the European model. In the USA, however, universities developed a modular system in which practical vocational subjects could be mixed in with academic subjects. As a result, journalism education, at degree level, is firmly embedded and recognised – though still debated.

It seems unnecessary, then, on the basis of the evidence, to prescribe the kind of degree which is most useful to would-be journalists. The project on 'employability and the Media Studies curriculum' (Thornham and Ball 2003), while it did not look specifically at journalism, found that employers in the media were looking for a combination of critical and vocational skills. Vocational skills were not seen as more important than general education. What employers were after was young people who were bright and 'trainable' and would bring in new ideas. A survey of UK employers in radio also found that the transferable skills such as team working and flexibility were more highly rated than technical skills (Purdey 2000).

Those who are doing a degree which includes some element of journalism practice, may be able to avoid the additional post-graduate training which most other degree holders will require. They will certainly have skills which are immediately useful to employers – such as the ability to write concisely and handle a range of computer programs. Nevertheless the evidence available tends to demonstrate that it is the thinking part of higher education which is most prized by employers. Vocational skills are important and do need to be learned but, whatever journalists themselves might say, they are not more important than learning to think.

How should vocational skills be taught?

The reality of employment patterns is not reflected in what employers actually say. They may recruit sophisticated thinkers but, when asked what should be taught, they often seem to be concerned only with narrow vocational skills (Thorham and Ball 2003). James Curran (2000), in his paper on press reform in the UK, comments that as far back as the first commission on the press in 1949 there was a demand for journalists to be better educated. The Third Commission on the Press in 1977 called again for more journalists to be university educated and for journalism training to be better organised. These objectives were never fulfilled because, according to Curran:

> Press employers steadfastly opposed the introduction of critical 'media theory', a liberal education or even the learning of creative skills. What they wanted was training that imparted basic skills (shorthand), relevant knowledge (law) and an unquestioning attitude.
>
> (2000: 42)

These attitudes live on. At a meeting of the UK Periodical Training Council held in June 2003, the chair listed the concerns of those editors who had been visiting journalism courses. They were the standard of grammar and spelling, and the students' knowledge of 'Customer Magazines'. There seemed to be little appreciation of the different kinds of courses represented and there was little regard at all for the expertise of the educators. As one journalism lecturer put it: 'I felt that we were there to be told what to do, not to be consulted.' This tension was noted ten years earlier:

> On the one hand the media employers have tended, collectively, to the view that the main function of journalism education is to provide the necessary technical skills to people already having a general level of education ... They tend to be less interested in the academic content of such education. In contrast the journalism educators and their national educational authorities ... tend to be as much or more concerned with developing this side of their activities.
>
> (Stephenson and Mory 1990: 33)

When employers were recruiting well-educated young people and then providing their own training, this tension could be contained. Today, having run down much of their in-house training, and recognising that new technologies require new skills, the industry is looking towards the universities and colleges to fill the gap.

Judging by the evidence, the education sector in the UK has risen to this challenge. According to the 2002 Journalism Forum study, 61 per cent of journalists hold (or are working towards) some form of specific journalism qualification, the majority of whom feel that such a qualification is 'relevant' or 'very relevant' to their work. The research doesn't clarify the type of course (degree, post-graduate) or the length (three months, one year, three-year degree or day release). It does indicate that qualifications are most common in regional newspapers (75 per cent) and least common in magazines, and that the most usual qualification was that provided by the National Council for the Training of Journalists (NCTJ). This lack of specificity means it is impossible, for example, to discover how those with journalism degrees compare, in terms of employment prospects, to those with post-graduate NCTJ qualifications or with master's degrees or post-graduate diplomas. Judging by anecdotal evidence, the broader and more academic university-based post-graduate qualifications are highly thought of by broadsheet newspapers, magazines and new media. It may well be that the different types of courses are tending to prepare entrants to different levels or sectors of the industry.

As far as can be judged on this evidence, then, the system is working pretty well. New courses have grown up to provide training and education combined. The old vocational courses are still operating but fulfilling a different purpose, often recruiting post-graduates, rather than school leavers, and providing an alternative route from the more academic university-based post-graduate courses. The UK media prides itself on its diversity and independence and this rather *laissez-faire* system provides a matching diversity. Some courses are tailored to the needs of the provincial press, others to the magazine sector and still others aim to be innovators rather than providing only traditional skills.

The industrialisation of education?

In 2001, in the UK, a new voice was added to this mix. The Audio Visual Industries Training Group (AVITG), on behalf of employers, decided to move in and shake up media education. Chaired by Roger Laughton, Director of the University of Bournemouth Media School and formerly a senior TV executive, the AVITG produced a document called *Skills for Tomorrow's Media*. Written by Laughton (2001) and published by Skill Set (the training arm of the UK audio-visual industry), it is seen as a blueprint for what could be described as the industrialisation of media education.

The pressure for change seems to have come from the burgeoning New Media sector. In 1999/2000, when the research for this report was done, the internet and cable sector were developing rapidly (rather too rapidly it is now clear, as large numbers of companies in the field have failed). The industry wanted workers. They wanted them trained, and they wanted them now. The place to get them was the universities and the assumption was that the universities needed a good shake-up in order to provide what was required. So the committee recommended that:

- courses should be industry accredited;
- centres of excellence should be established which would attract extra funding;
- the numbers of training places should be restricted.

Although the document was addressed, at least partly, to educators, in its set of recommendation the words 'skills' and 'training' are used six times whereas 'education' is only mentioned once. Laughton's central argument to educators was that the media industry should be putting money into training, but that it would only do so if those working in education give something back in the form of greater control of the education process.

In whose interests?

Clearly it appears to be in the interests of industry and government to concentrate funds on a small number of colleges (which could then be tooled up to industry standards), rather than spreading funding, on the basis of student numbers, across a large number of courses. But is tying the work of colleges to national 'best practice' standards really the best way to encourage diversity in the delivery of education? If those on the 'best practice' body decided that students should be required to produce packages tailored to existing industry standards, then what would happen to those courses which currently allow students to mix drama and documentary, or use computer animation to muse on issues of world poverty? Would that be considered bad practice? Since colleges would be forced to compete with one another to attract 'excellence' status, even those innovative courses, which are interested in exploratory approaches to media, might find it very difficult to survive on the basis of their own reputations. They would be forced to 'join up' because the power of labelling is such that, those without such a label would lose both the bright students and the additional funding as well as access to that vital first step into the industry – work placements.

This effect could be accelerated by artificially restricting the number of colleges able to teach practice so ensuring that young people face stiffer competition to get into what they will assume are the best courses. We know that increasing competition has the effect of skewing the social-class balance (this is the issue which underpins the debate in the UK about selective versus comprehensive education and one can see the effect most clearly in the intake to the universities of Oxford and Cambridge). This is surely not something that one would wish for in an industry which has already been castigated, by Greg Dyke, then Director-General of the BBC (8 January 2001), for being 'hideously white' (see Deans 2001).

Norway has gone for just such an approach to media education. The country has few places where media training of any kind is possible and the courses are massively over-subscribed. The result is that large numbers of Norwegian students find their way to the UK for training. Few manage to survive without heavy parental subsidy because, although the Norwegian government offers generous loans, they are not generous enough to cover the high cost of overseas fees and living costs. If, over the past ten years, the UK had similarly limited the numbers of students (as our critics in the media here have so often said we should), it is hard to see how the country would have found the recruits to staff the industry we have today. It has to be said that those working close to the ground don't always have the best view of the way ahead.

The role of accreditation

While it is hard to see any merit in the plan for 'centres of excellence', the question of accreditation can be viewed quite separately and perhaps ought to be. It is clear that a great many of those teaching practical courses in universities are attracted by the idea of accreditation. Many feel that their skills are underrated by academic colleagues and see industry accreditation as a means of improving their status within the academy (see Thornham and Ball 2003: 15). Accreditation is often seen as the means by which journalism will rise from being a mere trade to the lofty heights of a profession. Often the training of doctors and lawyers is cited as a near equivalent and accreditation of courses is suggested as the means by which 'professionalisation' can be attained. Absent from this debate is any discussion about what accreditation would actually achieve other than giving the industry greater control over the education of its new recruits. In most other fields accreditation is used to protect public safety or promote public confidence.

Lawyers and accountants are licensed to practise via training schemes which are accredited by the profession. Bad advice can have a devastating effect and the public has a right to be protected from bad practitioners. Similarly it is in the interests of lawyers and accountants that these standards are enforced in order to protect their position and increase public confidence in their skills. It could be argued that journalists similarly would benefit from a professionally accredited training which reassures the public. But journalists don't have direct client relationships. On the contrary, their job is to reveal confidences rather than keep them, and to avoid close and confidential relationships with sources except in so far as they are useful in uncovering information. In most countries, press excesses are regulated by the law. While there is no doubt that the teaching of media law should provide a central plank of journalism education, the public interest will still, in the end, be upheld by the courts, and teaching of media law is, on the whole, aimed at protecting the proprietors from lawsuits rather than public from harm.

When safety considerations are paramount, it is clear that some form of standard setting, overseen by an independent body which has a specialist knowledge of the field, is important. The public needs to be assured that doctors, engineers and electricians, for example, are undergoing training which prioritises public safety and that they are tested rigorously to ensure that they are, as far as possible, certified as safe practitioners. Journalists also have an effect on public safety. They can do as much harm with an ill-judged article as a surgeon can inflect with an ill-judged knife. It is possible that accreditation could help to enforce standards in this arena and to bring a discussion of ethics into as central a position in the training of journalists as is currently held by the teaching of media law. This would be the most compelling argument for accreditation and it does underpin the American journalism accreditation schemes. According to the AEJMC:

> Professional programmes should prepare students with a body of knowledge and a system of inquiry, scholarship and training for careers in which they are accountable to:

> - the public interest for their knowledge, ethics, competence and service;
> - citizens, clients or consumers for their competencies and the quality of their work; and
> - employers for their performance.

> (AEJMC website)

While this may be the most important reason for accrediting journalism courses, it is not a reason I have seen offered in any context in which accreditation has been discussed in the UK. The major newspaper-accrediting body in the UK is the National Council for the Training of Journalists. Its website uses the words 'exciting', 'glamorous' and 'hard work' to describe what journalism is all about. It doesn't mention ethics or press freedom at all. The drift towards accreditation in the UK has none of the high mindedness of the American scheme. It is being pushed by industry with the enthusiastic support of a government which is keen to see universities more closely tied to industry (see speech by UK Secretary of State for Education, Charles Clark: 2003) and its purpose seems merely to render transparent to the employers just what it is that the college has been teaching. Certainly it is this aspect of training which seems to be of most interest to British accrediting bodies and the organisations which are pushing for such schemes to be adopted by the universities.

Maintaining vocational standards

If the object of accreditation in the UK is not to ensure high ethical standards but to ensure high vocational standards, perhaps one should judge its usefulness in that context. Journalism courses in training colleges have been accredited by the National Council for the Training of Journalists (NCTJ) since 1952. NCTJ training is provided within a minority of degree courses too. Although the NCTJ has no mandatory course on ethics, it does provide very detailed curriculum instructions in other areas. For example it insists that students should visit courts and council meetings on at least five occasions. While knowledge of the law and local government is important, in a degree programme in which practical journalism is only one of a number of subject areas, it would seriously skew the curriculum, leaving little time for equally important study in other areas.

This training model, in which the course and the assessment are prescribed by an external body, fits very uneasily within a higher-education framework in which the individuals in charge of the courses write the curriculum which is approved and validated by the university. Nor can it adapt quickly to change. It was the un-accredited colleges which were first to move into the field of web journalism, for example, and to shift the emphasis from news gathering to feature writing in order to accommodate changes in the content of newspapers.

The NCTJ has been heavily criticised by university journalism lecturers and the Association for Journalism Education (AJE: http://www.shef.ac.uk/aje/) for being rigid and insufficiently responsive to the requirements of the university sector. It has also had its share of criticism from the industry. The UK Guild of Editors issued its own 'Green Paper' on training in 1997 with a view to setting up a new system. The paper was, unfortunately, just as narrow, and still took no account of the burgeoning internet sector. It was prescriptive and entirely without intellectual content. One memory which sticks in my mind was that the only specialist area thought necessary for training was sports journalism. I could imagine the boys who had sat around a table to dream that one up. Then, two years later, the Society of Editors announced another draft training strategy and sought to establish itself as 'an approving if not accrediting body' (Society of Editors 1999).

In addition to all this, Skill Set is also interested in accreditation and has established the Journalism Forum which also has a training brief. The Forum does at least intend to address the proliferation of accreditation schemes. At present there is the NCTJ (for newspapers), the Periodical Training Council (PTC) and the Broadcasting Journalism Training Council (BJTC). The BJTC is currently working closely with Skill Set and seems to have made a bid to gather the on-line sector into its remit. While it might make sense, from an employers' perspective, to divide up by sector, it makes little sense for students. In my experience, journalism is a cross-sectoral activity. Students from the Goldsmiths' Journalism MA are as likely to end up as BBC television researchers or web producers as print journalists (newspapers and magazines) and I have even had a few move into radio. Yet departments which offer hybrid courses currently have to seek accreditation from three different bodies, with separate criteria and separate inspection regimes, not to mention separate fees.

On the basis of this evidence it would seem that accreditation is not, in and of itself, a guarantee of quality. Accreditation schemes which are too narrowly focussed can work as a brake on innovation. In a converging industry, where someone working on a website may be called upon to handle pictures, video, sound and text, courses need to be capable of responding quickly to changes in the industry. Innovation is often spearheaded by the Young Turks. Training bodies (and indeed courses) are more often the preserve of those coming towards the other end of their careers. Their expertise is important but it may well be looking backwards, to what used to be done, rather than forwards to what might be done in the future. Any workable accreditation scheme needs to have a sufficiently light touch to allow courses to make their own adaptations. Otherwise they can too easily become a monolithic, centralised training structure, incapable of responding to market change.

Accreditation: whom does it serve?

I recently surveyed a random sample of my ex-students to find out if the lack of accreditation (prior to 2002) had hindered their job seeking. Only one had ever been asked about accreditation. She went straight into a job on a local newspaper and took the exams in her own time, paid for by her employer. When I contacted her she had just been taken on by the BBC as a trainee. She comments:

> To be honest, I think the only people who really care about it are local newspapers, and if you don't have the exams, they get you to do them while you're working there. Once you've got experience, national papers only really care about that. I like the fact that on the MA we got to do some creative feature writing ... you wouldn't have the chance to do that on an NCTJ course, which is more concerned with turning people into formulaic reporters, rather than journalists with individuality.

However, in a world in which branding is becoming increasingly important, is it possible for any course to resist accreditation and still maintain a reputation with students and industry? In the same survey, the majority said that although it hasn't been relevant to them, they still think accreditation would be an advantage. One who was working on a BBC website said:

> I personally think that anything that adds to the prestige of the course is a good thing. I'm sitting in an office with former print journalists (one of whom did the accredited course at Cardiff about six years ago). Talking to them right now, they feel that applying for a job on a paper, accreditation does help.
>
> (personal communication 2003)

The lecturers I canvassed had similar reasons for favouring accreditation. Tim Crook teaches a Radio MA at Goldsmiths which is accredited by the BJTC. Crook lists the advantages as:

- It is a positive marketing tool in an increasingly competitive market.
- It ensures a continual liaison and engagement with professional standards and industry.
- It gives the students additional confidence about their course participation.
- The branding marks the course out as a centre of excellence.

Tony Dowmunt, who teaches television documentary, had the opportunity to pilot the RVQs (Related Vocational Qualification) which Skill Set had intended to use as the first step towards accreditation. He found:

> We would be doing very badly if we did not already teach and assess those competencies. Piloting the RVQ was therefore a help to us in identifying the basic research skills we should be teaching, and (mostly) re-assuring us that we were.
>
> As an employer in the industry (which I am when I'm not at Goldsmiths), I recognize that the RVQ would be some limited help when interviewing ... As a teacher I am worried by the incursion of narrow vocational demands from the industry on the content and conduct of media courses in HE.
>
> We should accept that employers and their representative organisations (like Skill Set) are going to continue to push HE courses towards accreditation of some sort, and that maybe RVQs offer us more control than whole course or institutional accreditation.

In the observations of two very different schemes (the BJTC, in common with the PTC do not dictate the curriculum, they send a team of inspectors every few years to check what the course provides), the major advantage as seen by both students and staff is that accreditation would 'improve the *status* of the course'. No one suggested that it would actually improve the courses. On the contrary, there was concern that in achieving status, the course might actually lose quality. The only positive effects were thought to be:

- Liaison and engagement with professionals.
- Reassurance that we are teaching what we should be teaching.

These seem to my mind to be very slender grounds on which to accept nationally dictated accreditation of courses. For my own part, and in the experience of colleagues teaching journalism elsewhere, professional involvement with courses does not seem to be very hard to arrange. Indeed, in Skill Set's own survey, 100 per cent of those post-graduate courses deemed to be 'practical' had industry professionals lecturing on courses. Many also have industry professionals as external examiners who advise on the curriculum.

The question of reassurance is another matter. Most of those teaching on practical courses have come directly from the industry. They are well acquainted with the industry norms of their particular sector. What they may lack is an overview of their industry, a feel for where the industry is moving (people often come into teaching towards the end of their career) and, above all, any knowledge of teaching. This is where industry bodies really could help – organising symposiums for educators on innovation and change, and providing support to those who are often moving into teaching for the first time. But are they interested in supporting media educators – or only in controlling them? It is the Association for Journalism Education, with its membership of journalists who work in higher education, which has established workshops where members can share professional practice. Ironically, in my experience, it isn't the professional skills which we lack, but the knowledge to teach them. Accrediting bodies which took on board the need for training, reassurance and inspection could well be an asset.

Conclusion: bringing hands and minds together

The complete separation between the practical and the intellectual in British universities (Stephenson and Mory 1990: 31) has for too long forced students to specialise in one or the other: to study drama rather than producing it, to analyse literature rather than to write, to study History of Art rather than making art. These artificial divisions are breaking down and media courses have been at the forefront of responding to this shift, allowing students to analyse media uses, as well as trying out their skills as TV directors, radio producers or journalists. On these programmes students bring the, often confusing and unsettling, lessons of their academic study into their practical work. They may get stuck because the ideas they have are bursting out of the box of their practical abilities. Often students learn more from heroic failures to change the traditional forms than they ever would from a perfectly executed package written to an existing, and easily mimicked, format. But those who create these courses do so because they believe that education should help students to challenge the existing paradigms rather than slotting neatly into them. Some employers agree. Steve Geimann (2001) of Bloomberg News had this to say to American journalism educators:

> Editors and TV producers generally agree that journalists with strong writing and critical-thinking skills, who can adapt quickly, have an edge over prospective reporters able to work in just one medium. Professional journalists have been encouraging universities to prepare students with those skills, and leave equipment training and style issues for the newsroom.

While there is certainly a role for the industry to play in education, there is a real danger that the current push for vocationalisation will have the effect of re-building the barriers between courses which prioritise intellectual enquiry and those which focus on vocational skills. It cannot be useful for either students or industry to move backwards in this way. There are other ways in which industry could involve itself in education. The training bodies could set themselves up to enable, rather than to control, education. They could provide training for educators and organise conferences where practice could be shared between those in industry and those in education. They could help to arrange work experience (both for staff and students) and ensure that courses have access to industry professionals to advise on content and standards. Those of us in the UK university sector are used to working with others in this way. Our courses have external examiners, new courses are subjected to the scrutiny of independent readers, we have to operate with the oversight of a 'Quality Assessment Agency' and our subject benchmark. There is no reason why the industry could not be brought in to participate in some of these existing structures rather than establishing a whole separate structure of its own.

When hot metal disappeared it was the highly skilled compositors who lost their jobs – the more flexibly trained journalists moved in and took over. Should we then confine journalism training to the kind of vocational courses which were used to train printers? Even if such schemes were broad – non-sectoral and light of touch – they could still end up by stunting the very flower they intend to nourish if they don't also acknowledge the importance of education. Given the increasing rate of technical change, what is most needed by employers is innovative, flexible thinkers. Where are they most likely to come from? When it comes to education, the universities and university lecturers should be acknowledged as the experts and given the lead in deciding what should be taught and how.

Vocational training certainly has its place as part of the education of journalists, and employers can help to provide it by offering equipment grants, work-experience opportunities and advice to universities and colleges as well as providing in-service training to staff (perhaps in partnership with universities).

But prospective journalists need a lot more than training. The fact is that serious journalism (both broadcast and print) requires a steady influx of innovative thinkers who can adapt quickly to new situations and respond to changing world events. It needs people who can talk their way into any situation and then talk themselves out of it again, while at the same time keeping a grip both on the broad picture of the event and the immediate detail. They need to be able to absorb information quickly, think critically, and go straight to the heart of a story. And then they need to convey what they have discovered in terms simple enough for busy people to take in over their breakfasts.

Last, but not least, we must consider which system is more likely to fulfil the public-interest aspects of journalism by offering a context in which students examine the ethics of journalism and the role of journalists in a democracy. I would suggest that a good education for a journalist is one in which learning how to write good intros, putting together a news package and learning the elements of media law sit alongside lectures and discussions which encourage them to think about where the power lies.

Note

1 John Humphrys is one of the anchor men on *Today*, the BBC Radio 4 flagship current-affairs programme in the UK.

References

Alves, Rosental Calmon (2003) The Challenges Democracy Created for Journalism Education in Latin America. *http://www.thedialogue.org/publications/programs/policy/politics_and_institutions/press_freedom/FinalAlves.doc*

Castells, Manuel (1999) 'An introduction to the information age', in Mackay, Hugh and O'Sullivan, Tim (1999) *The Media Reader: Continuity and Transformation*, London: Sage.

Clark, Charles (22 Jan. 2003) Speech: *http://www.guardian.co.uk/special reports*

Cohen, Nick (1998) 'The death of news', *New Statesman*, 22 May.

Cole, Peter (1996) 'The Case for Media Degrees', *British Journalism Review* vol. 7, no. 2, pp. 42–48.

Curran, James, (2000) 'Press Reformism 1918–98: A Study of Failure' in Tumber, Howard (ed.) *Media Power, Professionals and Policies*. London: Routledge

Deans, Jason (2001) 'Today's medias stories'. *http://www.GuardianUnlimited.co.uk*, 9 January.

de Burgh, Hugo (2002) 'Skills are not enough: the case for undergraduate degrees in journalism', *Journalism* vol 4(1): 95–112, December.

Gaber, Ivor and Phillips, Angela (1996) 'The case for media degrees. Response', *British Journalism Review*, vol. 7, no. 3, pp. 62–65.

Geimann, Steve (2001) 'Task force on the professions in the new millennium and beyond': www.AEJMC.org.

Guild of Editors (1997) 'Tomorrow's journalists: a Green Paper on editorial training', Guild of Editors internal paper.

Hann, Michael (2001) 'Media Studies? Do yourself a favour — forget it', *http://www.GuardianUnlimited.co.uk,* 3 September.

Hough, Graham (1988) 'Crisis in Literary Education', in Barrow, Robin and Woods, Ronald (eds) *An Introduction to Philosophy of Education,* 3rd edn. London: Routledge.

Hume, Ellen (2004) *The Media Missionaries: American Support for Journalism Excellence and Press Freedom.* Knight Foundation.

Journalism Training Forum (2002) *Journalists at Work,* London: Skill Set.

Laughton, Roger (2001) *Skills for Tomorrows Media,* London: Skill Set.

Medsger, Betty (1996) *Winds of Change,* Arlington, VA: Freedom Forum.

Phillips, Angela (2003) *Cultures of Journalism* 'Contesting control in the newsroom', conference paper, Goldsmiths College.

Purdey, Helen (2000) 'Radio journalism training and the future of radio news in the UK', *Journalism,* vol. 1, no. 3, pp. 329–352.

QAA Media Studies Benchmarking Group (2001) 'Communication, Media, Film and Cultural Studies Benchmarking' document. London: QAA.

Rusbridger, Alan (2003) 'Who is to blame for Brittany?' *Guardian* Weekend, 8 May.

Samuelson, Robert (2003) 'Snob Journalism' *Washington Post,* April, p. A35, 23 April 2003.

Society of Editors (1999) Society of Editors News: *http://www.ukeditors.com/may/train.htm*

Stephenson, Hugh and Mory, Pierre (1990) *Journalism Training in Europe,* Luxembourg: Commission of the European Communities.

Thornam, Sue and Ball, Tim (2003) 'Chasing the real', conference paper from 'Bridging the Gap' employability project, University of Sunderland.

Varlaam, Andreas, Walker, Adrian and O'Conner, Kate (1995/6) *Media Courses:* Vol. 1 *Survey and Consultation,* London: Skill Set.

13

RUNNING THE
TECHNOLOGICAL GAUNTLET
Journalism and new media

John V. Pavlik

New media, or digital information technology and their convergence in a networked environment, are transforming the world of journalism fundamentally. This chapter examines new media and their impact upon journalism, including benefits and costs, intended and unintended consequences.

Overview of trends in information technology

Here I offer a five-part conceptual framework for understanding the new media terrain. These five parts are: (1) acquisition devices; (2) storage technologies; (3) processing technology; (4) distribution technology; and (5) display or access devices. Increasingly, these five areas are interconnected or "converged," through the process of digitization.

Each of these areas of technological change presents enormous opportunities and challenges to journalism. These impacts include a transformation of how journalists do their work, including the ways that reporters gather and edit the news. In particular, portable, handheld and even wearable devices (e.g., mobile email devices or cellular telephones with cameras) are becoming ubiquitous. On February 18, 2004, the *New York Times* ran its first front-page news photograph taken with a mobile-phone camera. Such developments will become increasingly common in the future. Few reporters will go into the field without the technology to capture not just words but images and even video, regardless of whether their employer obtains most of its revenue or audience from off-line or print media. Similarly, the content of news is evolving as a by-product of these technological developments. Not just cell-phone camera photos but Web-logs, or Blogs, and other new media content forms are emerging that offer a dramatic departure from traditional news models. Blogs, for example, are much more interactive and "stream of consciousness" in form than news produced through more traditional editorial processes. In many cases, new ethical problems are arising or old ethical concerns take on new meaning. For instance, digital imaging not only makes it possible to manipulate photographs, but it also makes it far simpler and harder to detect. At the same time, there are technologies, such as the digital watermark and the GPS stamp that could be an effective weapon against such transgressions (and protect the intellectual property of news organizations and journalists), if only news organizations and journalists would begin to use them routinely.

Newsroom structures, management and culture are also changing in response to technological developments. For instance, a growing proportion of journalists are working as freelancers, and are not working full-time or exclusively for a single news organization. Others are not even working on the same continent they are assigned to cover. For example, in March, 2004, Reuters announced it was hiring six new reporters to cover American companies. All six reporters would work out of India. Apparently, the reporters there know business reporting and can cover American companies adequately, at least for Reuters' needs, via the Internet and the telephone. The Internet and the World Wide Web are making such structural and cultural changes possible, in combination with the economic advantages of going off-shore or into freelance reporting. Finally, all these changes are bringing about a shift in the relationships between or among news organizations and their publics. Clearly, hiring reporters off-shore creates different relationships to those familiar to the conventional newsroom.

But beyond that, Blogs, interactive media and ubiquitous imaging and its further developments are all influencing the relationships between news organizations, reporters, the general public, news sources, regulators, sponsors and others.

I begin with an examination of the five broad areas of technological change affecting the media, and then proceed critically to examine four fundamental ways that these technologies are influencing journalism and the media.

Acquisition devices

Acquisition devices are those used in gathering information, images, sound. They are in most basic terms "sensors." Cameras and microphones are the most familiar acquisition devices, and there have been many important developments in these technologies. In general, as with all five parts of the new media revolution, acquisition devices are digital. Because they are digital, they can be connected and communicate with each other and via the online world.

There are at least four major trends in sensor technology worth mentioning here because of their implications for journalism. First, sensors of all types, but especially audio and video sensors, are increasingly powerful. They are capable of detecting images and sounds at increasing levels of resolution (such as digital high-definition cameras), distance, speed and large fields of view—in other words, they can sense the world in all directions, 360 degrees. Second, they are getting smaller, lighter, cheaper, more portable and less obtrusive. In development are insect-sized cameras and audio sensors that can fly and transmit audio and video wirelessly to remote locations. Consider the possibilities the next time you see a large flying insect go by. New miniature video sensors are also available in new so-called 3G (third generation wireless) cell phones permitting pretty good quality two-way video conferencing from one mobile phone to another. These video cell phones could be thought of as a potentially massive news-gathering force. Third, they are increasingly "intelligent." That is, they have imbedded chips capable of performing other functions simultaneously, such as detecting motion, recognizing patterns, colors, textures, faces or other objects. For example, one omnidirectional camera, what is called a "computational camera," invented by Columbia Computer Science Professor Shree Nayar, not only sees a 360-degree field of view, but can monitor that space in real time by detecting any motion, even something as small as an incoming page received on a fax machine located within the camera's field of view. Finally, these sensors are increasingly ubiquitous, and will become even more so in the near future.

A variety of sensors are located in space or other aerial environments, making it increasingly possible to survey the earth, urban environments or other areas on land or sea. In autumn 1999, the first one-meter resolution commercial satellite, IKONOS, was launched, making high-resolution satellite imagery available to media and other organizations.

Unmanned air vehicles complement these orbital sensors with the capability of monitoring earth-based activities and structures with even higher granularity. These sensors have the ability to observe areas in which civilians might otherwise be restricted.

Cameras on the Internet have also become not only ubiquitous but of increasing quality. In New York City one television news organization alone has positioned 31 web cams around town permitting viewers to tune in any time of the day or night to 31 different locations, most of them in Manhattan, to watch the activity on the streets. Consider the live web casting system, called WebView, now available from Canon (http://www.canon.com/wvw/)

WebView cameras are offering live and navigable near-broadcast quality views of literally dozens of locations around the world, from the Acropolis in Greece to Times Square in New York to Orchard Road in Singapore to Harajuku Takeshita-dori Street in Tokyo. Using the Canon system, the viewer can pan, tilt or zoom anywhere in a panoramic view. This "interactive video" is a new form of broadcasting possible on the Internet today.

Storage

Storage is the second area of the new media transformation. Now all digital, storage technologies are increasingly powerful, fast and inexpensive. Where just a few years ago a powerful desktop computer might have the ability to store up to 100 megabytes of data, it is now standard for even an inexpensive PC to come equipped with 60 or more gigabytes (GB) of storage, frequently up to 100GB or more. With the rise of rich media, especially digital audio and video, the storage needs are already in the many gigabyte range and beyond. One minute of audio, even compressed at MPEG-audio level 3, or MP3, requires about a megabyte of storage. A minute of video compressed using MPEG-2, the standard for broadcast digital video, requires more on the order of 100 megabytes. Every ten minutes of compressed video requires nearly a gigabyte (GB) of storage, and an hour of digital video requires about 4–5 GB of storage. The Digital Video Disc, also known as Digital Versatile Disc, or DVD, is a fixed optical storage medium for video, audio, and data, and is an accepted standard established by a consortium of major consumer electronics companies. A DVD can store some 16 GB of data on one double-sided, dual-layer disk. A single-sided, single-layer disc can store up to 4.4 GB of data which, using MPEG-2 compression technology, can store 2 hours of high quality video and 8 channels of high quality stereo sound.

High-resolution satellite imagery can require many gigabytes of storage. High-resolution full-motion 360-degree video, such as that from iMove (www.imoveinc.com) can similarly require many gigabytes of storage. As a result, high-end storage devices are now delivering terabytes of storage. These devices will be soon available to consumers at very little cost. If you want to see the latest in storage technology, go to a U.S. military contractors' trade show. You'll see desktop devices with petabytes of storage needed for 3D maps and more. It is now standard operating procedure for all U.S. fighter jets to come equipped with video cameras for monitoring all flight activity, and the demand for storage is growing exponentially. On a consumer level, digital television recording devices such as Tivo (www.tivo.com) already offer low-cost high-capacity storage options, making it possible for consumers to record many hours of their program choices, and watch them on-demand, with or without advertising.

More than storage capability is needed. Advances in digital storage have revolutionized the process of indexing and retrieval of video stored digitally. Technologies such as Virage (www.virage.com) make it possible to search, sort and retrieve video and audio as easily, seamlessly and quickly as words from a text file. Not only is it possible to search and retrieve audio and video from key word indexing, but the indexing of the video content itself is automatic, done in real-time and features key-word extraction 90 percent reliable. Face recognition is now an increasingly standard part of the retrieval process as well.

Processing

Processing technology is continuing to follow Moore's law: it is growing in power and speed by 100 percent every 18 months. In other words, every year and a half the speed of the computer chip doubles. This means that what now fits on the head of a pin is as powerful, or even more so, than the most powerful mainframe computer 50 years ago. In fact, the world's smallest Internet server is now the size of a pin, thanks to a student inventor at the University of Massachusetts. Of course, that was in mid-year 2000. According to Moore's law, by the end of 2004 that server could now fit onto an object about one-sixteenth the size of that pin. My Palm Pilot or devices such as the Treo or iPac are not just personal organizers. They are in fact powerful hand-held computers (with communications capability). Using Avantgo software, I download into my Palm much of every day's *New York Times*, *Wall Street Journal*, CNN and half a dozen other web sites (in fact, any that I choose), including not only the full text, but images, graphics and animations; other tools enable me to download play high-quality digital audio and video.

New types of processors are also emerging, including DNA and optically based processors that promise exponentially faster, more powerful processors.

All of this means that processors are being put into everything from chairs to clothing. We are rapidly entering the age of ubiquitous computing. Only we will not call it computing any more. We will simply have "smart" even "intuitive" devices, and these devices will be equipped with sensors that detect everything from sound to images to pressure (i.e., touch, weight) to scent. These sensors will store, process and transmit that information.

More than that, these powerful processors are making it a simple, low-cost matter to produce and manipulate digital audio and video. As a result, a wide range of organizations and individuals are now producing their own audio and video content, many of them calling it news.

Distribution

Distribution refers to networking, or telecommunications, technologies for publishing or moving content from one location to another or many others. Increasingly, all digital devices are linked to a network, either local or wide-area, most commonly the Internet and the World Wide Web. Increasingly, these networks are interactive, broadband and wireless. Broadband refers to high-bandwidth, or high-speed networks. Established broadcast technologies are broadband, but are not interactive. That is, they have no ability for the user to communicate with others on the network; the user merely receives transmissions, although of high quality. All this is being transformed. As cable modems, digital subscriber lines and various wireless technologies, including satellite and terrestrially based wireless digital distribution technologies deploy, users and consumers of all types are accessing high-bandwidth interactive networks for costs as low as traditional cable and telephony. In the U.S., cable modems and DSL services can now be installed for about $50–100, and carry a monthly service charge of about $50. This provides high-speed, unlimited Internet access. This means that the consumer's Internet access device is left in continuous operation and provides up to some 2 megabytes per second of transmission capacity. Of course, in the case of the cable modem, this is shared bandwidth; in other words, if others in your node are simultaneously using the service, your bandwidth will be reduced in proportion to the numbers online. In the case of DSL, or xDSL (high speed, or advanced DSL), the network is switched and there is no sharing of bandwidth, giving telephone providers an upper hand, although they have had their own problems in rolling out DSL service, including incompatibility of certain existing installations.

Being continuously connected to a high-speed Internet service means a transformation of how people use the Internet. Increasingly, they use the Internet as a news and information and entertainment appliance. Since they don't have to go through the laborious dial-up process, those with broadband simply click whenever they want news, entertainment, communications or commerce. They access text, audio and video on-demand. And, many providers of audio and video increasingly offer near-broadcast quality audio and video. Whether MP3 (for near CD-quality audio, especially music) or high-resolution, full-screen MPEG digital video, companies such as Digital Bitcasting, which streams video and audio via Real Networks, Apple's Quick Time (with about a third of a screen) or other services are delivering a media experience almost equivalent to that of traditional broadcasters—all via today's Internet with connection speeds of at least 300 kilobits per second, what we might call "minimum broadband." In fact, with sufficient bandwidth (at least 700 kilobits per second), they can deliver better than standard analog broadcast quality video (NTSC), plus additional interactive services. They can deliver MPEG-2 quality video, which is the standard for digital broadcast video.

There are essentially four differences between Internet-delivered multimedia and that delivered via customary news providers. One, the programming is delivered on demand via the Internet. Two, Internet delivered programming is subject to network congestion. Three, original Internet programming today is relatively limited in terms of quality content—speaking in terms of the substance, not the technical features. And four, Internet content, including audio and video, is interactive. Differences one and four make Internet delivered news superior to that provided by customary, analog news providers, such as newspapers, magazines, analog radio or television. Differences two and three make it inferior. Limitations in content are rapidly disappearing, however, and the only real advantage customary news providers have over online media is the occasional network congestion which can interrupt a user's media experience. Will ubiquitous broadband eliminate this advantage? Will network congestion solutions such as that provided by Akamai provide the answer? I do not know, but many investors seem to think so; Akamai's initial public offering, in the autumn of 2000, broke most of the records for an Internet company IPO.

The convergence of broadband, advanced processing and massive storage capabilities is also making it possible to edit video in entirely new ways. One Silicon Valley company, Javu Technologies, has introduced a new Internet-based approach to non-linear video editing on the web. Although most television news producers today work with nonlinear video editing systems such as the Avid Media Composer, or the software-based non-linear video editors such as Adobe Premiere or Apple's Final Cut Pro, these systems require the editor to sit at a workstation and edit digitized video in a non-linear fashion, cutting and pasting video and audio anywhere in a file for later viewing.

Javu's non-linear video editor for the web enables this capability via the Internet. The digital video is put on a server and an editor, who might be anywhere in the world, can edit it remotely. The implications are profound:

> as footage is stored and edited on remote servers, individuals will not have to invest in state-of-the-art hardware or worry about clogging their hard drives with megabytes of video footage. In addition, the editing technology has been developed with user friendly graphic user interfaces, allowing even the newest of computer users to easily store, edit, and enhance their own video footage, pictures and music.
>
> (www.javu.com)

The only real obstacle is bandwidth, which is rapidly increasing in availability.

Wireless technologies such as Wi-Fi (or 802.11B) or Bluetooth offer low-power high bandwidth wireless local area networks or connecting devices to each other or the Internet at high speeds (e.g., www.bluetooth.com).

Where does the name "Bluetooth" come from? The origins are not dental. In fact, Bluetooth comes from the King of Denmark Harald I Bluetooth (Danish Harald Blåtand), the Viking who ruled between ad 940 and 985 and unified Denmark and Norway. 'Bluetooth technology' means technology which unites computers with telecommunications.

Ericsson Mobile Communications initiated the modern Bluetooth initiative in 1994 to study the feasibility of a low-power low-cost radio interface between mobile phones and their accessories. In 1998, four companies joining Ericsson were four other companies, Nokia, IBM, Toshiba and Intel formed a Bluetooth Special Interest Group (SIG). By 2004, the Bluetooth standard and other wireless technologies such as Wi-Fi are widely expected to transform much of how a wide variety of digital technologies communicate without the need for physical connectors. The notion of a virtual broadcaster may soon become a reality.

Combine Digital distribution with search and storage technologies, and you get powerful peer-to-peer computer-based file-sharing applications such as Napster or KaZaa, which have exerted powerful influences on music distribution and may transform movie and other forms of entertainment and content distribution.

Display

Display devices relevant to the world of journalism include not only HDTV sets, flat-screen displays, computer monitors and Web TVs. Today, a wide range of other devices are also relevant, including Personal Digital Assistants (PDAs), mobile phones, and much more that connect to the Internet and are increasingly capable of not only two-way communications but multimedia display.

CNN.com is already designing video for display on mobile phones. Electronic books are only the beginning. E-ink (www.e-ink.com) is a type of electronic ink developed at MIT. It provides a flexible, light-weight, and portable electronic display on paper and promises to one day replace not only traditional ink on paper, but may also deliver audio and video playback capability.

Such digital display devices are increasingly inexpensive and ubiquitous, giving mobile, nomadic consumers the ability to connect to the online media system at will, continuously, for better or worse. A variety of wearable displays, such as head-worn visors and glasses provide an immersive media environment, either opaque or translucent. Using this technology, it is possible to create either virtual or augmented reality. In augmented reality, the user still sees or hears the natural environment, but sees or hears overlaid against that reality additional computer-mediated content, which can be text or multimedia, including audio, video, images or graphics. In fact, working collaboratively with colleagues in the Columbia University Department of Computer Science, we have created "situated documentaries" in which multi-media information is presented on head-worn displays enabling the wearer to walk the Columbia campus (or elsewhere), and see not only information such as the names of the campus buildings, but to relive, or re-experience, historic events, such as the infamous 1968 Columbia student revolt, or the pre-history of the campus when it was the Bloomingdale Asylum for the Insane. The head-worn display is linked to a high-speed wireless Internet connection permitting the transmission of real-time multimedia. The system, which we call the Mobile Journalist Workstation, also includes a GPS receiver, or global positioning system, as well as a head-tracker for measuring the orientation of the wearer's head. Together, the GPS and head-tracker enable the display of multimedia information in a precise location in the environment surrounding the user. Details are available online at http://www.cs.columbia.edu/graphics/projects/mars/mars.html.

Augmented-reality systems may seem like science fiction, but they are already being developed commercially and are already in wide use in medicine, manufacturing and media (http://www.sciam.com/article.cfm?articleID=0006378C-CDE1–1CC6-B4A8809EC588EEDF).

An analysis of four impacts of new media journalism

New media, including acquisition, storage, processing, distribution and display technologies, are transforming the world of journalism. This transformation can be seen in at least four areas: the impact of new media on production tools and techniques; content, including storytelling, advertising and e-commerce in a digital, networked broadcast environment; distribution channels and industry structure; and the relationships between and among broadcasters and their many publics, including audiences, advertisers, competitors, program producers and regulators.

Production tools and techniques

Digital technologies have already begun to transform news media production tools and techniques. Inexpensive, lightweight, highly portable digital video (DV) cameras and audio recorders are making it increasingly simple and cost-effective for a wide variety of organizations, broadcast, cable, newspapers and others, to produce broadcast quality audio and video programming. Frequently, this content is broadcast on television or cable TV, but increasingly it is trans-mitted via the Internet (e.g., www.nytimes.com). In many cases, organizations such as universities, foundations, corporations and others are producing their own broadcast-quality programming for online distribution. Columbia University is among the first major private universities to launch such an online video production and distribution operation. One of the major advantages these new DV cameras provide is their unobtrusiveness. It is now relatively simple to shoot a class lecture, seminar or conference, or at least a portion of it, without expensive set-up and lighting, or without significantly affecting the organization of the event.

Other acquisition devices, such as new 360-degree cameras, remote-sensing satellites and unmanned air vehicles are, only beginning to find their way online, much less into conventional journalism, but they are poised to signifi-cantly transform the visual content of television and online media.

These various technologies, including today's inexpensive and increasingly ubiquitous cellular telephones equipped with cameras, are making the multi-media journalist a reality, for better or for worse. It is almost inevitable that most reporters will go into the field equipped to not only conduct interviews and observe the scene of breaking news, but they will have highly portable, unobtrusive devices to capture images, audio and video and transmit them live over the wireless telecommunications infrastructure. This suggests we are rapidly moving toward a much more visual journalism, one where images are an increasingly dominant part of the news landscape. Ethical issues arise here as well. Not only is digital image manipulation a concern, but the more funda-mental question of whether a news discourse that is dominated by instant photos and video will shed as much light or understanding as more textured and nuanced traditional reportorial techniques, often supplemented but not supplanted by news photos.

Content

Digital technologies are rapidly transforming the content of print, broadcast, and other broadband media. There are at least three basic ways this content is changing: first, it is increasingly visual, as was suggested above; second, it is navigable and user controlled; third, it is layered, with multiple levels and modalities of content interwoven, such as moving pictures, audio, 3D objects, 360-degree video, text, graphics, animation and 3D sound; and fourth, it is customizable, corresponding to a variety of factors, including the user's preferences, tastes and location. The user can pan, tilt, zoom, and interact with programming, frequently accessing web content to supplement their primary viewing experience. Research at Columbia University and elsewhere is introducing voice command and video as forms of input to manipulate the media experience. Customization is taking a variety of forms, including the ability to get information or programming targeted directly to each individual consumer, and dynamically updated when that consumer becomes mobile.

Or, consider the Digital Earth initiative (www.digitalearth.gov), a collaborative undertaking involving government agencies, including NASA, corporate and journalistic organizations, as well as educational institutions. The Digital Earth is intended to be an online virtual representation of the earth that enables anyone "to explore and interact with the vast amounts of natural and cultural information gathered about the Earth." One prototype already permits users to access and manipulate in real time 3D maps of the Earth featuring satellite-gathered meteorological data for any part of the planet, transforming the notion of weather information. Another prototype enables users to navigate, in real time, through a 3-D graphical representation of actual Earth landscapes created from elevation data and aerial images of that landscape, offering accurate and realistic imagery never before possible. The Digital Earth project illustrates the coming age of interactive media and user control of media experiences. Of course, these same resources are available to broadcasters to use in developing their own programming.

Distribution channels and industry structure

The growing abundance of broadband digital distribution channels is fundamentally restructuring the broadcast industry structure. Today, there is an unprecedented level of competition in the electronic information and entertainment arena. There are literally thousands of news sources online, many of them streaming audio and video, and increasingly in direct competition with broadcasters for the limited attention span of the world's consumers. Satellite-delivered programming is also emerging as a serious alternative means of digital distribution. In the U.S., DirecTV has accumulated more than 11 million subscribers nationwide, and offers high-speed Internet service as well. Legal and regulatory hurdles restricting DirecTV from carrying local programming are also falling, launching the direct-to-home satellite television provider into even more intense competition with established broadcasters and cable programmers.

What have broadcasters provided up to now? First, they bring a license, a franchise to use the public airwaves. They are a public trustee of a very valuable, limited resource (with compression of the digital signal, it is less scarce than it used to be in the analog age, and this has spurred deregulation of the airwaves). Second, to use that resource, broadcasters have invested in very expensive newsroom equipment. These start-up costs as well as the broadcast license have constituted a very tall barrier to entry to the broadcast industry, effectively keeping out competition. The Internet changes both these conditions in a fundamental way. It negates the need for a broadcast license, it overcomes the spectrum scarcity problem, and it reduces the cost of "broadcast" equipment to a low level affordable to a much wider spectrum of potential webcasters. Just as the Web has made it possible for millions of people to publish content to a global audience, so is the Web today making it possible for millions to broadcast programming—but to make that programming, rich in audio and video, available on demand and interactively. This takes away a fundamental mechanism of control basic to all broadcasting of the past—scheduling. Now, only at the time of a "premier" or "live" transmissions is a schedule of significance. After a premier or live transmission, the audience can have complete control over when, where and how they experience programming. Similarly, cable providers, now operating increasingly digital systems, are increasingly offering video on demand, interactive and other digital programming that further erodes the once-dominant position of traditional broadcasters.

There is, though, at least one more important item provided by broadcasters. That is their ability to create quality programming. This is their ace in the hole—if they can keep it and capitalize on it. It is still expensive to make quality original programming. If broadcasters can amplify on their traditional strength as content or programming creators, they can still be important players in the digital, networked world of the new millennium. But if they think they can rely on their ownership of the distribution channel as an asset, they will soon find themselves as obsolete as an 8-track cassette player. Cable operators are increasingly producing quality digital programming, not only in the entertainment arena but also news.

Consider the implications for the traditional television networks, especially the national broadcasters in the United States, such as ABC, CBS and NBC, traditionally major providers of television news. The networks have seen their share of the television audience fall precipitously over the past three decades. Where these three networks once captured 90 percent of the viewing audience, they today barely get 50 percent. The erosion of network audience share is due to the rise of a variety of new technologies introduced or expanded in the past 30 years, including cable and satellite television, the videocassette and today the digital video disc, or DVD, as well as the Internet. Some 3.9 million DVD players, many now priced less than $300, were sold in 1999 in the U.S., greatly exceeding industry forecasts, and people spent more than $6 billion buying DVD titles in 2001, for the first time exceeding the sales of VHS tapes. DVD is likely to continue to do well, although technology to enable "video on demand"—retrieving any movie or program via cable, satellite or the Internet may be a strong competitor. News applications of such technologies, especially "tell me more"-type requests for greater detail about breaking stories, may become popular.

Coming technological advances are likely to continue the erosion of network television audience share, including the coming of digital television broadcasting. University of Southern California telecommunications expert A. Michael Noll notes that in the U.S. viewers who watch their television via over-the-air broadcasting, that using UHF/VHF spectrum, has been falling in audience steadily the past thirty years, and now totals just 22 percent of all households. Cable, or CATV, reaches 64 percent, DBS reaches 6 percent, C-band satellite reaches 2 percent, as does Satellite master antenna, while 2 percent have no TV and 2 percent choose not to watch television. Noll (1999) predicts that by 2015, just 5 percent of all U.S. households will get their TV via UHF/VHF stations.

Although the networks may survive, and they are still today quite profitable, they will need to rethink their role in the media news and entertainment industry. Among the most important changes they will need to make is to redefine themselves not as "television" companies, but as communications media news and entertainment companies that use any and all digital means to reach the audience. Network audiences will be accumulated over time and media.

Notably, the networks have taken some significant steps in the right direction. ABCNews.com, for example, in 2001 offered the first live, broadcast-quality Internet news program, a weekly interactive public affairs talk show hosted by distinguished journalist Sam Donaldson. CBS News has integrated a variety of advanced digital technologies into its news coverage, including remote sensing satellite imagery, 3D urban imaging and 3D modeling. NBC has been testing interactive programs, including soap operas in which items that appear on screen, such as clothing or furniture, are actually digital objects that viewers can buy simply by clicking on them. Interactive programming is also being extensively rolled out via "enhanced television," which permits viewers with a Web TV to access additional material related to a show they are viewing, such as customized real-time sports statistics during ABC's popular *Monday Night Football*, or game shows such as *Jeopardy!* in which viewers can play along.

The broadcast networks have also embraced new digital imaging technologies, such as those provided by Princeton Video Image, or PVI. PVI offers broadcasters a variety of digital imaging tools for creating virtual signage, virtual game enhancements and virtual product placements. Networks such as CBS, ABC, Fox and ESPN have begun using these technologies extensively to place virtual logos in programs such as CBS's *The Early Show*, or to place a yellow line on the football field in National Football League games to indicate the so-called first down marker. CBS has also begun inserting virtual commercial messages in programs, such as red "bulls-eyes" for Target stores inserted in *Survivor*. This is partly a response to the easy ability of viewers to skip commercials using digital personal recorders and remote controls. Although these tools are highly effective in a commercial sense, their use has come under some criticism when used in news programming as being an unethical manipulation of "reality." When

CBS News with Dan Rather [a well-established US journalist] superimposed a CBS logo in Times Square on New Year's Eve in 2001, a number of critics were critical, especially competitor NBC whose physical signage in Times Square was obliterated by the CBS virtual sign.

Radio broadcasters have also employed new digital tools. One particularly interesting technology is called "time compression," or in the industry vernacular, simply "Cash." This technology enables radio broadcasters to speed up ever-so-slightly recorded or even live programs—unnoticeably to the listener—and thus squeeze in an extra four minutes or so into every hour—and thus have room to insert eight additional 30-second commercials into each program hour. This again is highly attractive commercially, but has been criticized as inappropriate. One New York station, WABC, has used "Cash" time compression in the Rush Limbaugh show—without first telling Limbaugh—and when he heard about it he was so upset he complained about it during a broadcast. About 50 radio stations around the U.S. have used Cash.

One thing the television networks have not done, unlike their counterparts in radio broadcasting, is fully embrace online delivery of their programming, both live and on demand. "Radio on the Internet" is common. Real.com and "Radio Locator" link to more than 1,700 radio stations worldwide now offering programming via the Internet, including more than 100 news or news/talk format stations delivering online (see http://www.radio-locator.com). Apple has introduced its iTunes service offering online radio in a variety of formats, as well, including National Public Radio.

By contrast, "television on the Internet" is far less developed. Real.com offers video Webcasts from ABCNews, either live or on-demand (from archives). Web-delivered programming direct from the major networks is somewhat limited (although major cable networks, such as CNN and MSNBC provide more extensive online video programming), mostly some news video and promotional video for other programs broadcast on conventional television.

A critical issue for broadcasters who enter the online arena is security. A recent spate of hacker attacks against such notable web sites as cnn.com, yahoo.com and etrade.com has exposed the vulnerability of the online world of computer criminals. These hacker attacks also underscore the importance of encryption technology designed to not only protect copyright of digital assets but also to provide a secure digital watermark to authenticate the source of media content. SARI is an interesting prototype available online for testing (http://www.ctr.columbia.edu/sari/).

Taken as a whole, these technological developments present fundamental challenges to the economics of news distribution. Reuters, for example, once largely a principal player in the wholesale news business (i.e., news distributed to other content providers) and high-rolling financial players, is now a major competitor in the retail news business, with its news reports frequently seen online in portals such as yahoo.com. News is increasingly becoming a digital commodity that is independent of any single distribution system. News organizations and journalists capture imagery, sound and other news items, produce reports incorporating text and other media elements, and then distribute that news through a variety of channels. News is packaged and repackaged for different audiences digitally accessing the news on their cell phones, laptop computers and handheld devices, not to mention traditional channels such as newspapers, news magazines, television and radio. All this means the news landscape is increasingly fragmented across channels and audiences. The business of news is undergoing a potentially significant transformation. In the conclusion of this chapter I will offer some speculative thoughts on where this transformation may be headed.

Relationships

Geographic, political and cultural boundaries which once defined broadcast media audiences are increasingly irrelevant. Instead, communities defined by interests, demographics and media and consumer preferences and patterns are of growing importance in planning online news programming. Moreover, the on-demand nature of online media, as well as the increasingly powerful storage media such as Tivo, are changing the nature of the viewing experience. Broadcast media have traditionally presented programming on a regular schedule for an audience that had no choice but to view or listen to that program at that time. Audience ratings were defined in terms of the percent of the potential audience present at that time. Today, a new model is emerging. Audiences are built over time and distance. The audience for a particular program may be relatively limited at any single moment, but over the course of a 24-hour period, week or even month that audience may accumulate into a substantial number. Moreover, the audience can accumulate over vast geographic regions, even on a global scale.

American audiences are spending their disposable income at an increasing rate on new media. Research by media ethnographer John Carey shows that after decades of relatively constant spending on media (McCombs and Eyal, 1980), American consumers increased their media spending steadily throughout the 1980s and 1990s. Citing data from the Consumer Electronics Manufacturers Association, Carey notes that consumer spending on electronic media increased dramatically from US$47 billion in 1992 to US$70 billion in 1997, a 49 percent increase.

Carey explains that a new technology must attract early users who are able and willing to pay a high price for it in order to achieve the economies of scale in manufacturing that lower the price for the general public. Carey notes that early adopters tend to be wealthy, have an insatiable desire for the product, or love electronic gadgets and are willing to pay a high price in order to be one of the first to own a new electronic device. Data from American Demographics and others reveal that early adopters in the U.S. tend to spend more than $3,000 a year on information and entertainment, especially for cellular communications, cable and satellite TV services, Internet services and information and entertainment hardware. Carey notes that there tend to be three groups of early adopters: males, especially those with higher incomes; telecommuters and those who maintain a home office; and two-income households, especially those with children. The data show that nearly two-thirds of the households with personal computers, for example, are households with children.

Although it's hard to forecast precisely how rapidly a new technology will enter American households, Carey shows that many new media technologies introduced in the twentieth century achieved 50 percent penetration into American households when the price was the equivalent of about two weeks' salary. Radio reached a 50 percent penetration of U.S. homes in 1931, nine years after its introduction and when the price was roughly 1.8 weeks' salary. Black and white TV followed a similar path, reaching a 50 percent penetration in 1955, eight years after it became widely available to the public (Sterling and Haight, 1978) and when it cost about 1.8 weeks' salary. The same is true of color television, which entered 50 percent of U.S. homes in 1972 and when the price was about 1.8 weeks' salary. But, later technologies have entered 50 percent of U.S. homes only when their price was even lower, approximately one week's salary. This was the case for the videocassette recorders (VCRs), which penetrated 50 percent of U.S. homes in 1987 when the price was just one week's salary. Personal computers only recently entered 50 percent of U.S. homes—when the price was about one week's salary, or about $750.00 U.S. Digital television sets are likely to reach 50 percent of U.S. homes only when the price falls considerably from the $2,000 or more of today.

Carey also notes that consumers buy new media technologies for a variety of reasons, including new services or capabilities and to replace old, worn-out devices. But one of the most important reasons is when a new device is adopted as a by-product of another purchase. This has been the case with the computer modem. Carey notes that the percentage of personal computer households with a modem grew from under 10 percent in 1988 to more than 60 percent in early 1997 (Veronis and Suhler, 1996; Odyssey, 1997). Modems are included in nearly all personal computers sold since 1994 and this has helped propel the adoption of modems in U.S. homes.

This audience transformation is increasingly fueling the development of a new commercial marketplace known as e-commerce. E-commerce operates relatively independently of temporal, geographic, political and cultural boundaries. The age of the 24/7 global consumer is arriving. Will the global online news provider be far behind?

Perhaps most importantly, the news media will need to transform their business model in light of the growth of e-commerce. Still relatively small today, e-commerce will likely grow to play a major role in the world's twenty-first-century global economy as broadband capabilities become commonplace. Research forecasts from a variety of government and industry groups, such as Jupiter Communications and Forrester Research, confirm this. They indicate that by 2004 global e-commerce will exceed $3 trillion U.S. One of the ways that e-commerce works most effectively is by combining the addressibility of online media—that is, the ability to target each individual—and the aggregation of individuals into mass buying and selling markets, thereby obtaining economies of scale. The news media will need to adapt to this new e-commerce model, and move well beyond the traditional mass audience advertising model, if they are to prosper in the coming decade or beyond.

Moreover, the world of wireless communications is set to exert profound influences on the world of journalism in the digital age. Wireless media, especially low-cost infrastructures such as Wi-Fi, are rapidly transforming how many people go online. Based on capabilities inherent in wireless media, one notable new content form with significant implications for news providers is called "location-based media." Using Wi-Fi or other high-speed wireless media, content providers can deliver news or other information customized to specific places or locations, such as a city street, block, or building. News about those locations, either of a contemporary or historical nature might have particularly high appeal to tourists, shoppers or community residents exploring and interacting with their neighborhoods. News organizations who have covered their communities for generations are in a unique position to provide quality news and information about their localities. Wireless media present an efficient vehicle to deliver that content on demand and at a fair price.

Conclusion: envisioning the future of news

The challenges and opportunities outlined in this chapter suggest the news media of the U.S. and around the world are undergoing potentially dramatic changes. These represent more than an incremental change; it is a sea change in the world of news. Yet, few have a clear grasp of where these changes will lead. Following is a speculative view of the future of news, particularly new business models that will arise and how they might influence both matters of public interest and journalism ethics.

In March of 2004 the Project for Excellence in Journalism (PEJ) and the Committee of Concerned Journalists (CCJ) released their inaugural report on the state of the news media in the U.S. (www.stateofthenewsmedia.org). In the study, the authors present data on trends in eight major news media, including newspapers, online, magazines, network television, local television, cable television, radio and ethnic/alternative media. Their findings, based on data culled from a variety of national, regional and local sources, suggest that only three sectors of the news media show audience growth: ethnic, alternative, and online media. Meanwhile, the dominant media of the twentieth century—newspapers, network TV and local TV—are suffering steady long-term audience declines.

The study shows that growth in ethnic media is particularly dramatic. Since 1991 years, Spanish-language newspaper circulation has almost quadrupled to 1.7 million. Moreover, advertising revenues have increased sevenfold.

Circulation of English-language daily newspapers has fallen 11 percent since 1990. Network evening news ratings have decreased 34 percent since 1993.

Consequently, many of newsrooms are seeing dramatic reductions in news staffs. There are one-third fewer network TV correspondents than in 1985. There are 2,200 fewer people at newspapers than in 1990. There has been decrease of 44 percent in full-time radio newsroom employees since 1994.

Moreover, the PEJ study shows that technology continues to play a vital role in the transformation of news. The authors observe: "Convergence seems more inevitable and potentially less threatening to journalists than it may have seemed a few years ago. At least for now, online journalism appears to be leading more to convergence with older media rather than replacement of it."

If an economic model doesn't develop for the online world, there is this troubling prediction: "The move to the Web may lead to a general decline in the scope and quality of American journalism." The PEJ report states: "The web increases the ability for people to get news in an unfiltered way, but it also increases the need for journalists to act as referees and synthesizers to help identify what information is reliable and what is not."

Cable TV is similarly suffering from the 24/7 cycle, with just 5 percent of stories on cable providing updates with new information. "Two thirds of stories are rehashing the same facts."

The PEJ report concludes that "the basic problem in journalism is too many news outlets are chasing a relatively static and in some cases a shrinking audience for news." Further, "much of the new investment in journalism today is in disseminating the news, not in collecting it." Journalistic standards are slipping. News is often gathered in its raw form, without extensive and expensive fact checking.

This forecast is on track and consistent with the evidence provided in this chapter. As the news media move inexorably into the digital age, they need to make a new commitment to investing in the future. This means building new audiences and engaging them in an interactive dialog. Ethical standards must be maintained. Any further slippage will erode public trust beyond repair. A new business model based on the unique qualities of the digital environment must be developed. Simply adapting the old business plan will not work. A lesson from history may be of use here. In the 1830s, most newspapers targeted an elite audience who were willing to pay a relatively high price for a partisan press. Then, advances in printing technology made it possible to print a newspaper far more cheaply. One innovator, Benjamin Day, saw a unique opportunity to reinvent the newspaper. He began offering the first penny paper, and the audience swelled. Advertisers were drawn to this new opportunity to reach a mass audience. Almost overnight, the press was transformed.

Journalism of the twenty-first century needs a similar innovator to step forward and offer a similar bold new business model for news in the digital age. What might such a new model look like? That's very hard to say, but in the USA its attributes would likely include the following:

- Spanish-language versions.
- Interactive features drawing young audiences.
- Adherence to high ethical standards providing quality original news.
- File sharing communities ... something young lovers of music have already shown an aptitude for.
- Diverse revenue streams that provide a menu of services, including free, premium and on-demand content.
- Mobile media, with computer-assisted design aiding in the efficient production and dissemination of news for a variety of wireless and wearable devices, thereby dramatically reducing the production and distribution costs.
- Off-shore production to reduce costs.
- Cross-media convergence to leverage economies of scale inherent in repurposing content.
- Audience input (e.g., web logs).
- More reporters spending more time in the field reporting using digital, wireless technologies to operate in a "virtual newsroom," dramatically reducing the cost of news gathering and production.

If these opportunities are exploited in a responsible and ethical way, news organizations can recapture their central role in modern democratic society and provide not only the foundation for an informed citizenry but also a lucrative investment opportunity. The alternative is to fade gradually away into little more than an interesting historical footnote.

References

Bluetooth [On-Line]. (2004). Available: www.bluetooth.com

Carey, J (2001). The First 100 Feet For Households: Consumer Adoption Patterns, Available: http://www.ksg.harvard.edu/iip/doeconf/carey.html, pp.3–5.

CNN [On-Line]. (2004). Available: www.cnn.com

Digital Earth [On-Line]. (2004). Available: www.digitalearth.gov

Feiner, S. (2004). *Argmented Reality: A New Way of Seeing* [On-Line]. Available: http://www.sciam.com/article.cfm?articleID=0006378C-CDE1–1CC6-B4A8809EC588EEDF

Feiner, S., Hollerer, T., Gagas, E., Hallaway, D., Terauchi, T., Guven, S., and MacIntyre, B. (2004). *Mars—Mobile Argmented Reality System* [On-Line]. Available: www.cs.columbia.edu/graphics/projects/mars/mars.html

iMove [On-Line]. (2004). Available: www.imoveinc.com

Java [On-Line]. (2004). Available: www.java.com

McCombs, M. and Eyal, C. (1980). Spending on Mass Media. *Journal of Communication,* 30(1), 153–158.

New York Times [On-Line]. (2004). Available: www.nytimes.com

——(1996) *The Veronis, Suhler and Associates Communication Industry Forecast.* New York: VSA.

Noll, A. M. (1999). The Impending Death of over-the-air Television. *Inform*, 1 (5), 389–391.

Radio-Locator [On-Line]. (2004). Available: www.radio-locator.com

SAR [On-Line]. (2004). Available: www.ctr.columbia.edu/sari

Sterling, C. H., and Haight, T. R. (1978). *The Mass Media: Aspen Institute Guide to Communication Industry Trends.* New York: Praeger.

The Project for Excellence in Journalism (2004). "The State of the News Media" http://www.stateofthenewsmedia.org/index.asp, p. 2.

The State of the News Media 2004: An Annual Report on American Journalism [On-Line]. (2004). Available: www.stateofthenewsmedia.org

Virage [On-Line]. (2004). Available: www.virage.com

WebView World [On-Line]. (2004). Available: www.canon.com/wvw

What is Electronic Ink? [On-Line]. (2004). Available: www.e-ink.com

What is TiVo? [On-Line]. (2004). Available: www.tivo.com

14

CAN WE MAKE JOURNALISTS
BETTER?

Theodore L. Glasser and Lise Marken

Journalism and journalists face two sets of challenges, one intellectual and one structural. The structural issues boil down to questions of mastery and control: Do journalists enjoy the freedom and autonomy that good journalism demands? Who or what undermines that independence? What can be done to retain or regain—or perhaps even establish—journalism's authority in the community? And how should journalists reconcile their autonomy and authority with the pleas for accountability that a democratic press needs to take seriously? In short, what would it take, to recycle the title of a famous American report, published in 1947 but still very much on target today, to bring about a genuinely "free and responsible press"?

Answers to these and related questions too often devolve into platitudes and clichés, a conventional wisdom that illustrates in painfully obvious ways the need for journalists to develop and debate the foundations of their craft. Whatever the urgency to provide answers to questions about the practice of journalism and the performance of the press, these answers need to be checked by and grounded in a larger intellectual framework that deals with journalism in overtly normative terms. In other words, it makes some sense to assign a priority to intellectual issues, particularly ones having to do with basic questions of quality and value, because the treatment of these issues will impose very real limits on the treatment of structural issues. It may be true, as Michael Schudson recently observed, that "[w]e are a long way from a coherent normative theory of journalism" (1995: 29), but that only underscores the importance of moving the project forward.

Thus, without discounting the importance of structural issues and the tantalizing range of possible responses to them, and without implying that structural issues are not themselves intellectually interesting, we focus in this chapter on a few of the foundational questions that, in our judgment, most deserve our sustained and critical attention. We do this not so much to provide answers to these questions, though at times we do, but to sketch the contours of a response to the question posed by the title of this chapter. Any effort to "make journalists better," we believe, must begin with a commitment to prepare journalists to talk openly and eloquently about what they do and why they do it, an articulation of the purpose of the press that amounts to more of an explication of journalism than a defense of journalists.

Drawing from, but without confining ourselves to, the many interesting claims developed in the chapters in this volume, we look at some of the difficulties and dilemmas journalists face in three related but broadly distinguishable areas: the nature of news as knowledge, the tension between professionalism and multiculturalism, and the relationship between journalism and democratic participation.

The nature of news

More so today than ever before, news represents the triumph of epistemology over morality. In the United States and increasingly elsewhere, the absence of values stands out as journalism's chief value. News does indeed flourish as a genre of literature, where interpretation supersedes description, but in mainstream, mass circulation journalism—what Paolo Mancini in his chapter appropriately calls the "omnibus" press—news often succumbs to the American predilection for facts that speak for themselves. Many of the contributors to this volume document and at times celebrate different traditions of journalism and different forms of news, but no one discounts the consequences of what in the book's foreword James Curran unhappily describes as "journalists in different countries steeped in the ideology of American journalism."

Claims about an "ideology of American journalism" are more likely to resonate with academics than journalists, especially American journalists. Journalists in the United States cling tenaciously to the view that news at its best renders the world transparent. Despite decades of derision, including several thoughtful critiques by prominent American journalists (e.g., Wicker 1978; Fuller 1996), "objectivity" remains a regulative ideal; it stands as a cornerstone of American professionalism, a commitment and a conviction—an occupational ethos—that presumably transcends time and space. To the examples of "universalistic values" that Curran cites—'freedom, equality and mutuality"—most American journalists would add the value of being value-free.

Being value-free—being objective—denotes a set of protocols, not a pristine mind. In their recent but already widely read account of the principles of good journalism—now available in Japanese, Greek, French, Spanish, Turkish, Chinese, Korean, Portugese, and Indonesian, which underscores its global appeal—Bill Kovach and Tom Rosenstiel, two decorated American journalists who have turned their attention to press reform, lament any conception of objectivity that implies "free of bias." Objectivity, they maintain, refers to "a consistent method of testing information," a "discipline of verification," a way of assessing "the reliability of journalistic interpretation" (2001: 74, 82, 77). Objectivity, it follows, does not eradicate subjectivity; it more or less claims to confine it to the individual.

By confining bias to the individual, objective reporting moves journalism closer to "the truth," the pursuit of which is "journalism's first obligation";

accordingly, Kovach and Rosenstiel distance themselves from the "postmodern deconstructionist academics" who "reject that anyone can put facts into a meaningful context to report the truth about them" (ibid.: 42) and align themselves instead with scientists who, we are told, share with journalists the same intellectual roots. Just as science gets at the truth one step at a time, one study after another, journalism approaches the truth as "a protean thing which, like learning, grows as a stalagmite in a cave, drop by drop over time" (ibid.: 46). Kovach and Rosenstiel approvingly cite a historian, Gordon Wood, whose view of history provides them with a useful model for journalism: "'One can accept the view that the historical record is fragmentary and incomplete ... and that historians will never finally agree in their interpretations' and yet still believe 'in an objective truth about the past that can be observed and empirically verified'" (ibid.: 47) Like U.S. Supreme Court Justice Potter Stewart's "I know it when I see it" test for obscenity, Kovach and Rosenstiel remain confident that "people can tell when someone has come closer to getting it right, when the sourcing is authoritative, when the research is exhaustive, when the method is transparent," which brings them back to Wood: "Historians may never see and present that truth wholly and finally, but some of them will come closer than others, be more nearly complete, more objective, more honest, in their written history, and we will know it, and have known it, when we see it" (ibid.: 47).

Kovach and Rosenstiel's treatment of news and knowledge, truth and objectivity, illustrates what has been variously described as "foundationalism," "universalism" or "objectivism"—basically a belief in not only the possibility but the superiority of a permanent, transcendent, universal and objective knowledge that can "re-present" the world as it *really* is. To apply here and in subsequent paragraphs an argument developed elsewhere (Glasser 1992, 1996), journalists embrace this view of the relationship between knowledge and reality, and derive from it an understanding of their roles and responsibilities, whenever they explain themselves and their craft, as they often do, with reference to some metaphor of glass: a *window* on the world, a *mirror* of society, a *lens* that magnifies and clarifies what otherwise would be undetectable or unclear. To take a handy but hardly isolated example, when the editor of the local newspaper *San Jose Mercury News* was asked why nearly 75 percent of the paper's reporters and editors said they would publish a photograph of a woman in agony, legs badly shattered, being pulled from earthquake rubble, he replied: "The earthquake was a horrible event, and no matter how unpleasant the image, they say the newspaper must mirror reality" (quoted in Fedler *et al.* 1997: 534).

Metaphors of glass—journalism's "glassy essence," to appropriate one of Richard Rorty's terms—are the legacy of a seventeenth-century view of the mind as a mirror of nature and knowledge as the quality of its reflection: "To know is to represent accurately what is outside the mind" (Rorty 1979: 3). Or as Walter Lippmann (1965) put it three centuries later, the "pictures in our heads" amount to knowledge only insofar as they correspond to the "world outside"; the closer the correspondence, the better the knowledge. What undermines knowledge, then, is whatever interferes with the mind's image—whatever, that is, "causes" the mind to represent the world in inaccurate ways. "Without the notion of the mind as mirror," Rorty writes, though without reference to journalism, "the notion of knowledge as accuracy of representation would not have suggested itself" (1979: 12).

Journalists revel in their glassy essence by treating language—and communication in general—as a medium for meaning, which is very much the Enlightenment ideal that John Locke advocated when he made the case for the purification of language. Once purged of any of the imperfections associated with speech, discourse, rhetoric and so on, as John Peters reconstructs the argument, Locke was able to imagine ways of communicating "with as little corruption from language as possible":

> Using a notion that had direct use in physics and metaphysics to describe the unification of disparate entities via intangible or invisible forces, Locke was able to describe a kind of society in accord with his scientific and political principles. In it, men and women would not *speak*, with all the risks language involves; they would *communicate*. Once language was purged of its imperfections and organized on sound principles, ideas would flow from mind to mind with all the ease that a lodestone 'communicates' with a piece of iron.
>
> (Peters 1989: 394)

It is not difficult to see how this view of language, even in the crude summary of it here, sustains what James Carey (1989) describes as a "transmission" or "transportation" model of communication, where meaning is to communication what freight is to a train: one simply transports the other.

Popularized by journalists and others with aphorisms like "don't blame the messenger for the message," this view of language and communication reduces news and journalism to mere devices of conveyance. Indeed, objective reporting works precisely this way as it manifests itself as a set of routines and rituals that effectively shift the journalist's authority—and responsibility—away from the content of news and toward its form. This shift in authority and responsibility began in the early 1900s, a time of the "scientization of journalism," as Daniel Hallin (1985: 129) aptly describes the period, when the "changing conventions of journalism paralleled the rise of science as a cultural paradigm against which all forms of discourse came to be measured." This marked the beginning of the rise of what Carey calls the "professional communicator," along with a form of news that had no *necessary* relation to the writer's own "thoughts and perceptions":

> the journalist went through a process that can be fairly termed a "conversion downwards," a process whereby a role is deintellectualized

267

and technicalized. Rather than independent interpreters of events, journalists became reporters, brokers in symbols who mediated between audiences and institutions, particularly but not exclusively government. In this role they lost their independence and become part of the process of news transmission. In this role they principally use not intellectual skills as critics, interpreters, and contemporary historians but technical skills as writing, a capacity to translate the specialized language and purpose of government, science, art, medicine, finance into an idiom that could be understood by a broader, more amorphous, less educated audience.

(1969: 137)

For the journalist as professional communicator, the world can be known separate from—and independent of—any judgments about the world. Epistemology thus supplants morality by relegating questions of right and wrong and good and bad to the realm of values, which has no place in a system of communication that prides itself in being value-free. Under these circumstances, a watchdog press remains credible only as it takes for granted a moral order and focuses on violations of it (Gans 1979). Journalists can expose wrongdoing, of course, but only on empirical, not moral, grounds. This is how American journalism resolves the paradox of a morally disengaged press driven by a sense of moral outrage (Ettema and Glasser 1998), and it explains in part why even the most aggressive forms of reporting usually end up conserving, not challenging, the status quo.

To bring to the press a sense of moral independence would require a wholesale rejection of the proposition that an interest in the world discredits knowledge of the world, that values devalue truth, and that language—any language—can provide a finally "right" or "correct" description of anything. And it would require an acknowledgment that journalism always interprets what it ostensibly only describes, a point Carey (1974: 245) makes when he observes that the day's news "sizes up situations, names their elements and names them in a way that contains an attitude toward them"; that journalism is a fundamentally creative enterprise that "dissects events from a particular point of view" and therefore "brings a certain world into existence."

But what would remain of newsroom standards, beyond a witless relativism that reduces facts and truth—and good journalism—to individual preference or personal whim?

Neither a relativist nor a deconstructionist, Rorty embraces a form of pragmatism that accepts the existence of enduring standards but locates them in history instead of in nature, a position not always easy to accept given that values and purposes inhere in language and are, over time, often taken to be the "natural" property of what is being described. What is normally accepted as true, Rorty has argued on more than a few occasions, is a description that "embodies agreed-upon criteria for reaching agreement," and any effort to build a more enduring foundation for truth is "a self-deceptive effort to externalize the normal discourse of the day." Whether it comes from science or the arts, from the newsroom or the classroom, no description is *self-evidently* "truer" than another. Rorty rails against any "entrenched" or "final" vocabulary, especially ones that presuppose the possibility of an absolutely literal, strictly denotative, purely referential language. Facts, truth and knowledge are taken to be *social* phenomena, and the *community* is taken to be the source of their epistemic authority.

From Rorty's perspective, then, any defense of news, like any defense of knowledge, rests not on finding "the truth," an epistemological claim based on "privileged representations" of reality, but on "being truthful," a moral claim grounded in a discursive test of what in the end "is good for us to believe" (1979: 176). This is because, Rorty explains, "nothing counts as justification unless by reference to what we already accept, and there is no way to get outside our beliefs and our language so as to find some test other than coherence" (ibid.: 178). Or to extrapolate from the work of Sissela Bok (1989), another pragmatist, claims of "truthfulness," subject to a "test of publicity," will be finally settled by the "reasonable persons" in the larger community in which news and knowledge circulate.

Professionalism and multiculturalism

As several of the earlier chapters make clear, no one benefits from the pretensions of professionalism that prompt lame comparisons between the education of journalists and the education of, say, physicians and lawyers. Practicing law or medicine is a privilege, not a right; in most parts of the world, it requires authorization from the state, a requirement journalists understandably resist. If an education in journalism matters, for journalists or anyone else, it matters not because it credentials practitioners or trains them in certain ways but because it clarifies and maybe even heightens the public's expectations for a certain quality of public discourse. No one needs a degree in political science to win an election; or a degree in comparative literature to write a great novel; or a degree in business administration to succeed in the marketplace; or, alas, a degree in journalism to do well as a journalist. But we still know what it means to say that someone in politics or business or the arts—or journalism—acted unprofessionally. Studying journalism makes a difference to the extent that it instills among students a sense of moral purpose; educating journalists, rather than merely training them, makes a difference when it engenders the eloquence students need to respond publicly and candidly to questions about what they do and why they do it. Too much of the debate over whether journalism is—or could be or should be—a profession seems to us to miss the point: "It is not important to argue about which occupations qualify as a profession," as John Soloski (1989) put it a few years ago; "what is important is to ask what it means for an occupation to claim to be a profession."

In the case of journalism, claims of professionalism account for a proliferation of codes of ethics, beginning in France in 1918 and including a set of 10 "International Principles of Professional Ethics in Journalism" negotiated in a series of meetings between 1978 and 1983 with members of the International Organization of Journalists, the International Federation of Journalists and other regional and international groups (Traber and Nordenstreng 1992). In the United States alone, there exist hundreds of journalism codes: for editorial writers, for feature writers, for editors, for photojournalists, for broadcasters, for this newsroom and for that newsroom. If these codes mostly belabor the obvious—codes usually articulate "what most professionals do by habit and personal conviction"—they nonetheless serve the useful purpose of expressing in public a set of moral precepts: the very existence of a code "conveys the impression that a profession is concerned about ethics" (Kultgen 1988: 413–417).

But codes of ethics also serve to isolate and insulate journalists from the larger community. While they almost always cite the public and make commitments to it, the public seldom plays any role in a code's creation, application or revision. With a few notable exceptions—sometimes in the case of broadcasting, sometimes in the case of press councils (see Rønning's chapter)—codes tend to be in-house matters: Journalists write them, monitor them and enforce them (or not). Moreover, codes typically reify morality by creating lists of blameworthy and praiseworthy conduct, which might be satisfying to the small group of individuals who participated in the code's construction but which might also disenfranchise others, journalists and non-journalists alike, whose understanding of morality finds little or no recognition in a code's provisions. Given their brevity, codes invariably exclude more than they include, which implies, perhaps unfairly, that journalists will quietly tolerate that broad range of unmentioned conduct that falls somewhere between what practitioners get blamed for doing and what they get praised for doing. Finally and most importantly, by elevating practitioners above their cultural and social differences, codes of ethics have the effect of homogenizing the practice of journalism.

To be sure, professionalism means standardization; it accounts not for differences among individuals but for what individuals have in common. Being a professional means abiding by certain norms and accepting the uniformity of practice that this implies (Glasser, 1992). Put a little differently, professionalism, along with a professional education, functions to unify knowledge and practice by glossing over differences in experience (Schön 1983); it *depersonalizes* experience, as Larson (1977) argues in her social history of professionalism, by fostering a belief in the proposition that well-educated and properly trained professionals can and should transcend their circumstances. It is presumably reassuring to know that surgeons in one part of the country follow the same operating-room protocols as surgeons in other parts of the country; ideally, no one should be able to distinguish between an appendectomy performed in New Jersey and one done in Kansas. But how reassuring is it to know that reporters in one part of the country will end up with basically the same account of an event as reporters in other parts of the country—that they will rely on the same kinds of sources, organize their stories in basically the same way, and end up with essentially the same lead?

Journalism struggles with this dilemma as it tries to reconcile claims of professionalism with claims of multiculturalism. Earlier this year at the *San Francisco Chronicle*, to indulge in another local example, two women, one a reporter and one a photographer, were told they could no longer cover San Francisco's mayor's unprecedented and controversial decision to invite same-sex couples to City Hall to exchange marriage vows because they had themselves, as a couple, accepted the mayor's invitation. Although no one at the newspaper doubted the women's "professionalism"—"[n]ot once did any editor hint that they would abandon their fairness," as the paper's "public editor" explained in a column that defended the decision—the newspaper's management decided that journalists who participate in a controversy should not cover it: "Newspapers should want readers of all viewpoints to find their stories credible. Allowing journalists to take part in a controversy, then cover it, gives readers an excuse to discount the story" (Rogers 2004).

The *Chronicle*'s decision, widely debated in the gay and lesbian community as well as among journalists, highlights the difficulties the press faces as it seeks to navigate a course between its understandable aversion to conflicts of interest and its commitment to newsroom diversity. The recent and long overdue move to diversify American newsrooms, an initiative the *Chronicle* and other major news organizations take very seriously, rests on the premise that different kinds of people, experiencing the world in different ways, will bring to the newsroom new and different interests. But this runs afoul of the premise of professionalism, which in the United States posits a *dis*interested newsroom whose staffers must steer clear of even the appearance of partiality.

Unmoved by the question of why the public disclosure of an interest creates any more of a conflict than the same interest when it remains the knowledge of only friends, family and colleagues, the *Chronicle*'s policy of disengagement leaves journalists wondering why a newspaper would want to conceal the very interests it trumpets as evidence of its commitment to diversity. In this case, significantly, the two journalists' interest in gay and lesbian rights did not materialize with their very public wedding; it simply manifested itself there. Accordingly:

- Is it only the conspicuously public appearance of an interest that constitutes a conflict of interest?
- Do interests matter less when the public knows little or nothing about them?
- Where do newsrooms draw the line between private and personal interests and public and shared interests?
- How do newsrooms distinguish between legitimate interests and interests that run counter to the demands of good journalism?

271

What remains unclear, then, at the *Chronicle* and elsewhere, is what the American press plans to do with hiring policies that honor differences in gender, race, ethnicity and other markers of diversity when other newsroom policies insist that these differences should not make a difference.

Calls for a more open and inclusive journalism, now heard from around the world, invite a reconsideration of the meaning of professionalism; they call into question the viability of forms of knowledge that exclude experience as a legitimate source of knowledge; and they look askance at arguments that equate universal values with the homogenization of journalism. As any number of students of journalism have reminded us over the years, Edward Said prominent among them, the pretense of a disinterested and detached press, an objective press, does not dissolve interests or distance journalists from them; it only makes journalists less aware of their personal, cultural and institutional interests and unprepared to acknowledge and examine them. "There is never interpretation, knowledge and then understanding," Said (1981: 165) wrote in his classic study of journalism's treatment of Islam, "where there is no *interest*."

Journalism and democratic participation

Among the many ways to read Said's book, *Covering Islam*, is to concentrate on his discussion of agency in journalism. From one chapter to the next, Said emphasizes the importance of understanding journalists not only in terms of what they cover but how they cover it. The press gives us a certain picture of the world, as Said documents in some detail, but "also a communicable set of feelings about the picture" (1981: 47), which he also documents. Like Carey, cited earlier, and others whose work examines the power of the press to render the world intelligible and distinct, Said calls on journalists to understand and defend their choices—choices of topics, choices of images, choices of sources, choices of vocabulary. For these choices, treated historically, often reveal a purpose for the press not nearly as benign or as benevolent as journalists might assume; and they seldom reveal what Said would prefer to see from the press: news and knowledge "understood in human and political terms as something to be won to the service of coexistence and community" (ibid.: 160).

It is telling that one of the most contested set of claims from within American journalism in the last 15 years comes from the "public journalism" movement, which wants the press to promote and improve, and not merely report on and complain about, the quality of public life. A loosely organized but widely diffused response to the increasingly cynical tone of political journalism and the alienation and apathy associated with it, public journalism expects journalists to find better ways of engaging readers, viewers and listeners *as citizens* with a stake in the issues of the day; to emphasize substance over strategy, especially in their coverage of elections and campaigns; and to treat problems in a manner that highlights the prospects for their resolution (Rosen 1999; Glasser and Lee 2002). "Making the community work," the popular refrain of proponents of public journalism, excites some journalists but offends many more who recoil at the idea of the press playing any role in cultivating citizenship or increasing the likelihood of participation in politics. David Broder, one of the most highly regarded political journalists in the United States, put it succinctly when, in response to questions about what could be done to enhance the quality of political news, he insisted on the "still fundamental" distinction between engaging citizens and keeping them informed, between "what journalists do and what civic leaders or politicians do": The "essence of politics," Broder explained, is "getting people engaged," and that needs to be kept separate from "the function of the journalist." As much as he wanted to see journalism improve and political participation increase, he was not prepared to cross the line between politics and the press: "I honestly believe that once we take on the responsibility of being the agent for engaging them [citizens], that we are in politics" (quoted in Glasser 1999: 4).

Elsewhere in the world, however, being political, even being downright partisan, corresponds to, rather than contradicts, the prevailing standards of professionalism in journalism. In this volume and in his recent work with Hallin, Mancini examines forms of democracy, mostly in southern Europe, in which the press works to mobilize citizens as much as it tries to keep them informed. Under conditions of "polarized pluralism," the term Hallin and Mancini (2004) use to describe the "sharply polarized and conflictual politics" in Italy, Spain, Portugal and Greece, news content tends to be more politically charged than dispassionate. Through their coverage of polices and politicians, news media in these countries serve as "instruments of struggle" in the conflicts that animate local politics; the "notion of a politically neutral journalism," Hallin and Mancini observe, "is less plausible where a wide range of competing world views contend" (ibid.: 61).

Self-governance comes in many forms, as David Held (1987) illustrates in his widely cited account of various "models of democracy." So, too, does journalism.

From the commitment of journalists in Latin America to help secure democratic reform (see Alves' chapter) to the role of Arab satellite television in combating traditions of control and patronage (see Sakr's chapter), different forms of journalism contribute in different ways to the provision of what all forms of democracy require: popular sovereignty. These contributions differ not only with regard to the diffusion of technology, as Pavlik and McNair point out in their respective chapters, but in deference to very different conceptions of how democracy works.

However well established the principles of modern democracy might be, the practice of democracy shifts over time and varies considerably from one place to another. Crises of all kinds, from terrorism and war to financial instability and natural disasters, can quickly alter the role of the state and suddenly redefine what it means to live in a democratic society. In many countries, moreover, multiple forms of democracy co-exist; democracy in a small community might bear little or no resemblance to democracy at the national level. As useful as it is to talk about competing traditions in democratic thought—liberalism versus republicanism, for example (Young 2000; Habermas 1996)—"actually existing" democracies create their own traditions which need to be understood concretely and historically and with an awareness of how particular practices intersect with democratic ideals.

Imagining and realizing democratic roles for the press begins with an appreciation for the history of the industrialization of journalism, which in many ways amounts to a history of neglect of journalism's political economy. Insofar as it equates a free press with free enterprise, journalism leaves little room for a serious discussion of the conditions for democratic communication. This happens repeatedly in the United States, where there exists, as Michael Schudson puts it in his chapter "The US Model of Journalism', "a very stringent reading of the role of the government in sustaining a framework for freedom of expression." Although the U.S. Supreme Court has on occasion, particularly in the area of broadcasting, authorized a role for the state in promoting "uninhibited, robust and wide-open" debate—Mancini in his chapter overstates the case when he concludes that the "First Amendment makes it impossible for Congress to intervene in the field of mass communications"—the American judiciary generally honors the press's distrust of government by separating the "right to be heard," which the Constitution protects, from the "opportunity to be heard," which Americans prefer to consign to the marketplace.

The American predilection for letting a private press fashion a public purpose for itself, an important but limited conception of independent journalism, poses a problem only when it blocks plans by others, including the state, to create opportunities for public communication beyond what market forces accommodate. It poses a problem, for example, when Americans view subsidies for public broadcasting as illiberal and therefore undemocratic. But, given the global influence and at times dominance of Western, especially American, forms of journalism, this becomes something more than a domestic squabble. It was certainly more than a local issue a quarter of a century ago when, fueled by distorted accounts in the U.S. press (Raskin 1981) of a UNESCO report on the need for a New World Information Order, popularly known as the MacBride Report (MacBride 1980), the U.S. made clear its disdain for any model of journalism that violates the precepts of private ownership and individual autonomy. And it remains today something more than a local issue as a new generation of American journalists struggles to find its place in a world where journalism, augmented by satellites and computers, crosses borders and enters the lives of people for whom democracy and democratic participation demand more from the press than disinterest and detachment.

References

Bok, S. (1989) *Lying: Moral Choice in Public and Private Life*, New York: Vintage Books.

Carey, J. W. (1969) 'The Communications Revolution and the Professional Communicator', *Sociological Review* Monograph, no. 13 (January): 23–38.

—— (1974) 'Journalism and Criticism: The Case of the Undeveloped Profession', *Review of Politics*, 36 (April): 227–249.

—— (1989) *Communication as Culture: Essays on Media and Society*, Boston: Unwin Hyman.

Ettema, J. S. and Glasser, T. L. (1998) *Custodians of Conscience: Investigative Journalism and Public Virtue*, New York: Columbia University Press.

Fedler, F., Bender, J. R. Davenport, L. and Kostyu, P. A. (1997) *Reporting for the Media*, 6th ed., New York: Harcourt Brace & Co.

Fuller, J. (1996) *News Values: Ideas for an Information Age*, Chicago: University of Chicago Press.

Gans, H. (1979) *Deciding What's News*, New York: Random House.

Glasser, T. L. (1992) 'Professionalism and the Derision of Diversity: The Case of the Education of Journalists', *Journal of Communication*, 42, 2: 131–140.

—— (1996) 'Journalism's Glassy Essence', *Journalism & Mass Communication Quarterly*, 73, 4: 784–786.

—— (1999) 'The Idea of Public Journalism', in T. L. Glasser (ed.) *The Idea of Public Journalism*, New York: Guilford.

Glasser, T. L. and Lee, F. L. (2002) 'Repositioning the Newsroom: The American Experience with Public Journalism', in R. Kuhn and E. Neveu (eds.) *Political Journalism: New Challenges, New Practices*, London: Routledge.

Habermas, J. (1996) 'Three Normative Models of Democracy', in S. Benhabib (ed.) *Democracy and Difference*, Princeton, NJ: Princeton University Press

Hallin, D. (1985) 'The American News Media: A Critical Theory Perspective', in J. Forester (ed.) *Critical Theory and Public Life*, Cambridge, MA.: MIT Press.

Hallin, D. and Mancini, P. (2004) *Comparing Media Systems: Three Models of Media and Politics*, New York: Cambridge University Press

Held, D. (1987) *Models of Democracy*, Stanford, CA: Stanford University Press.

Kovach, B. and Rosenstiel, T. (2001) *The Elements of Journalism: What Newspeople Should Know and What the Public Should Expect*, New York: Crown.

Kultgen, J. (1988) 'The Ideological Uses of Professional Codes', in J. C. Callahan (ed.) *Ethical Issues in Professional Life*, New York: Oxford University Press.

Larson, M. S. (1977) *The Rise of Professionalism: A Sociological Analysis*, Berkeley, CA: University of California Press.

Lippmann, W. (1965 [1922]) *Public Opinion*, New York: Free Press.

MacBride, S. (1980) *Many Voices, One World*, New York: Unipub.

Peters, J. D. (1989) 'John Locke, the Individual, and the Origin of Communication', *Quarterly Journal of Speech*, 75: 387–399.

Raskin, A. H. (1981) 'U. S. News Coverage of the Belgrade UNESCO Conference', *Journal of Communication*, 31 (Autumn): 164–171.

Rogers, D. (2004) 'Journalists Shouldn't Take Part in Controversies They Cover'. Available online: http://www.stanford.edu/group/gradethenews/feat/makethecall/gaymarraige

Rorty, R. (1979) *Philosophy and the Mirror of Nature*, Princeton, NJ: Princeton University Press.

Rosen, J. (1999) 'The Action of the Idea: Public Journalism in Built Form', in T. L. Glasser (ed.) *The Idea of Public Journalism*, New York: Guilford.

Said, E. W. (1981) *Covering Islam: How the Media and Experts Determine How We See the Rest of the World*, New York: Random House.

Schön, D. A. (1983) *The Reflective Practitioner: How Professionals Think in Action*, New York: Basic Books.

Schudson, M. (1995) *The Power of News*, Cambridge, MA: Harvard University Press.

Soloski, J. (1989) 'News Reporting and Professionalism: Some Constraints on the Reporting of News', *Media, Culture and Society*, 11: 207–228.

Traber, M. and Nordenstreng, K. (1992) *Few Voices, Many Worlds: Towards a Media Reform Movement*, London: World Association for Christian Communication.

Wicker, T. (1978) *On Press: A Top Reporter's Life in, and Reflections on, American Journalism*, New York: Viking.

Young, I. M. (2000) *Inclusion and Democracy*, New York: Oxford University Press.

INDEX

277